Islam and Muslims in Victorian Britain

Islam of the Global West

Series editors: Kambiz GhaneaBassiri and Frank Peter

Islam of the Global West is a pioneering series that examines Islamic beliefs, practices, discourses, communities and institutions that have emerged from 'the Global West'. The geographical and intellectual framing of the Global West reflects both the role played by the interactions between people from diverse religions and cultures in the development of Western ideals and institutions in the modern era and the globalization of these very ideals and institutions.

In creating an intellectual space where works of scholarship on European and North American Muslims enter into conversation with one another, the series promotes the publication of theoretically informed and empirically grounded research in these areas. By bringing the rapidly growing research on Muslims in European and North American societies, ranging from the United States and France to Portugal and Albania, into conversation with the conceptual framing of the Global West, this ambitious series aims to re-imagine the modern world and develop new analytical categories and historical narratives that highlight the complex relationships and rivalries that have shaped the multicultural, poly-religious character of Europe and North America, as evidenced, by way of example, in such economically and culturally dynamic urban centres as Los Angeles, New York, Paris, Madrid, Toronto, Sarajevo, London, Berlin and Amsterdam where there is a significant Muslim presence.

American and Muslim Worlds Before 1900
Edited by John Ghazvinian and Arthur Mitchell Fraas
Anarchist, Artist, Sufi
Mark Sedgwick
Amplifying Islam in the European Soundscape: Religious Pluralism and Secularism in the Netherlands
Pooyan Tamimi Arab

The British Muslim Convert Lord Headley, 1855–1935
Jamie Gilham
Interrogating Muslims
Schirin Amir-Moazami
Islam and Nationhood in Bosnia-Herzegovina: Surviving Empires
Xavier Bougarel
Islam and the Governing of Muslims in France
Frank Peter
Islam as Critique: Sayyid Ahmad Khan and the Challenge of Modernity
Khurram Hussain
Muslims Making British Media
Carl Morris
Sacred Spaces and Transnational Networks in American Sufism
Merin Shobhana Xavier

Islam and Muslims in Victorian Britain

New Perspectives

Edited by
Jamie Gilham

BLOOMSBURY ACADEMIC
LONDON • NEW YORK • OXFORD • NEW DELHI • SYDNEY

BLOOMSBURY ACADEMIC
Bloomsbury Publishing Plc, 50 Bedford Square, London, WC1B 3DP, UK
Bloomsbury Publishing Inc, 1385 Broadway, New York, NY 10018, USA
Bloomsbury Publishing Ireland, 29 Earlsfort Terrace, Dublin 2, D02 AY28, Ireland

BLOOMSBURY, BLOOMSBURY ACADEMIC and the Diana logo are trademarks of Bloomsbury Publishing Plc

First published in Great Britain 2024
Paperback edition published 2025

Copyright © Jamie Gilham and contributors, 2024

Jamie Gilham has asserted his right under the Copyright, Designs and Patents Act, 1988, to be identified as Editor of this work.

For legal purposes the Acknowledgements on p. xv constitute an extension of this copyright page.

Series design by Dani Leigh
Cover image © Brian Stablyk / gettyimages.co.uk

All rights reserved. No part of this publication may be: i) reproduced or transmitted in any form, electronic or mechanical, including photocopying, recording or by means of any information storage or retrieval system without prior permission in writing from the publishers; or ii) used or reproduced in any way for the training, development or operation of artificial intelligence (AI) technologies, including generative AI technologies. The rights holders expressly reserve this publication from the text and data mining exception as per Article 4(3) of the Digital Single Market Directive (EU) 2019/790.

Bloomsbury Publishing Plc does not have any control over, or responsibility for, any third-party websites referred to or in this book. All internet addresses given in this book were correct at the time of going to press. The author and publisher regret any inconvenience caused if addresses have changed or sites have ceased to exist, but can accept no responsibility for any such changes.

A catalogue record for this book is available from the British Library.

A catalog record for this book is available from the Library of Congress.

ISBN: HB: 978-1-3502-9963-4
PB: 978-1-3502-9967-2
ePDF: 978-1-3502-9964-1
eBook: 978-1-3502-9965-8

Series: Islam of the Global West

Typeset by Newgen KnowledgeWorks Pvt. Ltd., Chennai, India

For product safety related questions contact productsafety@bloomsbury.com.

To find out more about our authors and books visit www.bloomsbury.com and sign up for our newsletters.

For Humayun Ansari

Contents

List of figures	xi
Notes on contributors	xii
Acknowledgements	xv
List of abbreviations	xvi
Note on quotations and spelling	xvii
Glossary	xviii
Introduction *Jamie Gilham*	1

Part 1 Discourse and Representations

1	The royal family's attitudes towards Islam and Muslims during the reign of Queen Victoria *A. Martin Wainwright*	13
2	Rival views on the Eastern Question, Muslims and Islam: William Ewart Gladstone, Benjamin Disraeli and Anglo-Ottoman relations *Clinton Bennett*	29
3	Thomas Carlyle, Islam, empire and after *Geoffrey P. Nash*	45
4	'Permission to go and see the ancient city': Women travellers' encounters with Islam in the nineteenth century *Anne-Marie Beller and Kerry Featherstone*	61
5	Translators, publishers and popular readerships: The Qur'an on the Victorian bookshelf *Alexander Bubb*	81

Part 2 Muslim Lives

6   Saiyid Mustafa Ben-Yusuf, an Arab Muslim convert to
    Christianity in Victorian Britain   99
    Jamie Gilham

7   From Arab *millet* to British Islam: Syrian Muslims in Victorian
    Manchester   123
    Riordan Macnamara

8   The last Nawab of Bengal: India and England, 1838–84   139
    Lyn Innes

9   Maulana Muhammad Barakatullah Bhopali in late-Victorian
    England   159
    Humayun Ansari

10 Feeding hungry Christians: The Liverpool Muslim Institute on
    Christmas Day   177
    Brent D. Singleton

11 Authority and legitimacy in Victorian Liverpool: Re-evaluating
    Abdullah Quilliam's title of 'Sheikh-ul-Islam of the British Isles' 193
    Matthew A. Sharp

Notes   209
Select bibliography   253
Index   257

Figures

1.1	Mohammad Abdul Karim with Queen Victoria at Balmoral, *c.*1890	18
3.1	Thomas Carlyle by Robert Scott Tait, 1855	46
4.1	Florentia, Lady Sale by William James Ward, after 1820	65
4.2	Emily Eden by Simon Jacques Rochard, 1835	66
4.3	Lucie, Lady Duff Gordon by Henry Wyndham Phillips, 1851	72
4.4	Amelia B. Edwards by August Weger, after 1876	77
6.1	Saiyid Mustafa Ben-Yusuf by W. and A. H. Fry, *c.*1869	108
6.2	Saiyid Mustafa Ben-Yusuf with boy servant by Hills and Saunders, *c.*1874	116
7.1	Mustapha Karsa Bey, Ottoman consul for Manchester and Salford, *c.*1900	129
7.2	Selim Mokaiesh in Manchester, *c.*1900	132
8.1	The Nawab Nazim of Bengal by Matt Somerville Morgan, 1870	154
9.1	Maulana Muhammad Barakatullah Bhopali, *c.*1890s	161
11.1	Abdullah Quilliam presenting as 'Sheikh-ul-Islam of the British Isles', *c.*1905	196

Notes on contributors

Humayun Ansari (PhD) is Emeritus Professor of the History of Islam and Cultural Diversity in the Department of History at Royal Holloway, University of London, UK. His research interests include radical Islamic thought, ethnicity, identity, migration and multiculturalism. His publications include '*The Infidel Within': Muslims in Britain since 1800* (2004, 2018), *The Making of the East London Mosque, 1910–1951* (2011), *The Emergence of Socialist Thought among North Indian Muslims* (2015) and, as co-editor, *From the Far Right to the Mainstream: Islamophobia in Party Politics and the Media* (2012).

Anne-Marie Beller (PhD) is Senior Lecturer in Victorian Literature at Loughborough University, UK. Her research interests include sensation fiction, New Woman Writing and Neo-Victorian Studies, with a focus on issues of gender, race, disability and sexuality. She has published books, chapters and articles on the nineteenth-century novelist Mary Elizabeth Braddon and her contemporaries, Wilkie Collins and Ellen Wood. Recent research includes projects on the neo-Victorian slave narrative, the sensation short story and the intersectionality of race and disability in the sensation novel.

Clinton Bennett (PhD) teaches at the State University of New York at New Paltz, United States. A Fellow of the Royal Asiatic Society and the Royal Anthropological Institute, he specializes in Christian-Muslim relations and interfaith dialogue and is Western Europe research team leader for the series *Christian-Muslim Relations: A Bibliographical History*. His publications include *Victorian Images of Islam* (1992), *Muslims and Modernity: An Introduction to the Issues and Debates* (2005), *Understanding Christian-Muslim Relations: Past and Present* (2008), *The Bloomsbury Companion to Islamic Studies* (2012) and *Islam as Imagined in Eighteenth- and Nineteenth-Century English Literature* (2023).

Alexander Bubb (PhD) is Senior Lecturer in English at Roehampton University, UK. He has written extensively on nineteenth-century literature and cultural history, with a particular interest in how the British print marketplace was diversified and enriched by foreign languages and translations. His publications include *Meeting without Knowing It: Kipling and Yeats at the Fin de Siècle* (2016) and *Asian Classics on the Victorian Bookshelf: Flights of Translation* (2023).

Kerry Featherstone (PhD) is Lecturer in Creative Writing at Loughborough University, UK. He has published on travel writing and has a particular research interest in representations of Afghanistan from the nineteenth century onwards in a range of genres. He is also a poet and his creative practice involves writing about landscapes, involving a combination of personal memory and historical research.

Jamie Gilham (PhD) is an independent historian and biographer in the UK and Taiwan. A Fellow of the Royal Historical Society, UK, his research focuses on the history of Islam and Muslims in Britain and Western travellers to the Middle East. His publications include *Loyal Enemies: British Converts to Islam, 1850–1950* (2014), *The British Muslim Convert Lord Headley, 1855–1935* (2020) and, as co-editor, *Victorian Muslim: Abdullah Quilliam and Islam in the West* (2017) and *Muslim Women in Britain, 1850–1950: 100 Years of Hidden History* (2023).

Lyn Innes (PhD) is Emeritus Professor of Postcolonial Literatures at the University of Kent, Canterbury, UK. She has published many books and articles on African, African American, Irish and Indian writers, including *A History of Black and South Asian Writing in Britain* (2002, 2008), *The Cambridge Introduction to Postcolonial Literatures in English* (2007) and *The Last Prince of Bengal: A Family's Journey from an Indian Palace to the Australian Outback* (2021).

Riordan Macnamara is Lecturer at the Institute of Cultural and International Studies, University of Paris Saclay, France. He has translated to French Ibn Ata Allah's *Miftah al-Falah* (2002) and is co-editor of the English edition of Yusuf Samih Asmay's *Islam in Victorian Liverpool* (2021). He is currently writing a PhD at the University of Bourgogne, France, about conversion to Islam in late-Victorian and Edwardian Britain, specifically looking at gender, class and power dynamics at the Liverpool Muslim Institute and the influence of other religious, denominational and ethnic groups on the evolution of its discourse and practices.

Geoffrey P. Nash (PhD) has taught in universities in Qatar, India and the UK. He is a specialist in recent and contemporary Muslim and Anglophone Arab writing, travel writing on the Middle East, Orientalism and modern Muslim movements. He is the editor of *Marmaduke Pickthall, Islam and the Modern World* (2017) and *Orientalism and Literature* (2019), and author of *The Arab Writer in English* (1998), *From Empire to Orient: Travellers to the Middle East, 1830–1926* (2005), *Writing Muslim Identity* (2010) and *Religion, Orientalism and Modernity: Mahdi Movements of Iran and South Asia* (2022).

Matthew A. Sharp (PhD) is an independent scholar in the United States. He has a PhD in Near Eastern Languages and Civilizations with a concentration in Middle Eastern Literatures and Societies from the University of Pennsylvania. His work explores entanglements between British and American converts to Islam and Ottoman state officials and Arab and Turkish Muslim intellectuals in the late nineteenth and early twentieth centuries.

Brent D. Singleton is a faculty member and Coordinator for Reference Services at the John M. Pfau Library, California State University, San Bernardino, United States. He has published chapters and articles relating to Mohammed Alexander Russell Webb, Abdullah Quilliam, West African Islam and enslaved African Muslim in the Americas. He is the editor of *Yankee Muslim: The Asian Travels of Mohammed Alexander Russell Webb* (2007) and *The Convert's Passion: An Anthology of Islamic Poetry from Late Victorian and Edwardian Britain* (2009).

A. Martin Wainwright (PhD) is Professor of History and Chair of the Department of History at the University of Akron, Ohio, United States. A specialist in modern British history and the history of India under British occupation, his books include *Inheritance of Empire: Britain, India, and the Balance of Power in Asia, 1938–55* (1993) and *'The Better Class' of Indians: Social Rank, Imperial Identity, and South Asians in Britain, 1858–1914* (2008).

Acknowledgements

I am very grateful to the chapter authors for their contributions and commitment to this volume. I thank Kambiz GhaneaBassiri and Frank Peter, Islam of the Global West series editors, for their encouragement and feedback on the manuscript; the anonymous reviewers of the original book proposal and the first draft for their constructive comments; and Lalle Pursglove, Stuart Hay and Lily McMahon at Bloomsbury Publishing for their guidance and advice. Thank you to Yen-Ting and my family for their help and support.

Completion of this book coincided with the retirement from Royal Holloway, University of London, of Professor Humayun Ansari – a pioneering and inspirational historian of Islam and Muslims in Britain. This book is dedicated to him.

December 2022

Abbreviations

BL	British Library, London
BOA	Başbakanlık Osmanlı Arşivi (Ottoman Archives of the Prime Ministry)
CMS	Church Missionary Society
EIC	East India Company
GRO	General Register Office, England
IOR	India Office Records (British Library)
LMI	Liverpool Muslim Institute
MMS	The Moslem Mission Society
MP	Member of Parliament
PCUMA	Palestine Christian Union Mission to the Arabs
QVJ	Queen Victoria's Journal
RCT	Royal Collection Trust, UK
TC	*The Crescent*, Liverpool

Note on quotations and spelling

To ensure that the sources retain their authenticity, all quoted material is *verbatim* unless otherwise stated. This accounts for the various spellings of the same word, for example, 'Mahommedan', 'Mohamedan', 'Moslem' and 'Mussulman' for Muslim, 'Mahomet' for Muhammad and 'Quran' and 'Koran' for Qur'an. Spelling of Muslim names and place names, italics, capitalization and inconsistent punctuation within quotations are also *verbatim*.

Glossary

adhan	Muslim call to prayer.
al-Fatiha	The first *sura* (chapter) of the Qur'an, which is recited during daily prayers.
alim	Learned scholar qualified to offer Islamic legal opinions.
ayah	Nanny, lady's maid, historically from South Asia and working for Europeans; or, a verse in the Qur'an.
bastinado	Foot whipping as a form of punishment or torture.
Begum	An honorific title for a Muslim woman of high social status or rank in colonial India and elsewhere.
bey	Lord, sir, master; a courtesy title used in the Ottoman Empire (see also *effendi*).
bid'ah	Innovation in religious matters.
binbaşi	The rank of Major in the Ottoman imperial cavalry.
bismillah	Arabic phrase meaning 'In the name of Allah'.
Caliph	The successor of the Prophet Muhammad as leader of the *umma*.
Caliphate	The office or government of the Caliph.
dar al-Islam	Territory of Islam.
da'wah	Lit. 'invitation'; the act of inviting or calling to people to embrace Islam.
du'a	Prayer of supplication.
effendi	Lord, sir, master; a courtesy title used in the Ottoman Empire (see also *bey*).
fahri	Turkish equivalent of the Arabic *fakhri*, in the possessive form meaning 'honorary' and used as a name or surname.
fatwa	Juridical opinion.
ghazeeas	Derived from *ghazis*, Muslim warriors who fight in a war against non-Muslims; also used by Western Victorian writers to denote a religious fanatic.
hadith	Report of the traditions (words, actions) of the Prophet Muhammad.

Hajj	Pilgrimage to Mecca. The greater of the two pilgrimages to Mecca (see also *'umra*) undertaken during the last month of the Islamic calendar; the fifth 'pillar' of Islam.
harem	Women's quarters in a domestic space.
hijrah	Journey.
houris	In the Qur'an and Islamic belief, women with beautiful eyes described as a reward for faithful Muslim believers in Paradise.
'Id	Muslim religious festival.
'Id al-Adha	Feast of the sacrifice celebrating the end of the annual Hajj.
'Id al-Fitr	Feast that marks the end of Ramadan.
imam	Muslim religious leader.
Imambara	Assembly hall for Shi'i Muslims to observe *Muharram*.
irâde	Sultanic decree.
jahiliyah	Lit. 'ignorance'; the period and state of affairs in Arabia before Islam.
jihad	Striving or struggling in the path of God.
kalima	Islamic statement of faith.
keffiyeh	Headdress worn by men.
Khedive	Honorific title used for sultans and grand *viziers* in the Ottoman Empire; in Egypt, the Ottoman viceroy.
khutbah	Sermon.
kitabi	One who believes in a book of sacred scripture.
lascar	A sailor, often Muslim, from Asia, Africa and the Middle East employed on European ships.
Maulana	Lit. 'master'; title given to a Muslim religious scholar.
Mawlid	Observance of the Prophet Muhammad's birthday.
millet	An Ottoman semi-autonomous minority community.
mohur	A gold coin minted in colonial India and elsewhere.
muezzin	A Muslim elected to call other Muslims to prayer (anglicized from the Arabic, *mu'adhdhin*).
Muharram	The first month of the Islamic calendar.
mullah	A male Muslim learned in Islamic theology and law, religious leader.
munshi	Instructor, attendant.
namaz	Worship or ritual prayer (see *salat*).
Nawab	Prince; Muslim nobleman, regional governor.
nikah	Islamic marriage ceremony.
nikah mut'ah	Temporary marriage contract.

Nizam	Hereditary ruler in colonial India.
qadi	Magistrate, judge.
rak'ah	A single iteration of prescribed movements and supplications performed by Muslims as part of *salat*.
Ramadan	Muslim month of fasting.
Saiyid	Also 'Sayyid', 'Syed'; a signifier of eminence used by Muslims who are descendants of the Prophet Muhammad; title to denote a prince, lord or chief in Arab societies.
salat	Worship or ritual prayer; the second 'pillar' of Islam.
salat al-fajr	Dawn prayer; if counted from midnight, the first mandatory prayer of the day.
salat al-'isa	Night prayer; if counted from midnight, the fifth mandatory prayer of the day.
salat al-janazah	Islamic funeral prayer.
salat al-jum'a	Friday prayer, congregational prayer.
salat al-magrib	Sunset prayer; if counted from midnight, the fourth mandatory prayer of the day.
sawm	Fasting/abstinence during Ramadan; the fourth 'pillar' of Islam.
sepoy	Indian infantryman.
şeyh	The Ottoman Turkish for shaykh.
shahada	The Islamic testimony of faith and first of the five 'pillars' of Islam: 'I declare that there is no god but God and I declare that Muhammad is His Messenger.'
shaykh	or 'sheikh'; a religious leader, or the leader of a community or family/tribe.
Sufi	A follower of Sufism, or Islamic mysticism.
Sultan	Ruler, king.
sunna	Custom; practice and example of the Prophet Muhammad and the early Muslim community, which is for Muslims an authoritative example of the correct way to live a Muslim life. The second authoritative Islamic source after the Qur'an.
sura	A division, or chapter, of the Qur'an.
takbir	The name for the Arabic phrase *Allahu 'akbar*, meaning 'God is the Greatest'.
tariqa	Lit. 'the way'; a Sufi order, led by a spiritual teacher.
ta'zieh	In South Asia, a miniature mausoleum used in ritual processions during *Muharram*.

thawb	Ankle-length robe, usually with long sleeves.
ulama	Plural of *alim*.
umma	The universal Muslim religious community.
‘umra	The lesser pilgrimage to Mecca, which can be made at any time of the year.
vilayet	Ottoman administrative division or province.
vizier	High-ranking official.
waqf	Property, land or other assets that are an inalienable charitable endowment under Islamic law.
zakat	Almsgiving; the third 'pillar' of Islam.
zamindar	In colonial Bengal, hereditary landlords.

Introduction

Jamie Gilham

Prior to the nineteenth century, Britons had been visiting and settling in Islamic countries and Muslim communities for hundreds of years.[1] From at least the sixteenth century, a small but regular number of Britons had, for diverse reasons, converted to Islam abroad,[2] and Muslims from overseas – initially diplomats, merchants and sailors – began to enter and live in the British Isles.[3] However, it was not until the Victorian period, that is during the long reign of Queen Victoria, from 1837 to 1901, that Muslim communities were properly established with basic institutional structures (including prayer rooms and Islamic societies) and Britons converted to Islam in Britain. Moreover, both immigrant and indigenous Victorian Muslims began to propagate their faith on British soil. The first purpose-built mosque was opened at Woking in England in 1889, the year that Abdullah Quilliam (1856–1932), a British convert to Islam, created a permanent base for his Liverpool Muslim Institute (LMI), which became the centre of Islamic missionary activity in late-Victorian Britain.[4] These demographic, social and religious changes were integral to the growth of multicultural British society as it developed in the Victorian era. The origins of these changes are to be located in the process of industrialization that had begun in the previous century, but they were driven during Victoria's reign by rapid globalization. The enablers were major developments in the technologies of transportation, especially steam power and print, a potent combination which quickly led to more plentiful, efficient, cheaper and extensive trade, migration and communication that connected ostensibly Christian European (and American) societies with Muslim societies like never before.[5]

These connections meant that non-Muslims and Muslims discovered or became better acquainted with the other (and with each other, across communities and borders) in the second half of the nineteenth century. However, as James L.

Gelvin and Nile Green have noted in relation to Muslims, though the same can be said of non-Muslims, they 'defined themselves in relation to these contacts, and synthesized new ideologies and rethought older doctrines'.[6] As the British succeeded in dominating the globe through imperial expansion and control, new Muslim settlement, conversions to Islam and its propagation in Britain by people like Quilliam occurred in a context of hardening of attitudes towards Muslims and their faith. By the end of the Victorian era, British Christian attitudes tended to reflect the spread of an emotional and zealous evangelicalism, which was highly critical of non-Christian faiths, including Islam. In turn, this stimulated a huge effort among missionary societies to 'save the souls' of 'heathen' Muslims and other non-Christians throughout the British Empire and beyond.[7] Given the shared Abrahamic roots of Christianity and Islam, Muslims were deemed to be especially ripe for conversion, and there was a very large number of them within the British Empire. As Queen Victoria wrote to her last prime minister, Lord Salisbury (1830–1903), in 1895: 'I have more Mohammedan subjects than the [Ottoman] Sultan.'[8] Indeed, by the end of Victoria's reign, Britain governed more than half the world's Muslims, 80 million in the Indian subcontinent alone.[9] In Britain, the permanent Muslim population was very small but increasing: official statistics are unavailable, but one scholar estimated that the number in 1897 was 2,700, compared with 2,600 Muslims in France and 800 in Italy.[10] The Muslim population in Britain swelled at least sixfold (and probably much higher) annually with temporary visitors and occasional settlers comprising seafarers (around 10,000 each year), traders, diplomats, students, intellectuals, professionals such as lawyers, servants and affluent tourists.[11]

Writing the history of Islam in Victorian Britain

By the 1980s, a century after Woking mosque and the LMI opened, there was renewed academic and public interest in the Victorians and Victorian Britain, including religious thought and practice. However, only modest attention was given to Victorian attitudes to Muslims and Islam,[12] let alone the lives and experiences of Muslim communities or individuals in nineteenth-century Britain.[13] Consequently, at the end of the decade, when Muslims in Britain were in the public spotlight due to protests following the publication of Salman Rushdie's *The Satanic Verses* (1988), little was known about the history of Islam in the British Isles beyond, at best, orthodox Christian attitudes and discourse which tended to denigrate Islam and demonize Muslims.

However, two scholarly books appeared between 1989 and 1992 which shed light on Victorian British attitudes to Islam and Muslims – that is, from the non-Muslim perspective – and especially those writers and public speakers who diverged from conventional approaches. The first of these studies, by Phillip C. Almond, focused on mainly British images of the Prophet Muhammad and Islam.[14] Almond built on the pioneering – but then, as now, rather overlooked – research about Western images of Islam by Norman Daniel published in the 1960s[15] and also Edward Said's important but sweeping analysis of Western Orientalism.[16] Almond challenged Said's methodological emphasis on the unity of Orientalist discourse by emphasizing the plurality of approaches to Islam in Western Europe, especially Britain, in the Victorian era. Whilst Almond conceded that archaic images of Muhammad as 'heretic, anti-christ, ambitious imposter, profligate politician' persisted throughout the period, he also identified alternative images which characterized Muhammad as 'a sincere hero, noble Arab, and even true prophet of God'.[17] Almond showed that some Victorian British writers and philosophers had a much more sympathetic understanding of the Prophet and Islam than was commonly assumed.

The second study, by Clinton Bennett, presented new biographical case studies of six British Christian men who wrote and spoke about Islam and Muslims.[18] Like Almond, Bennett underlined that Victorian images of Islam were not monolithic, and that some public religious men presented a more positive approach to Islam and Muslims at a time when negative and hostile opinions and perceptions dominated British political and cultural imperial discourse. Almond and Bennett's studies were followed by or, in some cases, triggered new historical research about British relations with the so-called Muslim world,[19] as well as pioneering scholarship about Muslim engagement with British society and Muslim experiences in nineteenth-century Britain.[20] Notably, in 1997, the Open University and Manchester University Press addressed the neglect of Islam and Muslims in their four-volume *Religion in Victorian Britain* series of books.[21] Almost a decade after that series was first published, a fifth and final volume included a chapter about the institutionalization of Islam, Hinduism and other 'South Asian religions' in Victorian Britain and a primary sources section with extracts of material relating to Quilliam and the LMI.[22]

The increased public scrutiny of Muslims in Britain and elsewhere in the West following the 9/11 and 7/7 terrorist attacks in the United States and UK respectively led to a new wave of scholarship about Christian-Muslim relations and the modern history of Islam and Muslims. In terms of Britain in the Victorian era, scholars have examined discourse about and representation of Islam and Muslims in fiction and by academic and literary Orientalists,[23] Christian missionaries[24] and travellers to Islamic countries and Muslim societies.[25] Many of these studies identify increasing prejudice against Islam and Muslims in Britain and amongst the British abroad during Queen Victoria's reign, but they also show how some Britons, as well as Muslims, presented Islam as a legitimate living faith and Muslims as equally capable of virtue and vice as Christians and members of other faiths. Valuable work produced from the perspective of Christian-Muslim relations includes analysis of Victorian writers and thinkers from many walks of life, including politicians, philosophers and travellers, most of them men but also some women.[26] Additionally, there are a number of useful general and focused studies about the British and other European empires as they interacted with Muslims in the nineteenth century.[27]

Over the past two decades, more has been discovered and written about Muslim lives and experiences in Victorian Britain, gradually bringing to the fore the stories and voices of those Muslim visitors and immigrants as well as indigenous converts mentioned earlier.[28] This is a fertile area for research, yet it is complicated by a lack of primary sources, especially for working- and middle-class Muslims and women and immigrants in particular. Inevitably, research has tended to focus on public or quasi-public figures, whose lives are better documented than the majority of Victorian Muslims, such as Queen Victoria's Muslim instructor-attendant, or *munshi*, Mohammad Abdul Karim (1863–1909) and Quilliam and his Muslim community.[29] However, the digitization of primary sources by libraries and archives worldwide is greatly enabling research, helping to expose details about both well-known and lesser-known, even marginal, Muslims in Britain in the past, leading to further discussion and analysis of their lives and experiences.

Researching and communicating Muslim histories in Britain (and elsewhere) has been revitalized in this twenty-first century, not least by scholars from diverse backgrounds and Muslims from all walks of life – including community historians and activists, educators and students, artists, designers and makers, museum and gallery curators, journalists and writers, politicians and interested citizens. The breadth of new research and vitality of discussion about attitudes towards Islam and Muslim experiences in the Victorian period is a testament to its importance to our understanding about the modern history of Britain: it complicates existing narratives and understandings about Britain, its peoples and its global interactions; and, whilst the subject matter and the subjects must be considered in their own historical period, they help to contextualize contemporary beliefs about and attitudes towards Islam, and they point to resilience and achievement as well as the struggles of class, poverty, racism, prejudice and sexism experienced by Muslims in Britain today.

Scope and chapters

This book presents eleven case studies to offer new perspectives and insights about Islam and Muslims in Victorian Britain and to encourage further research. By revealing nineteenth-century attitudes towards and beliefs about Islam and Muslims, the contributors demonstrate the plurality of voices – from, for example, politics, academia, literature, the press and other forms of popular culture – and their different approaches to and representations of Islam and Muslims in Britain's past. Indeed, the chapters show a complex web of motivations for Victorian non-Muslim engagement with Islam, including curiosity, Orientalist fantasy, academic interest and colonial and imperialist ideology. Equally important, the contributors to this book also bring to life the stories of Muslim visitors, settlers and British converts to Islam to examine and better understand their experiences as Muslims in the Victorian period.

The contributors are from a variety of academic disciplines – history, Islamic studies, religious studies, philosophy, literature and languages, and Victorian, cultural and postcolonial studies – but they all use historical research methods. Their chapters focus on the Victorian era, but some naturally dip into the pre-Victorian years and others stray into the twentieth century; some also explicitly show how the past influences the present. Whilst Britain is the main focus, inevitably all of the chapters are broadly or significantly concerned with Britain's global history, especially its relationship with Muslims in the Ottoman Empire (including Turkey, Syria, Palestine and Egypt) and India. Besides empire and imperialism, cross-cutting themes include religion, faith and religiosity, 'race' and ethnicity, gender, class, citizenship, confrontation, prejudice and discrimination, conciliation and tolerance, and resilience.

The eleven chapters are divided in two parts. Part one examines discourse about and representations of Islam and Muslims in Victorian Britain. To begin, A. Martin Wainwright (Chapter 1) looks at the British royal family's attitudes towards Islam and Muslims during Queen Victoria's reign. Wainwright shows that their attitudes evolved in the context of Britain's expanding rule over Muslims and the increasing presence of Muslims in Britain. Unlike some of her children, Victoria never travelled to Islamic countries or Muslim societies and only encountered Muslims when they visited Britain. Wainwright argues that royal views of Islam were thus generally grounded in Orientalist fantasies of the exotic. However, the queen herself partly transcended this late in life through her relationship with the Indian-born Muslim attendant, Mohammad Abdul Karim. Although Karim excited Victoria's interest in Islam by appealing to her love of the exotic, he imparted perspectives that she had not gained through earlier brief encounters with Muslims or Western visitors to Muslim lands.

Clinton Bennett (Chapter 2) concentrates on Anglo-Ottoman politics from the British perspective in the mid-to-late-Victorian period. He focuses on the rival views of the two titans of Victorian British politics, William Ewart Gladstone (1809–1898) and Benjamin Disraeli (1804–1881), as they related to the so-called Eastern Question, which asked whether Britain and its European allies should prop up the Ottoman Empire to maintain the balance of power and curb Russian expansion or support nationalist movements and allow the empire to collapse. Bennett analyses how Anglo-Ottoman relations were impacted by their different views on the Eastern Question, which saw Disraeli's friendly policy replaced by Gladstone's policy of disengagement. Bennett also looks at Christian support for both leaders in order to gauge how the wider public responded to their policies. He describes too the reactions of Gladstone and Disraeli's successors to the Armenian massacres of 1894–5, and Queen Victoria's involvement in the debate, to assess the continued impact of Britain's shift in attitude towards the Ottoman Empire and, by extension, Muslims and Islam. Bennett points to how the outcome of this rivalry between the two prime ministers, which was the withdrawal of friendship from the Ottomans, affected British and European politics and continues to reverberate in the modern world.

Geoffrey P. Nash (Chapter 3) also identifies strong connections between the past and present in his analysis of the content, reception and impact of Thomas Carlyle's (1795–1881) famous lecture about Muhammad, published in his *On Heroes, Hero-Worship, and the Heroic in History* in 1841. Nash reveals that Carlyle's ground-breaking reappraisal of the Prophet's character and his creed opened up possibilities for broader views about Islam as a faith conceived in Arabia by an Arab for Arabs which, by the close of the nineteenth century, co-existed alongside a troubled appraisal of the decline of the Ottomans and the potentially disruptive presence of a large Muslim population within the British Empire. Nash shows that, at the end of his life, Carlyle expanded his view to include India and Ottoman Turkey. Consequently, while in Britain Carlyle was either forgotten or confined to the category of proto-fascism, in a kind of afterlife, his lecture about Muhammad held purchase in India and the Middle

East as a statement on cultural relativism in which a British writer appeared to valorize the spiritual history of a non-Western people or nation.

Whilst political, historical and philosophical writing in Britain in the nineteenth century was dominated by men like Gladstone, Disraeli and Carlyle, the genre of travel writing enabled Victorian women, albeit largely from the middle and upper classes, to express in print their views about and experiences of other lands, peoples and cultures. Anne-Marie Beller and Kerry Featherstone (Chapter 4) analyse the published accounts of four educated women to show the diversity of responses to Islam, Muslims and European colonial ideology across the nineteenth century. They consider the work of Florentia Sale (1790–1853), Emily Eden (1797–1869), Lucie Duff Gordon (1821–1869) and Amelia B. Edwards (1831–1892), which includes representations of Islam and the daily lives of Muslims in Afghanistan, India and Egypt. Beller and Featherstone evaluate the extent to which these writers' religious, ideological and social positions shaped the encounters about which they wrote. Focusing on their responses to Muslim peoples and cultures reveals the contradictions and complexities of religious and racial prejudice in a time of heightened imperial fervour in Britain.

As the nineteenth century progressed, literate Victorians were deluged with books, tracts, pamphlets and articles that sought to undermine and condemn as well as understand and explain Islam and Muslims. They also had the opportunity to read new English editions of the core religious text of Islam, the Qur'an. In the final chapter of part one, Alexander Bubb (Chapter 5) examines the place and impact of the Qur'an on the Victorian bookshelf. Bubb documents the transition, between the 1840s and the early twentieth century, from expensive scholarly English editions of the Qur'an for the preserve of scholars and Orientalists to cheap, accessible, popular copies for the layperson. Bubb compares three English editions that were commonly available in the late nineteenth century to show how they gave starkly different impressions of the Qur'an to the neophyte reader. He demonstrates that the book was widely read by Victorians, suggests motivations for their interest and provides examples of individual readers in order to show their particular responses to Islam's most authoritative source.

Part two examines the lives and experiences of Muslims in Victorian Britain. As noted above, this is a growing but challenging area of research. Jamie Gilham (Chapter 6) tests what newspapers and public records can tell us about a Muslim immigrant whose life and work has largely been forgotten over time. When he arrived in Britain from Algeria in the early 1860s, Saiyid Mustafa

Ben-Yusuf (*c*.1847–1931) identified as a Muslim, but soon afterwards converted to Christianity and achieved a modest public profile by becoming an evangelical missionary. Gilham compares and contrasts press reports, supplemented by traditional genealogical records such as Census returns, to reconstruct Ben-Yusuf's life in England. He shows how this marginal working-class Arab Muslim became a minor celebrity by virtue of his conversion to Christianity and, against the odds, had some agency in the mid-to-late Victorian period.

As the pioneering research of the late Fred Halliday revealed in the 1990s,[30] some of the earliest Muslim communities in Britain comprised Ottoman Arab Muslim merchants and traders from Syria and what is now Lebanon, who took advantage of the manufactured goods, especially cotton, produced in Lancashire in the nineteenth century. Riordan Macnamara (Chapter 7) takes a fresh look at these communities through the lives of some key personalities and their families to show that they formed a broad, self-segregated interest group with a shared ethnic, linguistic and cultural background, intermarrying and associating in business, coalescing in a singular recreation of a *millet* (an Ottoman semi-autonomous minority community). Whereas the Arabic-speaking Jews opened synagogues in Manchester, the Syrian Muslims did not establish a formal religious institution in that city. Macnamara shows that, instead, from the late 1880s, the Manchester Muslims visited and became members of Abdullah Quilliam's LMI. There, they congregated with other Muslim immigrants, as well as British converts to Islam, and participated in an inter-ethnic network of Muslims that shared a common interest to profess allegiance to the central Ottoman authority. By the end of the First World War, however, most Syrian Muslim merchants had relocated to the Levant, to witness the partition of the Ottoman Empire and the French Mandate for Syria and Lebanon.

The majority of Muslims who came to Britain from overseas in the Victorian period were visitors or temporary rather than permanent settlers. Many were from India, who chose Britain to work, study or sightsee. Lyn Innes (Chapter 8) examines the case of Mansour Ali Khan (1830–1884), the Nawab Nizam (hereditary ruler) of Bengal, Bihar and Orissa, who visited Britain for quite different reasons to the norm. Innes explains the fraught relationship between the Nawab Nizam, the de facto independent Shi'i Muslim ruler of a nominally sovereign princely state, and British government officials in India. She shows how the British sought to control the Nawab and undermine his position in Bengal, ultimately forcing him to leave India for Britain in 1869 to appeal to the Crown for the restoration of his rights. The intended short stay in Britain turned out to be a twelve-year exile from India, during which time the

Nawab pleaded with Queen Victoria and her government to settle his financial and titular status. Innes explores how the British press received and perceived the Indian Muslim prince and how the authorities used the Nawab's marriage to a working-class Englishwoman in London as one of the reasons for eventually forcing his abdication.

Humayun Ansari (Chapter 9) examines the life and times of a very different Indian Muslim visitor to Victorian England, Maulana Muhammad Barakatullah (*c*.1859–1927). In contrast to the Nawab of Bengal, who described himself as 'the oldest ally of the British Government', Barakatullah came to desire and campaign for Muslim freedom from imperial rule. Ansari focuses on Barakatullah's short but formative years in Britain in the 1890s, explaining how he was drawn into a range of pan-Islamic as well as transnational, predominantly secular, networks that emerged in that decade. Ansari explores the process by which, in response to his experiences of hostility to Islam and Muslims in wider society, in England Barakatullah developed his own critique of Muslim subjection and his radical vision of political liberation, which effectively combined pan-Islamism and secular nationalism.

It is likely that Barakatullah was in part persuaded to visit Britain because of reports circulating in India in the late 1880s concerning Abdullah Quilliam and his propagation of Islam in Liverpool. Indeed, as Ansari shows in his chapter, Barakatullah eventually settled briefly in Liverpool, where he became a close associate of Quilliam and a champion of the LMI. The final two chapters of this book examine aspects of Quilliam's life and work in late-Victorian Liverpool. As was noted earlier, scholars of Islam and Muslims in Britain and elsewhere have devoted much energy to researching, unravelling and assessing Quilliam's complicated life and work. In a research field where sources are often difficult to locate, Quilliam is, for the scholar of British Islam, the gift that keeps on giving. He was a prolific writer, editor and public speaker, an avid self-publisher and self-promoter, who achieved such a wide global reach and influence in the 1890s and early years of the twentieth century that there are many primary sources still to be properly evaluated and received narratives reassessed and inevitably much more original material to be discovered in archives and libraries around the world.

In a sign of the vitality of what might be termed 'Quilliam studies', the final two chapters take quite different approaches to the subject. Brent D. Singleton (Chapter 10) looks at, for the first time in any detail, the LMI's tradition of feeding the Liverpool poor on Christmas Day and occasionally on Islamic religious holidays. Singleton uses LMI publications, mostly edited by Quilliam himself, to help reconstruct the events, explain why they were celebrated and evaluate their success in terms of philanthropy and propaganda for Islam and the Institute. He also introduces a few non-LMI sources to highlight both local (non-Muslim) press and critical Muslim opinion about the feedings. Matthew A. Sharp (Chapter 11) avoids the LMI's self-supporting, public-facing publications in favour of external sources to reassess Quilliam's claim to the title of 'Sheikh-ul-Islam of the British Isles', which effectively made him the leader of Muslims in Britain. Quilliam claimed that the title was bestowed on him by the Ottoman Sultan-Caliph 'Abd al-Hamid II (1842–1918) in the mid-1890s. Sharp, however, uses newly discovered English newspaper articles, Ottoman archival documents and other Ottoman Turkish and Arabic sources to argue that the sultan did not in fact give Quilliam the title. Sharp also contests that the sultan did not publicly refute the narrative that Quilliam perpetuated well into the twentieth century. Instead, Sharp argues that both Quilliam and his community, as well as the sultan and his court, benefited from the story of an Ottoman-appointed 'Sheikh-ul-Islam of the British Isles'; it gave Quilliam legitimacy and authority and helped the Ottomans to cultivate ties with non-Ottoman Muslims at a time when their very survival was being debated by the European powers, not least Great Britain.

Part 1

Discourse and Representations

1

The royal family's attitudes towards Islam and Muslims during the reign of Queen Victoria

A. Martin Wainwright

Introduction

When, in 1858, Queen Victoria proclaimed her accession over former East India Company territories, she also became sovereign of a third of the world's Muslims. Subsequent British acquisitions further increased Britain's share of the Islamic world. By the end of Victoria's reign, Muslims constituted nearly a quarter of her subjects, outnumbering Christians, who amounted to only a seventh.[1] Moreover, as Britain's jurisdiction over Muslims expanded overseas, so did the number of Muslims living in or visiting Britain, from an average in the low hundreds during the Napoleonic Wars to well over 8,000 in 1877.[2] Yet, residing as they did amid an overwhelmingly Christian population, thousands of miles from the vast majority of their Muslim subjects, the royal family knew little about the latter or their religious beliefs. This situation changed over time. Throughout Victoria's long reign, the royal family encountered Islam and Muslims in various ways, through fiction, travel literature, journeys abroad and visits of Muslim dignitaries and servants to Britain. These encounters with Islam and its adherents shaped royal attitudes towards the religion in complex and sometimes conflicting ways.

This chapter examines the Victorian royal family's attitudes towards Islam, the Islamic world and Muslims. Although the precise focus of this chapter is new, it builds on existing scholarship dealing with the British monarchy's involvement and role in the British Empire. Much of this scholarship examines the monarchy's central role as an institution in the ideology of the empire, although more from the perspective of official Britain than that of the royal family.[3] Miles Taylor has written an extensive examination of the Victorian royals' relationship and interaction with India, and Mohammad Abdul Karim's (1863–1909) relationship with Victoria has been the subject of a popular biography and movie based on it.[4] The royal family's attitudes towards Islam and Muslims were complex, evolving during Victoria's reign. Some overarching characteristics, however, were consistent. The royals viewed Muslims through an exotic lens, applying a romanticized past to the present. Just as the royal family essentialized aspects of British culture and society, they did the same to Muslims and the Islamic world. The royals, therefore, interacted within a world of their own imagining but grounded in British dominance.

The complexity of royal encounters with the Islamic world lends itself to a combination of chronological and thematic analysis. This chapter approaches these themes as they arose and discusses how each evolved during Victoria's reign. It begins with Victoria's early encounters with Islamic culture, interpreted through Western romantic fiction and travel accounts, and follows this approach to Muslims as denizens of the exotic East through the rest of her reign. It then shifts focus to the royal family's religious views, which it argues became more tolerant of non-Christian religions over time. Moving from the ideological to the political, the final theme centres on concerns over Muslims as political agents, particularly as they encountered Victoria in person.

While this chapter discusses the royal family generally, its focus is the queen. Victoria was a prolific writer, whose diaries and extensive correspondence provide a clearer window on her views of Islam, the Islamic world and Muslims than do those of other family members. Also, since this analysis deals with Victoria's reign, she appears in it more than any of her contemporaries. Much of the rest of the royal family's encounters with Islam, the Islamic world and Muslims must be gleaned less directly than is possible for Victoria herself. This is not necessarily a major shortcoming, since the other royals' relations with the Islamic world usually centred on Victoria, who was the embodiment of the Crown for nearly sixty-four years.

The Islamic world in the royal family's imagination

Victoria's earliest encounters with Islam were through entertainment. At age fourteen she attended a ballet, *The Revolt of the Harem*, which depicted a rebellion of enslaved women against an oppressive sultan in the Islamic Kingdom of Granada. Victoria was struck by the elaborate costumes, which she described in detail in her journal.[5] The following year, she read Washington Irving's

(1783–1859) *The Alhambra* (1832), 'a most delightful book', and followed it with his *A Chronicle of the Conquest of Granada* (1829).⁶ Victoria's fascination with the 'Orient' surely began with accounts such as these.

Several attitudes are identifiable in this worldview. The first two are the contrast between condemnation of Islamic misrule and sympathy for the suffering of its people and disappearance of its culture. 'I do so pity and admire those poor Moors who were (though cruel & fickle) a noble & most brave set of people', wrote Victoria in 1836, while regretting 'the way in which these poor people were driven step by step from their beloved & beautiful land'.⁷ Of course, in this instance, the fact that the conquerors were Spanish, and therefore long-standing villains in the British imagination, would have strengthened Victoria's sympathy for the Muslim 'Moors'. Another attitude regarded the position of women in Islamic society. Irving describes a balcony in the Alhambra's 'women's apartment . . . from whence the dark-eyed beauties of the harem [women's quarters] might gaze unseen upon the entertainments of the hall below'.⁸ The sexually charged mystery of the harem was a common trope in nineteenth-century Western imaginings of Islamic society, even in the travel writing of some British women.⁹ Finally, these books reinforced Victoria's love of exotic settings and her longing to see them in person: 'The descriptions of the country of Granada & of the Alhambra are so beautiful, that they make me quite long, that I could see them myself, & wander through the deserted Halls & courts . . . But these are all Phantom Castles which I love to form!'¹⁰

This longing to travel continued through Victoria's life, although she never ventured beyond Europe. Writing to the Maharaja of Kutch (1866–1942) in 1887, Victoria declared: 'To me it is a source of deep regret that I cannot go myself to India, but alas! at my age and dreading sea voyages as well as heat, it would be impossible.'¹¹ Rather than visit India or Muslim lands, the queen contented herself to have their inhabitants come to her. Her frequent receptions of non-Western princes and aristocrats exposed her to the Islamic world amid the familiarity of her native land.

Eastern societies also interested Albert, the Prince Consort (1819–1861), albeit somewhat differently from Victoria. He approached the East from a more academic perspective than his wife. Before his marriage to Victoria in 1840, Albert studied at the University of Bonn. Although his education there focused on European humanities, he also encountered emerging European scholarship concerning India. One of his professors, August Wilhelm von Schlegel (1767–1845), was a leading scholar of Sanskrit and comparative linguistics of Indo-European languages. In the 1850s, Max Müller (1823–1900), a rising specialist in Sanskrit, advised the prince on the acquisition of titles for the Royal Library.[12] Although these connections extended Albert's interests beyond Western societies, they directed them towards Hindu and Buddhist culture rather than Islamic. By contrast, the visit of German prince and travel writer Carl von Hügel (1795–1870) to London in 1845 may have provided some balance in this regard. While promoting the English translation of his *Travels in Kashmir and Panjab*, von Hügel dined with Victoria and Albert on several occasions. The first half of his account deals extensively with predominantly Muslim Kashmir, whose wonders he described while confessing disappointment that the land did not quite live up to its reputation as 'the terrestrial paradise'.[13] For instance, he praises Lake Dal's Mughal gardens, discussing their fabled history, while criticizing alterations made by recent local rulers.[14] Albert acquired the book for the Royal Library.[15]

Indeed, the Royal Library's catalogue provides a further glimpse of Albert's interests, because he oversaw a major increase in the library's collection.[16] A comparison of the library catalogues for 1843 (for which only the first of two volumes survive) and shortly after the prince's death is instructive. The 1843 volume lists almost no titles pertaining to Asia and Africa. It includes English and French translations of *The Thousand and One Nights*. Victoria and Albert might also have been familiar with Sir Walter Scott's (1771–1832) *The Talisman* (1825), with its romanticized depiction of Sultan Saladin during the Crusades, and Edward Gibbon's (1737–1794) description of the Ottoman conquest of Constantinople. Both Scott's and Gibbon's works were in the original collection.[17] By contrast, the later library catalogue lists extensive travel literature from Africa and Asia, many of them predominantly Muslim lands. It is impossible to know how many of these titles Victoria or Albert actually read, but their presence in the collection indicates an interest in the Islamic world.[18]

Complementing the royal couple's fascination with the exotic was their passion for the visual arts. Albert adopted the new technology of photography enthusiastically, collecting professional portraits and taking his own. When Duleep Singh (1838–1893), the deposed Maharaja of Lahore, first visited the royal family at Osborne House on the Isle of Wight, Albert participated in setting up a photograph of him in Indian dress, and the royal couple persuaded him to sit for a portrait by the painter Franz Xaver Winterhalter (1805–1873).[19] Victoria, an amateur artist, made several etchings of the Indian prince. Duleep was a convert from Sikhism to Anglican Christianity, but the royals also collected or recorded the images of Muslim visitors to their court. Albert's collection includes a photograph of Farrokh Khan (1812–1871), the Persian ambassador to

Britain, who was sent to negotiate the end of the Anglo-Persian War (1856–7).[20] Victoria's journal includes etchings of servants and soldiers in Middle Eastern or Indian dress, many of whom were likely Muslim. For the royal couple, the distinctions did not matter, since their attraction to Islamic culture, as with Hindu and Sikh, was in its visual trappings rather than its beliefs.

Following Albert's death, Victoria went into seclusion for several years, eschewing even the public functions expected of her position. Nevertheless, as she emerged from mourning, her romantic views of the East remained. She reveled in ceremony and costume, particularly accompanying her role as Empress of India, a title she actively sought and received in 1876. By 1880, she was requesting that Indian women she received at court 'should appear in Indian costume', and the expectation that non-Western guests wear their native apparel became so entrenched that an Indian prince attending the coronation of Edward VII (1841–1910) had to ask permission from the viceroy (the monarch's representative and governor-general in India) to wear Western dress at a garden party.[21]

Little wonder then that Victoria jumped at the opportunity during her Golden Jubilee in 1887 to have two Indians become a permanent part of her household staff. These table servants were both Muslim, as were all their successors during the remainder of the queen's life. The rise of one of them, Abdul Karim, to attain the new position of the queen's *munshi* (instructor, attendant), is a now familiar tale.[22] Partly out of desire for self-promotion, and partly out of a sincere affinity to the queen, Karim indulged Victoria's Orientalist imagination. He participated in *tableaux vivants* (living pictures) in which members of the royal family, household staff and occasional visitors would dress up for scenes from the Bible, literature, art and history. These were often photographed for private use. For the royal family, the presence of Indian servants at court added a seeming level of authenticity to any theme occurring in the Middle East or India. For instance, on one occasion, Indian servants took part in two *tableaux*, one based on the biblical book of Esther, the other recreating an Arab Bedouin camp. Karim 'helped arrange the oriental draperies for the ladies'.[23] On another occasion, Indian servants served as backdrops to a *tableau* of the meeting between Richard the Lionheart and Saladin in Scott's *The Talisman*.[24] These photographs, taken at home, substituted for visual records of the exotic that other royals were encountering abroad, such as photographs in the Prince of Wales's private album of Alexandra, the Princess of Wales (1844–1925), seated on a camel, taken during their 1869 tour of the eastern Mediterranean.[25]

Tableaux vivants, whether in ancient or contemporary settings, echoed in private the very public displays that official Britain coordinated equating

Figure 1.1 Mohammad Abdul Karim with Queen Victoria at Balmoral, *c.*1890.
Source: Courtesy of Royal Collection Trust / © His Majesty King Charles III 2022.

the exotic with the past. Bernard S. Cohn refers to the Imperial Assemblage of 1877, which formally celebrated Victoria's acquisition of the title Empress of India, as the realization of the 'British conception of Indian history . . . as a kind of "living museum" '.[26] The same could be said of the queen's Golden and Diamond Jubilees, and of the participation of Muslim Indian servants in these *tableaux vivants*. It was, in the view of the royals and their friends, perfectly appropriate for brown-skinned Muslims to play any exotic role that arose. Significantly, these servants rarely performed in titled character roles. For instance, in the 'Talisman' *tableau*, Prince Henry of Battenberg (1858– 1896), who was the husband of Victoria's youngest child, Princess Beatrice (1857–1944), played Saladin.[27] Royals and household staff might dress up as characters from the Bible. In one *tableau*, for example, Princess Beatrice played the queen of Sheba across from Queen Victoria's private secretary, Henry Ponsonby (1825–1895), who posed as King Solomon.[28] But in this case, the Indian servants played Hebrew servants; they never posed in European roles in any of the performances. While most *tableaux* were set in the past, those set in contemporary settings tended to depict the Indian servants in primitive roles, as with the Bedouin scene, or subordinate ones, as in 'India', in which Beatrice personified the 'Indian Empire' with the Indian servants attending her.[29] The continuity of scenes from the Bible and contemporary Asia and Africa suggests a sense of timelessness in these non-European settings that contrasts with the dynamic nature of Western society.

In this context, the arrival in 1893 of Karim's wife and her mother in purdah thrilled the elderly queen. This was not the first time that a member of Victoria's family had seen Muslim women in purdah. During the Prince and Princess of Wales's 1869 tour, Alexandra visited the harem of Khedive Ismail Pasha of Egypt (1830–1895) as the dinner guest of the latter's mother. On the couple's return to England, the princess's travelling companion, Theresa Grey, published a journal of the tour describing the scene as reminding 'one of the descriptions one reads in the *Arabian Nights*'.[30] But the princess was not quite finished immersing herself in this Oriental fantasy, for she returned from the dinner to her husband disguised as a harem slave.[31] Later on the tour, Alexandra became the first woman outside the Ottoman royal family to dine with Sultan 'Abd al-Aziz (1830–1876).[32] Queen Victoria's knowledge of these encounters had set up her expectations and excitement at finally meeting women in purdah. Karim used these expectations to his advantage. The decision of his wife and mother-in-law to wear veils complemented his own efforts to elevate his social background in Victoria's eyes, since veiling was a marker of high social status in much of the

Islamic world. Karim's supervisor at the Agra jail, where he had worked before coming to Britain, claimed to have 'constantly seen the Munshi's wife and female relations in India, as they were never shut up there from public gaze, belonging as they do to quite a low class; and that the idea of their being in purdah was never dreamt of until they came to England to pose as ladies'.[33]

None of this mattered to the queen, who dismissed accusations that Karim's family was posturing above its social rank. Writing to her eldest daughter Victoria, Princess Royal (1840–1901), the queen declared that her visitors were 'I believe the first Mohammedan purdah ladies who ever came over ... and keep their custom of complete seclusion and of being entirely covered when they go out, except for holes for their eyes'.[34] As usual, regarding visitors in exotic attire, she appraised the appearance of Karim's wife: 'She was beautifully dressed with green and red and blue gauzes spangled with gold, very gracefully draped over head and body'.[35] Victoria then asked Karim to allow her daughter to visit his wife, once again stressing the exotic clothes she should wear (within limits) for the occasion: 'I know you wd. like her to be seen in her fine clothes, only I think the large nose rings spoil her pretty young face'.[36] Indeed, Victoria's other daughters visited the Muslim women on a number of occasions.[37] Access to Karim's female relatives was a privilege that only the women of the royal family could exercise, since the practice of purdah prevented men from seeing their faces. And Victoria exercised it as if she were a member of Karim's family, referring to the couple as 'my dear Indian children' and even arranging for a 'Lady Doctor' to examine the *munshi*'s wife, because they were having difficulty conceiving a child.[38] Such interventions were part of the personal approach Victoria took to most issues she encountered. As the matriarch of the world's largest empire, she saw her relationship with Karim as the personal manifestation of her relationship with all her Muslim and Indian subjects.

Perhaps the most remarkable of the elderly queen's efforts to compensate for not actually travelling beyond Europe was her study of Urdu. Karim introduced her to the dominant language of north-central India, which drew extensively on the subcontinent's Islamic culture and was written in Arabic script. His recitation of Urdu poetry enchanted the queen, and her exercise books demonstrate her ability to write simple passages in the language. She also spoke it occasionally when addressing her Indian servants and greeting high-ranking Indian visitors.[39] Victoria's willingness to learn about Muslim Indian culture showed her desire to glean more knowledge about her non-European subjects while satisfying her love of the exotic.

Royal attitudes towards Islam as a religion

Interest in Islamic culture, however, did not necessarily translate into an interest in Islam as a religion. Notably absent from the Royal Library's collection was scholarship on the Islamic religion. The collection includes only two titles that focus on the early history and doctrines of Islam. One of them describes the Prophet Muhammad as 'one clever but unprincipled imposter'.[40] The other is a French translation of George Sale's (1697–1736) somewhat sympathetic 1734 commentary on the life of Muhammad, which accompanied a more recent French translation of the Qur'an along with other sacred writings from non-Christian religions. While Sale similarly accuses the Prophet of making 'use of an imposture', he also argues that '*Mohammed* gave his *Arabs* the best religion he could, as well as the best laws, preferable, at least, to those of the ancient pagan lawgivers'.[41]

For most of their twenty-one-year marriage, the royal couple's sentiments may have echoed those of Sale. Both were devout Protestants, who initially saw the British Empire as a field for proselytizing. The first two Indians whom the royal family took under their supervision were Princess Gouramma of Coorg (1841–1864) and the Maharaja Duleep Singh. Of Hindu and Sikh background respectively; both were baptized into Anglican Christianity, with Victoria as their godmother. Alexandra followed suit in 1869 when she returned from her visit to Egypt with Ali Achmet, a ten-year-old presumably Muslim Nubian boy, who was baptized at Sandringham.[42] Writing to the governor-general of India in 1854, the queen anticipated that the 'progress of the railroad' would 'tend more than anything else to bring about civilization, and will in the end facilitate the spread of Christianity, which hitherto has made but very slow progress'.[43]

Nevertheless, just as Victoria and Albert believed in the power of modern technology to spread the Gospel of Christ, so they allowed science to shape their views of Christian doctrine and their tolerance of other religions. Always fascinated with scientific advancement, Albert joined with Prime Minister Viscount Palmerston (1784–1865) in supporting a knighthood for the naturalist and geologist Charles Darwin (1809–1882). The proposal died amid opposition from Anglican clergy.[44] Moreover, since Victoria and Albert came from different national branches of Protestantism, they centred their faith on domestic piety and frowned on rigid doctrinal tests for membership in the established church. This sentiment led them into direct conflict with the emerging Tractarian movement, which sought to position the Church of England in the Catholic line of apostolic succession and rein in the variations of doctrine that the Reformation had unleashed.[45] Although the British monarchy reigned over a growing empire, most of whose inhabitants were non-Christian, its primary religious concerns were those that had occupied European monarchs since the Reformation. The royal family was more concerned about the threat of Catholicism than Islam.

Victoria and Albert's children varied from their parents' convictions in different ways. Beatrice was considered the most devout. Her maid of honour claimed that the princess focused on 'theology and all religious questions' while 'science was a dead letter'.[46] By contrast, Victoria feared that her third child, Alice (1843–1878), who was married to the Grand Duke of Hesse, was falling too much under the influence of rationalist and agnostic German intellectuals.[47] In terms of interaction with the Islamic world, however, it was the Prince and Princess of Wales' attitudes that mattered most, because they (particularly the Prince) represented the British monarchy when they visited Muslim lands. Although Alexandra was a devout Lutheran, Albert Edward's (later King Edward VII) interests focused on the worldly. While he may have been secretly attracted to Catholicism, he spent most of his time hunting and socializing rather than engaging in intellectual discourse.[48]

Nevertheless, the Prince of Wales's journal from his first visit to the Middle East, in 1862, reveals considerable knowledge of its historical importance to Western civilization. He acknowledges as much in his description of the Pyramids of Giza as 'wonderful mementoes of *our* forefathers'.[49] Throughout his journal the prince refers to Jesus as 'Our Lord' when visiting sites associated with the Gospels. He also displays considerable knowledge of biblical traditions. However, he uses more sceptical language when referring to Muslim holy sites, for instance: 'We then saw the Pillar of Mahomet, where the Mohamedans fancy he will come & judge the world.'[50] Such references indicate a passing acquaintance with Islamic beliefs, probably learned while the prince was touring the Middle East.

Victoria and Albert's broad church beliefs within Protestantism facilitated their shift in attitude following Britain's successful suppression of the Indian Rebellion of 1857–8. Although the British government easily passed legislation to replace the East India Company with direct rule through an India Office and viceroy, the manner in which the queen should characterize her assumption of sovereignty presented a dilemma. On the one hand, evangelical Christians wanted the queen to make the Christian nature of British rule explicit in her proclamation of accession. On the other hand, doing so would surely inflame Indian opposition. Victoria urged a conciliatory tone, forcing a major revision of the original draft of the proclamation. The result modelled the queen's approach to other religions on the royal couple's inclusive approach to religious doctrine within Protestantism: 'Firmly relying Ourselves on the truth of Christianity, and acknowledging with gratitude the solace of Religion, We disclaim alike the Right and the Desire to impose our Convictions on any of Our Subjects.'[51] Victoria's own sincere beliefs were now analogous to those of her non-Christian subjects. This willingness to respect the beliefs of others through the prism of her own set the stage for the most remarkable phase of the queen's encounter with Islam as a religion.

By elevating Karim to be her personal instructor on India's cultures, Victoria exposed herself for the first time in her life to a Muslim perspective on a regular basis. Hitherto, she had known Islam almost exclusively through the filter of non-Muslims. The occasional exception might have been comments she encountered from visiting Muslim dignitaries. Karim, however, exerted unprecedented influence over the queen's understanding of Islam. Writing in 1891 to Lady Harris (1851–1930), wife of the governor of Bombay, Victoria cautioned against interfering with the practice of purdah among Muslim women: 'I think no attempt should be made to induce them to alter their mode of living, or to interfere with their religion, which, when well-known and understood, contains so much that is fine and to be respected and admired.'[52] She contrasted Islam to Hinduism and Parsi Zoroastrianism, both of which she described as 'idolatrous', and made clear her reliance for this information on 'my young Mohammedan Munshi', from whom she had 'learnt a great deal'.[53] The queen's lady-in-waiting recalled Victoria wishing that 'the Mohamedans be left alone by Missionaries'.[54] Perhaps more astonishing was the way in which the queen's knowledge of Islamic beliefs modified her acceptance of Christian doctrine. Under Karim's influence her understanding of divine intervention in human affairs became more deterministic and her Christological views veered in a Unitarian direction, the latter to the point where she argued with a Conservative politician against the doctrine of the Trinity.[55]

Whether Victoria was fully aware of how dramatically her views were departing from orthodox Christianity is unclear. She approached so many aspects of her life from the perspective of personal interaction that her statements of sympathy with Islamic doctrines may have simply amounted to momentary expressions of her affection for Karim and her other Muslim servants. What alarmed British officials most over the last decade of Victoria's reign was not the queen's tendency towards unorthodox beliefs but the threat to imperial security that they believed her friendship with Muslims created.

Islam as a political issue for the British monarchy

Britain's political relations with the Islamic world in the Victorian period had two dimensions. One was with subjects and vassals of the Crown within the empire, whose loyalty British authorities sought to ensure. The other was with strategically important Muslim powers, whose friendship the British government sought to nurture. The two dimensions overlapped inasmuch as poor relations with independent Muslim powers could inspire disloyalty among Muslim subjects of the Crown. British strategic policy supported the Ottoman Empire as a bulwark against Russian and French designs on the Middle East and India. It was Britain and France's support of the Ottoman Empire that led them into war with Russia in the 1850s and nearly did so again in the 1870s. As British sovereign, the queen played an important role in all these considerations.

Victoria tended to receive negative reports of the Ottoman Turkish and Egyptian governance and military organization. This became more pronounced during the Crimean War (1853–6), when Britain, France and the Ottoman Empire were allies. In 1854, Soliman Pasha al-Faransawi (1788–1860), a French convert to Islam who had directed Egyptian Khedive Muhammad Ali's (1769–1849) military academy, told Queen Victoria that the deceased khedive's descendants were lazy. Victoria recalled in her diary: 'After dinner [Soliman] made us die with laughter with all he said about the Turks, – their vanity, venality, &c.'[56] A few months later, Victoria reacted to news of the Battle of Balaclava (October 1854), famous for the disastrous 'Charge of the Light Brigade', by contrasting heroic British actions with those of 'the Turks', who 'ran away shamefully'.[57] However, she subsequently decided that Ottoman Turkish soldiers had been 'placed in a most unfair & exposed situation'.[58] In an era when Europeans regularly questioned the masculinity, and therefore right to autonomy, of people of colour, Victoria's willingness to entertain mitigating circumstances for such apparent acts of cowardice was important. In her analysis of British efforts to portray Bengali men as effeminate, Mrinalini Sinha notes that Muslims 'were usually exempted' from this treatment.[59]

Whatever the queen's impression of Muslim men-at-arms, some of their rulers were simply too important for her to ignore. Ironically, for all the official concerns about Muslim intrigue later in her reign, the prominent visits of three Muslim rulers helped to rehabilitate the monarchy after Victoria had gone into extended seclusion following Albert's death. This seclusion had led to increasing public criticism that she was failing to attend to her royal duties. Worse still, French autocrat and British rival, Napoleon III (1808–1873), was outshining Britain with the pomp and entertainment he afforded visiting heads of state. Unfavourable comparisons among these visitors could harm British interests abroad. The need and opportunity coincided in the summer of 1867 when Napoleon III invited Ottoman Sultan 'Abd al-Aziz to Paris. After much resistance, Victoria assented to receive the sultan at Windsor Castle for lunch and again at Osborne House for a naval review. To complicate matters, the government learned that Khedive Ismail Pasha of Egypt also wanted to visit England. Although the khedive was theoretically ruling Egypt on behalf of the Ottoman sultan, he was in reality an independent monarch of a country that, from the British perspective, was strategically of equal importance to Ottoman Turkey.[60]

The arrival of both rulers in July 1867 presented some curious cultural dilemmas, particularly regarding the sultan, with whom British officials were less familiar than they were with the khedive. Rumours abounded as to what the sultan could eat, whether he would bring slaves and how he would use a water closet. Similar concerns arose in 1873 when Persian Shah Naser al-Din (1831–1896) visited England. Henry Ponsonby warned the queen that the Shah might wipe 'his wet hands on the coat-tails of gentlemen next to him', drink out of the spout of a teapot and use his fingers to eat his food. Worse still, he might bring concubines on his journey and make improper advances to women in Victoria's household.[61] Ultimately, however, such fears either misrepresented the customs of these Muslim visitors or failed to take account of their knowing more about Western habits than British officials or the queen did about theirs. Freda Harcourt notes ironically: 'Despite the fact that Britain ruled many millions of Moslem subjects, officials in London were strangely ignorant of their habits.'[62] Victoria enjoyed the opportunities to see her expectations of the Islamic world fulfilled without too jarring an encounter with the 'Other'. Regarding lunch with the Ottoman sultan, she remarked: 'He [ate] of most things, but (which I was glad to see) never touched wine. He seemed to cut his meat with difficulty, this generally being done for him.'[63] The sultan's efforts to eat with European cutlery made him approachable, while his refusal to drink wine made him authentically Muslim, just the right combination for the queen.

Muslims, however, represented a potential threat to Britain as well as an opportunity. Islamic movements challenging British rule were ever present. Of particular concern, especially in India, were Wahhabis, or Muslims who sought to restore the moral and political world of the first generations of Islam.[64] Such aspirations were incompatible with the rule of a Christian power. Rather, they required a caliph committed to expunging secular and Christian Western influences. Although he claimed the title caliph, 'Abd al-Aziz was not such a ruler, since he adopted various aspects of Western culture. It was not surprising, therefore, that when, in 1872, a Muslim ex-convict assassinated India's viceroy Lord Mayo (1822–1872), the latter's private secretary told the queen that the assailant was a 'Wahabee'. This even though the investigation into Mayo's assassination had already determined that the perpetrator had committed the crime for personal reasons.[65] Moreover, as Britain's relations with Russia improved during the 1880s and 1890s, supporting the Ottoman Empire became less of a strategic priority. British officials increasingly saw Sultan 'Abd al-Hamid II's (1842–1918) role as caliph a threat to the internal stability of the British Empire, particularly among Muslims in Britain itself. An 1898 India Office intelligence report warned: 'The supreme authority of the [Ottoman] Sultan as Caliph, and measureless laudation of the diplomatic ability and good qualities of Abdul Hamid II form the staple of the speakers at all their meetings.' As a result, it questioned 'whether the Moslem considers his prime allegiance due to his Queen or to his Caliph'.[66]

In this context, Abdul Karim's influence over Victoria became a cause for concern, particularly when it manifested a pro-Muslim bias or threatened to compromise security. The former became apparent when, in 1893, the juxtaposition of the Muslim lunar and Hindu solar calendars caused the two communities to celebrate festivals simultaneously, resulting in communal riots in India. The queen wrote to viceroy Lord Lansdowne (1845–1927) claiming that 'Hindus are, I believe, mostly the aggressors', an assertion both Lansdowne and the governor of Bombay refuted.[67] Concerns over security were more acute regarding Rafiuddin Ahmad (1865–1954), an Indian Muslim barrister and journalist, who gained access to Victoria through their mutual friendship with Karim. Ahmad flattered the queen by publishing an article about her knowledge of Urdu in *The Strand Magazine* in December 1892.[68] Their friendship continued over the next few years, leading to her recommend him to Prime Minister Lord Salisbury (1830–1903) for service as a diplomat in the British embassy in Constantinople. Failing to include a Muslim on the staff would, she argued, imperil imperial security: 'You know how serious wd. be the injustice or supposed injustice on our part towards the Moslems, for I have more Mohammedan subjects than the [Ottoman] Sultan.'[69] British officials, however, regarded Ahmad himself as a security threat. Rumours circulated that Karim was passing to Ahmad information from confidential papers intended for the queen's eyes only. Victoria's personal physician, James Reid (1849–1923), even bluntly suggested to the queen that he might declare her 'insane' if she continued under Karim's spell.[70] He did not follow up on this threat, but concerns over Karim ended only with Victoria's death.

Conclusion

Victoria's relationship with Karim culminated a lifelong evolution in her attitudes towards Islam and its adherents. Starting with romantic imaginings of exotic 'Moors', her views expanded as she faced the practical demands of her office regarding British rule over India and diplomacy with Muslim powers. Only during the final thirteen years of her life did her relationship with Abdul Karim push her further than any member of her family in her sympathy for Muslims and their beliefs. Other royals joined her on this journey only part of the way. While Albert supported Victoria's inclusive approach to religious diversity in India, he died too soon to interact with Muslim monarchs or servants. Just as Victoria entertained Muslim royalty in Britain, so some of her children represented her when travelling in the Middle East and India, thereby projecting British power abroad and in the empire. Sometimes, as in the case of Alexandra abroad or Beatrice at home, they indulged in fantasies about the Orient. Indeed, such fantasies seem to be the most consistent aspect of the royal family's attitudes towards the Islamic world, since many members (including Victoria herself) continued to indulge in them through ceremony and *tableaux vivants* during the last years of her reign. The presence of Muslim servants and the visits of Muslim royalty forced the royal family to adapt to some cultural differences, but for the most part they continued to view Islam through an Orientalist perspective on their own terms.

2

Rival views on the Eastern Question, Muslims and Islam: William Ewart Gladstone, Benjamin Disraeli and Anglo-Ottoman relations

Clinton Bennett

Introduction

This chapter examines the contrasting views of the Ottoman Empire (commonly called 'Turkey' in Victorian Britain) and of Muslims and Islam found in the writing and parliamentary speeches of the rival politicians and sometime prime ministers, William Ewart Gladstone (1809–1898) and Benjamin Disraeli (1804–1881).[1] It analyses how their different views impacted Anglo-Ottoman relations, which saw Disraeli's friendly policy replaced by Gladstone's policy of disengagement. Throughout the second half of the nineteenth century, debate about the future of the Ottoman Empire was known as the 'Eastern Question', which asked whether Britain and its European allies should prop up the Ottoman Empire to maintain the balance of power and curb Russian expansion or support nationalist movements and allow the empire to collapse. If the latter, the assumption was that the British would gain control of some former Ottoman territories. Since England had signed its first treaty with the Ottomans in 1579, Britain had usually sided with the Ottomans – most recently against Russia in the Crimean War (1853–6). Russia was regarded as a major threat to British interests in the East generally, and in India especially, and featured large in discussion about the Eastern Question.

As well as becoming a major trading partner with the Ottomans, Britain also supplied military advisers and engineers to establish and maintain such machinery as blast furnaces and steam drills that British companies sold to the

Ottoman Empire.[2] After Gladstone withdrew military advisers in 1880, and as trade declined, Germany filled the gap with loans, engineers to build railways and with military advice. Responses to the Eastern Question by Christian clergy and others are described to show that people in Britain generally supported Gladstone's anti-Ottoman and specifically anti-Turkish policy but that Disraeli's pro-Ottoman view had some sympathizers. The Armenian massacres of 1894–5 revived discussion of the Eastern Question. Gladstone and Disraeli's successors' responses, and Queen Victoria's role in the debate, are briefly discussed to assess the continued impact of Britain's change in attitude towards the Ottoman Empire and, by extension, Muslims and Islam. Compared with the contributions of academic writers or of Christian and Muslim leaders or religious thinkers, the chapter demonstrates that Gladstone and Disraeli's rival views on the Eastern Question, Muslims and Islam had enduring and serious consequences, including reluctance in Western Europe to see present-day Turkey as a European state and current conflicts in the Middle East which are exacerbated by how Britain and its allies drew up national boundaries after the First World War.

Introducing the rival politicians

William Ewart Gladstone was born in Liverpool in 1809. His father, Sir John Gladstone (1764–1851; born as Gladstones; he changed the family name in 1835), was a wealthy merchant and slave owner who had moved to Liverpool from his native Scotland in 1787. His mother was Anne MacKenzie Robertson (1772–1835), who was also born in Scotland. William attended a preparatory school near Liverpool, then Eton College, followed by Christ Church, Oxford, in 1828. Although he enrolled at Lincoln's Inn in 1833, Gladstone had no intention of pursuing a legal career because he had set his sights on entering Parliament, which he did as the Conservative Member for Newark, Nottinghamshire, in 1832.

After holding several junior posts in the government, in 1843 Gladstone became president of the Board of Trade. He switched constituencies several times during his parliamentary career, ending as MP for Midlothian, Scotland. He was chancellor of the exchequer four times. In 1859, Gladstone left the Conservatives and joined the Liberal Party. He became prime minister for the first time in 1868 (until 1874), succeeding Disraeli, and served three more terms in 1880–5 (when he again succeeded Disraeli), 1886 and 1892–4.

A devout Christian who identified with high church Anglicanism, Gladstone disliked Disraeli's pro-Ottoman policies. In 1856, when the Treaty of Paris ended the Crimean War, Gladstone objected in Parliament to the claim that this bound the Christian powers to maintain 'Turkey as a Mohamedan state' and instead spoke of Christians living under 'the Mohamedan yoke'.[3] When, in 1876, the Ottomans crushed a rebellion in Bulgaria, killing thousands of Christians, Gladstone wrote a pamphlet, *Bulgarian Horrors, And the Question of the East*, which succeeded in shifting public opinion against the Ottoman Empire by vilifying its leaders, the Turks, as a 'race' of monsters who should be driven out of Europe.[4] Despite his attempt to blame Ottoman Turkish barbarity on their 'race' and not on their religion, this confirmed for many the idea that Islam 'retarded' human progress. The pro-Ottoman British writer and Muslim convert Marmaduke Pickthall (1875–1936) later claimed that Gladstone once declared 'that so long as there were followers of that accursed book (the Koran), Europe would know no peace'.[5] Lack of any record that Gladstone said this has not deterred people claiming that Gladstone did so while holding up a copy of the Qur'an in the House of Commons. In his second term as prime minister, Gladstone withdrew military advisers from Ottoman territory. British trade with the Ottoman Empire quickly declined owing to the Ottoman's suspension of dividend payments and the general belief that their empire would not survive. However, while Gladstone supported autonomy for Christian populations under Ottoman rule, he did not call for their complete independence, but allowed that the Ottoman Empire could retain titular sovereignty. Gladstone tended to be more pro-Russian than Disraeli because, for Gladstone, the Russians were Christian, if of a dubious type. He stepped down as Liberal Party leader in 1875, but uprisings in Bulgaria against the Ottoman state caused him to return to the centre of British politics. Gladstone retired from Parliament in 1895 and died in 1898.

Benjamin Disraeli was born in London in 1804, the elder son of the writer Isaac D'Israeli (1766–1848) and Maria Basevi (1774/5–1847). His father ceased practicing as a Jew after a quarrel with his synagogue and had all of his children baptized into the Church of England. Benjamin was baptized in 1817 and, a few years later, dropped the apostrophe from his name. He was sent to a private school in Walthamstow between 1817 and 1821, when he entered a law firm and, like Gladstone, enrolled at Lincoln's Inn (1824), though his uncle, who was a barrister, advised him to switch to a literary career. Disraeli's first novel, *Vivien Grey*, was published in 1826–7. Inspired by Lord Byron's tour of the East, he set out on his own travels of the Middle East in 1830, but these ended precipitously when his companion, his sister's fiancé, died of smallpox in Egypt.

Politically ambitious, Disraeli stood for Parliament unsuccessfully three times as an Independent Radical and once as a Conservative before winning his first seat in Maidstone, Kent, in 1837. In 1841, Disraeli was elected Conservative MP for Shrewsbury, then, in 1847, for Buckinghamshire, which he represented until he was raised to the House of Lords as Earl of Beaconsfield in 1876. He served twice as chancellor of the exchequer. In February 1868, he became prime minister, serving until December that year. In 1874, the Conservatives won the general election and Disraeli began his second term as prime minister (to 1880).

Known for his pro-Ottoman sympathies, Disraeli's response to the massacres carried out by Ottoman troops in Bulgaria in 1876 was that the reports were exaggerated. However, public opinion sided with Gladstone's anti-Ottoman stance and, at the Congress of Berlin in 1878, which followed the Russo-Turkish War (1877–8), Disraeli had to accept the formation of four independent Balkan states. The Congress also allowed Austria-Hungary to occupy Bosnia-Herzegovina and ended Russia's threat to the Ottomans, which Disraeli had feared, though Russia was able to keep some territory in the Balkans. Gladstone was unhappy with aspects of the Treaty of Berlin because he objected to the European Powers taking over any territory in the Balkans. The treaty also failed to address Greece's border disputes with Turkey. Gladstone would have been happy with autonomy for the Balkans, rather than full independence. The motion to censure the treaty failed, but Queen Victoria created the Knights of the Garter and inducted Disraeli and Lord Salisbury (1830–1903), his foreign secretary and later his successor as Conservative Party leader, for their role in the Congress. Disraeli led the government from the House of Lords after 1876. Though he was a practicing Christian, Disraeli was proud of his Jewish heritage, strongly supported the emancipation of the Jews and peopled his novels with heroic Jewish characters to help instil pride in Jewish past accomplishments and future possibilities.[6]

In his novels, Disraeli depicted Islam and Islamic civilization sympathetically, and he wanted to encourage a Jewish-Christian-Islamic alliance. Opponents made spiteful remarks about his Jewishness behind his back and were suspicious that his 'Semitic' and 'Turcophile prejudices' might compromise British interests.[7] Gladstone wrote in 1878 that he thought Disraeli's 'crypto-Judaism' resulted in policies that were harmful to British interests.[8] Disraeli was referred to as 'Jew Earl, Philo-Turkish Jew, and Jew Premier', 'the traitorous Jew, veritable Jew, haughty Jew or even the abominable Jew'.[9] Disraeli retired in 1880 after Gladstone won the general election. He died in 1881 in London and was buried in the parish graveyard of St Michael and All Angels, Hughenden, Buckinghamshire, where Queen Victoria erected a memorial to him. It is known that Victoria preferred Disraeli over Gladstone, famously remarking that the latter spoke to her as if she 'were a public meeting'.[10] Like Disraeli, Victoria has been described as a Turcophile.[11] She was markedly cold with the Russian Romanovs, whom she distrusted and saw their clinging to autocracy as out of step with the trend towards constitutional monarchy elsewhere in Europe, which she had personally embraced. In 1867, she awarded Ottoman Sultan 'Abd al-Aziz (1830–1876) the Order of the Garter during his London visit (see Chapter 1) and even contemplated her daughter, Princess Louise (1848–1939), marrying the sultan's nephew and successor, Murad V (1840–1904). During Victoria's Golden Jubilee celebrations in 1887, the Ottoman ambassador's red fez was conspicuously visible; as were Turkish uniforms at her state funeral in 1901, where the Ottoman ambassador was the first diplomat to arrive in Westminster Abbey.[12]

Rival politicians and the 'Eastern Question'

Gladstone's anti-Turkish view

Throughout their careers, the Conservative Disraeli and the Liberal Gladstone disagreed on British policy towards the Ottoman Empire and held opposing views on Islam. Their very different perspectives clashed dramatically in 1876 following the anti-Ottoman uprising in Bulgaria (April to May), during which approximately 15,000 Christians were massacred and about thirty-six villages were burned by the Ottoman army and irregular troops. In June 1876, politicians in the House of Commons began to debate how Britain should respond. Under Disraeli's government, Britain was an ally of the Ottomans committed to defending the integrity of the Ottoman Empire. News of the massacres was slow to reach Britain and broke in the media before the government released any information. Although some mention was made of Christian fatalities in May 1876, it was an article by Edwin Pears (1855–1919), a British barrister and historian who lived in Constantinople, on the 'Moslem Atrocities' in the *Daily News* (23 June 1876) that prompted questions in Parliament. The *Daily News* sent the American journalist J. A. MacGahan (1844–1878) to Bulgaria to investigate. MacGahan's correspondence from Bulgaria, which had already enjoyed a wide readership through reprints in various newspapers, was republished as *The Turkish Atrocities in Bulgaria* (1876). On 26 June 1876, William Edward Forster (1818–1886), Liberal MP for Bradford and a social reformer, asked the British government to confirm or deny the allegations that Ottoman Turkish troops and irregulars had massacred Christian civilians in Bulgaria, citing the *Daily News* articles. Prime Minister Disraeli replied that the government had 'no news' in its possession 'which justifies the statements' to which Forster had referred. Disraeli suggested that perhaps Christians had attacked Ottoman Turkish settlers who 'were then obliged to defend themselves'.[13] Later, while they admitted that atrocities had occurred, Disraeli's government took the position that both sides were to blame.

Speaking on 31 July 1876, Disraeli stated that he was not prepared to say that the atrocities had 'all been committed by one side', and he disputed the number of fatalities.[14] Gladstone, in his reply, saw no alternative but to call on the European Powers to oversee the granting of autonomy to the Christian-majority provinces where there were insurrections, since the Ottoman government could not be trusted to carry out reforms that would address subject peoples' grievances, although he greatly desired to 'maintain the integrity of the Turkish empire'.[15] In July, Walter Baring (1844–1915), second secretary at the British embassy in Constantinople, was sent to Bulgaria to investigate what had happened. His report, published on 10 September 1876, largely confirmed the version of events reported in the *Daily News*. While Disraeli thought that this did not merit any change in British policy and that Britain should honour its treaties with the Ottoman Empire, Gladstone began to campaign to end Britain's support for the Ottomans and quickly wrote his *Bulgarian Horrors*. Gladstone had officially retired from leadership but, returning to the front benches, he succeeded in reversing Britain's policy towards the Ottomans.

Bulgarian Horrors, a tract of sixty-four pages, is dated 5 September 1876, five days before the release of Baring's report that had been privately submitted to the British government on 1 September. The Bulgarian revolt followed insurrections in Herzegovina and Bosnia and triggered the Russo-Turkish War, in which Russia intervened to liberate Bulgaria, Romania, Serbia and Montenegro from the Ottoman Empire. Claiming to be the protector of Eastern Orthodox Christians within the Ottoman Empire, and regarding the Balkan Slavs as their kin, Russia both defended Bulgaria's demand for autonomy and supported the independence of Romania, Serbia and Montenegro.

Gladstone's aim was to inform the British public of the Ottoman government's 'true character' and the reasons why Britain's policy was 'questionable and erroneous'.[16] Referring to the 'Turkish race', he stated that it was not a question of 'Mahometanism simply, but of Mahometanism compounded with the peculiar characteristic of a race'. Ottoman Turkish Muslims were neither the 'mild Mahometans of India, nor the chivalrous Saladins of Syria, nor the cultured Moors of Spain', but 'the one great anti-human specimen of humanity'.[17] Wherever they went, 'civilization disappears from view'. They governed solely by force as opposed to law. Their guide for this life was a 'relentless fatalism', while their promise for the next life was 'a sensual paradise'.[18] Their advance 'cursed' the whole of Europe, which, Gladstone argued, was united in opposing this 'common enemy', who, since they lacked intellectual capability, devolved a lot of authority onto ethnic and religious minorities, which helped to compensate for the 'deficiencies of Turkish Islam'.[19] Now, an empire that had borrowed large sums from European banks was 'at war' with the peoples of its Balkan provinces. Twenty years previously, Britain and other European powers had tried to remodel Ottoman Turkey's 'administrative system' and, helping the Ottoman's win the Crimean War, they had given 'the Turks' two decades of 'repose'.[20] Gladstone argued that the Bulgarian atrocities revealed the viciousness and barbarity of Ottoman Turkish rule, yet the British government was slow to admit that the massacres had occurred and tried to obscure what happened by attributing blame to both sides.

In *Bulgarian Horrors*, Gladstone referred to newspaper reports, and to questions and responses in Parliament, about the massacres of Christians. He cited a report of 22 August 1876 by Eugene Schuyler (1840–1890), the American consul-general in Constantinople, who had joined MacGahan's team in Bulgaria. Schuyler stated that he had found no evidence of anyone who was Muslim (as opposed to Christian) being killed in 'cold blood', of women who were Muslim being violated or of a mosque being 'desecrated or destroyed', which all pointed to Muslims, not Christians, as the aggressors.[21] Gladstone judged that Schuyler's reporting was especially reliable because America had no vested interest in the matter, whereas the European states did.[22] Gladstone described a British fleet in the region at the time that stood by while the insurrection was proceeding. This, for him, implicated Britain in the atrocities. Such a fleet should be used to 'protect innocent lives'; instead, British inaction had 'gravely compromised' the 'honour of the British name'.[23]

Gladstone insisted that Ottoman Turkish 'executive power' must be 'excluded' from the Balkans but, since he remained committed to maintaining the territorial integrity of the Ottoman Empire, he recommended that 'titular sovereignty' could be retained. Thus, no European powers should exercise sovereignty within 'the present limits of the Turkish empire'. He argued that Disraeli, in defending the status quo, wanted to perpetuate the Ottoman Turks' 'airy promises, his disembodied reforms, his ferocious passions, and his daily, gross, and incurable misgovernment'.[24] Britain should withdraw 'moral and material support' to 'the maintenance of Turkish administration in Bulgaria', cease being the 'evil genius' whose support for the Ottoman Turks baffled civilized people and join the Central Powers (comprising Germany, Britain, France, Italy and the Austro-Hungarian Empire) in overseeing Ottoman Turkey's withdrawal from the Balkans.[25] The new autonomous states would need to reach an accommodation with their Muslim minorities, but 'in none of these provinces has it been in the main a case of war between conflicting religions or local races: nearly the whole of the mischief has lain in the wretched laws, and the agents at once violent and corrupt, of a distant … Power'.[26] Gladstone argued that the only reparation that could be made for Bulgaria's tragedy would be the Turks' eviction from Europe 'one and all, bag and baggage'.[27] Three days after publishing *Bulgarian Horrors*, which sold 40,000 copies in less than a week, Gladstone spoke to a large crowd at Blackheath, London, making the first speech to rouse public support for his proposed change in policy on the 'Eastern Question'.

The Russo-Turkish War took place before the next general election in Britain, which Gladstone won. Disraeli supported the Ottomans during the war, although the only direct British intervention took place in February 1878 when Disraeli sent a fleet to protect the Ottoman capital, Constantinople. With the Treaty of San Stefano of 3 March 1878, which ended the war, the Ottomans were to grant independence to Romania, Serbia and Montenegro, give autonomy to Bulgaria, and cede territory in the Caucasus to Russia. However, other members of the Central Powers objected and convened the Congress of Berlin to revise these terms (June – July 1878). In Berlin, the independence of Romania, Serbia and Montenegro was ratified, and Bulgarian autonomy confirmed, though the territory was divided into three provinces, only one of which was returned to the Ottomans. This was to thwart Russia's aim of controlling a satellite Greater Bulgarian state in the region. Austria-Hungary was allowed to occupy Bosnia, and some territories that had been ceded to Russia were returned to the Ottomans, as was part of Romania. In agreeing to the independence of Romania, Serbia and Montenegro at Berlin, Disraeli went further than Gladstone in supporting their autonomy. On 4 June 1878, immediately before the Congress, Britain signed a convention with the Ottomans, negotiated in secret, that placed Cyprus under British administration for a fee. If Russia relinquished her newly acquired territories in Asia, however, Britain would leave Cyprus. The Cyprus Convention also pledged continued British military support for the Ottoman Empire in return for promises of reform.

Gladstone responded to the Treaty of Berlin and to the Cyprus Convention in a speech on 30 July 1878. He criticized the treaty for failing to include a resolution of Greece's border disputes with the Ottomans (Greece's independence had been recognized in 1832), for obliging Britain to defend Turkey's Asian provinces and for lacking parliamentary approval.[28] Regarding Cyprus, he disliked the secrecy of the negotiations and again objected that it undermined parliament's treaty-making prerogative. Gladstone ridiculed the British government's claims that it would provide a strategic port to protect access to the Suez Canal, asking where the funds to build such a port or to garrison it were coming from: Cyprus was not even on 'the road to India'; it was '250 miles away'.[29]

In November 1880, Prime Minister Gladstone withdrew Britain's military advisers from the Ottoman Empire, and soon afterwards Germany sent replacements. British banks also ceased making loans to the Ottoman Empire; they had already stopped buying bonds when the Ottomans halted dividend payments in 1875. The consequent collapse of the Ottoman financial system led to the creation of the European-run Ottoman Public Debt Administration in 1881. Britain's occupation of Egypt the following year reduced any remaining political influence she had in Constantinople. Although an anti-imperialist, Gladstone justified intervention in Egypt on the grounds that the latter was technically still governed by the Khedive (the Ottoman viceroy) with British advisers, and that this was essential to prevent anarchy and to maintain peace and order.[30] This same argument would be routinely used in India to resist Indian demands for Independence right through to the end of British rule there in 1947. Increased German involvement, and the departure of the British, prepared the way for the Ottomans' decision in 1914 to enter the First World War as an ally of Germany.

Gladstone thought that Disraeli's Turcophile views placed his Jewish interests above those of the state, although his own more favourable view of Russia was also based on religious sympathy. 'Russia', he had declared, was 'the natural leader of Christendom in the east' and had been sucked into 'Turkish affairs' by the decay and abuses of the Ottoman Empire during the Bulgarian atrocity debate; Disraeli's Jewishness and his defence of the Ottomans were 'turned against him and utilized to present him as dangerously un-English'. Much of the criticism of Disraeli's views focused on 'his being a Jew'.[31] Disraeli's pro-Ottoman policies were likely linked with his idea that Jews, Christians and Muslims enjoyed a 'theocratic unity', and that, as soon as their differences were resolved, a spiritual renaissance would replace the West's preoccupation with materialism and lead to civilizational renewal.

Disraeli's pro-Turkish view

Disraeli's ideas about religion informed several of his novels, especially *Coningsby* (1844) and *Tancred* (1847), in which some of the same characters featured, including Sidonia, a Jew who extolls Muslim tolerance in Spain. In *Coningsby*, Sidonia tells the novel's hero that it 'is difficult to distinguish the follower of Moses from the votary of Mahomet' since 'both alike built palaces, gardens and fountains; filled equally the highest offices of state, competed in an extensive and enlightened commerce, and rivalled each other in renowned universities'.[32] In *Contarini Fleming* (1832), Disraeli reveals that his East was a source of wisdom from which Europeans could learn, rather than the despotic, backward desert of the Orientalists: 'Why not study the Orient? Surely in the pages of the Persians and the Arabs we might discover new sources of emotion, new principles of invention, and new bursts of fancy.'[33] In *Tancred*, Disraeli's hero travels to Palestine in the hope of penetrating the 'mystery' of the East and gaining a better understanding of the origin of Christianity. He visits Mount Sinai and is told by an angel to preach the 'doctrine of theocratic equality', which meant that he was to promote Jewish-Christian-Muslim cooperation.[34] Jews are 'Arabs on horseback' and Christianity is 'Judaism for the multitude'.[35] Disraeli also called Jews 'Mosaic Arabs' and wrote that God had always communicated to the descendants of Abraham, never 'to a European'.[36] Tancred (Lord Montacute) says that he would not 'impugn the divine commission of any of the seed of Abraham when asked whether he would affirm Muhammad's divine inspiration', and continues: 'there are doctors of our church who recognise the sacred office of Mahomet, though they hold it to be … limited and local'.[37]

Christian response and the national debate

Gladstone tried to avoid blaming Islam for everything he saw as wrong with the Ottoman Empire by attributing its faults to the combination of 'race' and religion. However, when he contrasted Muslim (Ottoman) Turks with the 'mild' Muslims of India, the 'cultured' Moors of medieval Spain and the 'chivalrous' Muslims of crusader Syria, he was in fact saying that, just as the Ottoman Turks' barbarism and cruelty were racial and not religious characteristics, so too the finer qualities of Indians, Moors and Arabs were due to their 'race', not to Islam. Islam was responsible for neither positive nor negative qualities and was therefore bankrupt as a force for good in the world. Thus, he could use the term 'Mahometan fanaticism'[38] and object to Christian powers being committed to help preserve

Islamic government, which he thought was required by the Treaty of Paris. Speaking in the House of Commons, Gladstone complained that the treaty 'bound' the allies to maintain 'Turkey as a Mahomedan State, and of the internal institutions of that country as a Mahomedan country'.[39] Although, in his writings, Gladstone tried to tell his readers that they should not believe that all Muslims behaved like 'the Turks', given the popular conflation of the words 'Muslim' and 'Turk', few would have been inclined to follow his advice. He also saw religion as part of national identity, which meant that, for him as a committed Christian, Islam was an alien faith that belonged elsewhere, and certainly not in Britain.

Muslims (and non-Muslims) have sometimes described Gladstone as hating Islam, and this is epitomized in the story perpetuated by Marmaduke Pickthall mentioned earlier, and which has circulated among the Muslim Brotherhood, the transnational Sunni organization committed to restoring its version of authentic Islamic government in Muslim majority states, since the 1950s. Gladstone is supposed to have held up a copy of the Qur'an in the House of Commons and declared that there would be 'no peace for the Empire … as long as this book exists', with another version of the story describing him tearing up a copy of the Qur'an as he spoke.[40] There is no official record of any such event, but this has not prevented the story from being repeated by, among others, the Indian politician Rafiq Zakaria (1920–2005)[41] and the Pakistani-American academic Akbar Ahmed (b.1943).[42] Eugenio Biagini also comments that Gladstone's 'dislike of Islam' influenced his policies in Egypt, where the Egyptian education department, run by Douglas Dunlop (1861–1937), a former missionary, replaced Arabic and French with English and dropped religion from the curriculum.[43]

Public opinion over the Bulgarian atrocities and Ottoman Turkey's culpability for this sided with Gladstone, which contributed to his electoral victory in 1880. Disraeli's supporters found themselves on the losing and unpopular side of a national debate. The anti-Turkish campaign became known as the 'Bulgarian agitation'. Official statements by representative church bodies solidly supported Gladstone. National newspapers such the *Daily News* and, though less consistently, the *Times*, lined up behind Gladstone, while the *Daily Telegraph* supported Disraeli. The British and Foreign Unitarian Association, the Baptist Union, regional bodies of Methodists, Presbyterians and Congregationalists, together with trades unions, condemned the 'Turkish atrocities'.[44] Among other prominent preachers, Charles Haddon Spurgeon (1834–1892) of the Baptist Metropolitan Tabernacle denounced Disraeli's 'immoral policy' and 'heartless epigrams' from his pulpit.[45] Although the Church of England did not issue an official statement, a petition was presented at the Province of Canterbury's

Convocation, signed by fifty-three members' favouring Gladstone, but this was not put to the vote.[46] The Bishop of Manchester, James Fraser (1818–1885) strongly urged the public to demand an end to Disraeli's Eastern policy.[47]

Fraser was one of only three bishops who signed the Clerical Declaration against Britain 'going to war on behalf of Turkey', which, by 2 February 1878, had attracted over a thousand signatories.[48] Canons Henry Liddon (1829–1890), Malcolm MacColl (1831–1907) and William Bright (1824–1901) were among the most outspoken supporters of an anti-Turkish policy and promoted the Clerical Declaration. Many Christian leaders were organizers of the National Conference on the Eastern Question, which met in London in December 1876 and was attended by 1,200 people, including Gladstone as keynote speaker, church leaders including the Bishop of Oxford, politicians, artists, literary and legal figures. Thomas Carlyle (1795–1881) sent a letter of support for the 'immediate and summary expulsion of the Turk from Europe'.[49] Richard Shannon describes this as 'the most brilliant array of intellectual figures ever brought together to intervene in a question of politics in England'.[50] The conference, where pro-Russian sentiment was expressed, condemned Ottoman Turkish tyranny and resolved that 'a war in support of the integrity and independence of their Turkish Empire would be injurious to the interests of England, opposed to the interests of the English people, and an offence against the world'.[51]

Disraeli did, however, gain some support from prominent Christian writers. Among these, the Harrow schoolmaster and biographer, Reginald Bosworth Smith (1839–1908), contributed an article to *The Contemporary Review* for December 1876 responding to Gladstone. Although Smith's writing on Islam, which he saw as an ally rather than as a foe in the task of spreading humanness, civility and improving society (even if less desirable than Christianity), alienated some, he remained a devout Christian and often spoke at missionary gatherings.[52] In his 1876 article, Smith criticized Gladstone for failing to distinguish between the Ottoman Turkish people and their rulers. The Ottoman Turks might be 'violent, cruel and corrupt' but the Muslim masses were victims as well as Christians.[53] Yet the Ottomans did possess certain moral qualities, or they could not have held onto their empire for as long as they had.[54] The Qur'an, Smith wrote, 'inculcates not in isolated precepts merely but in its whole drift and spirit, self-reliance and self-respect, truthfulness and hospitality, justice and mercy, the care of the sick and the aged'.[55] Aspects of Islam might too easily encourage its professors' 'baser passions', but it did not lack virtues to remedy this; nor should the 'abuse of a religion' be confused with 'its use'.[56] Smith argued that Bulgarians had, in the past, willingly served in the Ottoman army against 'Christian neighbours', while Spain flourished intellectually under Muslim rulers to which the Christian response, 'the thumbscrew and the boot, the rack and the stake', was far worse than the recent atrocities in Bulgaria.[57] Smith also contrasted Christian mistreatment of Jews with their comparatively more humane experience under Muslim rule. Smith supported autonomy for the Balkan provinces but thought it possible for Ottoman Turkey to implement reforms that would facilitate retaining sovereignty. He opposed Russian hegemony; Russia had dirty hands and could not claim to be a 'disinterested advocate of humanity' as it pursued its 'sacred mission' of expansion.[58] Smith also wrote several letters to the *Times* expressing sympathy for 'the Turks', arguing that they deserved 'another chance to set [their] house in order'.[59]

Another Disraeli ally, Edwin Arnold (1832–1904), aligned the *Daily Telegraph* – then the most popular newspaper in Britain – firmly behind the Conservative Party. Its proprietor, Edward Levy-Lawson (1833–1916), had invested heavily in Ottoman Turkish bonds.[60] More widely known for his writing on Buddhism and Indian religion, Arnold received awards from the Shah of Iran and the Ottoman sultan for his books on Islam.[61] The *Daily Telegraph*'s pro-Ottoman stance provoked Gladstone's comment that London was the centre of 'mischief: through money, rowdyism, and the *Daily Telegraph*'.[62] The newspaper argued that Muslims as well as Christians had been victims of the Bulgarian massacres and that foreign agitators had fomented the Bulgarian uprising. It took aim at those who contended that, as a Christian country, Russia merited Britain's support by denigrating the Eastern church. Arnold, who sometimes attended a Unitarian church, has been described as a 'liberal Christian'.[63] Although Gladstone won the 1880 election on the success of the Bulgarian agitation, the *Daily Telegraph*'s influence was such that London remained mainly pro-Ottoman. In 1878, Arnold drafted the foreign policy section of the Queen's Speech for Disraeli, which stated that the government had maintained neutrality during the Russo-Turkish War because 'the interests' of Victoria's empire 'were not threatened', and overtures had been made to both the Russian tsar and to the Ottoman sultan-caliph to end the conflict.[64]

The role of Queen Victoria, Lord Rosebery and Lord Salisbury during the Armenian massacres, 1894–6

When Gladstone retired in March 1894, Lord Rosebery (1847–1929) succeeded him as Liberal leader and prime minister. The Eastern Question loomed large during Rosebery's short term in office, between March 1894 and June 1895, as reports of the massacre of Armenian subjects of the Ottoman Empire reached London. Hampered by a tiny majority in the Commons, Rosebery, who sat in the House of Lords, had an uneasy relationship with William Harcourt (1897–1904), who led the Liberals in the Commons and had hoped to become prime minister. Between 1894 and 1896, an estimated 1,000,000 (possibly much higher) Armenian Christians lost their lives at the hands of Ottoman soldiers, although the Ottomans blamed Kurd irregulars and Armenian provocation. A mixed Ottoman-foreign commission reported in July 1896 that accounts of the massacres were exaggerated. However, in a separate report, the European member accused Ottoman Turkish troops of 'indiscriminate massacre'.[65] Article 67 of the Berlin Treaty had called for reforms in relation to the Ottoman administration of Armenia, which had not been implemented.

As British newspapers covered the massacres, Liberals and Conservatives of all classes recoiled in horror and, once again, anti-Ottoman and anti-Turkish sentiment was rampant. On 27 November 1894, the British Cabinet 'resolved to take a strong attitude' and to ask Russia and France to task their consuls with investigating the reports.[66] The Ottoman response was that the United States ought to undertake the inquiry, which it refused to do, and the Consular Commission was formed. From retirement, Gladstone quickly intervened and demanded action, calling for Britain to act alone if the other Berlin Treaty signatory powers would not do so. Initially, believing that Rosebery was 'willing to dismember the Ottoman Empire', Russia and France agreed to intervene with Britain.[67] Then Russia changed its position when Britain declined to send its navy to assist them in a dispute with Japan, which led to France also dropping out. The French National Assembly did not discuss the massacres until 3 November 1896.[68] Rosebery's military chiefs seemed unable to advise how Britain might accomplish an independent intervention. This convinced him that it would be foolhardy for Britain to act alone. Rosebery was about to issue an ultimatum to the Ottoman Empire to undertake reforms when his government was defeated in the Commons, and he resigned. Disraeli's successor as Conservative leader, Lord Salisbury, who had already served two terms as prime minister, won the subsequent general election in July-August with a clear majority, which was increased when the Liberal Unionists joined his government. He acted as his own foreign secretary until 12 November 1900. Salisbury, who had overcome his initial suspicion of Disraeli to serve in his Cabinet, did not share his predecessor's Turcophilia, but he was wary of Russian ambitions in the East. Salisbury tried to convince France and Russia to act on behalf of the Armenians, but he met with no more success than Rosebery had, especially when he made it clear that he did not favour dismemberment of the Ottoman Empire. Russia and France hoped to gain territory as a result of its collapse.

When concern was expressed that any intervention might spark Muslim insurrections in European colonies, Queen Victoria instructed her viceroy in India to 'dispel any feeling among Muslims' that, 'in consequence to the dreadful events in Turkey', her government was 'ill-disposed towards them'.[69] The queen also sent a 'personal appeal' to the Ottoman sultan, 'Abd al-Hamid II (1842–1918), begging him to restore peace for the sake of humanity 'and earnestly discussed with her prime minster the wisdom of similar approaches to Russia and Germany'.[70] She described the massacres and the 'misrule in Constantinople' as 'too dreadful'.[71] Salisbury, who believed that a single-handed British intervention would precipitate a much larger war, rejected independent British action aware that, while the navy was strong, 'Britain had very few soldiers'.[72] He thought that the moral obligation to act lay equally with all the Berlin Treaty powers and that there was no obligation for Britain to act alone, which he explained in a speech in January 1896. In September 1896, Tsar Nicholas II (1868–1918), who had married Victoria's granddaughter Alexandra (1872–1918), visited Britain. Victoria and Salisbury engaged in negotiations with the tsar, aimed at reaching a joint Russian-British response on the Armenian massacres. Salisbury proposed regime change in Constantinople, but the tsar thought this risky and no agreement was reached. Although the six Berlin Treaty powers drew up a list of actions that the Ottoman Empire was to take under their supervision, such as introducing devolved local government in Armenia and allowing freedom of the press, this was not implemented due the outbreak of war between Greece and Turkey over Crete in April 1897. Now, Russia, Britain and France intervened to force the Ottoman army, newly organized by a German general, to withdraw. This time, Britain's navy could carry out the operation without the need for soldiers.

Conclusion

The Armenian massacres further fuelled the British public's already widespread anti-Turkish sentiment initially enflamed by the Bulgarian atrocities. By then, with Egypt under British control, increased British influence in Persia (Iran), and a series of British protectorates around the Gulf, the route to India was much easier for the Royal Navy to protect, which made preserving the Ottoman Empire redundant. In fact, after the Anglo-Russian Agreement of 1904, relations between Russia and Britain were also much improved and, arguably, the 'Great Game' that had dominated the nineteenth century was over.[73] Having won the debate against Disraeli's Turcophile policy, Gladstone can be credited with ending Anglo-Ottoman friendship, and even with paving the way for the Ottoman Empire's costly alliance with Germany, which brought the Ottoman Empire – and the Sunni Caliphate – to an end. Had Disraeli's policy prevailed, history may have taken a different path. Yet, Gladstone cannot be fully blamed for all the geopolitical changes that resulted in the Ottoman Empire's demise, when Britain was as eager as France to claim Ottoman territory. Literally creating states by drawing lines on the map, Britain and France ignored sectarian and ethnic differences and left some groups stateless, hence the Kurdish desire for a contiguous state in the region, and Shi'i-Sunni tensions in Iraq and elsewhere. By creating Palestine as a distinct political entity without making any accommodation for its non-Jewish population, Britain and France also inserted the prospect of a Jewish homeland into the mix, precipitating the Palestinian-Israeli conflict. Gladstone's wish to see Turks 'one and all' out of Europe probably did contribute to current reluctance, in Western Europe, to regard the Republic of Turkey as truly European, which revives the idea that Islam is an obstacle to progress and at odds with Western civilization. The way that, in 2016, some British politicians used Turkey's potential membership of the European Union as an argument for what became known as Brexit can also be seen as a by-product of Gladstone's legacy.[74]

3

Thomas Carlyle, Islam, empire and after

Geoffrey P. Nash

Introduction

Writing in the 1950s, the British Orientalist W. Montgomery Watt (1909–2006) proposed that Thomas Carlyle's (1795–1881) lecture about the Prophet Muhammad published in his *On Heroes, Hero-Worship, and the Heroic in History* (1841) amounted to the 'first strong affirmation in the whole of European literature, medieval or modern of a belief in the sincerity of Muhammad'.[1] This was no mean achievement, since 'none of the great figures of history is so poorly appreciated in the West as Muhammad'.[2] While others have assented to Watt's statements, they nonetheless require elucidation, not least because Carlyle's lecture on Muhammad, titled 'The Hero as Prophet', is often talked about out of context. To write about Carlyle and Islam has, until recently, largely meant producing an exegesis of the lecture explicating Muhammad and his conception of Islam as a historico-spiritual force. The manner in which Carlyle's lecture translated Muhammad and Islam into the terms of current Victorian debates, and its afterlife in a non-European setting, are the focus of this chapter.

Carlyle and *On Heroes* in context

Carlyle employed both as a tool to assail Victorian secularism and capitalism and in implied contradistinction to Anglicanism, Benthamite Utilitarianism and other materialist trends of the time. However, by the 1870s, in accordance with growing Western politico-cultural domination over most parts of the world, including the domains of Islam, Carlyle's statements on Islamic or Islamicate subjects largely focused on the Ottomans and slipped into the stereotypical

Figure 3.1 Thomas Carlyle by Robert Scott Tait, 1855.
Source: Courtesy of National Portrait Gallery (x5641) / © National Portrait Gallery, London.

tropes of Orientalism. After Carlyle's death in 1881 and into the early twentieth century, when in Britain he was either sidelined or confined to the category of the proto-authoritarian, in the Middle East his lecture on Muhammad had achieved currency and was read as a statement on cultural relativism in which a British writer appeared to valorize (rather than patronize) the spiritual history of a non-Western people and nation.

First of all, we need to understand the environment in which Carlyle's strongly revisionary statement about Islam was enunciated in order to appreciate its full significance. Born in 1795, the same year as John Keats (1795–1821), into a lowland Scottish dissenter background, as a young man Carlyle relinquished the strict Calvinist beliefs of his parents. Having completed his education at the University of Edinburgh, he acquired in the 1820s a limited reputation from the essays he published mainly on German literature in the *Edinburgh Review* and *Foreign Review*. Building on anti-rationalist tropes which he inscribed into the 'prophetic history' of *History of the French Revolution* (1835) and the philosophic transcendentalism of *Sartor Resartus* (1837), by the time he stood up to address the London audiences that came to his lecture series in 1840, Carlyle had begun to be known as a seer or prophet to the secular age. His apparent vindication of Islam's Prophet therefore needs to be set against the religious landscape of the first half of the nineteenth century, in which English Christianity faced the challenge of the growth of secularism and the expansion and dissemination of scientific knowledge.

Carlyle became one of the best known and most influential figures to withdraw from the canopy of conventional Christianity. A vivid recorder of the receding influence of religion, for the remainder of his lifetime he expended great energy in reminding his readership of the vital need to recover the spiritual belief missing from the Victorian age. Composed between 1833–4, *Sartor Resartus* pioneered the autobiography/autobiographic novel as a genre for expressing personal religious crisis, in Carlyle's case associated with the denigrating effects upon the interior self of the previous century's mechanistic thought. Pronouncing against the Enlightenment while also proclaiming the end of the old 'mythus' of religion, under the influence of J. G. von Goethe (1749–1832), Carlyle's strangely written book enunciated a mystic faith revealed through nature and the human heart that upheld the moral foundations of the world and which he called 'natural supernaturalism'.[3]

Although the intellectual criticism of Christianity in the Victorian period may not have forestalled evangelical revival and a boisterous struggle between established church and dissenting chapel, it was deep and wide ranging. Taking to task the prevailing English religious institutions, Carlyle's friend, the American critic Ralph Waldo Emerson (1803–1882), exemplified the critical trend. Emphasizing their wealth and complacency, he reproved the clergy for embodying the values of 'a religion devoid of subjective feeling and a theology devoid of criticism or science'. In addition to Emerson and Carlyle, 'similar criticisms of the Anglican Church and the major Nonconformist denominations' were made by F. D. Maurice (1805–1872), Francis William Newman (1805–1897), Mark Rutherford (1831–1913) 'and many of the other romantic, liberal critics of nineteenth-century Christianity'.[4] Despite the vitriol Carlyle directed against the eighteenth century, agnostics like John Stuart Mill (1806–1873), John Morley (1838–1923) and Leslie Stephen (1832–1904), who shared 'the general epistemological outlook of the Enlightenment', each at one time came under the influence of Carlyle. In fact, as Francis Turner has pointed out, 'Carlyle has not unusually been numbered among the friends of rationalism and science'; many emerging young scientists who campaigned against the Church/gentlemen-scientist hegemony in early Victorian science were 'initially spurred to social action by reading Carlyle' and he counted among his admirers T. H. Huxley (1825–1895), John Tyndall (1820–1893), Francis Galton (1822–1911) and Herbert Spencer (1820–1903).[5] Carlyle's 'The Hero as Prophet' lecture therefore requires situating against the background in England of the weakening influence of religion upon lay thinkers, 'in contrast to those [Tractarians like John Henry Newman, 1801–1890] who were vainly striving to restore the "old clothes" of Christianity'.[6] However, it stood equally in opposition to religion's replacement, Benthamite Utilitarianism.

On Heroes consists of six lectures. In the first group of four, the hero Odin stood for embodied divinity; 'Mahomet' as prophet; Dante and Shakespeare as poet; and Luther and Knox as priest. As David R. Sorensen has noted:

> The basis of [the heroes'] strength resided in their deep and abiding comprehension of the divinity of creation, the 'emblem of the Godlike'. This divine awareness was the primal 'Fact' of their existence, releasing them from doubt, checking their worldly ambitions, and imbuing them with the courage to seek the truth about themselves and their relation to God. Each conducted his search in a different historic environment, yet Carlyle traced the 'perennial fibre' of their quest to their mutual recognition that 'every object has a divine beauty in it'. Gifted with the intellectual power to penetrate the subterfuges of life ... they won trust and loyalty by the integrity of their aims and the sincerity of their motives.[7]

Setting aside the issue of his broad, some might say disparate, choice of heroes across the lecture series as a whole, Carlyle's portrait of Muhammad slowly acquired a distinctiveness of its own. If, in the early years of Queen Victoria's reign, one of the shrillest voices denouncing the Prophet's career and the early history of Islam was that of the Scottish missionary William Muir (1819–1905), by the end a still basically hostile Orientalist like D. S. Margoliouth (1858–1940) could write in an introduction to a new edition of the Qur'an: 'The eulogy pronounced by Carlyle on Muhammad in *Heroes and Hero Worship* will probably be endorsed by not a few at the present day.'[8]

Whilst Carlyle's interest in Islam developed out of his liberal early essays, the lecture itself was built upon eighteenth-century scholarship on Islamic history by Simon Ockley (1678–1720) and Edward Gibbon (1737–1794), and on the construction of a biography of Muhammad by George Sale (1697–1736) and Silvestre de Sacy (1758–1838).[9] In addition, formative influences were the tolerance of the German enlightenment, especially of Gotthold Ephraim Lessing (1729–1781) and Goethe, and the historicism of Friedrich Schlegel (1772–1829) and Johann Gottfried Herder (1744–1803).[10] The religious or spiritual dimension of the Prophet, lifted largely out of its epoch except in so far as its relationship to the Christianity of the seventh century was concerned, was mainly of interest to Carlyle. At its close, the lecture invokes a sense of Islam's timeless quality – the call to prayer that the Arabist Edward W. Lane (1801–1876) heard echoed across Cairo – as well as of its historical apotheosis in the spread of the domain of Islam from Delhi to Granada, exemplifying the eternal truth that belief was life-giving and produced greatness.[11]

A challenge to the sociolect of his contemporaries

As W. Montgomery Watt implied, Carlyle's innovation consisted in wholly breaking out of Christian prejudices rehearsed against Muhammad for more than a millennium; in addition, Carlyle enlisted Muhammad and his creed in his personal assault on the laissez-faire capitalist nostrums of the 1840s, culminating in the iconoclastic *Latter-Day Pamphlets* (1849). Carlyle found opportunities to apply ideas and images to undermine the public positions adopted by the contemporary religious institutions and the sociopolitical movement he most contemned. Towards the end of the lecture, Carlyle turned his exclamatory discourse against the sociolect of the emergent intelligentsia. Included in this class were political economists and Utilitarians, the foremost of who, John Stuart Mill, walked out of the lecture in response to the rhetorical remark: 'What is the chief end of man here below? Mahomet has answered this question, in a way that might put *us* to shame! He does not, like a Bentham, a Paley, take Right and Wrong, and calculate the profit and loss, ultimate pleasure of the one and of the other.'[12]

On the other hand, as Carlyle informed his mother in a letter, 'I had bishops and all kinds of people among my hearers.'[13] Clinton Bennett points out that, as a disbeliever, Carlyle took 'delight in shocking his audience, [and] had no desire to produce a Christian response to Islam'.[14] Reviewing *On Heroes* in *Christian Remembrancer*, starting from Muhammad's inclusion within the 'menagerie' of names on Carlyle's list of heroes, William Thomson (1819–1890), later to become Archbishop of York, condemned the 'eulogies' of Muhammad as 'simply ridiculous'. As regards Carlyle envisaging him in the desert 'alone with his own soul and the reality of things', he declaimed: 'There never was a phrase more shamelessly abused'. Thomson proceeds to dispute a number of Carlyle's assertions, before arriving at the key issue: 'But it is idle to insist on minor errors, when one predominant error poisons the whole book. *It is not a Christian book*.'[15] On the other hand, Ruth apRoberts's more recent summary confirms the presentation of a positive side of Muhammad which had scarcely been put before in Britain and which must therefore have presented a particular challenge to Victorian Christians:

> [The] portrait of Mahomet is a consistent and lively picture full of loving sympathy. He recounts the history: from the Kaaba to Mecca, through the *hegire* [*hijrah*, journey] to Medina, the Prophet's private life with his wife Kadijah, his handsome looks, his illiteracy, his amiability and cordiality, his sense of humour … his modest way of life … his alleged sensuality, his influence on his young Cousin Ali who was one of his first converts, and the spread of Islam.[16]

John Tolan points out that many authors who wrote portrayals of Muhammad in the eighteenth and nineteenth centuries were 'interested less in Islam and its prophet per se than in reading in Muhammad's story lessons that they could apply to their own preoccupations and predicaments'.[17] His brief summary of Carlyle's lecture closes with the statement: 'Islam itself is a "confused form of Christianity", a great improvement over what passed for Christianity in the seventh-century Orient, and of course over pre-Islamic Arab idolatry, but not, it seems, on a level with Anglicanism.'[18] That Carlyle could have had Anglicanism in mind in this context is a quite astounding misreading: Samuel Taylor Coleridge (1772–1834) might have but, as a son of Annandale covenanters, Carlyle remained contemptuous towards the established church all his life. Tolan's mistake might have been avoided if he had read Carlyle's fourth lecture, 'The Hero as Priest', let alone consulted Carlyle's *Oliver Cromwell's Letters and Speeches* (1845). The act of Muhammad's cleansing of the Kaaba[19] idols reverberates in Carlyle's redaction of Cromwell's Puritan revolution, where he envisages an Anglican priest as a 'two-legged Rhetorical Phantasm' against whom he would set 'an Oliver [Cromwell] without Rhetoric at all … a Mahomet, whose persuasive-eloquence with wild flashing heart and scimitar, is "Wretched mortal, give up that; or by the Eternal, thy Maker and mine, I will kill thee!"'[20] In short, Tolan fails to see the affinity in Carlyle's thought between Puritanism (or Calvinism) and Islam.[21] The evolution in thinking about Carlyle's relation to Islam and how it might have relevance to later Muslim articulations of religio-political dissent from Western secular liberalism is discussed below.

Carlyle, Islam and the Victorian world

In approaching the Islamic world, few Victorian writers were able to progress very far beyond boundaries of language, geography and culture.[22] Carlyle's near contemporary, the Arabist Edward W. Lane, author of the groundbreaking ethnological study, *An Account of the Manners and Customs of the Modern Egyptians* (1836), was the most obvious exception. In addition, we should cite the gifted travellers and outsiders who penned works on Arabia and who deserve to be incorporated into a specialized and enlightened Victorian corpus on Islam. Richard F. Burton (1821–1890), Charles M. Doughty (1843–1926), Wilfrid Scawen Blunt (1840–1922) and Lady Anne Blunt (1837–1917) adopted varied and sometimes extreme strategies to penetrate the lands of Egypt, greater Syria and undiscovered Arabia, but they did not entirely dispense with an umbilical cord connecting them to their race and native land. However, William Gifford Palgrave (1826–1888), whose paternal ancestry was Jewish, stepped furthest outside the circle by choosing to become a Jesuit. Later it was rumoured on his journey through Arabia he may have identified as a Muslim.[23]

In 1840 Carlyle seems to have been conscious of the Islamic world as a historico-religious space cohering around the *kalima* (Islamic statement of faith): 'There is none worthy of worship except God and Muhammad is the messenger of God'. The lecture conveys a strong sense that, for Carlyle, Islam was a faith conceived in Arabia by an Arab for Arabs. Islam was therefore mainly Arabian or in its geographical extent a domain of Arabic-speaking lands: 'To the Arab Nation it was a birth from darkness into light: Arabia first became alive by it'. In terms of 'belief', Carlyle delimited Muslim domains by conceptualizing a space of faithful believers stretching 'from Delhi to Granada'. He seems to have considered that Muslims exceeded Christians in their degree of faith and the seriousness with which they carried out their religious duties:

> These Arabs believe their religion and try to live by it! No Christians, since the early ages, or only perhaps the English Puritans in modern times, have ever stood

by their Faith as Muslims do by theirs [...]. A greater number of God's creatures believe in Mahomet's word at this hour than in any other word whatever.[24]

Numerically, then, as now, a greater number of Christians lived in the world than followers of Islam or any other single religion, and they were most widely spread through it, so Carlyle's estimation of Muslim numbers as in excess of Christians is mistaken.[25] In his lecture, however, he is mostly silent about the scope of the nineteenth-century Islamic world. No specific reference is made to the still widely flung Ottoman domains. Despite the eclipse of the Mughals, India's huge population of Muslims – including those residing in Delhi – are not addressed in their present condition. Nor is mention made of the Caucasian lands that only recently had been prised by Russia from the Persian Empire, or the independent Khanates that would also be in the near future. Islam's contemporary valence, confirmed by ongoing conversions in Africa and the East Indies, is nullified by the historical phenomenon of Arab Islam.

For a while after the lecture, Carlyle continued to hold a positive view of Muhammad's influence on his followers, as evidenced from his meeting with the Indian Muslim modernist Syed Ahmad Khan (1817–1898) in 1869. Khan's biographer relates that 'he had an interview with Carlyle, and the Chelsea Sage was unusually gracious to him: They talked long and earnestly over "Heroes and Hero-Worship," especially about Mohammed, of whom Carlyle expresses a very high opinion in that work; and also about Syed Ahmed's "Essays on the Life of Mohammed," then in the press'.[26] However, in his advancing years, Carlyle's attitude towards Islam changed. While it is going too far to suggest, as Clinton Bennett does, that he reneged on the positive assessment of the Prophet enunciated in his lecture,[27] Carlyle's perspective shifted away quite significantly from the generative force of Muhammad's original message. As Shaden Tageldin notes: 'With the decline of Mughal power in India and of Ottoman power across the Mediterranean world and the ascent of British dominion in these regions, the British Empire had begun to supersede the imperiums of Islam.'[28] As the 'ailing Ottoman Empire ... deteriorated', Jamie Gilham adds, it 'adversely affected British attitudes towards Muslims and Islam'.[29] The two decades separating the Crimean War (1853–6) and the 'Bulgarian Horrors' (1876–8) nurtured in Carlyle the view that the Ottomans were unworthy of Britain's protection, and he endorsed the Orientalist image of the Ottoman Turk as 'dark, fanatical and sensual ... *waiting*, these last three hundred years, to be thrown into the Black Sea'.[30]

In spring 1873, Charles Eliot Norton (1827–1908) reported to Edward FitzGerald (1809–1883) a conversation he had had with Carlyle regarding FitzGerald's *Rubaiyat of Omar Khayyam* (1859):

I told him what I had heard, that the translation was made by a Rev. Edward FitzGerald, who lived somewhere in Norfolk ... I told him I would send him the book .... Two or three days later, when we were walking together again, he said: 'I've read that little book which you sent to me, and I think my old friend FitzGerald might have spent his time to much better purpose than in busying himself with the verses of that "old Mohammedan blackguard"' .... He held the whole thing as worse than a mere waste of labour.[31]

In spite of his being a Persian sceptic and materialist, and so scarcely a Muslim, Omar Khayyam is conflated by Carlyle with contemporary Ottoman decay in his use of the curiously garbled epithet 'old Mohammedan blackguard'. Carlyle counted FitzGerald among his long-standing friends, as did he Alfred Tennyson (1809–1892), who, taking a cue from the translator of the *Rubaiyat*, dabbled a little with Persian. Tennyson's poem 'Akbar's Dream' demonstrates an awareness of the seventeenth-century Indo-Persian culture of the Mughals, about which Carlyle remained incurious. (But in his poem 'To E. FitzGerald', Tennyson calls Omar 'that large infidel').[32] In this realignment of his formerly positive Islamic predilection, Carlyle might be said to have done no more than move in line with a common perception. Although he did not live long enough to see the debacle of General Gordon's (1833–1885) death in Khartoum, we might guess that the Mahdi's army, recently termed 'an early example that presaged the later emergence of Islamic resistance movements', would most likely not have impressed him.[33]

Orientalism and empire

'Much of what Carlyle had to say on England's imperial mission', according to John Murrow, 'was framed implicitly by a view of empire in which settler colonies were a predominant concern'. Carlyle's vision was global to the extent that it promoted settlement of the world's empty expanses by 'the "surplus" population of Britain and Ireland', a project which he believed had most purchase with respect to Australasia, Canada, the West Indies and India.[34] At the time of the Indian Rebellion of 1857–8, Carlyle's letters show that, far from being a religious, nationalist or imperialist chauvinist, the savage reprisals visited on the Indian sepoys drew his sympathies. During the Crimean War, he condemned the ineptitude of the British government and generals more than of the Ottoman Turks.[35]

Carlyle's pronouncements on Muhammad and Islam were for a long time read in isolation from the nineteenth-century British imperial background, but postcolonial scholars have grounded them more firmly within contexts of empire. Taking his cue from Arab historian Albert Hourani, who stated that Carlyle's rendition of 'The Prophet as Hero' was 'an early and rather crude attempt to classify historical events',[36] Edward W. Said characterized Carlyle's portrayal of Muhammad as an exercise that 'forced [the Prophet] to serve a thesis totally overlooking the historical and cultural circumstances of [his] own time and place ... show[ing] us that the Orient need not cause us undue anxiety, so unequal are Oriental to European achievements ... the Orient in itself was subordinated intellectually to the West'.[37] Humayun Ansari considers: 'All British historians during this period assumed the intellectual and moral superiority of contemporary Britain over the Muslim world'. Adducing close connections between empire, Orientalism and Christianity, Ansari considers that Carlyle too 'uncritically deployed Orientalist tropes and attitudes in his rhetoric: Islam for Carlyle was "a confused form of Christianity", fit for semi-barbaric Arabs'.[38]

From a postcolonial perspective, it is highly important to foreground a remark Carlyle makes near the beginning of his lecture, almost as an aside: 'We have chosen Mahomet not as the most eminent Prophet; but as the one we are freest to speak of ... as *there is no danger of our becoming, any of us, Mahometans*'.[39] Shaden Tageldin confirms the significance of these remarks in her comments on Carlyle's reversion to the topic of Muhammad in the third lecture, 'The Hero as Poet'. Here Carlyle takes issue with Muhammad's claim to 'supreme Prophethood', and manipulating the Latin term *vates* to emphasize the dual meaning of 'poet' and 'prophet' diminishes Muhammad in favour of those icons of European culture, Dante and Shakespeare. Carlyle postulates: 'Even in Arabia, as I compute, Mahomet will have exhausted himself and become obsolete, while this Shakspeare [*sic*], this Dante may be still young; – while this Shakspeare may still pretend to be a Priest of Mankind, of Arabia as of other places, for unlimited periods to come!'[40] These comparisons, Tageldin argues, must be construed as 'imperially motivated and imperially implicated':

> [Carlyle's] insistence on the geographic and temporal universality of Dante and Shakespeare and on their capacity – Shakespeare's especially – to supersede the Prophet of Islam '[e]ven in Arabia' pits European literature against Arab Islam in a geopolitical competition not only for territory (Dante and Shakespeare will claim Arabia and all 'other places') but also for time (Shakespeare, like Dante, will rule 'unlimited periods to come,' overwriting other histories).[41]

Tageldin stretches her postcolonial analysis of the Prophet as he appears in *On Heroes* to scrutinize the position adopted towards the text by the Egyptian translator, Muhammad al-Siba'i (1881–1931). He viewed Carlyle's lecture from an opposite point of view to a European – that is from the inside of a non-Western national literature, Arabic, from where he performs a translation (published in 1911) of the Western text of *On Heroes* under the illusion that the European is endorsing the pre-eminence of an Easterner, the Prophet Muhammad, and his religion, Islam. We are now looking at 'The Hero as Prophet' as a translated Arabic text, as seen from the point of view of an early twentieth-century Egyptian context. Tageldin argues that an apparently positive representation of Islam conveyed by Carlyle's lecture has been translated by an Egyptian in such a way as to produce 'the hallucination of an Islam shared by colonizer and colonized'.[42] Al-Siba'i's enthusiasm causes him 'to ignore Carlyle's assertion that Shakespeare would eventually render the Prophet of Islam "obsolete" (even in Arabia!) and to insist – against the evidence of Carlyle's full text – on the radical translatability of the native Islamic "religious" and the Western colonial "secular"'.[43] Caught in the secular trap that (Western) literature is the new religion, 'if al-Siba'i's translation of Carlyle enabled Egyptian writers to view secular literature (English especially) as religion, it also enabled them to subsume religion (Islam especially) within the secular and thus to reconcile religion to the political project of colonial modernity'.[44] Overall, 'by fostering the illusion that Carlyle – and by extension Britain – have been "taken" by Islam', al-Siba'i's translation 'beckons its unintended Muslim reader to imagine the Islamic world as not just sovereign (in possession of itself) but also imperial (in possession of Christian Europe) and thus to forget that Carlyle's text and history itself have already taken Islam for the British empire'.[45] As a footnote, we might add that the Christian pan-Arabist writer and traveller Ameen Rihani (1876–1940) was clearly aware of this self-deception when he took the view that the Arabic translation of the 'Hero as Prophet' lecture had induced a group of local Muslims in Jeddah into believing that England was endorsing the Prophet.[46]

Coda: Carlyle's Victorian dissidence and twentieth-century Islamism

From the perspective of postcolonial scholarship, we have seen how Carlyle's revision of Muhammad and Islam's significance continued to function at least within one different, colonial context. Shaden Tageldin makes a persuasive case for Carlyle's lecture on Muhammad operating in Arabic translation as a secular colonial Trojan horse that is misguidedly received as a championing of Arab Islamic superiority. Even so, Carlyle's remark 'there is no danger of our becoming, any of us, Mahometans' is ironic when we know that the late-Victorian

British Muslim leader, Abdullah Quilliam (1856–1932), often quoted Carlyle in his proselytising literature on behalf of Islam.[47] In general, twentieth-century Carlyle scholarship was much exercised by his writings' perceived aberration from principles of Victorian liberalism, and with scrutinising the ways in which his creed of hero-worship could be collapsed into the horrors of twentieth-century totalitarianism. While C. F. Harrold (1897–1948) and Watt proposed that Carlyle's affinity for the Prophet Muhammad arose from his Calvinist roots, it awaited the twenty-first century for that confluence to be stretched so far as to align aspects of his partially dissident religio-political thought with stances adopted in contemporary Middle East politics. In what I intend as a coda to the arguments so far presented, I shall attempt to parallelize Carlyle's views on society and belief with those of modern Islamism.

According to one of his biographers, 'Carlyle's sensibility was basically Christian and his politics antiliberal.'[48] He is situated by another biographer as a man who did not come 'from the mainstream of English thought, or shared in the education of his contemporaries. ... He lacked sympathy with their society, and attacked it fiercely as an outsider. He was no liberal thinker in a conventional sense'.[49] Works such as *Chartism* (1839), *Past and Present* (1843), *Oliver Cromwell's Letters and Speeches* and *Latter-Day Pamphlets* were intended to assuage 'the underlying spirit of wilful delusion in electoral politics and government administration, and in various characteristic cultural, literary and social forms' which Carlyle believed had gained a hold on Britain and to a comparable extent France.[50] In so far as the prognosis for present ills and their remedies were concerned, this might be said to rest on his conviction that a historical fall from grace had occurred. Modern history had taken an infernal turn, and in Carlyle's idiolect this notion is comprehended in the phrase 'the two godless centuries'. For him, the Puritan age, which ended two hundred years before his own, constituted a punctuation of the heroic vision leaving him 'impatient that the New Era does not come'.[51]

Comparing Carlyle's secular Calvinism and the influential Egyptian writer Sayyid Qutb's (1906–1966) revivalist Islamism, we might see a convergence in their respective diagnoses of a painful dichotomy or gulf between a time now lost in which society was built on faith and its subornment by present unbelief. Qutb composed the pamphlet *Milestones* (1964) to propagate the thesis that a thousand years separated the true Islam from the Islamic practice of today.[52] Islamic history's ideal moment belonged with the pious elders, the first rightly guided caliphs who directly succeeded the Prophet. Since then, external importations had corrupted Islamic practice to such a degree that, in modern times, the situation amounted to a recrudescence of the state of affairs before the Prophet's appearance when Arab society had existed in its 'days of ignorance' (*jahiliyah*). Qutb proposed the present's annexation and replacement by the worldview of the elders. Both he and Carlyle agreed on the need to summon the people back to the straight path. This might be achieved through admonition, although Qutb in particular believed struggle and some coercion would be necessary to effect change: *jihad* (striving or struggling in the path of God) features in his thought somewhat differently to how coercion does in Carlyle's. Admittedly, there are significant further differences and discontinuities between the work of the British Scot from the Victorian imperial age and the Egyptian writer-cum-activist of the mid-twentieth century: not only in terms of their separation in time but in their respective positions with regard to power and religious allegiance. Some nineteenth-century reformers like Jamal al-Din al-Afghani (1838–1897) believed in the need to reassert Islamic suzerainty within *dar al-Islam* (territory of Islam), and this necessitated struggle against the Western conqueror. Revived Islam has not infrequently had an anti-imperial dimension. Carlyle, on the other hand, held an ambiguous attitude towards the spread of Western power which he associated with the racial predominance of the Anglo-Saxon/Germanic peoples who would succeed as long as they strove through work, effort and heroic leadership to 'drain the swamps', to conquer lethargy and overcome the innate darkness within human nature.

Laying aside the imperialist issue, however, when it comes to weighing how modern Western society is viewed, there are congruent aspects in the writings of both. Carlyle's contest the problematic role Western liberalism played in Victorian praxis, hence the blasts against Utilitarianism in *On Heroes* and *Latter-Day Pamphlets*. Twentieth-century Islamist thinkers might be said to share a similar antagonism towards the liberal value system's continuation into the modern world, particularly in respect to its perceived imposition on Muslim societies. In trying to account for the factors underwriting this negative appraisal in these societies more generally, Sharoukgh Akhavi quotes the following analysis by Crawford B. MacPherson in *The Political Theory of Possessive Individualism: Hobbes to Locke* (1964):

> The individual was seen neither as a moral whole, nor as part of a larger social whole, but as an owner of himself. The relation of ownership, having become for more and more men the critically important relation determining their actual freedom and actual prospect of realizing their full potentialities, was read back into the nature of the individual. The individual, it was thought, is free inasmuch as he is proprietor of his person and capacities. The human essence is

freedom from dependence on the wills of others, and freedom is a function of possession. Society becomes a lot of free equal individuals related to each other as proprietors of their own capacities and of what they have acquired by their exercise. Society consists of relations of exchange between proprietors. Political society becomes a calculated device for the protection of this property and for the maintenance of an orderly relation of exchange.[53]

In response to the aforementioned, Akhavi proposes:

In all Muslim outlooks the arrant individualism that MacPherson has described is simply missing. Efforts to establish liberalism in the Muslim world have been resisted because it conflicts with the central idea of salvation in Islam, according to which God has placed the human being on earth as His trustee, whose full potential can be realised only by membership in a community of believers, a community whose existence and welfare is warrant for the religious injunctions.[54]

David R. Sorensen is the Carlyle critic of present times who has most clearly co-referenced the Victorian sage's advocacy of the Prophet Muhammad and Islam and the liberal values discussed earlier:

There is a Carlylean familiarity to the pattern of events of the late twentieth century. In the sanguine aftermath of the Cold War, latter-day 'Progress of the Species' philosophers such as Francis Fukuyama too confidently assume 'there is a fundamental process at work that dictates a common evolutionary pattern for all human societies – in short, something like a Universal History of mankind in the direction of liberal democracy'.[55]

In a reading that dismisses Carlyle's postcolonial critics summarily and endorses Sacy's essentially humanistic view of Muhammad, though he parallels Carlyle and Islamism in a similar way to us, Sorensen still insists:

Were he alive today it is safe to assume that Carlyle would have regarded the emergence of radical Islamism as a threat to civilization, both Eastern and Western. But he would have insisted that the motives of its leaders, however violent and destructive, had to be gauged in relation to larger 'affinities with the higher powers and the senses of man'.[56]

Carlyle, while paying silent reverence to a divine text (not the Bible, in which he had ceased to believe), looked to the hero to ascertain what God's laws might be. But Islamism (in its absolutism?) is too certain of what these are and in applying them 'violates the sacred distinction between the will of the finite and of the infinite' in 'an idolatrous Idolatry'.[57]

Carlyle was aware of the dangers of fanaticism from his own copious research on the French Revolution and the Cromwellian period. In spite of his outsider position with respect to much that was considered 'progressive' in Western Europe, the argument runs, he remained connected to humanist values. In practice this looks like an imposition on Carlyle of a twenty-first century Western view of Islam and Islamism in which the former is held to be capable of tolerance and coexistence with other religions, while the latter is inherently violent and destructive.[58] One wonders why the comparison with Islamism is being invoked in the first place. By recuperating Carlyle into the Western fold the political dynamic of the conflict Sorensen sets up in his parody of Fukuyama returns once more into deficit. However, postcolonial readings of Carlyle's view of Islam need not undermine his radicalism, even though they might at first appear to do so. Rather, they can be said to amplify the aporia within Carlyle's writing, whereby the West is both glorified and despised, granted intellectual assent at the same time as it is denounced. This deepening bifurcation in Carlyle's thought drew in the Prophet Muhammad and Islam in the 'The Hero as Prophet' lecture. In spite of his reassertion of Western cultural hegemony in 'The Hero as Poet', it was a pyrrhic victory that could not arrest Carlyle's descent into 'the valley of the shadow of Frederick' – the last phase of his career associated with the writing of *History of Frederick the Great* (1858–65), when reactionary and illiberal modes in his thought decisively asserted themselves.

4

'Permission to go and see the ancient city': Women travellers' encounters with Islam in the nineteenth century

Anne-Marie Beller and Kerry Featherstone

Introduction

Representations of the Islamic world in Victorian culture and popular imagination drew largely on romantic texts such as *One Thousand and One Nights* (known chiefly in nineteenth-century Britain as *The Arabian Nights*) and the *Rubáiyát of Omar Khayyám*. As Clinton Bennett has suggested, 'Many allusions to Muslim life in Victorian fiction had roots in these fabulous tales, which, however, have little if any relationship with any corresponding Muslim reality.'[1] Images of Islam permeated myriad cultural forms in nineteenth-century Britain. There were, of course, Orientalist scholars publishing erudite (if frequently prejudiced) works on the languages, art, religions, philosophies and histories of Asian cultures. More mainstream were accounts of the African journeys of famous explorers such as David Livingstone (1813–1873), John Hanning Speke (1827–1864), Richard Francis Burton (1821–1890) and Henry Morton Stanley (1841–1904), which were highly popular with general readers and 'experts' alike. Most Victorian readers increasingly derived their ideas about Eastern life and religions through narratives such as these and through the burgeoning genre of travel writing more broadly.

Whereas popular novelists such as Charles Dickens (1812–1870) and George Eliot (1819–1880) worked from cultural stereotypes and exoticized imagery, the significant rise in the publication of travel writing as a genre provided readers with first-hand accounts of foreign lands, customs and people. The four women discussed in this chapter – Florentia Sale (1790–1853), Emily Eden (1797–1869), Lucie Duff Gordon (1821–1869) and Amelia B. Edwards (1831–1892) – published travel accounts in different formats and for different reasons, but each of them drew on their personal experience of encounters with Muslim peoples and Islamic cultures in Asia and North Africa. In this way, they offer distinct insights into the ways in which representations of Islam were mediated for readers in Britain by women whose experiences imbued such representations with a form of authenticity.

Victorian women on the move

Although there is now an extensive body of research into Victorian women travellers, relatively little criticism exists about their negotiations with the religious cultures they encountered. Sale, Eden, Duff Gordon and Edwards, in their travel accounts of Afghanistan, India, and Egypt respectively, included representations of Islam and the daily lives of Muslims in the countries through which they travelled. We evaluate the extent to which their own respective religious, ideological and social positions shaped the encounters about which they wrote. In doing so, we are less concerned with their understanding of, and attitudes to, the Islamic faith in its spiritual and doctrinal dimensions; instead, we focus on their responses to Muslim peoples in a bid to understand the complexities of religious and racial prejudice and presumptions in a time of both heightened imperial fervour abroad and rising debate about the 'Woman Question' at home.[2]

Lady Sale and Emily Eden were both implicated in the power dynamic and hierarchies of the colonial project, in military or political spheres – most directly, the First Anglo-Afghan War (1838–42). Importantly, neither woman had control over their reason for travel, the route, the timing or travel companions. What is more, both women complicate the line between private and public writing: in Sale's case, she is aware of the publication and reception of individual letters written by her whilst she was in captivity. Following the retreat from Kabul, on 8 January 1842, the women travelling with the force, their servants, and the commander-in-chief, Major-General William Elphinstone (1782–1842), were taken into captivity by the Afghan General Akbar Khan (1816–1847), who was hoping to gain ransom money. Frequent communication between British and Afghan forces allowed Sale the opportunity to send letters to her husband. Both Sale and Eden are therefore part of networks of information exchange, public and private, and both reflect these networks – and their frustrations with them – in their writing.

Lady Sale accompanied her daughter and son-in-law to Kabul with the army that, in 1839, placed Shah Shuja Durrani (1785–1842) on the throne of Afghanistan instead of Dost Mohammad Khan (1792–1863). Emily Eden was the sister of George, Lord Auckland (1784–1849), who, as governor-general of India, was largely responsible for the Simla Manifesto (1838) that led to the campaign.[3] Regime change was a failure: British and Indian troops, as well as 12,000 camp followers, were slaughtered on retreat from Kabul to Jalalabad. Sale was an eyewitness and her diary was published to great acclaim in 1843 after she had been rescued by her husband, General Robert Sale (1782–1845).[4] Each writer engages in different ways with the religious practices and the cultural markers that they encounter. Sale's even-handed account of Islam is the more astonishing because of what she experiences; Eden's response to events in Afghanistan is shock, but it does not override her concerns with the minutiae of her own life. Both writers are insightful and articulate, able to comment on British military and political events whilst observing at first-hand the local cultures through which they are travelling and the role that religion plays in them. In the first section of this chapter, we argue that Sale's depiction of Islam is inevitably bound up with the Kabul campaign and the military conflict that she witnesses. Eden, by contrast, sees Muslim architecture and religious observance as a tourist might: with interest but no personal engagement in their meanings.

Amelia Edwards and Lucie Duff Gordon lived very different lives, but both underwent life-changing encounters with Islamic culture, and were posthumously defined through their identification with Egypt. Both have been celebrated as independent Victorian women who challenged, to varying degrees, dominant gender and racial orthodoxies. Yet such readings overlook the complexity of their responses to Islam, to Muslims and to British colonial ideology. We seek to address these complexities through close analysis of key passages in their respective accounts. In much early scholarship of women's travel writing from this period, it was suggested that many of the women who produced accounts of their travels in Asia and North Africa offered more positive representations of Islamic culture and people than their male counterparts. Dea Birkett, for instance, argues that nineteenth-century women's different relationship to dominant power structures and ideologies enabled female travellers to challenge (and critique) prevailing British imperial attitudes and assumptions due to their own positions as 'colonialized women living in a patriarchal Victorian society'.[5] Such readings have more recently been challenged, or at least qualified, and there is currently an acknowledgement that women's representations of colonized people frequently replicate male depictions. As Carl Thompson has suggested: 'The rather utopian hope, in the first wave of feminist recovery, that women might be innately opposed to imperialism and more sympathetic than men to colonialism's victims, has been largely disproved.'[6] Yet important differences in women travellers' responses *are* apparent and, as Sara Mills, in her landmark study of women's travel writing argues, their accounts are often marked by more extensive 'interaction with members of the other nations', which allow female writers to present people not simply as 'other' or as 'representatives of the race' but as 'individuals'.[7] Of course, a key reason for such differences in interaction was bound up in women travellers' ability to access spaces closed to their male counterparts. One result of this privilege was a challenge to the tendency in many male writers' accounts to exoticize, accounts which, in Susan Bassnett's words, 'overtly sexualized whole areas of the globe, contrasting the "masculine" northern regions with the softer, eroticized, feminine Orient'.[8]

While accepting that gender plays an inescapable part in the negotiations of the peoples and cultures female travel writers encountered and presented in their writing, we agree with current scholarship that such distinctions are over-simplified, ignoring not only the diversity of positions displayed within the genre, but also the specific circumstances and individual agency of these women. We have therefore chosen to focus on four women from different points of the nineteenth century whose distinct experiences of travel in Asia and North Africa highlight the complex and often contradictory nature of their written responses.

Lady Florentia Sale and Emily Eden

As mentioned in the introduction, Sale's depiction of events in Kabul does not focus on her own emotional responses but rather purports to be a chronological report – sometimes hour-by-hour – of events taking place around her: 'I am not attempting to shine in rounded periods, but give everything that occurs as it comes to my knowledge.'[9] For this reason, and because she is trapped in the British cantonment, and then held prisoner, her diary does not show as much of the appreciation of Islamic culture that Eden displays in her letters. Sale does, however, show an acute awareness of the role of Islam in Afghan society. Because the actors in state affairs and the warring tribesmen to which she refers are all Muslim, the terms 'Afghan' and 'Muslim' are effectively conflated.[10] For Eden, the situation is different: she is almost constantly on the move and can observe the intersection between Muslims and their culture with that of Sikhs and Hindus.

Figure 4.1 Florentia, Lady Sale by William James Ward, after Sir Thomas Lawrence, mezzotint, after 1820.
Source: Courtesy of National Portrait Gallery (D4150) / © National Portrait Gallery, London.

Figure 4.2 Emily Eden by Simon Jacques Rochard, watercolour and pencil on paper, 1835.
Source: Courtesy of National Portrait Gallery (6455) / © National Portrait Gallery, London.

Both women comment on British colonialism but are nonetheless part of the hierarchies that colonialism introduces and enforces. So, although benefiting from positions of privilege, neither writer is party to the decisions or able to influence the events that they are writing about. Sale, of course, was not in the army, but she had enough experience as the wife of an army officer to judge the efficacy of leadership, strengths and weaknesses of military and political position. Indeed, her writing is marked by criticism of British leadership and strategy. She contrasts the expertise and demeanour of her son-in-law, Captain Sturt, with that of the army's commander-in-chief: 'Gen. Elphinstone vacillates on every point.'[11]

Bijan Omrani comments that Sale's 'tone, indeed, is like that of Austen, a dry wit and laconic irony: imagine Eliza Bennett transplanted to the Hindu Kush.'[12] This is an interesting observation about literary style, but it is also a revealing comparison: like Jane Austen (1775–1817), the focus of Sale's writing is on people from a certain class, whilst the behaviour, duties – and even survival – of the lower serving classes is seen as separate: 'Our fever cases today consist of Mackenzie, Waller, Freddy Eyre, Mrs Waller, Mcgrath, two ayahs [nannies, maids], one or two Hindostanee servants and several soldiers.'[13] Sale's keen sense of hierarchy, both in military and class terms, is demonstrated in her writing: 'Of so incorrect a person as Mrs Wade, I shall only farther say that she is at Mohamed Shah Khan's fort with her Afghan lover.'[14] Mrs Wade is the wife of a sergeant and, due to this lack status and her behaviour, she is, for Sale, 'a person', not 'a lady'. This demonstrates that Sale's writing is filtered by hierarchy, and that she sees Afghan society in the same terms, claiming that 'I give everything that occurs to my knowledge', but actually offering what occurs through the lens of social class, for example, when she discusses a 'saying of an Afghan gentleman, and also several of the lower classes'.[15] In this instance, it is the levels of social hierarchy that use the saying rather than the saying itself that is the focus. Sale is able to see parallels between Afghan and British society and judges people accordingly: whereas Mrs Wade is 'a person', the Afghan who sends food to Captain Sturt is 'a native *gentleman*'.[16] During captivity, the male members of the party meet to discuss their situation and what deputation they should make to their captors. Sale responds: 'I protest at being implicated in any proceedings in which I have no vote.'[17] Interestingly, she assumes that she has an equal right to voice opinion, despite this being more than seventy years before female suffrage in Britain. This is as much about class and hierarchy as about gender: at no point does Sale suggest that servants, female or male, should have a voice or a vote in this debate.

Eden is also aware of the constructed nature of the British situation in India – and refuses to see it as a consequence of natural hierarchies or God's will:

> Perhaps two thousand years hence, when the art of steam has been forgotten, and nobody can make out the meaning of the old English word 'mail-coach', some black governor-general of England will be marching through its southern provinces and will go and look at some ruins, and doubt whether London was

ever a large town, and will feed some white-looking skeletons, and say what distress the poor creatures must be in.[18]

This striking, imagined inversion of the colonial project and its consequences demonstrates a sense that Eden is aware of the artifice of British colonial structures, from which she nonetheless benefits. This inversion reflects her mindfulness that there is much to be appreciated about the cultures through which she is travelling. Eden is personally shielded from the events in Kabul and therefore has a different view from Sale; although, as will be seen below, she later generalizes about the 'savagery' of the Afghans, she is also able to appreciate some aspects of Islamic culture. Similarly, despite her situation, Sale is capable of appreciation of the Afghan character: 'They are no cowards, but a fine manly looking set … they show no cowardice in standing against guns without using any themselves, and in escalading forts which we cannot retake.'[19]

In Eden's comments, it is clear that her party respect the sobriety of Muslims, so that exceptions are seen as shocking: he 'took good care to drink nothing but water himself, and persuaded two others to get very drunk with what he called Sherbet, and then they began to quarrel. It is such an extreme disgrace for a Mussulman to be drunk, and so degrading in the eyes of the others, that J. turned them off forthwith.'[20] Here the reader sees the detail of human interaction but also appreciates Eden's understanding of its significance in the context of Islam. Eden is particularly keen on Islamic architecture, visiting and sketching mosques. She describes the mosques as 'tempting', 'the finest we have seen so far', and the reader's attention is drawn to the materials used to build them and the forms of the minarets: 'It is built of beautiful red granite, is 240 feet high and 50 feet in diameter, and carved all over with sentences from the Koran, each letter a yard high, and the letter interlaced and ornamented with flowers and garlands. … As it stands it is perfect.'[21] Whereas Sale, as we demonstrate below, sees the mosque in the light of its role in politics, here Eden focuses on aesthetics and Islamic heritage. Again, there is detail in the description, and again it is made explicitly in the context of religion.

As events in Kabul move towards disaster, the focus and tone of Sale's account naturally change. Of interest in this respect is her awareness of the role of Islam in wider Afghan society, an awareness of the intersections between state and religion in a way that the British had perhaps not anticipated, coming from a state in which politics and religion were, formally at least, separate. In the first instance, the regime change that the British are trying to effect is subject to the approval of the *mullahs* (religious leaders), without which it will not be accepted by the general population:

> The insurgent chiefs have set up a king, and a wuzeer [*vizier*, high-ranking official]; they went to the mosque, and read the fatcha [*al-Fatiha*[22]], or prayer, for the reigning monarch. Several of the Moollahs refused to recognize the name of Shah Zeman: they said they would allow that of Shah Shoojah as a legitimate monarch.[23]

Shah Shuja was the puppet king of the British, and this observation by Sale shows that the initial military success in the march on Kandahar, and then Kabul, was not the only process necessary in setting Shah Shuja in a position of authority. As well as playing a role in regime change, the *mullahs* can be held responsible within Afghan power structures when their decision-making is shown to be flawed, or when they appear on the losing side: 'Much of the obloquy was allowed to rest on Moollah Shekoor, who had paid the penalty of other state crimes.'[24] In this instance, with Shekoor already dead, he can also take the blame for political stances which are viewed in hindsight as blunders.

In due course, the military authorities in Kabul recognize the vital role of the *mullahs* in controlling the local population. As part of her criticism of Elphinstone, Sale shows the folly of allowing the *mullahs* to play this role without a military force to make sure it is enforced: 'Sturt proposed to destroy the Rikabashees' fort, and throw a party that was in it into the small fort near the bridge; but it was disapproved by the Envoy, who said he would place a moollah he had confidence in, in it, as the General said he could not afford twenty men to garrison it.'[25] Elphinstone recognizes the power of the *mullah*, stating that he can play the role of a twenty-man garrison, but overestimates the loyalty of the *mullah* to the British cause. Eventually this is seen more directly in the role of the *mullahs* in the insurrection: as well as having a voice in political decision-making, they carry weight with public opinion: 'Khojeh Meer says that he has no more grain: we only got 50 maunds in to-day. He also says that the moollahs have been to all the villages, and laid the people under ban not to assist the English, and that consequently the Mussulman population are as one man against us.'[26] This comment is also indicative of the relative positions of Sale – and most of the British force – and the *mullahs*: whilst the British are held in the Kabul cantonment, the *mullahs* are able to travel freely about their territories, and can therefore affect public opinion far more easily, and from a position of greater authority, than the static invaders. The extent of quotations from other sources such as 'Khojeh Meer' throughout Sale's diaries is testament to the limited view that she has of the situation.

Further evidence of the role of Islam in the ongoing situation can also be found in Sale's account. The appeal of joining a Muslim force plays a role in desertion: 'A man of Warburton's artillery has deserted, as also a havildar of Hoskins' regiment; the latter was received by Zeman Shah Khan with great honour, and told that all good Mussulmans were welcome. A house and shawls were given to him.'[27] Even in the arena of war, religious observance is reported by Sale: 'A body richly dressed was found, but the head was carried away. This they do when they cannot take the body, as the head then receives Mussulman burial, which the Afghans are very particular in observing.'[28] The link between Islam and war develops from Sale's previous comments on Islam and the state, as the situation deteriorates. As well as wielding political influence and being able to affect popular opinion, *mullahs* play an active role in violence against the British: 'Sultan Jan uttering an opprobrious epithet, calling him a dog, cut poor Trevor down, as did also Moollah Momind.'[29] This entry recounts a significant moment in the escalation of tension between the British and the Afghans: at what is supposed to be a peace talk, the British envoy is taken away and later killed, whilst the others are attacked. The *mullah* is directly involved in what Sale describes as 'a decided piece of treachery'.[30]

Sale goes on to make explicit the link that she sees between religion and warfare, going beyond this individual instance to generalize about the role of Islam in the male population:

> Here, every man is born a soldier; every child has his knife, that weapon which has proved so destructive in the hands of a hostile peasantry, incited against us by the moollahs, who threaten eternal perdition to all who do not join in the cause of the Ghazeeas; whilst heaven, filled with Houris, is the recompense for every man who falls in a religious war.[31]

The image of the Afghan with his knife is a powerful one, reinforced by many anglophone depictions of Afghanistan. As Corinne Fowler argues, the landscape itself comes to be associated with blades in several works, including Rudyard Kipling's *The Man Who Would be King* (1888) and his poem 'The Young British Soldier' (1892).[32] In this quotation, Sale makes explicit the link between resistance against the British and access to heaven, noting again the role of the *mullahs* in communicating this to the wider population. Here Sale presents a powerful combination of two factors that will dominate representations of Afghan men from this point onwards: they are inherently violent, and they are religious fanatics who dream of achieving heaven through death in battle, as ordained by religious leaders who play the role of catalyst. Eden is also capable of generalizations on this subject, although she does not refer to Islam in any of her responses to the massacre of the British army; as well as blaming the failings of British leadership, she is clear that the actions and dangers are specifically Afghan: 'Knowing what a savage people the Afghans are, I never can get the horrors that may happen out of my head.'[33] Later, as more details of the events in Afghanistan arrive in India, she bemoans the fate of 'those unfortunate women, in the hands of such savages'.[34] By contrast, in response to Sale's news from captivity, Eden notes that 'it is comfort to know that the ladies are well treated by the Afghans, and everything is going on well in other parts of Afghanistan; but the loss of life occasioned by local mismanagement is fearful'.[35] In this instance the characterization of Afghans as honourable is to the fore, rather than a generalization about their savagery. These texts and their contradictions will establish the Afghan character in the minds of British readers.

Both Sale and Eden, then, are aware of the role that Islam plays in the societies and events that they witness. Although their experiences differ greatly, they each make some positive comments about Islam, but the events of the First Anglo-Afghan War inevitably colour their writing. Eden's diaries are more nuanced in differentiating between Muslims and Afghans, as she sees and describes examples of the former in the wider cultural context of British India. For Sale, as we argued at the start of this section, Muslim and Afghan are conflated, and it is more difficult to untangle Sale's descriptions of one from the other. She nonetheless shows an awareness of the role of religion in the response to the British attempt to affect regime change. Sale also, due to the wide dissemination of her letters, and the success of the diary publication, lays down one of the first descriptions which will conflate violent Afghans with violent Muslims: her statement, quoted earlier, that 'here, every man is born a soldier; every child has his knife', will resonate through depictions of Afghanistan to the present day.

Lucie Duff Gordon

As in the case of Lady Sale, Lucie Duff Gordon's account of Egypt consisted of letters to family and were not originally intended for publication. Married to Sir Alexander Cornewall Duff Gordon (1811–1872), a senior civil servant, Lucie Duff Gordon was the daughter of the linguist and translator Sarah Austin (1793–1867), and was herself a published translator and writer. She moved in

Figure 4.3 Lucie, Lady Duff Gordon by Henry Wyndham Phillips, oil on canvas, 1851. *Source:* Courtesy of National Portrait Gallery (5584) / © National Portrait Gallery, London.

intellectual, political and creative circles, with Dickens, Alfred Tennyson (1809–1892), William Makepeace Thackeray (1811–1863) and other writers of the day being frequent visitors to the Duff Gordons' house. By the early 1860s, she had become seriously ill with tuberculosis and was advised by her doctors to travel to a dryer and warmer climate. After spending some time in South Africa,

Duff Gordon moved to Egypt, arriving in Alexandria in October 1862. Barring two brief visits to England in 1863 and 1865, she remained in Egypt until her death in 1869, making Luxor her home. Like the texts of Sale and Eden, Duff Gordon's *Letters from Egypt* (1865) are an important example of the epistolary travel account which, as Susan Bassnett suggests, 'tends to be more frequently produced by women' and blurs the margins 'between the autobiographical, the anecdotal, and the ethnographic'.[36]

Carl Thompson has suggested that nineteenth-century travel accounts by women are characterized by contradiction. He writes: 'The situation of being simultaneously "colonized by gender, but colonizers by race" seems to have produced in women an unconscious unease, and a psychological anxiety that finds expression in various forms of discursive uncertainty and contradiction in the female-authored travelogue.'[37] Arguably, this quality is perceptible in Duff Gordon's *Letters*, which reflect simultaneously the prejudices of her British, upper-class culture and a growing sense of affinity with the Arab people she comes to know and respect. The letters trace her psychological journey from a fairly stereotypical English disdain for a culture she neither knows nor understands to a resentful indignation at the way Arabs were treated and represented by the British. Yet, her narrative remains riddled with contradictory responses, embodying at times an exoticizing of Black and Arab men bordering on sexual objectification,[38] and at others an implicitly racist dismissal of specific Muslim peoples as 'children' innately inferior to 'civilized' and educated Westerners. Within these instances, there is a growing sense of comradeship with Egyptians, which occasionally takes the form of shame at her own country's actions and attitudes.

Patronizing comments about local people are more frequent in the early period of Duff Gordon's residence in Egypt. Often, such observations are affectionate, yet underpinned by an implicit superiority: 'My crew are dear, good, lazy fellows, or rather, children; their ways amuse me infinitely.'[39] The designation of adult men as 'children' here replicates contemporary racist discourses which perceived non-white people as less advanced than white Westerners and thereby helped to justify the colonial mission. Yet, more often, Duff Gordon records positive characteristics of the people she encounters, which she increasingly frames in opposition to British deficiencies: 'I can't describe how anxiously kind these people were to me; one gets such a wonderful amount of sympathy and real hearty kindness here.'[40] Elsewhere she describes her shame of her own religious culture, for example, when a Muslim man she meets informs her that 'he would like to come to England. When there he would work to eat and drink, and then sit and sleep in the church. I was positively ashamed to tell my religious friend that, with us, the "house of God" is not the home of the poor stranger'.[41] Such instances reflect her growing critical reflection regarding the respective virtues of Christianity as practiced in Britain and the Islamic faith that she witnesses daily; she increasingly questions many of the preconceptions with which she arrived: 'The thing that strikes me most is the tolerant spirit that I find everywhere. They say, "Ah, it is your custom!" and express no sort of condemnation; and Muslims and Christians appear perfectly good friends.'[42] Implicit here is an admission that such tolerance is less evident between faiths in her homeland.

Sarah Austin edited the first published edition of her daughter's *Letters*, and in the preface noted that 'nothing less than Humanity, in its most literal and its largest sense, – not circumscribed by race or religion, by opinions or customs, but the purely human sympathy which binds together those between whom no other tie exists, – could have made life under such conditions tolerable.'[43] Yet, it is perceptible that, for all her openness to the humanity of the Arab and Nubian people, Duff Gordon still replicates British class prejudices in a similar way to Sale, as we saw earlier. She shows pity for the peasants and the poverty that she witnesses in cities and villages alike, but the people she socializes with all hold a certain level of position and wealth in Egyptian society. Duff Gordon writes affectionately of Omar, her dragoman-cum-chef-cum-general factotum – but there is always the implicit distance of mistress and servant; he is treated as a confidential and trusted British servant would be at home. This contrasts with the accounts written by Sale and Eden, in which Muslim servants are invisible: Duff Gordon's position as not being directly involved in the mechanics of politics and the military perhaps allows her to deal with Omar as an individual in ways that Sale and Eden do not.

If Duff Gordon's class prejudices remain relatively entrenched throughout her time in Egypt, her attitudes to religion are much more tolerant and enlightened. In a representative passage, she writes: 'I am very puzzled to discover the slightest difference between Christian and Muslim morality or belief – if you exclude certain dogmas – and in fact, very little is felt here. No one attempts to apply different standards of morals or of piety to a Muslim or a Copt. East and West is the difference not Muslim and Christian.'[44] The *Letters* are replete with challenges to British stereotypes of Muslims. Early on, she notes that 'I have yet to see the much-talked-of fanaticism'.[45] In the later letters, fanaticism is relocated away from Islam and onto her own countrymen: 'I have been really amazed at several instances of English fanaticism this year. Why do people come to a

Muslim country with such hatred "in their stomachs" as I have witnessed three or four times?'[46] She also repeatedly refutes more general offensive assumptions about Egypt:

> I suppose I shall be thought utterly paradoxical when I deny the much talked-of dirt. The narrow, dingy, damp, age-blackened, dust-crusted, unpaved streets of Cairo are sweet as roses compared to those of the 'Centre of Civilization'; moreover an Arab crowd does not stink, even under this sun.[47]

Here, as elsewhere, England (or perhaps London) as the 'Centre of Civilization' is denigrated, and prejudice and hypocrisy countered.

This critical tone is increasingly evident as Duff Gordon grows in respect for the people among whom she lives, and there are critical musings on dominant British representations of Muslim culture and faith alongside her own gradual questioning of such assumptions. One example relates to the received wisdom concerning gender relations in the two respective cultures: 'The English would be a little surprised at Arab judgments of them …. They are shocked at the way Englishmen talk about hareem among themselves, and think the English hard and unkind to their wives and to women in general.'[48] A number of critics have pointed out the ways in which Victorian women's travel accounts provided a corrective to masculine fantasies about the harem (women's quarters) through women's ability to access and observe Muslim female-only spaces. As Susan Bassnett has noted, Duff Gordon describes 'the daily lives of Egyptian women in terms that contested the fantasizing of her male contemporaries' and 'refuted the growing tendency towards the eroticization of the unfamiliar that characterizes so many texts by male travellers'.[49] Arguably, Duff Gordon was conscious of these important insights and corrections to false depictions; in her final letters, she wrote: 'I honestly believe that knowledge will die with me which few others possess. You must recollect that the learned know books, and I know men, and what is more difficult, women.'[50]

All this is not to idealize Duff Gordon's outlook on the respective virtues of Britain and Egypt: the *Letters* also expose her blind spots and unconscious adherence to aspects of the colonial mission and its encoded sense of racial superiority – so much so that the British colonial administration made *Letters from Egypt* required reading in all Egyptian schools after the occupation of that country in 1882. Mervat Hatem explains this by pointing to 'The *Letters*' simultaneous portrayal of Egyptian rulers as corrupt and the Europeans as benevolent', which was cynically used as a tool both to legitimize British control and to suppress increasing 'nationalist sentiments among the students'.[51] At the same time, Duff Gordon's writing offered an authentic, largely respectful and more accurate picture of ordinary Egyptian lives to British readers more used to negative images of Islamic culture, which by turn demonized, exoticized and falsified. As Amelia B. Edwards noted when she visited Duff Gordon's house after her death, 'Every Arab in Luxor cherishes the memory of Lady Duff Gordon in his heart of hearts, and speaks of her with blessings.'[52]

Amelia B. Edwards

In the churchyard of St. Mary's in Henbury, near Bristol, an unusual Victorian grave marks the final resting place of a remarkable woman. Situated in a privileged spot, close to the church wall, the grave, absent of any Christian inscription, is marked by an obelisk, in front of which lies a stone ankh, the ancient Egyptian hieroglyphic symbol that represents life itself. It is, in many ways, an extraordinary monument for an Anglican church to sanction in the late-Victorian period, but it is a fitting tribute to the woman for whom it was erected – a woman whose devotion to the scholarship of Egyptology formed the major passion of her life. An inscription on the obelisk identifies Amelia Ann Blandford Edwards as a novelist and archaeologist, 'who by her writings and her labours enriched the thought and interests of her time'.

A trip to Egypt in 1873–4 proved to be a turning point in Edwards' life and instilled in her a passion for ancient Egyptian culture and archaeology that would inform her activities for the next two decades. On returning from Egypt, Edwards set herself upon an exhaustive reading programme, studied hieroglyphics and corresponded with various specialists in the field of Egyptology. In 1877, her account of the Egypt trip was published as *A Thousand Miles Up the Nile* to enthusiastic reviews. Edwards was instrumental in establishing in 1882 the Egypt Exploration Fund (later renamed the Egypt Exploration Society) and was elected one of the honorary joint secretaries, a position she retained for life. There followed a successful lecturing tour of the United States and various honorary degrees from American universities and colleges. Edwards' Egypt trip and subsequent travelogue, then, were pivotal in her self-fashioning of a new identity as a cultural authority and public intellectual. In her later writings, it becomes clear that the attraction of the country for Edwards lies in both her genuine personal response to its ancient culture and also her realization (not without self-interest) of the potential for 'even an amateur to make important contributions to knowledge of its ancient civilization'.[53]

Figure 4.4 Amelia B. Edwards by August Weger, after Elliott and Fry, line and stipple engraving, after 1876.
Source: Courtesy of National Portrait Gallery (D7713) / © National Portrait Gallery, London.

What is striking about Edwards' response to Egypt is her apparent disconnect between its ancient heritage and its modern-day inhabitants. Throughout *A Thousand Miles Up the Nile*, she rarely, if ever, references the current political situation in the country – surely a surprising omission given the unstable position of Egypt in the 1870s. Edwards' interest lies in her intellectual response to the antiquity of the country, leaving little room for any appreciation of modern Egyptians or Islamic culture. Unlike other female travellers to Egypt in this period, she is largely unmoved by the sight of ornate architecture or local customs – her attention is all on the ancient monuments. Though occasionally she speaks with respect and admiration of notable mosques that she visits, such as Sultan Hassan in Cairo, her attitude to local Muslims seems always distanced and uncomprehending. Representations of the people she encounters are often problematic, such as when she describes 'groups of wild-looking, half-savage figures in parti-coloured garments'.[54] As Patricia O'Neill states, Edwards' 'discussions of modern Egyptians consistently echo the opinions and attitudes of her European predecessors in the field', and she 'assumes the role of an imperial spectator, within a burgeoning discourse of Orientalism'.[55] Where Edwards *does* make connections between the ancient civilization that fascinates her and the modern people she encounters, her observations are marked by cultural distance and a negation of individuality. In her preface to the first edition of *A Thousand Miles Up the Nile*, she writes:

> I brought home with me an impression that things and people are much less changed in Egypt than *we of the present day* are wont to suppose. I believe that the physique and life of the modern Fellah [labourer, peasant] is almost identical with the physique and life of that ancient Egyptian labourer whom we know so well in the wall paintings of the tombs … we see him wearing the same loin-cloth, … ploughing with the same plough, preparing the same food in the same way, and eating it with his fingers from the same bowl, as did his forefathers of six thousand years ago.[56]

The disjunct between the people of Egypt and 'we of the present day' places Victorian Britain clearly in the realm of modernity, with the Muslims in a static, undeveloped past. The implications here all infer the inferiority of Egypt in contrast to the developed civilization of Britain.

Passages like these lead some critics to judge Edwards harshly for her lack of concern over the social problems of the country she visits and her blindness to the individual humanity of the people she meets. For instance, Billie Melman claims that Edwards' 'impersonal' and 'neutral' narrative renders her 'panorama of Egypt … strangely devoid of human figures'.[57] In part, this effect is a result of Edwards' deliberate attempt to de-gender her narrative voice, in a bid to appropriate masculine authority for her account. As Patricia O'Neill has also noted, this 'de-gendering' (and, arguably, her deliberate distancing and objectifying of her subject) allows Edwards to 'participate in the scientific discourse of her male contemporaries'.[58] But in this way, she arguably becomes complicit in the British imperial project, as are Sale and Eden, and the more general Orientalizing of the non-Western subject.

One of the strategies Edwards employs to facilitate this scientific objectivity, and presumably therein, authority by Victorian standards, is the abstract nature of her representation throughout. This reduces Egyptian people to mere parts of the landscape for much of her narrative. However, it is worth noting that she applies this technique equally to both Egyptians and the Europeans in her party. People who accompanied Edwards on her journey up the Nile become generalized as 'the Idle Man', 'the Painter', 'the Happy Couple', and so on, although we might argue that Edwards' third-person designation of herself as 'the Writer' imbues her with a certain observational distance, authority and power within this abstracted entourage. In this aspect, Edwards' narrative conforms to a broader trend in female travel writing whereby, as Susan Bassnett has noted, 'many of the works by women travellers are self-conscious fictions, and the persona who emerges from the pages is as much a character as a woman in a novel.'[59]

What is notable about Edwards' early responses to the Islamic culture she encounters is her ignorance of religious practices and observances. In Chapter 2, she writes:

> This was the first time we had seen Moslems at prayer, and we could not but be impressed by their profound and unaffected devotion .... So absorbed were they, that not even our unhallowed presence seemed to disturb them. We did not then know that the pious Moslem is as devout out of the mosque as in it.[60]

Edwards goes on to describe her initial surprise that Muslim men in her entourage pray five times a day, revealing a telling lack of understanding of the five 'pillars' of Islam and religious habits of daily life.[61] There was a relatively small, but growing number of Muslims in Britain at this time – several thousand by the end of the century, some of whom were British converts to Islam. In the decade immediately following Edwards' trip to Egypt, the first purpose-built mosque was established in England, at Woking in Surrey.[62] The fact that a woman as erudite and well-travelled as Edwards seems ignorant of the core beliefs and practices of Islam (unlike Sale, whose glossary includes several terms relating directly to Islam, thereby establishing her knowledge of the subject from the outset), speaks to its marginalization as a faith by the British at home and relates back to the influence of those cultural stereotypes mentioned at the outset of this chapter.

Edwards, then, presents herself as a complex figure: as an independent woman, travelling in remote regions of Egypt, and self-fashioning as a public intellectual and cultural authority in the male-dominated realm of Egyptology, she poses a challenge to dominant gender ideology. Yet, she is only able to do so by appropriating masculine discourses – scientific, historical, imperial – through the privilege of her own class and racial position; in doing so, she tends to replicate colonial and gendered stereotypes in many of her encounters with Egypt's inhabitants.

Conclusion

On the whole, most of the women discussed in this chapter were not writing because of their (privileged or otherwise) position in a binary of colonizer and colonized: this is too mechanistic and removes agency. Christine Bolt has argued that the unreliability of travel narratives by women are 'so lacking in objectivity as to be almost useless as the base for an accurate assessment of African societies'.[63] While not denying the subjectivity of the accounts discussed here, we refute the notion that this renders them 'useless'; on the contrary, these biases, along with the contradictions and ambiguities in each narrative, offer valuable insights into the complex interactions between West and East at this time. Clearly all four women were products of class, gender and their historical and cultural contexts; but they were also insightful, knowledgeable and articulate individuals. It is therefore worth paying attention to their accounts as writers of texts that complicate and inform our view of British responses to and representations of Islam and Muslims in the nineteenth century. Given the variations in region, time, background and forms of writing, we should be wary of assuming a homogenous response. Even when granted 'permission to see the ancient city',[64] the writing of these women travellers shows the undeniable stamp of personal response, as well as a sensitivity to the intersections of Islam with nationalism, local culture, history and politics.

5

Translators, publishers and popular readerships: The Qur'an on the Victorian bookshelf

Alexander Bubb

Introduction

In December 1877, George Campbell, the 8th Duke of Argyll (1823–1900), had engaged to give his opinions on something that he did not know much about: 'I may have occasion soon to give a little popular lecture here on the Koran', he wrote from his estate at Rosneath in Scotland, 'and there is a point on which I will ask yr help'.[1] His correspondent, in Edinburgh, was the retired colonial administrator and Orientalist Sir William Muir (1819–1905), known principally for his 1861 book, *The Life of Mahomet*. Having sat down with an English translation of the Qur'an and, presumably for the first time, carefully consulted the text, some points of confusion had arisen, which the Duke hoped a specialist like Muir might clarify for him:

> I do not see in the Koran so far as I have read it any full justification of much that is said against Mahomedanism and I can't help suspecting that subsequent tradition has added much to the evil of the original doctrine. For example in the current no. of the 'Nineteenth Century' in an article by G. D. McColl I find it said 'It is an axiom of Mussulman morals that faith need not be kept with an Infidel.' Now I can't find any passage of the Koran to bear out this: of course it is notorious everywhere that such has been practically the doctrine of Moslems – just as it has been practically the doctrine of Rom[an]. Catholics towards Protestants. Can you refer me to any passage in the Koran on this subject? Even as regards 'Persecution' the passages are few, and less direct than

I had been led to expect. Nor is it true as McColl states in the same paper that the Koran directs war against all Infidels till either they submit or are destroyed. It seems clear that Mahomet did not contemplate actual persecution against either Jews or Xns. Wd be glad to have y. opinion on this.[2]

It is unclear whether the lecture actually took place, and Muir's reply to the Duke appears to have been lost or destroyed. However, the Duke's experience echoed that of many literate Victorians who, in the last three decades of the nineteenth century, were enabled to consult a variety of Qur'anic translations and expositions – including cheap, mass-produced editions – and some of whom found in due course that the Muslim Holy Book was by no means what they 'had been led to expect'.[3]

The Qur'an was not a novelty in nineteenth-century Britain. As Ziad Elmarsafy has demonstrated, translations into English, French and other languages had been distributed and fervently discussed by the intelligentsia during the European Enlightenment.[4] Voltaire (1694–1778), Joseph Priestley (1733–1804), Edward Gibbon (1737–1794) and Thomas Jefferson (1743–1826) had all read George Sale's (1697–1736) *The Koran, Commonly called the Alcoran of Mohammed* (1734).[5] What changed after the 1860s was the breadth of distribution, and variety of translations, available to interested readers. In 1861, the clergyman John Medows Rodwell (1808–1900) published his version, followed in 1880 by the Cambridge professor Edward Henry Palmer (1840–1882), so that, by the end of the century, three different English translations were in common circulation. Moreover, in 1877, the publisher Frederick Warne (1825–1901) decided to issue the first cheap edition (using Sale's text) in his popular reprint series, 'The Chandos Classics'. The Qur'an (as well as the Talmud and an abridged version of *The Arabian Nights*) was to be had from Warne and Company for one shilling and sixpence in a paper wrapper, or bound in cloth for two shillings – and therefore affordable to the middle classes, though somewhat extravagant for the bulk of the labouring population.[6] It was the first of several affordable Qur'ans to be published in general 'classics' series over the following decades. This chapter offers an overview of the translators and publishers whose motives and strategies for bringing the Qur'an to a general audience established its place on the late-Victorian bookshelf. Through several case studies of individual readers, it also explores the Victorian experience of the Qur'an and identifies some key points of interest driving its steady permeation of literate culture and public discourse.

A choice of translations

A crude but perhaps enlightening statistic we might begin by trying to obtain is the total number of copies issued of English Qur'an translations after 1860. Though we cannot be exact, a consultation of surviving publishers' archives, combined with some appropriate inferences as to probable print runs, offers an approximate figure. When Warne issued his first 'people's edition' – as such cheap and portable volumes were commonly known – in 1877, it is likely that he ordered between 1,000 and 2,000 copies, which would have been typical of new books at the time. In 1880 a second print run was ordered, and thereafter the work was regularly reprinted. The year 1904, which is as far back as the firm's ledgers survive, saw the 31st edition, and after this point we can track its progress closely, alongside other bestselling titles. New editions were ordered in January 1906, April 1908, March 1909, June 1910, November 1911 and January 1914, totalling 15,500 copies printed. This made it one of the most popular works in the entire series for the Edwardian period, with only the *Works of Shakespeare* and Longfellow's poems being printed in greater numbers between 1904 and 1914.[7] Intriguingly, it was also one of only three volumes Warne reprinted amidst the rising costs and paper shortages of 1915–17. That one of the others was the Talmud suggests an anticipated public for religious texts, possibly soldiers – but let us curtail our census at the outbreak of war in summer 1914.[8]

Overall, at a conservative estimate, the total number of 'Chandos Classics' Qur'ans printed by this point was 70,000. However, Warne was not the only publisher to re-issue Sale's translation, which was most popular by far because it was out of copyright. In 1892, the Routledge brothers borrowed Warne's stereotypes, at a charge of £20, to print another 2,000 copies for their series of the 'One Hundred Best Books', as selected by the Victorian polymath Sir John Lubbock (1834–1913).[9] Moreover, several American firms, including Lippincott and A. L. Burt, also distributed Sale's translation. As for Rodwell, his translation went through two editions in his lifetime and, as soon as his posthumous copyright expired, it too was immediately re-issued, by J. M. Dent and Company, in the most celebrated of all cheap reprint series, 'Everyman's Library'. Print runs for 'Everyman's' titles typically numbered 10,000 copies, and Dent's presses rolled in March 1909, October 1909, 1911 and 1913 (and like Warne's, they continued to turn out Qur'ans during the First World War). According to Seymour Terry, over time the Qur'an established itself in the top five per cent of bestselling titles for 'Everyman's', exceeding even George Eliot's (1819–1880) *Silas Marner* (1861) and the works of John Stuart Mill (1806–1873).[10] Palmer's translation, meanwhile, commissioned for a limited-issue Oxford prestige project, the 'Sacred Books of the East' series, was little read until its inclusion in the Oxford 'World's Classics' in the 1920s. But, to the piles marked 'Sale' and 'Rodwell', we can also add the Duke of Argyll's correspondent, Sir William Muir (*Extracts from the Coran*, 1880), along with Sir Edwin Arnold (1832–1904; *Pearls of the Faith*, 1882), Nathan Haskell Dole (1852–1935; *Selections from the Koran of Mohammed*, 1903) and Arthur N. Wollaston (1842–1922; *Religion of the Koran*, 1904) – all of whom, like Edward William Lane (1801–1876) before them in 1843, edited selected passages from the Holy Book. Without going any further, we may safely say that well over 100,000 copies of the Qur'an entered circulation in the English-speaking world between 1860 and 1914. Probably the figure is closer to 150,000, and this does not include the not-insignificant number of copies that had already been printed before that period.

When describing the impression made on an individual Western reader by a religious or philosophical text from Asia, scholars have frequently neglected to consider which particular translation the reader was using. In a way this is unsurprising, because the evidence for that experience, which is usually the reader's own account obtained from their diary, correspondence or autobiography, often enough does not provide us with that information. In November 1897, Abdullah Quilliam's (1856–1932) newspaper *The Crescent*, a weekly record of the pioneering Liverpool Muslim Institute (see Chapter 10), carried a letter addressed by a recent convert to Islam: 'I have studied Sale's translation of the Koran, and now we have reached that point when the last lingering shadows of misgiving must be dispelled, and allow us to gaze with unclouded eyes on the glorious radiance of the truth.'[11] This, however, is an exception. The vast majority of the conversion narratives recounted in *The Crescent* do not mention the translation or edition favoured by the convert, including Quilliam's own account (though his preference for Sale has been determined from other evidence).[12] But a personal copy of the Qur'an does frequently play an instrumental role in such narratives, and occasionally we can make an identification based on the context. In November 1900, for example, the British Muslim convert Fatima Cates (1865–1900) recounted having to carry her Qur'an about on her person for fear that, if she left it at home, it would be burnt by relatives who objected to her religious conversion.[13] This could hardly have been the large octavo volume in which Rodwell's text was at that time issued (in spite of its handsome green binding with arabesque gilding), but is much more likely to have been the handier 'Chandos Classics' edition, in plain blue wrapper, of Sale's version.

The comparative inattention afforded to this crucial matter is particularly surprising, given that the three principal translators – Sale, Rodwell, Palmer – differed so much in their choice of language, syntax and register, in their organization of the text, and in their attitudes towards Islam. Notably, Rodwell decided to reorder the *suras* (divisions, or chapters, of the Qur'an) in what he judged to be the chronological order of their revelation to Muhammad over the course of twenty-three years. In preference to Sale's relatively plain English prose, tinged with some of the archaisms of the King James Bible, Rodwell employed a more elaborate Old Testament diction to impart, as he saw it, the appropriate sense of gravity and antiquity to the scripture. Choosing a different path again, Palmer opted for plainer and more modern expressions – dispensing with 'thou' and 'hath' – but he also rendered phrases and imagery more literally than his two predecessors, even when the original Arabic veered into 'low' vernacular register. Thus, God may 'leave you in the lurch' if you do not follow his precepts, reads a passage in the Family of Imran (Al Imran) *sura*, while in the Cattle (Al-An'am) the Muslims are urged to meet disputation with the challenge, 'Come on then with your witnesses'![14] This certainly baffled some contemporaries: 'Because Mohammed sometimes talked Arabic slang to Arabs who spoke Arabic slang', asked the *Saturday Review*, 'is Professor Palmer justified in writing what is very like English slang for English readers who do not speak, and would rather not read, English slang?'[15]

A short comparison of the first five *ayahs* (verses) of the Clot (Al-'Alaq) *sura* as given by Sale, Rodwell and Palmer illustrate the differences between them:

Sale:

Read, in the name of thy LORD, who hath created *all things;* who hath created man of congealed blood. Read, by thy most beneficent LORD; who taught the use of the pen; who teacheth man that which he knoweth not.[16]

Rodwell:

RECITE thou, in the name of thy Lord who created;—

Created man from CLOTS OF BLOOD:—

Recite thou! For thy Lord is the most Beneficent,

Who hath taught the use of the pen;—

Hath taught man that which he knoweth not.[17]

Palmer:

Read, in the name of thy Lord!

Who created man from congealed blood!
Read, for thy Lord is most generous!
Who taught the pen!
Taught man what he did not know![18]

Traditionally believed to constitute Muhammad's first revelation, these are the words with which the Archangel Gabriel summoned him to his calling. With their dramatic evocation of the act of divine creation, recalling the first chapter of Genesis, they form a striking overture to Rodwell's translation, but one quite at variance with the canonical order of the *suras* – in fact, the Clot appears towards the end of the Qur'an. Another of Rodwell's innovations was to arrange the *ayahs* on individual lines – giving the text the appearance of poetry – a tactic reprised by Palmer, who shared Rodwell's concern for expressing the Qur'an's vocal, exhortatory quality, and who made liberal use of the exclamation mark. This concern intersects, in a telling manner, with the two translators' mutual claims to literalism.

As noted, Palmer determined to follow the Arabic as closely as possible, and his policy of not interpolating any word without an equivalent in the original results in the curious elision 'taught the pen'. But Rodwell too makes claims to literalism, insisting that 'recite' is a more accurate rendering of the verb *qaraa* than the conventional 'read'. By way of justification, his footnote points out that *qaraa* is the root of Qur'an – 'the recitation' – but the proclamatory bearing this gives the text is not quite consistent with the emphasis laid in the Clot *sura* on literacy. This may be the first step in Rodwell's concerted effort to undermine the legitimacy and historicity of the Qur'an as a written document. For, as has been hinted, underlying these contrasts in style and editorship were dramatically different attitudes to the text itself. Palmer – an enthusiast from his youth for Arabic and Persian, well-travelled in the Middle East and a Cambridge academic – approached the Qur'an in a spirit of cultural relativism and generosity, whereas Rodwell, an eccentric High Church clergyman targeting a missionary readership, seems to have translated the Qur'an chiefly to discredit it.[19] Rodwell's commentary, in the form of copious footnotes, brings to the text a continuous undertone of scepticism that evidently grated on less prejudiced readers.

A fascinating document is Richard Francis Burton's (1821–1890) much-used copy of Rodwell's edition, the marginalia of which show the great intellectual renegade, whose sympathies were professedly with Islam over conventional Christianity, constantly chafing with disgust and frustration. On page xxii, where Rodwell avers that Muhammad was an epileptic ('of a highly nervous and excitable mother'), and thus susceptible to the delusion that he was appointed God's final and definitive prophet, Burton has inserted the blunt contradiction, 'So he was'. Where Rodwell criticizes Islam for condoning slavery and polygamy, Burton points out that Christian scripture is not free of these blemishes, while the suggestion that the charismatic Muhammad wilfully deceived his followers is dismissed by Burton as the narrow thinking of a 'man who cannot understand what genius means'.[20] Regrettably perhaps, Rodwell's version would continue to be distributed widely well into the twentieth century, owing to its reissue in 'Everyman's Classics' – a decision originally prompted, according to a company memoir, by the personal recommendation of George Bernard Shaw (1856–1950).[21]

In spite of its shortcomings, Rodwell's translation was not without its own unique merits, and while it may have been ubiquitous, it was not hegemonic. Late-Victorian readers could choose their own preferred text, as is evident from an article that appeared in *The Edinburgh Review* in 1881, in which 'Sale's well-meaning but prosaic work' was weighed against the 'poetic inspiration' of Rodwell and the 'freshness and buoyancy' of Palmer.[22] Three years later, the writer Lafcadio Hearn (1850–1904) wrote a letter to a friend in which he similarly considered the factors prior to purchasing a copy (Hearn's facility in several languages also permitted him to consult the Qur'an in French):

> There are two English translations besides Sale's – one in Trübner's Oriental Series, and one in Max Muller's 'Sacred Books of the East' (Macmillan's beautiful Edition). Sale's is chiefly objectionable because the Suras are not versified: the chapters not having been so divided in early times by figures. But it is horribly hard to find anything in it. The French have two superb versions: Kazimirski and La Beaume. Kazimirski is popular and cheap (3fr 50); the other is an analytical Koran ... and designed for the use of the Government bureaux in Algeria.[23]

With so many alternatives readily available, the *Edinburgh Review* critic deplored the habits of idle conversationalists who insisted on airing their opinions of the Qur'an without having actually bothered to read it. Length, the writer added, is 'no excuse' for not giving one's time to the Qur'an, for 'the Sunday edition of the *New York Herald* is three times as long', though they conceded that the plainness of Sale's version ('not a bad translation, but ... insufferably dull') may have put off more than one reader during the course of its long shelf life.[24]

Experiencing the Qur'an

This brings us to the question of motivation, and why readers might choose to welcome into their homes a work that, as Elmarsafy remarks, was 'considered simultaneously desired and dangerous', and yet was also perceived – and this is often overlooked – as tedious and devoid of interest.[25] When, in 1830, the writer Harriet Martineau (1802–1876) was spotted on her way home from Norwich city library with a copy of Sale's *Koran* under her arm, she was not branded a heretic, but merely teased with the question, 'What do you bore yourself with that book for? You will never get through it.'[26] This tolerant bemusement may have reflected her class and religious persuasion: Martineau was a Unitarian, and her purpose in borrowing the Qur'an was in fact to enter a competition, sponsored by the Central Unitarian Association, for essays explaining their church to Roman Catholics, Jews and Muslims. Unitarians have not traditionally proselytized, and it is very unlikely the essay was intended to spearhead a mission to Arabia. Rather, the purpose of the exercise was to adopt the perspective of the imagined Muslim audience, using analogies from Islamic tradition to explicate the foreign doctrine. While probably only a progressive denomination like Unitarianism would encourage a public discussion of this kind in 1830 (just one year after Catholic Emancipation), it was characteristic of a growing climate of ecumenicalism in Britain, which by the middle of the Victorian period had entered the intellectual mainstream.

In 1867, the Orientalist Emanuel Deutsch (1829–1873) was employed as an assistant librarian in the British Museum when his essay on the Talmud appeared in *The Quarterly Review*. 'A mighty change has come over us,' the Jewish scholar told readers of the Tory periodical that, earlier in the century, had viciously attacked Martineau and her co-religionists:

> We, children of this latter age, are, above all things, utilitarian. We do not read the Koran, the Zend-Avesta, the Vedas, with the sole view of refuting them. We look upon all literature, religious, legal, and otherwise, whensoever and wheresoever produced, as part and parcel of humanity. We, in a manner, feel a kind of responsibility for it. We seek to understand the phase of culture which begot these items of our inheritance – the spirit that moves upon their face. And while we bury that which is dead in them, we rejoice in that which lives in them. We enrich our stores of knowledge from theirs, we are stirred by their poetry, we are moved to high and holy thoughts when they touch the divine chord in our hearts.[27]

It is significant that Deutsch names the Qur'an first. Unlike Hindu or Parsi theological texts, which were largely translated following the advent of the comparative study of world religions, the Qur'an had entered the English language considerably earlier and had been the target of a longstanding and determined school of refutation – an endeavour that, Deutsch suggests, strikes the 'utilitarian' mind of the later nineteenth century as futile and fundamentally *inefficient*. While his rationale assumes the pre-eminence of modern, imperial Britain, acting in a spirit of trusteeship to the cultures of antiquity (a category in which Islam is implicitly classed), for English readers to neglect what benefits they might derive from allegedly heathen texts is for Deutsch an irrational and perverse form of self-denial.

Some heterodox readers went further, using the Qur'an as itself an instrument of rebuttal to Christian doctrine. Though he received the bulk of his commissions from the Catholic Church, the Irish ecclesiastical sculptor James Pearse (1839–1900) was privately a sceptic who amassed a diverse collection of religious books – a practice not uncommon among Freethinkers eager to vanquish their orthodox opponents in debate.[28] It was presumably for this reason that he picked up a copy of Sale's *Koran* at J. Darcy's bookshop on the Dublin quays sometime after 1860. Pearse's opinions were hardly shared by his son Patrick (1879–1916), a fervent Catholic who went on to lead the 1916 Easter Rising against British rule, but nonetheless the Qur'an was retained in the library of the experimental nationalist school, St Enda's, that he set up in 1908 (now the Pearse Museum), where it can still be found today.[29]

Sometimes a single copy, when it has passed through multiple hands, can testify to the change in popular attitudes between the latter eighteenth and nineteenth centuries. Rudyard Kipling (1865–1936) possessed two copies of Sale's edition: one printed at Philadelphia that he probably acquired during his American years (1892–6), the other a 1764 copy autographed inside both of its two volumes by a previous owner, William Barton. The latter has been ornamented with a series of annotations whose spelling and vocabulary identifies them as the product of an eighteenth-century hand, presumably Barton's. He seems to have been particularly occupied with the eschatology of the Qur'an and attempts to point out fallacies or inconsistencies in its account of how men shall be judged on the day of resurrection. When called before God, it is said in the Sundering (Al-Inshiqaq) *sura*, the dead shall be presented with a book in which the deeds of their life are inscribed. The righteous shall take this book in their right hand while the wicked shall receive it, unwillingly, in their left. Surely this is to 'punish before judge[ment]', observes Barton, who similarly objects to the suggestion (actually in a *hadith*, the traditions of Muhammad) that evil-doers will plunge into hell when attempting to cross As-Sirat, the bridge into paradise ('why so unfairly used?'). In a later annotation, Barton queries how women can be damned if they have no souls (a common misapprehension about Islam at the time), and to a paragraph in Sale's preface where the translator compares the Qur'an's praise for courage in battle to a passage in the Kabbala, he has added the intemperate remark, 'intolerant bloody lyars'.[30] Kipling's more muted response (he has marked passages of interest in red pencil) does not engage directly with this eighteenth-century marginalia, but it seems unlikely that the Indian-born writer, who in a poem about cultural ambivalence offered thanks 'to Allah Who gave me two / Separate sides to my head', could have agreed with their dogmatic sentiment.[31] Kipling also owned a Qur'an in Arabic, a present from Captain F. H. Huth (1844–1918), though its whereabouts is unknown. 'My dear Captain Huth', Kipling wrote in gratitude, 'it is a most priceless gift that you have sent me – the finest Koran I have ever laid eyes – much less hands – upon. ... It shall take rank with the greatest of my treasures and I thank you most heartily for your Hatim-Tai-like spirit in giving it to me.'[32]

Jamie Gilham has observed two broad trends in Victorian writing about Islam: the first was effectively the continuation of refutation, in the form of sceptical expositions of the Qur'an and the Prophet's life usually produced by evangelical writers and missionary advocates, such as the author of the periodical article the Duke of Argyll had been reading, as well as – in a more sophisticated vein – his correspondent Muir. The second was an attitude of conciliation and secular interest that manifested in various genres of writing, including poetry and travelogue, and that was typified by Thomas Carlyle's (1795–1881) qualified admiration for Muhammad in his *On Heroes, Hero-Worship, and the Heroic in History* (1841; see Chapter 3).[33] The ongoing influence, and deep pockets, of the first party allayed my initial surprise when I came across a copy of Muir's *Mahomet and Islam* (1887 edition) stamped with a prize bookplate from 1892, indicating that it had been presented to Alice Taphouse, a student at Stepney Pupil Teachers' School in the East End of London. It was a common practice to reward schoolchildren for punctuality, good behaviour or academic achievement with books of an edifying character, and in this case the object was clearly to reinforce received principles – and prejudices – rather than to suggest overlaps between Christianity and Islam. After all, the book was published by the Religious Tract Society, who supplied copies *gratis* for presentations to 'the Pupil Teachers who Excelled in Biblical Knowledge in the London Board Schools' in 1892.[34] In contrast, it is hard to say which of the two biases was uppermost when a copy of Rodwell's translation, in the 'Everyman's' edition, was presented to another East End pupil-teacher twenty years later. On 19 December 1913, Nellie Turner was rewarded 'For Mathematics' by the head teacher at the Central Secondary School in Stratford. Turner had just turned eighteen, her father worked in a flour mill and it may have been the only book she received that Christmas.[35]

Turner read the book thoroughly, adding marginalia that match the handwriting in the name box on the prize certificate that has been pasted inside the front cover. She did what many an older reader would have done (we must bear in mind, of course, that years may have elapsed before she actually read the book), highlighting passages of note and indexing them on one of the rear endpapers. In an unusual arrangement, however, this index takes the form of a table:

Christian	Moham.
Christ son of God.	Christ apostle of God p 428
Trinity	God is one God
Christ conceived by Holy Ghost	Christ created by God 391
Divine birth	Divine Birth 119

In this way, Turner has visually aligned some of the fundamental tenets of the two faiths, supplementing her method with additional notes in the text ('see Genesis', 'see St Luke'), at points where she has detected Biblical echoes. The emphasis is on similarity rather than difference. What we are glimpsing here is an exercise in comparative religion, encouraged by the new preface to Rodwell's translation commissioned by 'Everyman's' publisher, J. M. Dent. In the preface, George Margoliouth (1853–1924) remarks even-handedly that 'Muhammed may in a real sense be regarded as a prophet of certain truths, though by no means of truth in the absolute meaning of the term'.[36] Turner has underscored these words. Whether by doing this Turner was following her own judgment, and thus reading transgressively, is difficult to say. Indexing and cross-referencing were, it is probable, practices that she was taught at school: was she therefore acting as she had been instructed, or turning the teachers' tools 'against' them? 'Reverend Margoliouth', as he is credited on the title page, may have enabled her discoveries by virtue of his office, as well as his enlightened views. The head teacher perhaps felt that he could safely put a Qur'an into a girl's hands if she might study it under the guidance of a clergyman, but in fact Margoliouth had only spent the early portion of his career in the church, as a curate – the title page would more accurately have described him as Assistant in the Department of Oriental Printed Books and Manuscripts in the British Museum.[37]

Tasked with editing Rodwell's translation, which had so infuriated Richard Burton forty years beforehand, George Margoliouth did not tamper with the text but tried to mitigate his predecessor's bigotry by encouraging readers to approach it in a relativist frame of mind. This may have signified an inadvertent betrayal of the head teacher's trust, or we might see it merely as furthering the established Victorian tradition of praising the Prophet as leader and legislator (counterposed against an equally strong tradition of vilifying him). Carlyle's influence was still strong at this point and was reflected in such contemporary publications as *The Story of Mohammed* (1914), a title in the 'Heroes of all Time' series that offered another popular source for school prize-books in the 1910s.

Leah Price is doubtful whether many germs of fancy, epiphany or heresy were sown at Victorian and Edwardian school prize-giving events, for 'to receive a book from a teacher or parent strips reading of its transgressive force'.[38] All things considered, it is perfectly possible that Nellie Turner's annotations were entirely in line with what her teachers had expected of her. Though even if her reading was really the opposite of transgressive, this episode may still prompt us to reassess what we think of as Victorian-Edwardian norms, which bear little resemblance to the phobic attitudes common in twenty-first-century Britain. It is not hard to imagine the reaction of today's right-wing press were white schoolchildren to be presented with copies of the Qur'an for Christmas.[39] In spite of widespread fears at the time concerning the influence that 'vicious' books might have on impressionable women and young people, there is little evidence of anxiety surrounding translations from Arabic or any other Eastern language. On the contrary, the Qur'an appears to have been one of the 'improving' titles with which Victorian – and Edwardian – directors of reading sought to flush out bad literature.

To the growth of Victorian ecumenicalism, then, we might add the sense of the Qur'an as an improving text – offering, even if its moral or religious character remained in question, useful historical and anthropological information – as a further stimulus to its consumption by late-Victorian readers. This tendency was supported by the autodidact movement, whereby people with limited formal education pursued self-improvement or 'self-culture' through reading, often in public libraries, and often following the guidance of gatekeepers like Sir John Lubbock, who first proposed his aforementioned list of the 'One Hundred Best Books' during a lecture at the Working Men's College in London in 1886. Controversially, Lubbock omitted the Bible (inadvertently, he later claimed) but chose to include a number of classic texts from Asia, defending his position in a preface to his self-help manual, *The Pleasures of Life*:

> The Ramayana and Mahabharata, and St. Hilaire's Buddha, are not only very interesting in themselves, but very important in reference to our great oriental Empire. Kalidasa's Sakoontala is generally regarded as the gem of the Hindoo Drama, and the Shahnameh is the great Persian Epic. Of the Koran, I suggest portions only. We must remember that 150,000,000 of men regard it not merely as the best of books, but as an actual inspiration. Surely, then, it could not have been excluded.[40]

Lubbock's liberal imperialism leads him to attempt to formulate a kind of 'Oriental' canon in which the British nation, if it is to properly understand and govern its empire, is expected to school itself, and the Qur'an is integral to this proposition – even if only a partial reading is considered sufficient for Lubbock's ends. That his advice was followed by the very audience to whom he originally directed his words is demonstrably true.

Lubbock's papers at the British Library contain a number of letters from appreciative working men, including one addressed 'Honored Sir' that asked him 'what are the best translations of the Koran'?[41] Autobiographies, likewise, often furnish us with dazzling but piecemeal evidence. *Shades of the Prison House* is a remarkable memoir by a petty thief, born in 1885, who, prior to his criminal career, spent many hours in the public library at High Wycombe in Buckinghamshire. At the outset of his cautionary narrative, Stuart Wood (a pseudonym) remarks:

> I have read somewhere in the Koran, 'The fate of every man have we bound about his neck'. That about sums up life for many of us; life is largely what we make it and if we have made a hash of it, it is no use whining or trying to shift the blame upon other shoulders.[42]

Wood has taken this lesson to heart, and he even reads it correctly – Allah, at least according to most interpretations, is proclaiming man's free will in this passage, not his predestination. Like Lubbock's correspondent, he is likely to have consulted the Qur'an in a public institution (unless he stole a copy). For those who could afford to purchase one, the volume in itself conferred cultural capital on its owner, its presence on the bookshelf betokening worldliness, travel and broad-minded learning. William J. Curtis (1854–1927), a New York lawyer, acquired the 'Chandos Classics' edition and pasted his ornate bookplate onto the front endpaper but never bothered to cut the internal pages – for him, the Qur'an functioned as a visible token of his education, even if he never read it.[43]

Finally, contemporary geopolitics stimulated both the distribution and consumption of Qur'anic translations, which brings us back to the Duke of Argyll. His preconceptions of Islam as a coercive and militant creed reflected longstanding prejudice and suspicion, but also the immediate context of the Eastern Question, in which politicians debated whether Britain, in the wake of the 'Bulgarian Horrors' of 1876, should continue to support Ottoman sovereignty in the face of Russian expansionism, or if it should instead speed the breakup of the Ottoman sultan's Balkan empire. The Qur'an became an instrument in this debate. For example, in May 1877, the member of parliament for Galway, Mitchell Henry (1826–1910), spoke in the House of Commons and referred ironically to a speech by a fellow parliamentarian who 'told us the other day that we ought to be tender with the Turk when he does not admit Christian testimony against a Mussulman, because the Koran forbids it'. 'Why, Sir, that is the very reason why we must get rid of the Turk,' Henry declared. 'So long as he is an orthodox believer, it is impossible for him to do justice to the Christian.'[44]

These public controversies naturally did not go unnoticed by the publishing fraternity, and Warne's decision to include Sale's translation in his 'Chandos Classics' series in 1877, along with the simultaneous decision by another publisher, William Tegg (1816–1895), to bring out his own edition, was attributed by *The Publishers' Circular* to the Eastern Question. The competing books, it claimed, 'attest the interest taken in Turkish affairs by a large party which regards the Turk as ill-used'.[45] Quite possibly it was even one of these 1877 reprints that the Duke of Argyll had to hand at Rosneath in December of that year. It would be naïve to interpret his letter to Muir as marking a decisive change of heart. After all, treachery among unbelievers is still 'practically the doctrine' of Muslims, the Duke was convinced, even when unsupported by Qur'anic injunction. But his reading may have contributed to the moderation of his views. In September 1876, he had spoken before a meeting in Glasgow, denouncing the Ottoman government to an impassioned audience, 'the crowd swaying to and fro in a frightful way', as he later described it.[46] But, in 1879, in a two-volume enquiry into the Eastern Question, he adopted a more conciliatory tone and argued that the British government must be prepared 'to do our best to see that [Ottoman Turkey] be treated with justice and moderation'.[47]

Translations would, of course, continue to proliferate in the twentieth century – notably, versions made by writers like Marmaduke Pickthall (1875–1936), who had been exposed to nineteenth-century popularization trends and inclined towards Islam by existing translations. Rather than negating earlier productions with new, authoritative translations, the early twentieth-century translators augmented the choice presented to readers and, by enabling people to discover for themselves the contents of the Qur'an, diluted the influence accorded formerly to self-appointed (and often highly prejudicial) authorities on Islam. They hastened the normalization of the Qur'an, no longer a specialist text in the care of clerics, Orientalists and their associated institutions but instead a commonplace and unremarked presence on the bookshelf.

Part 2

Muslim Lives

6

Saiyid Mustafa Ben-Yusuf, an Arab Muslim convert to Christianity in Victorian Britain

Jamie Gilham

Introduction

The photographic image of Saiyid Mustafa Ben-Yusuf (*c*.1847–1931) was reproduced and so widely circulated in Britain and Ireland in the 1870s and 1880s that he became one of the most recognizable Muslim faces in the UK. The proliferation of Ben-Yusuf's portrait was the consequence of his unique position as an Arab Muslim convert to Christianity and evangelical missionary who toured the four nations between the late 1860s and mid-1880s. Surprisingly little, however, is known about Ben-Yusuf's life and work in Britain. He did not write an account of his remarkable life and, as far as is known, his personal papers have not survived. This chapter, then, draws on genealogical records, contemporaneous newspapers and other sources to reconstruct Ben-Yusuf's life. In doing so, it shows what these sources can tell us about a 'forgotten' and marginal working-class Victorian like Ben-Yusuf and also reveals their limitations. The chapter focuses on why and how Ben-Yusuf converted from Islam to Christianity and propagated the latter in Britain and examines his relationship with the evangelical missionary movement. It looks at how Ben-Yusuf was received by the public and considers if he had agency in Victorian society. Finally, it explains why Ben-Yusuf's successful missionary career ended and briefly accounts for his final years.

Reconstructing a life

Saiyid Mustafa Ben-Yusuf was one of the most photographed Muslims in Victorian Britain. His image, reproduced by photographic studios as *cartes de visite*, or small printed portraits, was distributed widely in his lifetime and originals are relatively easy to find today. Paradoxically, very little is known about Ben-Yusuf's life and work. Despite his fame, or notoriety, in the second half of the nineteenth century, it is difficult to locate Ben-Yusuf in archives or official records. This is to some extent inevitable for a working-class immigrant to Britain in the mid-to-late-Victorian period, but the task of identifying him in contemporaneous sources is complicated due to the many variations of the Anglicized spelling of his name, not least by Ben-Yusuf himself. For example, at the beginning of his missionary career in 1869, he signed his name Mustapha Ben Youseph. At times, he said that his surname was Nathan, and some of his children were baptized accordingly. By the 1870s, he generally went by the name Mustafa Ben-Yusuf, which was the most common spelling (and is used in this chapter). Ben-Yusuf sometimes prefixed his name with Sayyid, or Saiyid, a signifier of eminence used by Muslims who are descendants of the Prophet Muhammad or to denote a prince, lord or chief in Arab societies. To complicate matters further, for reasons that are explained below, from the early 1890s until his death forty years later, Ben-Yusuf generally, but not exclusively, publicly identified as 'Henry Crane'. Moreover, throughout his long life, Ben-Yusuf's foreign name baffled civil servants, clergy and reporters, who used a wide range of spellings, such as Mustáfa Mûsa Ben-Yûsuf, Mustapha Moussa Ben-Youseph Nathan, Mustafa Mussa Ben-Yusuph and Mustafor M. Ben-Yusuf.

In the absence of Ben-Yusuf's private papers and published works by or about him, traditional genealogical research documents such as birth, death, marriage, baptism and Census records help recover basic facts about his life in Britain. Given that Ben-Yusuf was, for a short time, a minor public figure, there are also scores of references about him in Victorian provincial and national newspapers and periodicals. Some of these reports are biased and prone to exaggeration, or even falsify biographical details, but by comparing and contrasting them, they shed light on Ben-Yusuf's life and, especially, his work as a Christian missionary. Using Ben-Yusuf's different names and the many idiosyncratic spellings of them, a detailed search through the newspapers in the British Library's British Newspaper Archive, a digital resource, produces approximately 1,000 citations, from detailed accounts of his life to short notices and advertisements for his public appearances.[1] Collectively, the advertisements provide information about Ben-Yusuf's missionary lectures: their number, frequency, location (including venue) and broad subject matter. They show that Ben-Yusuf gave at least 360 public lectures in England, Wales, Scotland and Ireland (which was part of the UK until 1922) – and probably many more – between 1868 and 1886.[2] By cross-checking newspaper reports and citations with genealogical records and other sources, aspects of Ben-Yusuf's life and work in Victorian Britain can be reconstructed and examined for the first time.

Early years and conversion to Christianity

Inevitably, some of the most basic details about Ben-Yusuf's early life, before he settled in Britain, are elusive. That he was born in Algiers, the capital of Algeria, is certain; but the precise date of his birth is unclear. At one of his first public lectures, Ben-Yusuf claimed that he was born in 1844.[3] However, official records such as the Census of England and Wales and Ben-Yusuf's death certificate state that he was born in 1847.[4] His surname translates as 'the son of Joseph', an important figure in the Abrahamic religions and a prophet in the Qur'an. Ben-Yusuf never tired of telling the story of his childhood because it was fundamental to his evangelical mission. Published newspaper reports reveal that Ben-Yusuf embellished the story of his childhood for the benefit of his audience, but it is clear that his biological parents were Jewish, not Muslim.[5]

Ben-Yusuf claimed that, when he was very young, he was 'attacked by a severe illness':

> His mother, in accordance with the superstitious ideas of the Jews, thought if she gave him to another woman to adopt, and also to change his name, when the Angel of Death came for him at his old habitation, and found him absent, and his name being altered, the angel would not be able to follow him or find him. So an Arab adopted him, and whether it was through her agency or not, at all events he recovered.[6]

Ben-Yusuf added that, after his recovery, he was returned to his biological parents. However,

> it happened the Arabs, with whom he had been living, had taken a great fancy to him, and resolved to steal him. One day they tempted him from his home with sweetmeats, and carried him away, many days' journey, into the country. He lived with them for some time, and saw a great deal of their habits, manners, and customs. Ultimately his father discovered where he was, and carried him off by stealth.[7]

Some newspapers reported a more romantic ending to Ben-Yusuf's confinement:

> One day a travelling merchant came amongst the tribe, and seeing Mustapha's face was not so dark as the rest he at once asked him who he was … The traveller

found out that he was a captive, and determined upon tracing out his parents if he possibly could. A year elapsed before the news of his whereabouts reached his parents, and one day, after he had been in captivity for about three years, he was out flying his kite when two Arabs, belonging to another tribe, went to him and told him the gratifying news that his father was waiting for him behind some rocks … Here to his irrepressible joy he found his father waiting for him with two swift horses, and before the Arabs knew or dreamt of what had taken place Mustapha and his father was out of sight.[8]

Ben-Yusuf always stated that, since he was raised by Muslims and 'brought up in their creed', he was Muslim and not Jewish.[9] Regardless of his origins and the circumstances of his childhood, Ben-Yusuf identified as a Muslim before his conversion to Christianity and, crucially, the British public identified him as a Muslim turned Christian.

In 1862, when he was about fifteen years old, Ben-Yusuf accompanied his sister to Europe. According to most accounts, Ben-Yusuf went first to Paris, 'where his sister kept a shop for the sale of Eastern trinkets, and he became her assistant in the shop, and attracted many customers by his Arab dress'.[10] An alternative version of this account claimed that Ben-Yusuf's biological father feared that 'the Arabs would come and take his son away and perhaps kill him', so he 'sent him to Paris to live with his sister':

When he arrived there he was sent to a boarding school, but before long he had to leave this in consequence of the death of his father. He then went and assisted his sister in her business and a short time afterwards his sister, hearing that an Exhibition would be opened in London in 1862, resolved together with her husband that Mustapha should go to the north of Africa and obtain a fresh supply of goods. Having accomplished his commission he went to London, where he met his sister, who had engaged a stand in the Exhibition.[11]

Ben-Yusuf was certainly connected with the London International Exhibition of Industry and Art, a World's Fair staged in South Kensington between May and November 1862.[12] The exhibition ended at the beginning of winter and, 'fearing that she should become consumptive', Ben-Yusuf's sister left England.[13] Ben-Yusuf refused to accompany his sister: he had developed 'a great liking' for England, had learnt some English and 'obtained a situation in a shop very similar to his sister's'.[14] The shop was in the Crystal Palace, the mighty cast iron and glass structure which had housed the first of the World's Fairs, the Great Exhibition of 1851, and was subsequently reconstructed at Sydenham Hill, south London.

Almost all contemporaneous accounts of Ben-Yusuf's life state that, whilst he was walking through the Crystal Palace in 1864, he 'came to a shop where they distributed copies of the New Testament in many languages to give to foreigners' and, 'seeing he was a foreigner', the missionaries presented to him a copy in his 'native' language, Arabic.[15]

Ben-Yusuf maintained that his chance encounter with the missionaries at the Crystal Palace was the first time he discovered the New Testament and Christianity. The missionaries introduced Ben-Yusuf to 'a religious family'; he visited their home for prayers and, later, joined their local church.[16] Later, in 1875, Ben-Yusuf changed this narrative to suit his evangelical mission. He claimed that he had actually received a copy of the New Testament at the 1862 Paris Exhibition and, 'thinking it an extraordinary thing, he took care of it, and reading it to himself, the love of the Saviour so clung to his heart that he determined to come to London and hear more of the Word'.[17]

Worshipping in south London in 1864, Ben-Yusuf heard about the most famous Baptist preacher of the day, Charles Haddon Spurgeon (1834–1892), pastor at the Metropolitan Tabernacle in Southwark who later publicly denounced Disraeli's pro-Ottoman policy (see Chapter 2). Completed in 1861, the Metropolitan Tabernacle was a spectacular purpose-built church, with seating for 5,000 worshippers and standing room for 1,000. According to newspaper reports, before Ben-Yusuf heard Spurgeon speak at the Tabernacle, he 'had no very clear ideas concerning Christianity, but the simple words used by Mr. Spurgeon enlightened his mind'.[18]

The Palestine Christian Union Mission to the Arabs

Ben-Yusuf was baptized in London in 1865. Shortly afterwards, he was taken under the wing of C. G. Scott, a Protestant evangelical clergyman who was closely involved with a new organization, the Palestine Christian Union Mission to the Arabs (PCUMA). Victorian evangelicals like Scott took an emotional and zealous approach to their religion, emphasizing the authority of the Scriptures, Salvation by faith and individual conversion.[19] They were, therefore, highly critical of 'superstitious' Catholicism and other religions, including Islam. The PCUMA was one of the first attempts in Victorian Britain to undertake missionary work amongst Muslims. Its geographical target was Palestine and the Holy Land, which were part of the Ottoman Empire, and its aim was 'to educate and send out to Palestine as missionaries to the Mahommedan Arabs other natives who shall have been converted and educated for the work':[20]

> The more frequently we visit the Holy Land – with a population of nearly 600,000 souls, the more do we see that it has, notwithstanding all the Christian enterprise and activity of the last century, been strangely neglected by the Protestant world. The Jewish inhabitants number less than 20,000, but the country is tenanted by another race which is also of the seed of Abraham – the Arabs – a people whose present belief and intellectual qualities appear especially to prepare them for the reception of Christianity. For many ages past the whole land has lain under the depressing influence of Mohammedanism without any organised effort being made to bring the Arab the saving knowledge of the Gospel.[21]

Conversion from Islam to Christianity was illegal in the Ottoman Empire. However, the PCUMA committee, of which the Reverend Scott was a member, sought to capitalize on recent developments which made Christian missions in Ottoman lands viable for the first time in centuries:

> The sanguinary law which formerly inflicted the penalty of death on every Mussulman who forsook his faith, has happily been repealed by … a decree of the [Ottoman] Sultan, by which religious liberty is granted to all Creeds in the Turkish Empire. The 'word' has therefore 'free course' in Palestine, and every man is at liberty to adopt what religion he pleases. A great change seems to be passing over the Moslem mind; the old fanaticism is fast dying away, and a spirit of religious enquiry rapidly spreading.[22]

The PCUMA appointed its first missionary in December 1865. Youhannah El-Karey was an Arab Christian originally from Nablus in Palestine (present-day West Bank) who had settled in England and married an English woman. During 1866 and 1867, whilst he was waiting to return to Palestine, El-Karey visited several towns in England, Wales and Scotland to deliver a lecture titled 'Eastern Life and Manners, as Illustrative of Scripture'.[23] El-Karey drew on his personal experience of Palestine and its peoples to describe incidents and characters from the New Testament. Importantly, he wore traditional Arab dress – a headdress or *keffiyeh* and ankle-length robe or *thawb* – for authenticity. He also showed the astonished audience a number of 'Oriental objects', and volunteers modelled 'the Costume of Eastern Brides' and 'a Dress similar to that worn by John the Baptist'.[24] The lectures ended with a collection for the PCUMA. By mid-1867, sufficient funds had been raised to send El-Karey and his wife to Palestine.

'A real live Arab' on display

When they met in 1865–6, Ben-Yusuf told the Reverend Scott that he wanted to return to 'his native country' to preach the Gospel. Scott 'at once spoke to him of the mission to the Arabs' and agreed to prepare Ben-Yusuf for missionary work.[25] After El-Karey left England in 1867, Ben-Yusuf was designated 'the second future missionary to the Arabs' who would, 'as soon as the resources at the disposal of the committee will allow of it', proceed not to Algeria but Palestine.[26] Less than a year after El-Karey departed England, Ben-Yusuf began to deliver public lectures on behalf of the PCUMA. One of his first lectures, titled 'Arabs and Arab Life in the Desert', was given in Birmingham in June 1868.[27] Ben-Yusuf's appearance and the structure and content of his lecture was directly influenced by El-Karey, whose performance he had seen several times; and his message was identical. For example, at Portsea, Hampshire, in August 1868, Ben-Yusuf appeared on the platform

> attired in a very striking dress, similar to the one worn by … the late chief of Algiers, and was followed by five friends in Arabian dresses such as those worn by John the Baptist, a Moor, an Eastern Rabbi, a Drus[e] lady, and also one similar to that worn by Rebecca [the spouse of Isaac]. He gave illustrations of manners and customs of the East at the present day, which elucidate Bible narratives, consisting among others of a day and night among the tents, halt of the caravan, encampment, prayer call from the Minaret by the Mufti, salutations, life in the tent, and the Arab and his horse. He also gave specimens of songs sung by the Arabs when they bade farewell and when they went to war.[28]

Introducing Ben-Yusuf at Ryde on the Isle of Wight the following evening, the host, Reverend Wingate, said: 'Though there had been so many missions sent to other lands, the descendants of Ishmael had never yet heard the Gospel tidings. Sied Mustapha was yearning to teach these people the things which had taken so great a hold of his own heart.'[29] Ben-Yusuf was 'a young man, with a most intelligent cast of countenance, and speaks English, not quite perfect, but intelligibly'.[30] For as long as he was a public figure, throughout the 1870s and 1880s, the press, like the audience, was preoccupied and fascinated by Ben-Yusuf's physical appearance, accent and mannerisms. In 1872, a journalist stated that he was a 'handsome man, of expressive features, middle height, and graceful in his movements … his delivery was pleasant, with a light foreign accent'.[31] Other correspondents noted that 'Ben-Yusuf's (we will not say intentional) violation of the meaning of English words lent an additional attraction to his discourse';[32] 'he is of rather swarthy complexion, but of regular features and very pleasing countenance.'[33]

It is clear from newspaper reports of Ben-Yusuf's first PCUMA public lectures that there was significant demand for the events and very keen interest in the speaker. Ben-Yusuf's evangelical colleagues recognized that he was a curiosity as both an Arab and a former Muslim. They exploited Ben-Yusuf's foreignness in advertisements and advance notices of the lectures, emphasizing his Arab and Muslim background, not his Jewish ancestry.[34] Advertisements in 1870s excitedly declared: 'The lecturer is a "real live Arab"'.[35] It might be assumed that the evangelical missionaries exploited Ben-Yusuf too. Whilst he was not brought to Britain by the missionaries to perform on their behalf, Ben-Yusuf's presence and lectures resonate with the exhibition or display of imported foreign peoples – from Australian Aborigines to Zulus – which provided some of the most popular public entertainments in Victorian Britain.[36] As Sadiah Qureshi has shown, what began as small-scale 'shows' of single foreign persons or small groups led to, at the end of the Victorian period, the special importation of hundreds of primarily colonized peoples, including Muslims. These peoples were expected to wear 'native' dress, perform songs, dances and other ceremonies, and were often housed in purpose-built 'native' villages, where they were viewed by thousands of paying visitors. Notably, whilst Christian missionaries were among the shows' most vocal critics, some of them used foreign peoples to promote their campaigns and raise funds for their activities overseas.[37] Indeed, foreign peoples who had converted to Christianity were displayed in Britain as evidence of the successful advance of Christianity abroad.[38] Qureshi argues that, whilst the shows were entertaining spectacles and undoubtedly helped perpetuate Western imperialist notions of superiority through shaping and reinforcing hierarchical and racist arrangements of peoples, they were a much more complex phenomenon: 'They may be recast as intercultural encounters and topical events which both generated and stimulated public discussions on numerous issues, including foreign policy, missionary zeal, and slavery.'[39]

Ben-Yusuf was similarly a curiosity by virtue of his 'foreign' appearance and accent. From the start, the *cartes de visite* depicting Ben-Yusuf were sold at the end of each event. *Cartes de visite* were hugely popular and widely collected in Britain in the second half of the nineteenth century. The earliest known to feature Ben-Yusuf (wearing a fez, a symbol of the Ottoman Empire, presumably to denote his Muslimness) is dated on the reverse April 1869 (Figure 6.1). In the following two decades, at least twenty different portraits were produced, featuring Ben-Yusuf's head-and-shoulders or full body in different postures and with various props, but always wearing traditional Arab dress. Some of the *cartes de visite* included printed captions, usually Ben-Yusuf's name in English and/or Arabic. Unlike the imported foreign peoples discussed in Qureshi's study, however, Ben-Yusuf was not, as far as is known, contracted by an agent to 'perform'; nor is there any evidence to suggest that he was coerced by the PCUMA or other missionary organizations; and, as is related further on, he later toured independently.

Ben-Yusuf appears to have relished the limelight. Newspaper accounts indicate that he was a born performer who readily interacted with the audience. Whilst he was a curiosity wherever he went, he used this to his advantage, much as he had done when he wore Arab dress in his sister's shops in Paris and London. Ben-Yusuf always wore what the audience assumed was authentic Arab Bedouin dress onstage. Notably, when his *thawb* was not delivered in time for a lecture at Banbury in 1873, the event was postponed until it arrived by train the following day.[40] Ben-Yusuf played on Victorian romantic notions – or myths – of the 'noble' desert Arab, the Bedouin, whose loyalty to clan and tribe and respect for legitimate authority seemed almost to reflect that of the English gentleman.[41] Introducing Ben-Yusuf at Wrexham in 1871, Mr French explained to the audience that he had travelled in Arabia and knew the region and its peoples well: 'When the Arabs were leavened with pure Christianity, he thought they would make the finest nation on the face of the earth.'[42]

The fact that Ben-Yusuf had renounced Islam for Christianity and devoted his life to missionary work meant that he was taken seriously and to some extent respected by the white Christian audiences he met in the UK. They also tended to respond warmly to his show and personality. Building on El-Karey's format, Ben-Yusuf introduced more volunteer models to depict 'Biblical characters' and a wider variety of 'Oriental' artefacts. He was a more flamboyant and witty performer than his predecessor: at Sheffield in 1869, the press noted that 'the exceedingly grotesque appearance' of members of the audience dressed as Biblical characters 'excited at first considerable merriment', but 'the attention of the audience, however, was quickly concentrated upon Seyd [*sic*] Mustapha, who in a vivacious conversational style proceeded to speak fluently and well of the cities of the East, and the manners and customs of their inhabitants'.[43]

Ben-Yusuf toured England and Scotland for the PCUMA between 1868 and 1869. He attended the PCUMA annual general meeting in early summer 1869 and spoke on the same platform as the mission's president, Lord Shaftesbury (1801–1885).[44] In a sign of his growing reputation, a few weeks later, Ben-Yusuf gave two talks for the Church Missionary Society (CMS) in Margate. He went on

Figure 6.1 *Carte de visite* signed by Saiyid Mustafa Ben-Yusuf, W. and A. H. Fry (Brighton), c.1869.
Source: Author's collection.

to Brighton where, in August, he married Anna Kind (*c.*1845–1909). Anna was heavily pregnant and she gave birth to a daughter, Zegledda (or Zeghdda) Esther, known as Zaida (a name of Arabic origin, meaning 'prosperous', 'fortunate'), in Hammersmith, London, in November 1869.[45]

The Moslem Mission Society

Settled in London with his wife and child, all seemed to be going well for Ben-Yusuf, personally and professionally. However, a passing comment in the press ahead of a series of lectures he was due to give in Scotland at the end of 1869 hinted that he had some critics: 'As doubts were somewhat mischievously raised further south about the validity of Mustapha's credentials, we may say that the mission he represents has for its President the Earl of Shaftesbury, while the committee includes well-known influential ministers and laymen of various denominations.'[46] The following year, whilst he was living temporarily in Manchester, Ben-Yusuf was confirmed by the city's Lord Bishop.[47] Around that time, for reasons unknown, Ben-Yusuf left the PCUMA and joined another missionary organization, the Moslem Mission Society (MMS).

Like the PCUMA, the MMS is little known today. It was established in London mainly through the efforts of the Reverend Dr John Muhleisen-Arnold (1817–1881), a clergyman, missionary and author. Muhleisen-Arnold was born in Germany and it is possible that Anna Ben-Yusuf, who was also German, introduced her husband to the missionary. Muhleisen-Arnold was extremely antagonistic towards Islam and Muslims. He did not believe that Islam was a divinely ordained faith, and was troubled by its 'spread over nearly a fifth portion of the globe' and recent instances of Muslim political organization and unrest, notably in India, where the 1857–8 uprising against the rule of the British East India Company was blamed on Muslim insurgents.[48] In 1860, Muhleisen-Arnold published a tract appealing for funds to create The Society for Propagating the Gospel among the Moslems:

> The need of a separate mission to the Mohammedans is rendered specially urgent *at the present time*, when a spirit of inquiry is agitating the followers of the Koran, and when a great change has come over the countries devoted to Islamism, a change we can only ascribe to Him … The recent outbreaks of Moslem fanaticism are but the natural result of a humiliating conviction that the cause is in danger.[49]

Extracts from Muhleisen-Arnold's statement were reprinted in several British newspapers when his organization, renamed The Moslem Mission Society, was formally launched in 1861. The editor of *The Atlas* (London) added:

> Christendom cannot disobey this call … Will England be backward in the good work? Millions of Mohammedans are committed to her charge in India, and millions are indirectly subject to her influence in Turkey, in Persia, and in North Africa. Unless we use this power and influence to advance the cause of Christianity, we are unfaithful to our Christian profession. Unless we have sufficient charity towards the Heathen to impel us to joyfully embrace an opportunity of proclaiming the Gospel to them, we are *as sounding brass or a tinkling cymbal*.
>
> … The new crusade against the Saracen will surely excite our enthusiasm. We freely pour out our blood and treasure to carry on a war of dominion, and shall we, a *Christian* people, withhold our money when it is needed to carry on a war against Heathenism, and to make us prove a blessing to the nations even as we have been nationally blessed.[50]

Like the PCUMA, the MMS aimed 'to propagate the Gospel among the Moslems by Missionary operations, by the diffusion of the Holy Scriptures, and by such other means as may be deemed suitable'.[51] Although it had a powerful president in the Archbishop of Canterbury and a long list of prestigious patrons, the society had limited funds. When Ben-Yusuf offered his services for free, plus expenses, Muhleisen-Arnold was delighted. In return, Muhleisen-Arnold agreed to train Ben-Yusuf for missionary work, with a view to his being ordained and returning to Algeria. Presumably helped financially by Muhleisen-Arnold, in spring 1871 Ben-Yusuf was admitted as a fee-paying student to Downing College, University of Cambridge.[52] He left or suspended his studies at Downing soon afterwards, but returned there to study medicine in 1874. It is possible that he first left Downing, in 1871, to spend more time with his family: a second child, Miriam (a name of Biblical Hebrew origin), was born in January 1871, but died less than two months later; Miriam Haidee (known as Heidi) was born in 1872, followed by Leila (a name of Arabic and Hebrew origin) in 1876. A final child, Pearl (a name of English origin which was popular in Victorian Britain), was born in 1877.

In autumn 1871, Ben-Yusuf enrolled at King's College London 'to prepare for holy orders'.[53] Besides theology, he studied medicine because 'he had no doubt he would find it very useful to him; for while he preached the Gospel to the people as a remedy for the ills of the soul, he would also be able to cure their bodies'.[54] Ben-Yusuf took to the road during the long university vacations. He delivered more than thirty lectures for the MMS in England and Wales between 1871 and

1872. The lecture format was almost identical to those he had developed for the PCUMA, except that they were now promoted by and for the benefit of the MMS, with Ben-Yusuf billed as the society's 'Missionary-designate for Algeria'.[55]

The lectures were advertised in advance in the local press and handbills promoting them were pasted around the area that Ben-Yusuf was visiting. The venues varied but were most often public places: town halls, corn exchanges, schools, and church, mission and temperance buildings. Admission was usually by ticket, initially free of charge except for reserved seats, with a voluntary donation to the MMS at the door. Within a few months, entry to most of Ben-Yusuf's lectures was by priced ticket. Each lecture lasted approximately two hours and had a set format and content, though several stock titles were used depending on the venue: 'An Illustrative Lecture on the Manners and Customs of the Arabs and Other Mohammedan Peoples, with Interesting Incidents of Travel in the Desert'; 'An Illustrated Lecture on the Arabs'; 'Oriental Customs and Desert Life'; 'Town and Desert Life in Algeria'.

On entering the venue, the audience was immediately struck with an exotic tableau: the wall behind the stage or platform was decorated with 'Oriental textiles', and an 'Arabian carpet' was placed on the floor. The event began with an introduction by a local clergyman, who welcomed the speaker. Ben-Yusuf then walked theatrically onto the stage or platform:

> At eight o'clock, [Ben-Yusuf] came into the room in true Arabian garb, with flowing robes and the genuine head-covering of the Oriental nomadic tribes, whose customs have changed so little since two thousand years ago. Having ascended the platform, Seyyid Mustafa seated himself cross-legged on a carpet which had been spread in Eastern style for his reception.[56]

He began by relating the story of his life, which accounts for the inconsistencies and embellishments of his biography over time. Turning to the lecture proper, Ben-Yusuf outlined

> the manners and customs of the Arabs, and other Mahomedan people, describing an oriental city, its narrow streets, shops and bazaars, and the habits of the town Arabs – a journey in the desert, with the manner of living in the tents, the salutations, the great hospitality, the water carriers, the hour of prayer, the different meals, and other things, which were narrated in a most interesting and vivid manner, and in very good English when it was taken into consideration that the speaker was a foreigner.[57]

As he spoke, Ben-Yusuf introduced members of the public wearing 'Arabian and other oriental dresses, illustrating Biblical facts and Eastern habits'.[58] The staple characters represented ' "The Beloved Son" wearing the coat of many colours, a woman of Cairo, a Bethlehem bride, an Arab shopkeeper, a donkey boy, a Druse woman of Lebanon, wearing the horn, and a shepherd boy'.[59] At a lecture in Wrexham in 1870, the chairman for the evening 'kindly consented to represent an Ishmaelite, dressed in the "Raiment of Camel's hair", with the "Leathern Girdle about his loins" such as John the Baptist wore'.[60] Ben-Yusuf's 'living pictures' (or *tableaux vivants*; see also Chapter 1) fascinated the audience:

> Admirably as they become their eastern dresses, they appear totally ignorant of Arabic – in fact they are the *muta persona* of the old Greek drama – and whilst exhibiting themselves, and their varied habiliments (male and female) to an admiring audience, may defy – at least the men, by reason of their flowing beards – the recognition of their nearest relatives. The stoicism with which an Arab slave boy, who volunteered for the occasion, received the bastinado [foot whipping] on the soles of his feet, was particularly admired.[61]

Ben-Yusuf lightly mocked both the Arab 'culture' he described and the volunteers on stage: 'The lecture … was very amusing, the descriptions of the strange ideas, customs, and indolence of the orientals, together with the awkward movements of the lecturer's assistants … frequently invoked considerable hilarity.'[62] Although most audiences enjoyed this aspect of Ben-Yusuf's performance, some thought that it went beyond good taste. At Chelmsford in 1875:

> There was only one slight jar to the pleasure which everybody felt, and we only mention it here that the lecturer may avoid the mistake, as we are sure he will be anxious to do, at any other place he may visit. We mean that the susceptibilities of the audience were a little wounded now and then by his peremptory treatment, which may, perhaps, have been more apparent than real, of those whose had consented to assume the Eastern costumes and to stand forward from time to time, passively or in action, in illustration of various parts of the address and who, for their good service, had a right to expect a little gentler treatment than they seemed at some junctures to experience at Mustafa's hands.[63]

Ben-Yusuf showed the audience a number of 'Eastern Curiosities', including 'skin water bottles, Hagar's bottle, David's lantern, the Virgin's lamp … and other articles mentioned in scripture … to throw light on many incidents in the Bible'.[64] When the venue could accommodate it, 'Arabian music' was also played on the organ.

Having described 'the Eastern city' and its inhabitants, Ben-Yusuf explained that 'there was a large field for missionary enterprise open amongst the Moslems, and asked for aid to enable the [Moslem Mission] society to carry out its beneficent intentions'. He estimated that 'there were 200,000,000 of those people who were unacquainted with the Gospel'.⁶⁵ Ben-Yusuf then contrasted 'the Eastern city' with 'the Western city', or the urban centres of Britain in which he often lectured. This led him to invoke traditional negative stereotypes about 'the East' and 'the Arabs', specifically the dishonest and rapacious 'town Arab' rather than the noble desert Bedouin:

> From a distance an Eastern city looked very beautiful, but when the traveller entered it he found the interior dark, dirty, and miserable in every respect. In England people had omnibuses, carriages, and cabs to take them home, but in the East they had to ride upon donkeys, and at the corners of the streets in an Eastern town they would find donkey boys waiting for hire. The lecturer then introduced one of these boys in costume … The Easterns were great smokers, and if a well-to-do man went into the street he always had a slave following him to carry his long pipe, and another walking in front of him with a whip to clear the way. In describing an Arab merchant, the lecturer said that in the East the population was divided into two classes, the town Arab and the Ishmaelites. All the former classes were most lazy fellows, while the latter were active, hard working, and brave.⁶⁶

Ben-Yusuf said that his distinction between the 'town Arab' and the 'Ishmaelites' of the desert (Semitic-speaking tribes mainly from western Arabia) was based on personal experience. He claimed that his father was 'a town Arab and a merchant, and his mother (who came from the desert) could not at first endure his inert disposition'.⁶⁷

Ben-Yusuf did not deny Muhammad's existence, but he spoke little about him because he did not believe in his prophecy. When he did mention Muhammad, it was to illustrate a story that mocked Muslims and their faith. At Bath in 1874, for example, he said 'it was surprising that while Mahomet allowed his people to indulge in every sensual pleasure, they were deprived of wine, when Arabian wine was so delicious'. Here, Ben-Yusuf relied on crude Western accounts to explain Muhammad's reasoning:

> The prophet was one day returning home from an entertainment drunk, when he was met by a priest of the Greek Church, who said, 'Do you call yourself a prophet and go and get drunk?' The prophet was so enraged that he killed the priest on the spot, and the following morning was so terror-stricken that the only punishment he thought sufficient for himself and his followers was never to taste any more intoxicating drinks.⁶⁸

Focused on promoting the Gospel, Ben-Yusuf rarely mentioned, let alone discussed, Islam as a living faith. Arabia was, he maintained, 'the land of the Bible' and it was for that reason alone that he and his Christian audience should be interested in the region.[69] This is not to suggest that he was wholly critical of contemporary Arabia or neglectful of its history. Indeed, he occasionally admitted that 'the Arabians discovered mathematics, chemistry, and many other things'. Moreover, 'the most striking feature of the Arabians was how they had preserved the customs of their forefathers; … the Arabians still wore the same kind of clothes as in the time of Abraham, and it would appear God had preserved their habits as an abiding illustration of His word'.[70] For Ben-Yusuf, the failings of 'the Arabs' far outweighed any positives; it was time that they, like him, were converted to Christianity.

Independent missionary

Within two years after joining the MMS, Ben-Yusuf resigned as its missionary-designate for Algeria. Details of his departure were kept out of the press but is likely that he was forced to resign. A footnote in an MMS tract dated 1873 states simply:

> Mustafa Ben Yusuf, who has lectured in this country on behalf of the Society for more than a year, resigned at the close of 1872 on being urged to remit the large sums due to the Society, and on measures being taken to put his agency on a more satisfactory business footing.[71]

Ben-Yusuf's departure from the MMS ended his hopes of being ordained. He did not, however, lose his evangelical zeal and he realized that he could finance his studies in London or Cambridge by lecturing independently. Back on the lecture platform, his narrative shifted accordingly in 1873: he emphasized that his purpose was to preach the Gospel and, in doing so, 'to defray the cost of his college training' in England with a view to returning to Algeria to practice medicine.[72] This was, he said, imperative, because his conversion from Islam to Christianity had cost him dearly. He explained that his father was dead, but he corresponded with his mother in Algeria: 'Having forsaken all for his new faith, however, he has not the least prospect of any fortune from a family source, and he now finds himself cast upon his own resources in England.'[73] It was a narrative that both the press and evangelical colleagues sympathized with: 'He gave these lectures in order to obtain money to support himself. At the close of the proceedings many persons evinced their interest in the lecturer by purchasing his photograph.'[74] Introducing Ben-Yusuf in Somerset in 1874, the Reverend Canon Pratt told the audience that the Bible had showed Ben-Yusuf 'his errors as a Mahometan, and he embraced Christianity – (hear hear). By this action he renounced his family, property and friends and he, therefore, decided that it would be best to remain in England and endeavour to obtain an education such as should enable him to gain his livelihood'.[75]

In 1873, the first year that Ben-Yusuf worked independently, he gave at least forty-four lectures across England and Wales, more than double the number he had given each year since he began missionary work in 1868. He took full advantage of improvements in transportation, including the expanded railway network and shipping, to traverse England, Wales and Scotland, Ireland (from 1875 onwards), the Isle of Man (1879) and the Channel Islands (1880). Entry to the lectures was by priced ticket; donations were collected from the audience and *cartes de visite* sold as mementos. Ben-Yusuf was not billed as having an agent or manager; events were advertised in advance in the local press and tickets were obtained from local businesses. The performance replicated the format of MMS lectures, with occasional alterations and additions. Notably, in early 1874, Ben-Yusuf introduced a new element, what *The Bath Chronicle* described as 'a real negro boy' who portrayed several characters on-stage: 'First as a donkey driver ... then as a baker, and lastly as a slave.'[76] Ben-Yusuf said that the boy had been a slave in the Caribbean island of Antigua but was released and ended up at the port of Liverpool, where he had 'engaged his services': 'Some little time ago Mustafa was at Trowbridge, and the negro had an opportunity of seeing the friends of the missionary who had obtained for him his freedom'.[77] Ben-Yusuf took the boy to a photographer's studio in Oxford, where a new *carte de visite* depicted the pair posing with artefacts from the lectures (Figure 6.2). The image, showing an African-Caribbean boy servant attending to an Arab, subverts a traditional image almost exclusively reserved in British photography of the period for white men. The boy worked with Ben-Yusuf for only a month and his fate is unknown.

Ben-Yusuf continued to lecture solo in public venues, and he also gave performances for organizations such as the Young Men's Christian Society and the CMS, which indicates that he had not severed ties with the latter after leaving the MMS. Over the following years, he was welcomed and introduced by many respected clergymen and important church leaders, including the Dean of Norwich. Having broken from the MMS, Ben-Yusuf had agency and he gave at least 220 lectures, and probably many more, between 1874 and 1880. The size of audiences varied depending on the success of publicity as well as the venue and time of year: for example, at Atherstone, Warwickshire, in July 1873, when many people were away from town on vacation, 'there was a very meagre

Figure 6.2 Saiyid Mustafa Ben-Yusuf with boy servant, *carte de visite* by Hills and Saunders (Cambridge and Oxford), c.1874.
Source: Private collection.

attendance'.⁷⁸ But more often than not throughout the 1870s, crowds flocked to see Ben-Yusuf and most venues were sold out. At Witham, Essex, in 1875, 'the Literary Institute was crammed to suffocation'.⁷⁹ The *Derby Mercury* noted that 'the lecture is unique, and has been attended by many of the most eminent clergymen and gentlemen of various denominations, who speak in the highest terms of its merits'.⁸⁰

Ben-Yusuf's church contacts led to an invitation to join another CMS annual meeting, at Guernsey, in 1880. Speaking on the platform, Ben-Yusuf said:

> He was himself a Christian, but unfortunately the whole of his countrymen in North Africa were heathens or Mahommedans. Formerly there were Christian Bishoprics in the country, but these had gradually been driven out by the intolerant Mahommedans. Much of the prejudice which existed against Protestants was caused by the influence of the Roman Catholics, who when the French conquered the country, had taken possession of it in large numbers, and the Mahommedans who had great reverence for God abhorred the worship of crosses, and the adoration of saints, and believing all missionaries to be alike, it was difficult to break down their prejudices, and induce them to believe in the Christian faith. He had often been urged to return to his countrymen as a missionary but he knew their character and disposition too well … Mahommedans were very stubborn but if you could once induce them to become Christians, they would remain ste[a]dfast, for they had a most exalted idea of God. He hoped therefore the good time would come, but if results were not seen at once, they must not be discouraged. It was not always by numbers that the amount of good done could be measured.⁸¹

After 1880, Ben-Yusuf's public appearances declined rapidly. From giving at least forty-four lectures in 1880, he gave thirteen lectures in 1881 and just fourteen in total between 1882 and 1886. There seem to be several reasons for this downward trend. First, Ben-Yusuf's credibility was further dented when, in December 1879, it was publicly reported that Hills and Saunders, one of the studios that produced hundreds of *cartes de visite* for Ben-Yusuf, took him to court for failing to settle a bill.⁸² Second, major changes in Ben-Yusuf's personal life put pressure on both his time and income. Shortly after the birth of Pearl, in 1877, Ben-Yusuf and Anna separated. Anna took their daughters to Ramsgate, east Kent. Ben-Yusuf abandoned his studies at Cambridge and enrolled at St. Thomas' Hospital in London, still 'with a view of returning to his native land to practise as a physician'.⁸³ He moved out of London to Speldhurst, a village in west Kent, more than sixty miles from his estranged family. Anna and her daughters later emigrated to the United States.⁸⁴ Third, it is likely that the novelty of Ben-Yusuf's appearance or performance, or both, began to wane, especially in towns that he had already visited, often on multiple occasions, to give almost identical lectures. For example, when Ben-Yusuf returned to Witham in 1876, the local newspaper commented: 'The lecture was precisely similar to the one which has been given in most of the provincial towns in Essex, and with which our readers are tolerably familiar.'[85] Ben-Yusuf revisited Stowmarket, Suffolk, the following month: 'The lecture did not differ much from that which the same gentleman gave about a year ago.'[86]

In autumn 1880, Ben-Yusuf went to Ireland for the first time since a brief visit in 1875. He gave a series of well-attended lectures in the north of the country, at Belfast, Coleraine and Ballymena. According to the local press, Ben-Yusuf's Coleraine lecture attracted 'by far the largest audience we ever saw assembled in the Town-hall'.[87] Buoyed by his success, Ben-Yusuf moved to Ireland in 1883. He gave lectures across the country, ending at Kells in County Meath in June 1886.

From performer to publican: Later years

Ben-Yusuf retired from public life and returned to London, where he met Henrietta Crane, who was eight years his junior. He did not divorce Anna but circumvented the law to marry Henrietta at Holborn registry office in February 1887. Having illegally married Henrietta, Ben-Yusuf took the name 'Henry Crane'. In a further move away from his life as an evangelical missionary, he became a licensed publican and landlord of The Windsor Castle, Holborn.[88] His first child with Henrietta, another daughter named Zaida (1891–1967), was born in 1891. A son, Mussa, was born in 1893 but died shortly afterwards. When Ben-Yusuf appeared in the press again, albeit as Henry Crane, in 1892, it was in the court circular columns because he had been charged with assaulting a drunk customer in The Windsor Castle.[89] Ben-Yusuf's life continued far removed from the world of mid-Victorian evangelical missions and missionaries. In 1895, he was charged with robbing a Mrs Winifred Gordon, who was 'in the habit of carrying about with her property of considerable value'.[90] Ben-Yusuf, referred to throughout as Henry Crane, had taken on the lease of a house in Clapham, south London. Aided by three accomplices, he lured Mrs Gordon to the empty property and threatened to kill her. The gang stripped the victim, handcuffed her and stole 'jewellery and securities of the value of £3,000'.[91] Ben-Yusuf was acquitted of robbery but pleaded guilty to assault at the Old Bailey in 1896.[92] He paid compensation to Mrs Gordon and settled court costs and was discharged without further penalty.[93]

It is unclear whether or not Henrietta Crane knew in 1887 that her marriage was unlawful but, in summer 1896, a few months after the robbery trial ended, she reported her 'husband' to the police. As he was being arrested, Ben-Yusuf reportedly said to a police officer: 'I thought my wife was dead years ago. My second wife made enquiries respecting her. She was satisfied that she was dead, and so I married her.'[94] The case was reported nationally, with headlines highlighting Ben-Yusuf's ethnicity: 'Charge of Bigamy against an Arab.'[95]

Ben-Yusuf appeared at Clerkenwell court charged with bigamy. The press claimed, incorrectly, that Anna would return to England to testify against her husband. In a curious turn of events, it was reported that

> in answer to the charge the prisoner said, 'Thank God, it has come at last.' Coming through the bar the prosecutrix, Henrietta Crane, said, 'Sit down; if you make it worth my while I will not charge you.' Mustapha replied, 'I would rather suffer the penalty of the law, if I have broken it, than be blackmailed anymore.'[96]

Henrietta allegedly demanded £200 from her 'husband' to settle the matter. Refusing the deal, Ben-Yusuf was remanded on bail. However, he reached an agreement with Henrietta, who subsequently dropped her complaint against him. Ben-Yusuf was released from prison at the end of August 1896 and, reconciled with Anna, returned to The Windsor Castle.[97]

Ben-Yusuf retired at the beginning of the new century. He moved with Henrietta and Zaida to West Green Road, a busy thoroughfare in Tottenham, north London. Neither the area nor the address was very respectable, but the Cranes took in a lodger (from Algeria) and had sufficient means to employ a live-in domestic servant.[98] A few years later, they moved up the social ladder by relocating to a large, nine-room house in Lansdowne Road, Tottenham.[99] Little is currently known about Ben-Yusuf's final years in Tottenham except that, in February 1904, almost eighteen years after his last missionary lectures, an advertisement in the local press announced a 'Lecture and Exhibition by Seyyid Mustafa Ben-Yusuf (Henry Crane, Esq.) in his Native Costume, Illustrating Eastern Life and Bible Customs'.[100] The lecture was hosted by the Downhills Board School in Tottenham, with proceeds donated to the extension fund of the nearby West Green Gospel Mission. Despite the trials and tribulations of the intervening years, Ben-Yusuf had evidently retained his Protestant faith and kept his missionary wardrobe and artefacts: he was joined on-stage by '13

Persons dressed in various Eastern Costumes'. In a sign of the times, the lecture included 'Selections by an Orchestral Band'.[101]

Two years later, in March 1906, Ben-Yusuf revived his performance for what was probably the final time: at almost sixty years old, he appeared at St. James' Church in Upper Edmonton, near Tottenham. The platform was decorated 'in oriental style with many objects of interest, and the lecturer, arrayed as a gentleman of Palestine, was accompanied by a dozen of the young men and lads of St. James' dressed in Bible costume'.[102] Ben-Yusuf's name had changed, but his message was the same as it had been forty years earlier: 'Mr Crane … spoke of the Bible as an Eastern Book that required a knowledge of Eastern customs and mode of thought to fully understand and appreciate.'[103]

Ben-Yusuf lived out his final years with Henrietta and Zaida in north London. Anna Ben-Yusuf died in New York in 1909; Henrietta Crane died in Tottenham in 1923, followed by Ben-Yusuf, aged eighty-four, in 1931.[104] At the time of his death, Ben-Yusuf had somehow accumulated a small fortune: his effects were valued at almost £36,000, the equivalent of around £2 million today.

Conclusion

In the absence of Ben-Yusuf's autobiography or other substantive first-hand accounts, Victorian newspapers, as well as missionary records and standard genealogical sources, help reconstruct the life and work of Mustafa Ben-Yusuf. The sources can be as unreliable as Ben-Yusuf's own telling of his story, which he adapted to suit his missionary narrative, including details about his early life, religious background, journey to Britain, conversion from Islam to Christianity and evangelical calling. However, comparing and cross-checking published and unpublished sources reveals a great deal about Ben-Yusuf's life and work as an evangelical missionary: his backers and relations with missionary organizations, evangelicals and other clergy; his methods, movements and reach across the UK; his audiences and their responses and reactions to him. They show that, early on, Ben-Yusuf was welcomed and nurtured by evangelicals and their fledgling missionary organizations, which focused on Muslims in the Ottoman Empire and elsewhere. The evangelicals' recognized Ben-Yusuf's intelligence and exploited his 'foreignness'. Ben-Yusuf drew large crowds wherever he went because he looked and sounded 'different'; yet he overcame prejudice and ridicule in Britain to gain the trust of his backers and large audiences. Despite personal setbacks, perhaps of his own making, during his missionary years Ben-Yusuf was respected by some very influential clergymen and missionaries.

It is difficult to gauge how successful Ben-Yusuf was as a missionary, but published accounts of his work suggest that, despite his difference, he was taken seriously and generally well received by communities in both urban and rural Britain and Ireland. If he was exploited by clergy and their missionary organizations, Ben-Yusuf's career after he left the MMS and set himself up as an independent missionary shows that he had significant agency on the lecture circuit for a solid ten years. That said, perhaps it was eventually his lack of organizational backing that led to a decline in bookings for lectures that had evolved little conceptually or intellectually since the late 1860s.

Ben-Yusuf's mission relied on the negative stereotyping of 'the East' and 'the Arabs' to show that evangelicals could penetrate Muslim lands to spread the Gospel and make conversions. His strategy was to focus on what he said he knew well, which was 'the Manners and Customs of the Arabs and Other Mohammedan Peoples', primarily in Arabia, rather than his native north Africa. His lack of explanation of or discussion about Islam is striking: perhaps Ben-Yusuf did not know Islam and the Qur'an as well as he knew Christianity and the New Testament; but it is certainly the case that ignoring Islam as a living faith suited his mission at a time when evangelicals were frustrated by the vitality of Islam and piety of Muslims around the world.

Ben-Yusuf never returned to Algeria. He died in London a wealthy man. He had come a long way, spiritually and materially, since arriving in the capital as a Muslim immigrant with little English or financial resources. Contemporary sources help reveal the circumstances of his religious conversion and life and work as an evangelical missionary; yet, when and how he accumulated the significant material wealth left in his will remains, for now, a mystery.

7

From Arab *millet* to British Islam: Syrian Muslims in Victorian Manchester

Riordan Macnamara

Introduction

This chapter outlines the features of a community of Syrian Muslim traders settled in Victorian Manchester and its suburbs and their integration into the social and cultural fabric of their immediate environment. It discusses their development of a relative biculturalism, through the acceptance of select British cultural codes, naturalization, intercultural marriage and attendance at the Liverpool Muslim Institute (LMI), founded and led by the British Muslim convert Abdullah Quilliam (1856–1932).

Primary documentation on the conditions of arrival and settlement of Levantine merchants in Lancashire, whether Jewish, Christian or Muslim, is sparse. Even less is currently known about their living conditions, social interactions, religious practices and their integration into the fabric of English society. The late Fred Halliday, in his pioneering study of Arab merchants in Manchester, argued that the Syrians developed a tight interreligious *millet* (an Ottoman semi-autonomous minority community), a social enclave formed around a common language and a transplanted set of cultural mores.[1] Yet was this community as homogeneous or ghettoized as depicted? Closer scrutiny shows that the more successful traders, or those from elite merchant backgrounds, tended to interact and identify with the British-born merchants with whom they established close business and personal ties. Other Syrians, such as clerks or newly arrived traders, lodged in British-owned houses and apartments. Halliday indicated that the majority of immigrant merchants and workers congregated in Didsbury,[2] but further research reveals that Syrian Muslim households could be found in the less remote and increasingly multi-ethnic suburbs of Moss Side, Hulme and Chorlton-on-Medlock. The cases of Abdullah Ydlibi (*c.*1820–1885), Mustapha Karsa (*c.*1848–1907) and the Mokaiesh family are discussed in this chapter to illustrate how they partially and temporarily acculturated with local society.

The Syrian Muslims were certainly a minority within a minority. Although their exact number has yet to be ascertained, in 1892 they travelled to the LMI – the nearest organized Islamic institution to Manchester, with a prayer room and other facilities – as a group of around fifty men led by the Ottoman consul to Manchester and Salford, Mustapha Karsa.[3] The Syrians discussed here are those who attested to belonging to the Islamic faith, either in the press or by their presence at the LMI, and confirmed by their descendants.

Ottoman Syria-British trade

From 1840 with the restoration of Ottoman rule in Syria,[4] Beirut profited from its new status of *vilayet* (administrative division) capital to grow from a small harbour town for Mount Lebanon to the most advanced East Mediterranean port city, linking traders in Damascus, Jaffa, Nablus and Aleppo. Improvement in infrastructure and transportation made the city a pivotal import and export trade centre, with regular maritime routes established between the major ports in the West. In 1863, a telegraph connected Beirut with Europe.[5] The British, who had supported Ottoman claims over Syria and negotiated the Egyptian retreat from Anatolia and Syria with the Alexandria Convention (1840), had already gained complete access to Ottoman trade markets through the Treaty of Balta Liman (or Anglo-Ottoman Treaty, 1838), a set of trade policies abolishing Ottoman monopolies and allowing British merchants to be taxed equally alongside local merchants.[6]

At the turn of the nineteenth century, Liverpool had become the major raw cotton port of Britain, and Manchester, within the county boundary of Lancashire, the leading centre of cotton manufacture.[7] At the Manchester mills, cotton was transformed into yarn and a large variety of fabrics – lace, satin, chintz, gauze, muslin and khaki cloth – to be shipped to ports worldwide. There they were sold to dealers working in diverse markets, such as the upholstery, military apparel and garment industries. At the time of the arrival of Manchester's first Ottoman consul in 1846, 70 per cent of the 1,105 cotton mills in Britain were located in Lancashire, providing work to over 40,000 people in Manchester alone.[8] By the 1860s, one-third of the Lancashire population was employed in the cotton industry, representing an unprecedented workforce in a small area leading in the manufacture of a global commodity.⁹ The marketing of yarn and cloth was carried out by a plethora of shippers, home trade houses and merchants. Although many Lancashire firms also acted as export houses, there was enough leeway for independent merchants who could make use of the available finishing, packing and shipping facilities and by specialising in a particular type of yarn or cloth to be sent to or shipped from Liverpool to be sold in a particular market.

A core reason for the popularity of cotton goods from Lancashire was their competitive price, with poverty encouraging the Syrians to turn to cheaper articles of Western production, of lower quality than the superior goods made from Syrian cotton. Articles of trade received from Europe were transferred to the interior, such as traditional fezzes from France and Italy and cotton twists from England. At Damascus, they were sold and forwarded by caravans to Baghdad, Bassorah and south Persia, or found their way from Aleppo into Asia Minor. In return, raw cotton, wheat, beans, barley, sugar, indigo and tobacco were exported to Britain from Egypt. Syrian ports such as Beirut and Tripoli exported mainly barley, goat's hair and opium.¹⁰

In Beirut, while the most privileged of the emerging middle-class stratum of merchants were Muslim notables, the majority of merchants were from Christian Arab, Greek Catholic and Greek Orthodox families.¹¹ Making the most of the new global trade connections that Manchester offered, they had moved chiefly to import and export with Europe, but they also aspired to create cultural, religious and political ties in the West.¹² From the 1860s, some of these merchants made their way to Manchester to establish cotton trade counters, followed by Armenian and Sephardic Jewish traders, the latter settling in the north of the bustling city.¹³ By 1880, among the eighty-two Levantine firms registered in Manchester and exporting to Syria, Egypt and Turkey, twenty bore Armenian names, thirty were owned by Greeks (mainly from Beirut), sixteen by Syrian Sephardic Jews and at least ten by Christian Arabs. Towards the end of the nineteenth century, 150 Middle Eastern merchant houses had been established in Manchester.¹⁴ These companies not only shipped cotton goods to the Levant and back but around the world to other Levantine traders who were established in the Americas and West Africa, creating a network of commerce across continents.

Abdullah Ydlibi, Manchester's first 'Mahommedan'

The Ydlibis were a family of Muslim notables in administration, politics and trade, with a branch in Damascus, and another in Beirut. The latter branch were importers and retailers of fabrics and cloth goods. Abdullah Ydlibi was born in c.1820 in Damascus into a family of Ottoman merchant notables originally from Idlib. He left Syria for Constantinople during the British-fuelled conflict between Egypt and the Ottoman Porte in the 1830s, and reached Manchester in about 1840, where he established the family trading business.[15] Appointed Ottoman consul for Manchester and neighbouring Salford in 1846, Abdullah Ydlibi became the first to occupy that position in Manchester and, according to the local press, was 'the only Mahommedan inhabitant of the town'.[16]

In 1846, Abdullah Ydlibi married Amelia Jones, a young Christian woman from Hulme, in a local church. They settled at Moss Side Terrace in Hulme, which was to become the home of the Ydlibis for two more generations.[17] The Ydlibis had a son, Ali, who was baptized into the Church of England at Amelia's parents' home. Amelia died three years later, aged twenty-five. Abdullah moved with his son Ali to Chorlton-on-Medlock and started buying cotton goods through a commission house,[18] before becoming independent and, like his earlier Moroccan counterparts, entering the market and buying in his own name.[19] He set up a partnership with a Syrian merchant, Paul Cababe, who in the early 1850s almost had a monopoly over the textile trade between England and Aleppo. Together, they exported goods such as shipping yarns, prints and shirtings to Damascus and Beirut, and imported madder roots and other Syrian produce. Cababe and Ydlibi's venture became the first extensive Syrian-led export and import business between England and the Levant.[20]

Ydlibi's main task as Ottoman consul was to protect the Levantine traders based in Manchester and Salford.[21] Given the negative image of the Ottoman Empire in mid-Victorian Britain, a defence of Ottoman economic interests inevitably led Ydlibi to respond to anti-Ottoman, specifically anti-Turkish, sentiment. The most controversial matter in this regard was the perceived ill-treatment and status of Christian minorities in the Ottoman Empire. In 1851, a group of visiting Syrian Christians gave an illustrated lecture on 'the manners and customs of the Turk' before 200 people at a Manchester school. The illustrations included an image reportedly showing where 'the Turks' congregated 'to lounge away their time, listening to the recitals of the public story-tellers, whilst they enjoy their pipes and coffee'.[22] The group also showed Ottoman officials prosecuting a Christian coffee-shop owner for illegally breaching the state monopoly over the coffee trade; European consuls had to intervene to prevent him from the *bastinado* (foot whipping), and he was released after paying a bribe. The lecture included a scene representing recent anti-Christian mob violence in Aleppo. Consul Ydlibi, who was present at the lecture, reacted vehemently. He said that the group's illustrations were false, which caused some unrest amongst the exclusively Christian audience and resulted in him being heckled out of the school hall. In a series of letters published in the local press, Ydlibi refuted that Ottoman law endorsed anti-Christian violence, and he argued that Ottoman Islamic society was liberal towards Christian minorities. Ydlibi said that the Syrian Christian group was playing fraudulently on anti-Turkish representations and eliciting Christian solidarity in order to gain support in England.[23]

As Ottoman consul, Ydlibi was granted a large house and grounds on Oxford Road, Manchester, where he held numerous events. These included a celebration of the victory of British, French, Ottoman and Sardinian allies over Sebastopol, leading to the Russian defeat in the Crimean War in 1856. Ydlibi opened his grounds to visitors and friends, illuminating the garden with lanterns, offering refreshments on behalf of the Ottoman Empire to over 200 people, who revelled and danced while listening to a local brass band.[24]

Ydlibi also acted as liaison between Manchester cotton manufacturers and Eastern traders. In 1848, the Persian secretary to the Residency at Indore, India, visited Manchester, where Ydlibi showed him around a cotton spinning and weaving establishment, a small-ware business and a locomotive engine factory.[25] A year later, Ydlibi received the Ottoman ambassador to the Court of St James for a similar tour of public buildings, factories and warehouses. In order to create a raw product that could be exchanged for imported Lancashire textile goods instead of for gold, the Ottoman ambassador sent on, through Ydlibi, a sample of cotton produced in Nablus. It was tested and the result was favourable, especially for candle wicks.[26] In 1863, following the shortage of American cotton due to the Civil War,[27] manufacturers were obliged to seek a larger supply of cotton from Ottoman Turkey and Egypt. Ydlibi imported to Beirut and Damascus the Manchester steam-powered cotton spinning wheel and ensured the plantation of cotton seeds.[28]

Although consul Ydlibi might reasonably be considered to have been 'the first resident in Manchester who regularly wore the fez'[29] (a trend among Syrian merchants and some Muslim converts into the early twentieth century), he chose to assimilate to the British culture of the middle-classes and the wealthier traders with whom he associated. Naturalized British in 1863, he was described as 'a pleasant man with much of the European and even a little of the Englishman in his ways and ideas'.[30] He was a patron of Manchester Theatre Royal and donated to the City of Manchester's Patriotic Fund during the Crimean War.[31]

During a depression of the Lancashire textile industry in 1861–5, consul Ydlibi returned to Constantinople with his son Ali and a British nurse, Emma, to enter into the service of the Ottoman Sultan 'Abd al-Aziz (1830–1876).[32] With Emma, he had another son, Hassib (b.1866), who was to become famous as a concession-chaser in Ethiopia and special advisor to Emperor Menelik II (1844–1913), before being ousted and deported to France at the outbreak of the First World War. By the late 1860s, Ydlibi's firm was still operating a counter at the other major European cotton trading port of Marseilles. Paralysed by a stroke, he died in 1885 in Beirut. He was replaced as Ottoman consul in Manchester and Salford by another Muslim merchant, Mustapha Karsa.

In Manchester, Abdullah Ydlibi's descendants were to further the process of assimilation that their patriarch had begun in the 1840s. His son Ali Ydlibi married an Irish woman, Rebecca Hinchley (1848–1938), with whom he had a son, Abdallah James (1871–1952). When consul Karsa left England, Ali Ydlibi and his family relocated to Egypt, then Beirut. Rebecca consented to her husband taking a second wife, a Syrian with whom Ali had two sons, Ozzat (1879–1943) and Abdulgani (1887–1953). Ozzat and Abdulgani went to Manchester at the beginning of the twentieth century, where they joined another trading family member, Selim Idielbe, to pursue the family business. Meantime, Abdallah James Ydlibi was educated at the British Protestant College in Beirut. He later moved to Wales, where he worked as a teacher. In 1904, Abdallah went to Cairo, where he opened the first school for the deaf-mute, funded by the Church Missionary Society. A British citizen by birth, Abdallah eventually resettled in England, where he married a Christian woman in 1915. He gave up his first (Muslim) name, Abdallah, preferring to identify as James Iddleby.

Mustapha Karsa, the second Ottoman consul

Mustapha Karsa, Manchester's second Ottoman consul, was born in Damascus to a wealthy landowning family. In 1880–1, he was sent to Manchester to develop the textile trade with England. Leaving his spouse and children in Damascus, Karsa first settled in Chorlton-on-Medlock, where Abdullah Ydlibi had lived and which, in the 1880s, was a lower-middle-class inner-city area of Manchester, littered with cotton mills and factories. He lodged with a Jewish clerk from Beirut, Kallil Hanna Koory (b.1854), who was to become his lifelong associate. Soon after arriving in Manchester, Karsa met and married a young local woman, Helen Saunders (1870–1939).[33] They had eight children, all of whom were baptized into the Church of England at St Peter, Swinton, certainly

Figure 7.1 Mustapha Karsa Bey, Ottoman consul for Manchester and Salford, c.1900. *Source:* Photographer unknown. Courtesy of Tamim Maamoum Mardam Bey.

as a condition for the Saunders's family to endorse the marriage.[34] The family eventually settled in Sale, a comfortable suburb in south-west Manchester.

Mustapha Karsa and Company's trading house flourished, with family firm bases in Izmir, Alexandria, Smyrna and Beirut. After being appointed Ottoman consul, Karsa moved with his family to a grander house in Sale. From one servant in their first house, the Karsa's now had four, and hosted important visitors such as the Liverpool Ottoman consul, Mehmet Kamil Bey. Unlike his predecessor, Karsa did not attempt to act upon British representations of the Ottoman Empire by taking polemical stances in the press or in public. Since the Russo-Turkish War (1877–8) and the British occupation of Egypt (1882), the relationship between Britain and the Ottoman Porte had deteriorated considerably. Karsa's diplomatic response was to hold cultural soirées open to all, and to host community events aiming to bind the local Syrian diaspora around a sense of belonging to the Ottoman Empire, such as the commemoration in 1900 of Sultan 'Abd al-Hamid II's (1842–1918) accession, to which all 'Turkish' citizens were invited.[35] Karsa presented himself as an assimilated Anglicized Muslim but a Muslim at heart. He was described in the press in 1892 as 'a Syrian Arab, but had long dwelt in England, and had become acclimated, but though he had got used to the climate, matter, customs and dress of the English people, he had never forgotten or changed the faith in which he was born'.[36] From his company premises on Whitworth Street, Manchester, Karsa remained consul until his death in 1907. Karsa's obituary in Quilliam's *The Crescent* newspaper stated that he left families in both Syria and England, with 'two wives and about seventeen children to mourn his decease'.[37]

Following Mustapha Karsa's death, his British-born children's ties to the Ottoman Empire, and their identification as Muslims, shifted in a variety of ways. As his widow under Islamic law, Helen Karsa relocated to Beirut with her five younger children. Of the latter, Eminie (Amina) Karsa married into the wealthy Beiruti Ardati family, who also had ties with the Mokaiesh family, both of which had family members trading in Manchester alongside the Karsas,[38] thus consolidating in Beirut the network of Muslim notables and merchants that had prospered in Manchester. The eldest Karsa son, Cecil Mustapha, who continued the family business in Manchester, married the daughter of a Sale bristle manufacturer at the local Wesleyan chapel. He chose not to give Muslim names to his sons, Anthony Herbert and Joseph Cecil. When Cecil Mustapha died in 1951, *salat al-janazah* (Islamic funeral prayers) was given for him at Victoria Park mosque, Manchester. His sister Fizie left Beirut to join her brother in Manchester. She was also given *salat al-janazah* at Victoria Park mosque following her death. Soon after consul Karsa's death, his second daughter Lily met Alexander Hamrah, an importer from a Christian Beirut merchant family trading in New York. They married and she moved to Brooklyn, where they had six children, all of whom were given Anglicized names: Elias, Edna, Alice, Claire, Louise and George. In 1909, Alexander founded with other Beirut family heads America's first Syrian masonic lodge, Damascus No. 867, the rites of which were said entirely in English.³⁹

The Mokaiesh family

The Mokaiesh (Muhayyeş) family were wealthy Muslim notables from Beirut. Professing allegiance to the Ottoman sultan through donations, and upholding their status and livelihood through honorary distinctions granted to them by him, they were a product of the 'politics of notables' that allowed the Ottoman Empire to garner support and allegiance from its more remote provinces.⁴⁰ In 1884, Mohamed Darwiche Muhayyeş sent his son Ali (b.1856) to Manchester to establish the family textile business in England. Although he was already married in Beirut, Ali met Amy Ogden (b.1866), the daughter of a paper merchant, and they settled, like many Levantine merchants, at Didsbury, Chorlton-cum-Hardy, where they had a daughter, Freda, in 1890. Six years later, Ali was declared bankrupt and absconded with his family to Beirut to avoid the proceedings and petitions presented by his creditors to the chamber of commerce. Notably, Abdullah Quilliam acted as Ali's defence lawyer.⁴¹

Subsequently, Mohamed Darwiche's brother, Amin Pasha, sent his son Kamal to establish a trading counter in Manchester. He created a partnership with Joachim Majdalany on George Street, joined later by his younger brother Selim (b.1879). By the end of the nineteenth century, the two Mokaiesh branches had developed trading firms. Kamal and Selim led a successful business, shipping goods to Syria and Egypt, as well as Constantinople and ports on the Black Sea and in South America.

Kemal, who was in charge of supervising the shiploads between Manchester and Beirut and selling the goods in the latter, did not settle within the Manchester community. He chose to return to Beirut to live in the Muhayyeş family home. By contrast, Selim, like his cousin Ali, had a stronger foothold in Manchester. He settled in Didsbury and married Fawzié al-Chamaa, whom he had met in Damascus. The latter's father was Rushdi al-Chamaa (1856–1916), a Syrian nationalist and politician in Damascus who was indicted with many others following the deposition of Sultan 'Abd al-Hamid II in 1909 and executed in 1916. Selim applied for British citizenship at the outbreak of the First World War and served with the British Army in France.

Figure 7.2 Selim Mokaiesh in Manchester, c.1900.
Source: Photographer unknown. Courtesy of Fady Mokaiesh.

Some Muslim families trading in Manchester, such as those described earlier, went back and forth between Syria and north-west England, forging and developing interconnected family ties. For example, Selim Mokaiesh's working partner in Manchester, Ali Ardati, had a brother, Muhieddine, in Damascus. Muhieddine married Eminie Karsa, who had returned to Syria with her British mother Helen upon the death of her father, Mustapha Karsa. Muhieddine

Ardati and Eminie Karsa's son Sami married Selim Mokaiesh's daughter Selma in Manchester.

Social and family life

Although the Syrian merchants – Christian, Jewish and Muslim – formed a distinct Arab community, they were, in the Victorian tradition, class-conscious.[42] They joined the value system of middle-class merchants, preferring the binding principles of class above those of ethnic belonging. Regardless of origin and religion, the merchants mingled and did business around the packing and export warehouses mainly on Princess Street and Whitworth Street in Manchester city centre.[43] On nearby Bloom Street, for instance, Syrian Muslim Mohamed Hallaby (1841–1902) shared an office with the Greek Georgiadis brothers and the Jewish trader R. M. Levi, shipping to Beirut, Greece and Egypt, and he was also a neighbour to British-led companies J. Whittaker, G. H. Clarke and Watson and Bogle, who shipped cotton goods to the Continent, as well as India, Japan and parts of South America.[44]

Another indicator of the aspiration of some Syrian Muslim merchants to partially integrate and develop a bicultural identity was their marriage to British Christian women. Syrian Muslim merchants tended to marry younger British women from the lower classes. For example, one LMI member, a merchant called Hassan Taweel from Beirut (b.1836), registered a marriage with the daughter of woollen cloth agent, Alice Shirley (b.1854), who was eighteen years old. From the LMI's inception, religious marriage ceremonies (*nikah*) could be and were celebrated by Abdullah Quilliam. The absence of a father figure for some of the British brides is notable. For instance, when Beirut merchant Selim Hanowye/ Henoway (1877–1931) married at the LMI a British woman, Emilie Bostock (1882–1961), who was the daughter of a deceased packer of manufactured goods from Chorlton-on-Medlock, another merchant, Mustapha Rekab (b.1863), acted as sponsor for the young bride.[45] Damascene Said Assha (1859–1930) married a fatherless servant, Marion Amina Sagar (1871–1940) at the LMI, with whom he was to have two children, both bearing Muslim names.[46]

Often middle-aged, the Syrian Muslim merchants generally wed younger British women despite having already been legally married in their homeland. Said Assha, for instance, had a Syrian wife and two children when he wed Marion Amina Sagar at the LMI. Indeed, the most regular Manchester-Syrian visitors to the LMI were those that had British wives taken as second spouses. The British brides tended to convert to Islam before the wedding ceremony. Although the Syrian Muslim merchants turned to British women from humbler backgrounds who would accept the status of unofficial second 'wife', some British-Syrian religious unions allowed the second spouse to gain middle-class respectability. Ali Mokaiesh, for example, took Amy Amina Ogden home to Damascus to meet his parents in 1892 when she was pregnant, and when Ali's first wife died three years later in Beirut, they discreetly registered a civil union in Liverpool, by which time their daughter Freda was five years old. To avoid showing that they lived together, the address of residence given by Ali was actually that of Abdullah Quilliam in Liverpool. The two witnesses to the discreet civil union were Selim Evans and Omar Byrne (1856–1901), both of whom were British converts to Islam and members of the LMI. To a certain extent, this indicates connivance between the Syrians and the Liverpool Muslims to enable polygamy. When Ali returned to Damascus with Amy a year later, Freda became a legal inheritor of the family *waqf* property.[47] Similarly, Selim Hanowye and Emilie Bostock, who had unofficially wed at the LMI five years earlier, registered a civil marriage in Chorlton in 1907.

The reproduction of an imported polygamous pattern in Manchester inevitably tested the strictures set by English law, which forbade polygamy. Consul Mustapha Karsa, who had an Arab wife in Damascus and an English wife in Manchester, met twenty-two-year-old Beatrice Cardus at the house of a Turkish merchant, Joseph Iliahoo, who happened to be having an extramarital liaison with Beatrice's sister, Ada.[48] Beatrice, who was an assistant at a theatre in the city, became intimate with Karsa. They travelled to Liverpool together, possibly to visit the LMI to arrange a religious wedding, and stayed at the Liverpool Ottoman consul's house as 'Mr. and Mrs. Karsa'.[49] Beatrice then charged Karsa for breach of promise, claiming not to have known that he was already married. Unable to defend his polygamous position, Mustapha Karsa denied that he had proposed marriage to Beatrice. The case was reported in the press: Karsa was dubbed a 'lustful Turk' by the judge and fined £200.[50]

Religious life

Whilst the Syrian Jews established synagogues in Manchester,[51] there was no mosque in that city in the nineteenth century. Perhaps this was simply because there was not an imam (Muslim religious leader) among the merchants capable of conducting a Friday *khutbah* (sermon). Rather than register a place of worship, the Manchester Muslims congregated at private dwellings until the LMI opened at its permanent Brougham Terrace premises in 1889.⁵² Thanks to the Liverpool-Manchester passenger railway, the Syrian Muslim merchants and their families could easily travel between the two cities. In practice, for the Syrians, taking membership at the LMI was to sign the register and support Quilliam's organization with donations and the input of Islamic practices imported from Syria. It was also to pledge to a movement that was, according to Quilliam, validated by the Ottoman sultan-caliph. Notably, the Manchester Syrian Muslims did not formally join the LMI before Quilliam's first visit to Constantinople in 1891, when he said he was endorsed by the sultan.⁵³

At least twenty-four Syrian Muslim visitors were mentioned in Quilliam's weekly newspaper, *The Crescent*, between 1893 and 1908. The first named Syrian LMI member was Mustapha Karsa, who, possibly through Liverpool Ottoman consul Lutfi Bey, hastened with his wife Helen to sign the LMI allegiance book.⁵⁴ Karsa donated generously to the LMI and remained an honorary vice-president throughout its existence, alongside other foreign Muslim notables. The Karsas soon became close friends of the Quilliams, visiting them at their summer residence on the Isle of Man in the 1890s, and Abdullah Quilliam and his family visited Karsa family members in Smyrna.⁵⁵ Ali and Amy Mokaiesh also joined the LMI, with Ali frequently acting as imam for the evening *namaz* (ritual prayer) that followed the LMI's regular Sunday service.⁵⁶ In 1892, consul Karsa travelled to Liverpool with a group of Manchester Syrians to meet Ibrahim Hakki Bey (1863–1918), Ottoman Imperial Commissioner for the Chicago Exhibition of 1893. They congregated at the LMI, expecting to attend the orthodox *salat al-jum'a* (Friday prayer), but had to wait until the evening, when the service was held. Said Adam acted as *muezzin* (prayer caller) and Ali Mokaiesh as imam. Mustapha Karsa was presented to Hakki Bey as the 'President' of the Manchester 'Institute' of Muslims. 'Liverpool and Manchester', proclaimed Karsa, 'were the pioneers of the English Moslem movement'.⁵⁷ Although there was not in fact a formal Manchester Muslim organization at that time, it is reasonable to suggest that Karsa, with his consular function, was considered to be a community leader for the Ottoman Syrian Muslims.

Syrian merchants and their British wives were regular visitors to the LMI, mostly for special occasions. The event that probably attracted the most Ottoman subjects at the LMI was on the occasion of the Ottoman sultan's silver jubilee in September 1900, with over fifty attendees, some of whom were Armenians and Orthodox Greeks.⁵⁸ For the 1896 *'Id al-Fitr* (feast that marks the end of Ramadan), the Karsas and Mokaieshs travelled by train to Liverpool with another Syrian Muslim merchant, Nejib Ramadan. Mustapha Khalil, from Damascus, who was acting that year as religious instructor and imam at the LMI, conducted the ceremony in English and Arabic. Both Karsa and Khalil praised Quilliam profusely as 'the man who had done the most to promote Islam in England'.[59] At least thirteen Syrian Muslims were present at Quilliam's fortieth birthday celebration held at the LMI in 1896.[60]

The Manchester Syrian Muslim community endorsement of Quilliam as a British Muslim leader contrasted sharply with the London-based Indian-led Anjuman-i-Islam's perception of Quilliam. Former LMI members Muhammad Barakatullah Bhopali (c.1859–1927; see Chapter 9) and Mustapha Khalil condemned Quilliam in 1896 as a confidence trickster and his institute a fraud,[61] and other Muslim visitors also denounced some of Quilliam's religious practices as *bid'ah* (innovations) and unlawful.[62] In light of this criticism of Quilliam and the LMI, why were the Manchester Syrians eager to praise him and his achievements? Their backing of Quilliam was as much political as religious because Quilliam was thought to have the patronage of the Ottoman sultan-caliph: Quilliam said that the sultan granted him the honorific title 'Sheikh-ul-Islam of the British Isles' – effectively making him the supreme authority on Islam in Britain (see Chapter 11) – and acted at times as a source of intelligence for the Ottoman Porte.[63]

Indeed, the Manchester-based Syrian Muslims considered that Quilliam was one of the sultan's 'notables', the influential Muslims of the decentred regions of the Ottoman Empire who received honours, and whose children were given military training in exchange for their loyalty and provision of intelligence, acting as intermediaries between the Ottoman government and its subjects.[64] Many of the Manchester Syrian Muslims were themselves from such notable families in Damascus, Beirut or Aleppo, or they were from Muslim families that acknowledged the power of the 'notables'. Like them, Quilliam certainly received important honours from the sultan, and his elder son Robert Ahmad (1880–1954) was appointed a lieutenant-colonel in the Ottoman army.[65] The leadership of an Ottoman 'notable' was built on two elements: his access to state authority and an autonomous, separate power in his own society.[66] Quilliam strove for both: a direct connection with the sultan and a function within British society as 'Sheikh-ul-Islam of the British Isles'. His function as a 'notable' within Ottoman terms explains the Manchester Syrians' acceptance of his autonomy and leadership in Britain.

At the LMI, British-born Muslims and Anglicized Ottoman Muslims cooperated to create a novel Islamicate environment. One can picture them on a Friday or a Sunday evening gathered around the fireplace in the LMI members-only room, listening to a female convert playing the piano,[67] discussing British politics or *da'wah*[68] methods in the West, before shifting to the mosque for the evening *namaz*, with the *adhan* (Muslim call to prayer) given in Arabic by a Syrian and in English by a local Muslim convert. Members of both communities bonded closely. For example, when Syrian merchant Selim Ydlibi died in 1897, the British Muslim converts postponed the *Mawlid* (observance of the Prophet Muhammad's birthday) festivities so that they could mourn their friend. Ydlibi's funeral ceremony was officiated by Mustapha Karsa at the LMI and then by Abdullah Quilliam at the burial site in the Merseyside Necropolis.[69]

Conclusion

Although the Syrian Muslim merchants of Manchester endeavoured to sustain an Islamicate remainder from their homeland, their arrival, settlement and tribulations tell a story of intercultural encounter and gradual, if partial, adaptation to British society. Towards the end of the Victorian period, Quilliam's LMI enabled them to practice their faith and bond with other Muslims. For Quilliam and other British Muslim converts, the Syrians were the contact they needed to represent themselves as part of a global *umma*, or universal Muslim religious community. The Syrians were also a physical reminder of the presence of the Ottoman sultan-caliph as 'Commander of the Faithful'. In an age of growing cosmopolitanism, the British Muslim converts could identify with these Anglicized Ottomans and their British wives and integrate into their British identities the otherwise exotic and distant 'otherness' of Islam. Notably, as a sign of a common cultural ground between converts and Syrian Muslims, men from both communities wore the red Ottoman Turkish fez. At the LMI, the Syrians brought to the converts their knowledge of Arabic and *sunna* (custom, practice of Muhammad). In return, they accepted the British converts' Anglicized religiosity and religious practices that offended Muslims such as Barakatullah Bhopali. For instance, they attended the LMI Sunday services, which included English hymns accompanied by a harmonium and led in Arabic the *salat al-'isa* (night prayer) with the *adhan* performed both in English and Arabic.[70] When Michael Hall, a Muslim convert and LMI member, died in Liverpool in 1893, a group of Syrians joined the British Muslims at his grave to perform a Muslim service: Quilliam said the funeral prayers in English, and Said Adam recited them in Arabic.[71]

The originality and subversion of this cultural amalgamation between Syrian and British Muslims can only be grasped in a context of persistent Victorian anti-Ottoman, and specifically anti-Turkish, sentiment. Culminating with reports in 1876 of the 'Bulgarian Horrors', depictions of 'the Turk' and Ottoman rule were generally negative.[72] Islamic laws and customs were considered, even in British official documents, to be incompatible with the European way of life and opposed to the betterment of mankind. As opposed to the subjugated Muslims of British India, Ottoman Muslims were seen as in enmity with Christendom and antagonistic with Western virtues of honesty, morality and courage. Such negative depictions persisted into the twentieth century and were to drastically impact the lives of the Syrian Muslims of Manchester. With the First World War, they were refused the status of 'alien friend': whether naturalized British or not, from 1915 they were designated for internment at the civilian prisoner camps of Knockaloe and Douglas, on the Isle of Man.[73] Around 300 Syrian Muslims and Jews were detained there during the war. Many of them suffered from malnutrition and depression, and ten of the Muslims died.[74] At the Armistice in 1918, an Alien Advisory Committee ruled which 'undesirable aliens' could be granted a British residence permit and which groups were to be deported. The urge to safeguard jobs for indigenous Britons led to the 1919 Aliens Restriction Act, which prolonged restrictions on work and trade for the former alien enemies, limiting property and key industry acquisitions and imposing the grant of licences to remain or to land on British soil.[75] Further research into the lives of the more low-profile Syrian Muslims – temporary settlers and those who did not feature in the press – will undoubtedly reveal a more accurate picture of the social fabric of this small network of Syrian Muslims in urban Lancashire that flourished for the seventy years prior to the Armistice. The children of those that could, or chose, to remain in Britain after 1918 forged a first generation of British Muslims of Syrian origin, becoming part and parcel of British society.

8

The last Nawab of Bengal: India and England, 1838–84

Lyn Innes

Introduction

Mansour Ali Khan (1830–1884), also known as Feradun Jah, was just eight years old when he became Nawab Nazim (hereditary monarch) of Bengal, Bihar and Orissa in India in October 1838, four months after the coronation of Queen Victoria.[1] Soon after his installation in the city of Murshidabad he received a letter from George Eden, Lord Auckland (1784–1849), then the governor-general of India, congratulating him on his accession to 'the throne of his ancestors' and affirming that 'the dignity and honour of the illustrious house you now represent will ever be an object of care and solicitude to this Government'.[2]

This chapter begins by examining British control of the young Nawab of Bengal with regard to his education, his removal from his mother's palace and his finances. It also explores reasons for British disapproval of his adherence to Shi'i rather than majority Sunni Islamic traditions.[3] The Nawab supported the British during the Indian Rebellion (or 'Mutiny') of 1857–8 but was not rewarded for his loyalty. Instead, he was threatened with further loss of status and treaty rights. The second half of the chapter, then, traces the Nawab's visit to Britain to appeal to Parliament and Queen Victoria directly for restoration of those rights, the press coverage of his visit, his marriage to an English chambermaid and his twelve-year residence in England.

Historical context

Behind Lord Auckland's official letter and anxiety to express respect and 'solicitude' for the House of Murshidabad lay a number of historical events and their repercussions. Chief among them was the Battle of Plassey (1757), when the British East India Company (EIC) defeated the Nawab of Bengal and his French allies, and British collaboration with the military general Mir Jafar (c.1691–1765) to replace Siraj-ud-Duala (1733–1757) as the ruling Nawab of Bengal, Bihar and Orissa. But also significant was the 1806 Vellore Mutiny, or Revolution, in Tamil Nadu, when sepoys (Indian infantrymen) tried to take over the fort in which the sons of the late Tipu Sultan (1751–1799), the Sultan of Mysore, were imprisoned. The rebels seized control by dawn and raised the flag of the Mysore Sultanate over the fort.[4] As in the later 1857–8 rebellion, violation of Muslim and Hindu religious practices (viewed by the British as superstitions), rather than opposition to British rule *per se*, was seen as the flashpoint for the revolts. In response to the Vellore Mutiny, Edward Parry, a member of the EIC Court of Directors, displayed a typical case of double-think when he wrote to the governor-general of India, Lord Minto (1751–1814):

> If the Sepoys of Vellore had been Christians they would not have conspired to restore a Mahomedan Power on our ruins. Nor would Christianity raise the natives to the assertion of a free Government or of Independence. The energy and boldness necessary for Achievements of this sort do not belong to the Asiatic Character.[5]

As with the 1857–8 rebellion, British officials were at one and the same time dismissive of 'Asian' desires for self-government, preferring to see the causes of unrest as relating to merely 'superstitious' practices, and anxious to avoid any offense which might be used as an excuse for an uprising.

The British government was indeed solicitous throughout the Nawab of Bengal's childhood and reign, continuing a tradition which had allowed the British to benefit from its oversight of the Nizamut, the House of Murshidabad, since 1757. As Mansour Ali Khan's father, Nawab Humayun Jah (1810–1838), declared bitterly, 'My ancestors and the British Government made treaties and the Government kept all the country, all the money, and left me nothing but old and useless paper.'[6] When the British agent in Murshidabad claimed that the Nizamut was now degraded, Humayun Jah responded that this was because the British had broken their promises. Thirty years previously, the EIC

Court of Directors had already noted the gap between titular power in India and the actuality: 'Half a century ago, our new and critical position among the Mahomedans of North Western India compelled us to respect the titular dignity of the kings of Delhi.'[7] However, the directors concluded, the experience of the half-century demonstrated that the inconvenience of an empty sovereignty descending from generation to generation was productive of more mortification than gratification to the royal pensioner. Before 1821, it was the Emperor in Delhi who swore each Nawab Nazim of Bengal into office. But, after this date, it was the British governor-general, based in Calcutta (Kolkata), who confirmed the new Nawab's status. Thus, the British government replaced the Indian Emperor as the supreme authority in the Indian subcontinent. In Bengal, as in many other principalities, this authority also included acting as regent for monarchs who had succeeded to the throne as minors.

Among other grievances expressed by Humayun Jah was the British governing body's habit of reducing the personal pension promised Mir Jafar and subsequent reigning Nawabs after 1757 upon the installation of successive Nawabs on the grounds that they were minors and hence did not need the full pension. However, in each case, the full pension was never reinstated. By the time Mansour Ali Khan became Nawab in 1838, the pension had been reduced to less than 10 percent of its original amount. The claimed 'inconvenience of an empty sovereignty descending from generation to generation' thus proved to be in significant ways very convenient for the British government.

Education policies

At the time of Humayun Jah's death, the governor-general's agent in Murshidabad was Colonel James Caulfield (1782–1852). He immediately took control of the new Nawab's finances and was also determined to shape and supervise the child's education. Now, for the first time, English language and literature would become not only a required subject but a major one, given greater importance than Persian, which had till then been the court language. Here, Caulfield was supporting Thomas Babington Macaulay's (1800–1859) famous 'Minute on Education' (1835) for the governor-general's Supreme Council, arguing that through encouraging upper-class Indians to obtain a command of English, the British should seek 'to form a class who may be interpreters between us and the millions whom we govern, – a class of persons Indian in blood and colour, but English in tastes, in opinions, in morals and in intellect'.[8]

When Macaulay wrote the Minute, he conceded that half the EIC Board of Control disagreed, arguing that Arabic and Sanskrit were more important languages for Indian students to study. Aware of such divisions about educational policy, and also in somewhat reluctant deference to court traditions in Murshidabad, including the royal family's strong commitment to Islam, Caulfield designed a curriculum which incorporated what was regarded as 'Eastern' as well as 'Western' learning. Half of the day was to be spent studying Persian and Arabic, the other half would involve instruction in English language and literature, as well as history, mathematics and the sciences.

For the 'Oriental' branch of the young Nawab's studies, Caulfield appointed Meerza Ali Azeem to provide Arabic and Persian tuition. Felix Seddon, Professor of Oriental Languages at King's College London, was recruited for what Caulfield deemed 'the more important duty of instructing [the Nawab] in English Literature and European Science'. Seddon was allocated a salary of 1,000 rupees a month; Meerza Ali Azeem's stipend was just one quarter of that amount. In Seddon's eyes, however, Meerza Ali Azeem was a man of learning and integrity, 'as good a man as ever I met ... and a sterling first-rate scholar'.[9]

The eight-year-old Nawab was ready to challenge his teacher, demanding to know why he was being forced to learn English. Seddon reported the Nawab asking: 'Since his father did not learn English, his grandfather did not speak it, none of his ancestors spoke it, why should he?'[10] While the Nawab's progress in English was at first slow and reluctant, he enjoyed becoming proficient at reading and writing Persian, perhaps an indication of his allegiance to his father's culture. When Robert Pemberton (1798–1840) replaced Caulfield as British agent in 1839, Lord Auckland directed him to keep a diary 'showing how His Highness the Nazim ... passes his time', recording his progress in his studies, and noting 'any particular traits of his general disposition and character' which might strike him as worthy of notice.[11] Pemberton took this request seriously, interviewing the young Nawab every Monday and examining him on his progress in English and Persian. Pemberton's report on the nine-year-old Nawab in 1840 criticized him for being 'too much aware of his status' and 'proud, unsteady, and volatile'.[12]

Robert Pemberton died in late 1840, just a year into his position at Murshidabad, and he was replaced by an exacting disciplinarian, Major-General Felix Vincent Raper (1778–1849), who had spent more than forty years in the Bengal Army. Raper promptly transferred Seddon to the Nizamut College, where lesser members and dependents of the royal family might be educated, and replaced him with a much stricter superintendent of studies, Captain G. D. Showers. The now ten-year-old Nawab was required to study English, history, science, mathematics and geography from seven in the morning till one in the afternoon, and then, after a brief meal break, resume lessons in Persian and Arabic till half-past five. Captain Showers would have preferred to scrap the study of Persian and Arabic but wrote that he had felt it necessary to allot several hours in the afternoon to the Nawab's four Muslim tutors because 'it was of importance that a Nobleman of his rank should possess a full share of Oriental acquirements ... and also on account of the jealousy and suspicion which would be created by any appearance of partiality for a course of English instruction'.[13]

Like Seddon, Showers expressed some respect for Meerza Ali Azeem or, rather, appreciated the latter's respect for him, for 'tho' a recluse and a Sheea, he possesses sufficient liberality to aid and assist me in all my views'. However, Showers thought it best to avoid including religion (meaning Christianity) as a formal part of the curriculum. He expected that the science lessons would gradually lead the boy away from 'superstitious beliefs in Omens, Auguries, and Supernatural spirits'. He hoped to 'install in his mind those more exalted Notions of Omnipotence, and of an over ruling Providence'.[14] That a belief in such notions might be seen as fundamental to Islam seems to have escaped Showers's notice.

Attitude to Shi'i traditions

Why Captain Showers expressed regret that Meerza Ali Azeem was a 'Sheea' rather than a Sunni is not entirely clear. Like Mir Jafar, who had come to India from Iraq, the Murshidabad family had always belonged to the Shi'i branch of Islam. They devoutly observed the ten days of mourning for the martyrdom of imam Husayn (626–680) during *Muharram* (the first month of the Islamic calendar) and had built one of the largest Imambaras (assembly hall for by Shi'is to observe *Muharram*) in the Indian subcontinent. But the Shi'is were a minority in India, where most of the provinces had Sunni rulers; Bengal and neighbouring Awadh were exceptions. Between 1810 and 1840, there had been many notorious attacks on Shi'is, encouraged by Sunni leaders such as Saiyid Ahmad Barelvi (1786–1831), who opposed the keeping of *ta'ziehs* (miniature mausoleums, including replicas of imam Husayn's tomb in Karbala), and urged his followers to destroy them as well as the Imambaras that housed them.[15] These conflicts might have persuaded British officials that their lives would be easier if majority Sunni beliefs prevailed in India (and elsewhere). Another cause of prejudice against Shi'is might have been that they had supported Tipu Sultan, whose fierce resistance to EIC armies in the late eighteenth century remained a traumatic memory.

As the Bengal historian J. Datta Gupta remarks, the British agent in Murshidabad had the challenging task of managing the Nawab's court and household, which was 'a latent threat to the [East India] Company's Government but which nevertheless had to be pampered and preserved, on administrative expedience, in an aura of respectability and splendour'.[16] Respectability, however, was an ambiguous term, with different meanings for different cultures. For Captain Showers and his compatriots, it did not include adherence to Islamic beliefs and customs, particularly Shi'i beliefs and customs. Nor did it involve Islamic concepts of *nikah* (religious marriage ceremony) and *nikah mut'ah* (temporary marriage contract) and the different attitudes and responsibilities they involved. Nevertheless, the British agents and education officials felt it was necessary to avoid creating 'the jealousy and suspicion which would be created by any appearance of partiality' not only for a course of English instruction but also for Christian beliefs and practices.

Excluding 'harmful' influences

Captain Showers sought not only to 'lead the [Nawab] away from "Superstitious Beliefs"', but also to remove him from anti-British influences. In a letter to the governor-general's secretary, Showers explained that when he took over as agent, 'the mind of the Nazim [sic] was essentially native, he was entirely under the Guidance of his relatives – suspicion of European[s] was apparent in his manner'.[17] The young Mansour Ali Khan had already been removed from the guardianship of his grandmother to that of his mother, who seemed, or perhaps pretended, to be more willing to cooperate with the British agent. But, in 1842, Showers and Raper agreed that the Nawab should be moved to a different building, away from his mother. In their view, it was the influence of the women and the atmosphere of the harem, or women's quarters, which was most harmful and which contributed to what Showers regarded as undesirable traits in the boy's character, such as a love of teasing and an emotional attachment to his religion. Showers hoped that the increase in time and conversation that this new arrangement allowed Mansour Ali Khan to have with him would prove 'so agreeable to him as shall lead him hereafter to associate the name of European gentlemen with many happy hours of his early years'.[18] Instead, the Nawab resented but felt helpless to resist Showers's decisions: 'I am obliged to do all that Captain Showers tells me', he declared, 'because if I do not, he will not allow me to visit my mother'.[19] It came as a surprise to Showers when the Nawab's mother refused to see him and the Nawab asked the governor-general's agent to fire him.[20]

Nevertheless, Mansour Ali Khan proved to be an able scholar. Although he excelled in and particularly enjoyed Persian and Art, he made such good progress in English that Showers reported in October 1843 that, when the Nawab could be heard speaking in another room, 'his voice can scarcely be distinguished from that of an Englishman'.[21] An examination report noted that he gave an expressive reading and analysis of Alfred Tennyson's (1809–1892) poem, 'The Lady of Shalott' (1832). Unlike upper-class boys in England, whose studies would have focused on Greek and Latin classics, the young Nawab was given a diet of English history (including *The Life of Wellington*), literature and language. Besides Shakespeare, he read contemporary English works such as the collected poems of Lord Byron (1788–1824) and Thomas Moore's (1779–1852) *Lalla Rookh* (1817). The choice of Moore's popular epic poem, which consistently depicts Muslims as despotic, fanatical, intolerant and puritanical colonizers, may have been deliberately confrontational. Mansour Ali Khan's opinion of it is not known. That Moore may have intended the poem to be an allegory of British colonial oppression (particularly in relation to Ireland) is especially ironic.

Finance and fraud

In 1846, when Mansour Ali Khan was sixteen years old, Henry Whitelock Torrens (1806–1852) replaced Raper as British agent. Unlike most previous agents, Torrens did not have a military background but had been employed as a secretary for the EIC in Meerut and Calcutta. In Calcutta, he was vice-president of the Bengal Asiatic Society, and he saw himself as a man of letters who published poems, short stories, essays and produced a translation of *The Arabian Nights*. Perhaps he was seen as a more companionable supervisor for the young Nawab than Captain Showers had proved to be, and indeed it appears that Torrens quickly gained the trust of his teenage charge. But Torrens bitterly resented the move from Calcutta to Murshidabad, feeling that he had been shunted there by an antagonistic 'Bengal clique', and that his job was one that 'any fool could do, an appointment in which he had little or nothing to do beyond seeing that things were kept straight in the petty court of the Nawab, an office which the most ordinary person might have filled'.[22] In his own eyes, Torrens was no ordinary person. His editor and erstwhile friend, James Hume (1808–1862), described his manner as 'a little coxcombical' for 'a strong feeling of self-satisfaction was often exhibited in every look and tone and gesture'.[23]

Torrens published a number of essays under the pseudonym 'Mark Matthews', claiming to be from 'the worst station in Bengal' and giving detailed descriptions of hunting expeditions in the company of a Nawab Nazim. Under his own name, he also wrote about his travels in Egypt. There, he declared, the Muslims were preferable to those in India because they followed 'the pure form of Islam', whereas by contrast the 'Indian Mussulman' had become corrupted and made intolerant by 'so much of the separatist spirit of Hinduism'.[24] Nevertheless, Torrens acknowledged an understandable bitterness on the part of Indians, since the British were 'a nation proverbial historically for insolent and overbearing demeanour among conquered or dependent races'.[25]

Torrens's condemnation of these aspects of British rule and of corruption among 'Indian Mussulmen' did not prevent him from contributing to a British history of self-enrichment at the expense of India. He persuaded the young Nawab to move his government securities, amounting to nearly 2 million rupees, to a firm based in Calcutta. These securities were then cashed in by the firm and placed in an account under Torrens's name. Six years later, after Torrens died of dysentery, Mansour Ali Khan discovered that all the money had disappeared. So too had many of the jewels belonging to the family and the estate, including the Hanoverian Cross given to his father by William IV (1765–1837), King of the United Kingdom and Hanover. Some of the jewels had been given to Torrens's mistress.

For the rest of his life, Mansour Ali Khan in numerous memorials protested and sought recompense for Torrens's swindling of his finances. He linked this fraud to the long depletion of the Nawab's pensions since 1757. He first turned to Lord Dalhousie (1812–1860), who had been appointed governor-general of India in 1848. Dalhousie, however, showed no sympathy. Under his administration, the Punjab, Burma and other princely states had been annexed, and the rule of the EIC expanded. On behalf of the British government, Dalhousie claimed any lands or states that did not have a direct heir when the title holder died. He also rejected the Nawab's claim that the annual stipend promised Mir Jafar on his accession was hereditary, despite the fact that it had been so regarded for nearly a century.

Then, in 1853, Dalhousie held the Nawab responsible during a hunting party for the death of two thieves who had been severely beaten by some of the Nawab's servants. Despite the fact that the two servants charged with the murder were declared not guilty by the Indian Supreme Court in Calcutta, Dalhousie ordered the Nawab to sack them, insisted that British police must accompany him on all future hunting parties, revoked the exemption historically granted Indian royalty from appearance in civil court and reduced his traditional nineteen-gun salute to thirteen guns. Mansour Ali Khan was deeply offended by this loss of status and thereafter avoided any occasion that would have called for such a salute. Finally, Dalhousie denied the Nawab Nazim supervision of the Nizamut Deposit Fund, which had been set up to cover expenses for the Murshidabad estate and public institutions. Thus, control of a large portion of the Nawab's finances went to the very agency under whose remit he had been so seriously defrauded.

Support for the British during rebellions

Nevertheless, when the Santhal rebellion against the EIC and local zamindars (hereditary landlords) broke out in Bihar in 1855, the Nawab supplied guardsmen and elephants to help suppress it. Nor did he hesitate to support the British during the so-called Mutiny, which began in Berhampore, just a few miles from Murshidabad in 1857. The Nawab supported the British, even though he claimed that the uprising was a response to Dalhousie's actions and a member of his household had urged him to 'wave the flag of rebellion', assuring him that he would find 5,000 men to fight on his side. Given that the British had annexed the neighbouring state of Oudh (Awadh) and banished its ruler the previous year, Mansour Ali Khan may have believed that the British were too powerful to resist. Moreover, he was more likely to sympathize with the zamindars than the peasants and sepoys. And he may also have believed that the British were more able to protect Muslim rulers and interests against Hindu nationalists. Above all, he expected his support to be acknowledged and to be followed by the restitution of his rights and his full pension.

These expectations were reinforced when, in August 1858, Queen Victoria affirmed that the rights, customs and religious beliefs of her Indian subjects should be respected, as well as the treaties made with Indian princes. The newly appointed viceroy and governor-general, Earl Canning (1812–1862), publicly thanked the Nawab for his assistance to the British. Moreover, the new British agent for Murshidabad, Brigadier-General Colin Mackenzie (1806–1881), appointed in 1858, supported the Nawab's case and (unsuccessfully) advocated that his personal stipend should be restored. However, British officials in India took care to remind Indian royalty that, although 'they ruled by right of birth', they were 'not members of the ruling race'.[26] Lord Canning's determination to reinforce acknowledgement of that hierarchy is illustrated by an incident that occurred when the Nawab went to Calcutta in 1859 to pay his respects to the viceroy. When Mansour Ali Khan arrived in Calcutta and proceeded towards the governor-general's residence, a problem arose. The Nawab's shoes were neither European nor black, and Lord Canning insisted that black European shoes must be worn in his presence; the Nawab's jewelled slippers, worn in Muslim courts, would not do. Nor could the requirement be waived for Shi'i Muslims, who avoid wearing black except during *Muharram* and other periods of mourning. Mansour Ali Khan was made to delay his visit until a pair of black boots had been bought.[27] He was also made to present a symbolic tribute of *mohurs* (gold coins) to the governor-general, a tribute formerly paid to the now exiled Emperor of India in Delhi. After the meeting, the Nawab was forced to remain in Calcutta for three weeks to await Lord Canning's return visit, which would only be made on condition that they did not discuss business. The Nawab was slightly mollified when, on the day of his return to Murshidabad, he was informed that his nineteen-gun salute would be restored.

Rupture

It was not long before Mansour Ali Khan's relationship with the British became even more fraught. The Torrens affair had led the Nawab to suspect anyone appointed to control his finances and, in 1861, he decided to replace Raja Prosunnu Narain Deb, the finance minister, and instead delegate his two elder sons to handle his estate. Brigadier-General Mackenzie, who supported Raja Deb, retaliated by refusing to authorize the Nawab's stipend, claiming that only the finance minister could do so. Mackenzie's letters to the Nawab Nazim become blunt, threatening and intensely contemptuous, bereft of the thin veneer of deference that he had previously expressed:

> But my office here is not only to protect the interests of the Nizamut, but also by advice and by other means (if necessary) to keep you … and the inferior members of your family, male and female, from committing gross errors and follies, alike injurious to yourselves and scandalous in the eyes of the British Government, who protects you and without whose protection and favour, your family would in a very short time principally through the utter absence in themselves of true dignity, common sense, and honourable principles of action,

fall to ruin, and be swallowed up by the population of the city of Moorshedabad [sic] who are notoriously the scum and refuse of Bengal.[28]

Mackenzie's diatribe went on to condemn the Nawab for having putting himself 'so completely within the hands of your mother', and to remind him that 'in defying the British agent you have literally defied the British Government'. He further regretted the Nawab's adherence to Shi'i rather than Sunni practice and belief.[29]

The Nawab responded by issuing all further correspondence with Mackenzie and his staff in Persian, thus asserting a court tradition that had long preceded British intrusion. In defiance of Mackenzie's ruling that all European visitors or staff had to be approved by the British agent, and his specifically forbidding his admission to the palace compound or holding 'direct intercourse with the gentleman', Mansour Ali Khan also employed William Austin Montriou (1810–1885), a distinguished lawyer, as his private secretary.[30] With the assistance of Montriou and a succession of other private secretaries, the Nawab composed a series of long memorials to the viceroy which outlined his grievances and set out his claims for compensation and the restoration of his rights. He expressed his indignation at the high-handed and patronising behaviour of the viceroy's agents, complained that his funds had been reduced to less than one-tenth of the original amount promised, whereas rewards had been heaped upon those who were merely 'not flagrantly rebellious', and he, 'the oldest ally of the British Government', was forgotten. He wrote that his status was equivalent to that of as a dethroned sovereign and that he should therefore be given the same respect and rights:

> If it was thought right to secure this position to the Prince of such a very small territory as Hollern Zollern [sic], how much more should the rights of the family who brought to the Crown of Great Britain the Sovereignty of three such provinces as Bengal, Bihar, and Orissa, be maintained! It is my desire to be to her Majesty the Queen the first, as I have always been the most loyal, of her Indian subjects, and it is to her most Gracious Majesty that I appeal for the fulfilment of the pledges, so repeatedly given, to maintain 'my dignity, rights, and interest,' the splendour of my court, and my ease, comfort, and prosperity.[31]

Visit to Britain

Mansour Ali Khan's memorials were ignored by the viceroy, and after 1865 officials refused to even forward them to him. Consequently, the Nawab decided to go to England and present his case to Queen Victoria personally. Perhaps encouraged by the queen's affirmation of treaty rights with Indian princes, and by Englishmen such as his secretary, who was not attached to the government officials India, the Nawab believed that the establishment in Britain, as distinct from its representatives in India, would give him a fair hearing and respond justly. Long negotiations began for permission to leave Murshidabad, and for funds to enable to him to visit England in a way that would reflect his status as an Indian monarch. Finally, in February 1869, the Nawab embarked for Europe along with a retinue that included a scripture reader, a musician, two scribes, a eunuch, three valets, a butler, a compounder of medicines, a barber and a cook.[32] He was also accompanied by two of his sons, his private secretary William Fox, and Colonel Frederick Layard, who had been assigned to supervise and guide the visit.

The group stopped briefly in Marseilles and Paris, where the Nawab was presented to the emperor of the French, Napoleon III (1808–1873), and where the local press commented sympathetically on his cause. Commentary by some English journalists was less supportive. The Paris correspondent for *The Illustrated Times* wrote:

> Just now we have among us the rich Nabob of Bengal, Synd Munsoor Ali, with a vast number of other queer looking names ... The Prince is not a very imposing person, but his costumes and those of his two sons are picturesque and attractive – the long silken robe with gold-embroidered sash, the religious green turban, chains, and rings.[33]

In contrast to Lord Canning's insistence on the wearing of European shoes, the correspondent went on to mock the acquisition of such footwear, remarking that 'Christian civilisation has already invaded the Indian legs and feet', and that the Nawab and his sons 'had already adopted the odious trousers of Christendom and highly varnished boots'. The Nawab was, in this correspondent's view, 'but a prince in name – a shadow of a shade'.[34]

Although the preoccupation with the Nawab's dress and appearance continued, the Paris correspondent's attitude was not typical. His fellow British journalists reported the Nawab's stay in Britain assiduously, noting every court reception and all of his almost daily visits to the theatre, the races and evening soirées hosted by the British aristocracy. When, on 9 April 1869, he was presented to Parliament by the Secretary of State for India, the Duke of Argyll (1823–1900), many papers reported the event, describing the Nawab as 'a great Eastern potentate': 'The distinguished stranger was none other than the Nawab of Bengal, who was accompanied by his two sons and suite. Their presence attracted much attention.'[35] A month later, *The Leeds Mercury* reported the Nawab's attendance at the Derby races, noting that 'another great attraction was very near the Royal Box ... the carriages of the Nawab of Bengal and his suite. These dusky Orientals, clad in silken vestments, and glittering with gold and jewels, formed a strange contrast to the carriages around them'.[36]

Perhaps, surprisingly, there is no mention in any of the British newspaper reports, nor indeed in the letters to and from government officials, of the Nawab's religion. French journalists noted that the Nawab refrained from eating or drinking at the official banquets for religious reasons, eventually returning to his hotel suite for 'a simple meal of mutton curry'. This abstinence must also have been apparent during the many long banquets and receptions Mansour Ali Khan attended in Britain, and yet with reference to the early years of his stay, none of the British newspapers commented on this or on the fact of his commitment to Islamic practices and beliefs. Perhaps the Nawab's status and exotic appearance outshone all other kinds of identity as far as the British elite and public were concerned, making his religion irrelevant. Or perhaps there lingered a faint consciousness of the purported role of religious belief in stirring the so-called Mutiny, together with a sense that the British role in ending Mughal rule, and murdering the sons of the Emperor of Delhi, was better forgotten. Nevertheless, Mansour Ali Khan remained a devout and practising Muslim, confirmed by the inclusion of the scripture reader, musician and cook in his retinue.

The Nawab's original plan had been to present his memorial soon after his arrival in London, quickly settle his claims and spend six months touring Britain and Europe before returning to India. But protocol demanded that the memorial should first be considered in India by the viceroy and governor-general, the Earl of Mayo (1822–1872). However, his papers were 'accidentally' delayed for many months and then lost in Calcutta. One Irish newspaper reported:

> This 'accident' has had the – of course, unexpected – effect of delaying for a whole season in India judgment of Lord Mayo on the facts. It also involved detaining the Nawab in England for another year at a ruinous expense, to say nothing of the peril of the Northern climate to an Eastern constitution. More than all it has a result of tiding over to the chances of another session, and the possibility of another Secretary of State for India, or another Governor-General, all questions of the policy pursued by the Indian government in regard to the native princes of India.[37]

Marriage to an Englishwoman

Now, having left his three wives in Murshidabad and desirous of female company, Mansour Ali Khan became enamoured of a sixteen-year-old chambermaid who worked at the Alexandra Hotel, where he was staying. Her name was Sarah Vennell (1853–1925), daughter of an impoverished tailor from East London. The Nawab sought the father's permission to marry Sarah, and a *nikah* marriage ceremony took place in the hotel on 15 May 1870. As Sarah was a Christian and therefore a *kitabi* (one who believes in a book of sacred scripture), the alliance was permitted under Shi'i Islamic law. The ceremony, probably conducted by Mansour Ali Khan's scripture reader, was witnessed by the Nawab's two sons and his courtiers. Nowhere was it reported in the British papers. The Nawab continued to reside in the Alexandra Hotel with his retinue, but Sarah was housed separately nearby, accompanied by an older sister. Although the Nawab's guide, Colonel Layard, and his secretary, William Fox, were probably aware of the marriage, it seems that for many years the relationship was not public knowledge. Certainly, on no occasion do any reports indicate that Sarah accompanied her husband to receptions or other events. However, by 1875, Sarah had given birth to four children, all girls, and in that year the Nawab affirmed before the Mayor of London that he was Sarah's husband and the father of her children. He added that she had been promised a dowry of £10,000. Sarah and Mansour Ali Khan were now living together, first at Borde Hill in Sussex, then in Edmonton, north London, and finally in Bedford Square, central London. They had two more children, both boys, born in 1875 and 1877.[38]

Appeals to the British government and public

During the twelve years that Mansour Ali Khan lived in London, he fought strenuously for the restoration of his full pension, the money stolen by Torrens and recognition of his royal status. With the assistance of his secretary, the Nawab embarked on a campaign of journalistic and political lobbying. He commissioned and contributed to several books supporting his cause, including *British Policy in India, With Special Reference to the Nawab Nazim of Bengal* (1870).[39] The books received some sympathetic reviews and features, including one in the popular and respected journal *Vanity Fair* with a caricature of the Nawab captioned 'A Living Monument of Injustice'.[40] Another, published in *The Tomahawk* with the caption 'Be Just and Fear Not!' (Figure 8.1), depicted the Nawab literally at the feet of Queen Victoria:

> It is utterly ridiculous to ask for justice on behalf of the Nawab of Bengal – once Prince of India – now suppliant at the foot of our throne, and always, through

good repute and ill repute, the firmest of our friends – the most powerful of our allies; because, to do him justice, and to keep our faith with him would cost the nation millions. Thus it is that we bring England into disgrace and save our pockets at the expense of our honour!⁴¹

Nevertheless, in April 1871, Parliament rejected by 122 to 64 (mostly Irish) votes a motion to consider the Nawab Nizam's petition. Speaking for the government, M. E. Grant Duff (1829–1906), the Under-Secretary of State for India, argued that the Nawab's titles and income were merely the personal gifts of the EIC and the British government, and that even if they were hereditary, the British need not be bound by any treaties made before 1857. While it was true that the Nawab had been loyal to the British during the uprising, Duff went on to argue that he had no other choice but to reject the motion.

The Secretary of State for India, Argyll, was triumphant. He had previously written to Mansour Ali Khan declaring that the Torrens case could not be reconsidered and that his title could not be regarded as hereditary. In fact, Argyll continued, the title of Nawab Nazim of Bengal, Bihar and Orissa should be abolished, and his successor be called the Nawab of Murshidabad, receiving a stipend not exceeding four lakh rupees. Now, in a private letter to viceroy Mayo, Argyll wrote:

> You will have seen that we have beaten the Nawab with the aid of your friends. But the radicals generally vote against the Indian Govt as a matter of course. We shall now try to get the Nawab to go home. But he is an obstinate Brute and difficult to deal with.⁴²

The Nawab was indeed obstinate. He remained in England, seeking to negotiate a more favourable outcome. Moreover, a return to India and the oppressive and patronising supervision of British officials there held little attraction for him. In England, he was free to come and go as he pleased and was treated by many with respect and deference. His name was often at the head of the court receptions and guest lists reported in the London newspapers. Whereas, in Murshidabad, the British agent and his staff sought to wean the Nawab away from 'Asiatic excesses', in England his role was that of an Oriental celebrity. As the Nawab of Tonk's representative, Hafiz Ahmed Hassan, reported in 1871, 'officials in India are haughty, rough, and overbearing in behaviour to all classes, including the native gentry'. By contrast, in England, Hassan was met with 'much kindness, affability, and courtesy from various members of the aristocracy and gentry'.⁴³

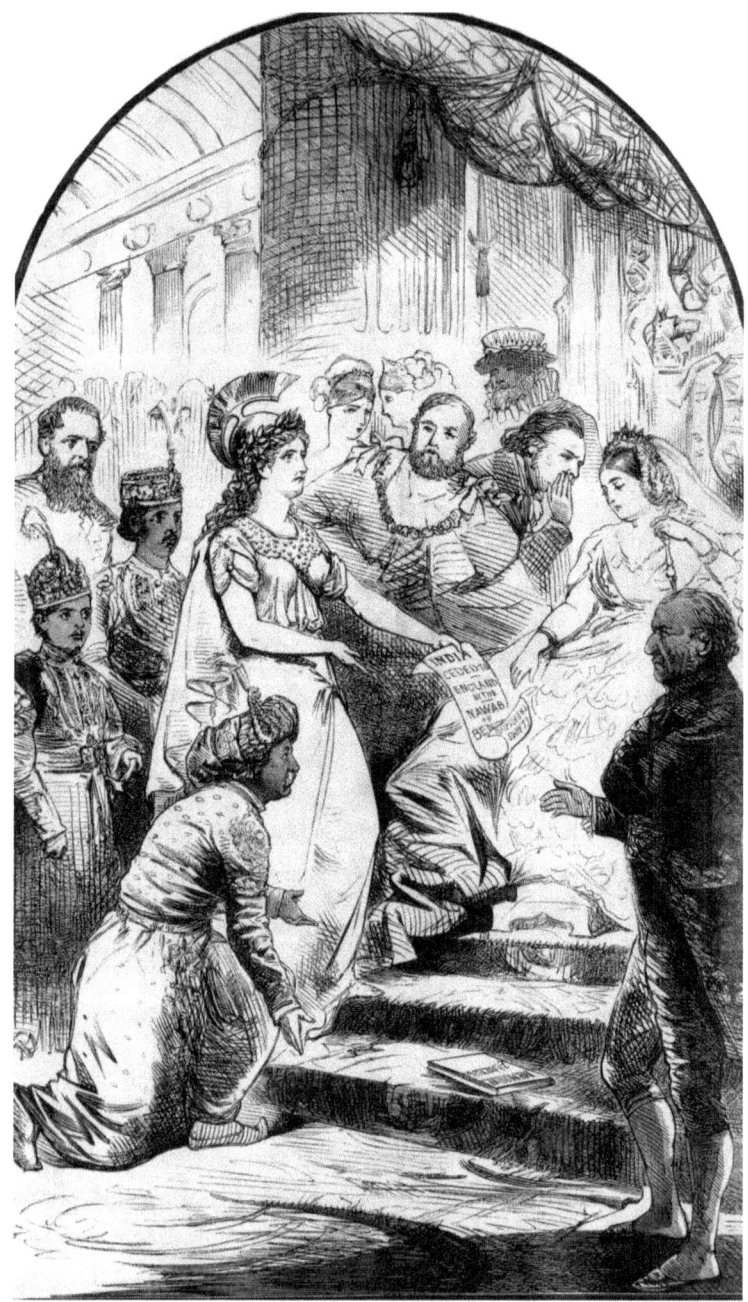

Figure 8.1 Lithograph by Matt Somerville Morgan depicting the Nawab Nizam of Bengal petitioning Queen Victoria, published in *The Tomahawk*, 16 April 1870.
Source: Private collection.

Forced abdication

Intermittent negotiations between Mansour Ali Khan and the British government faltered while the Nawab's debts increased. Horace Cockerell (1832–1908), secretary to the Government of Bengal, had scornfully dismissed the Nawab's claims, maintaining that, since being in England,

> he has lived a life of debauchery, and has disgraced his rank and position to such a degree that he is entirely excluded from all respectable society, and he has formed a connection with an English woman of low extraction, and lives with her in a suburb of London in a manner entirely unfitting to the position of a Mahomedan nobleman, and certainly in a manner which is inconsistent with his position as Nawab Nazim.[44]

Cockerell's assessment bears little relation to the reality and is poisoned by prejudice, snobbery and especially the desire to remove the Nawab. In fact, Mansour Ali Khan continued to be invited to events hosted by British aristocrats. But finally, in 1880, he accepted that his cause was lost. In return for a lump sum of £83,000 and an annual stipend of £10,000, as well as the promise of continuing provision for his wives and children, Mansour Ali Khan agreed to abdicate and also to allow the royal title to lapse; henceforth his successors would be known simply as the Nawabs of Murshidabad, and they would receive neither the gun salutes nor other privileges traditionally belonging to the Nawabs of Bengal.

For Cockerell, it seems, behaviour condoned when exhibited by the Prince of Wales or other members of the British aristocracy was not acceptable from a 'Mahomedan nobleman'. Despite opposition from the British government, which feared that the Nawab might stir up trouble, he decided to return to India. He took with him a new *nikah mut'ah* wife, Julia Lewis (d.1948), who had been a maid in the Bedford Square household, and the four surviving children from his marriage with Sarah, who was left in England without any provision.

Postscript: Sarah and the children

Mansour Ali Khan died of cholera at Murshidabad in November 1884. Prior to his death, he had let it be known that he wanted his 'English sons' to be sent to school in England, where they should receive 'a good Muslim education'.

Accordingly, Sarah's two sons, Syed and Nusrat, now aged nine and seven, were sent to England in May 1885 to stay with the Nawab's former secretary and lawyer, Mowbray Walker, who had been appointed their guardian. The 'English' girls, Miriam and Vaheedoonissa, remained in India for the rest of their lives.

More than thirty years later, Nusrat recalled his disorientation and dismay when, soon after his return to England, he attended a children's birthday party and was served ham sandwiches:

> Pig! Those pretty little fair-haired girls had offered me pig! Surely they knew it was a direct insult! Surely they realised that I could not sit at the same table with them and eat pig! How angry the great Queen would be if she knew how her loyal subjects were insulted.
>
> But I made no sign, of course. I am sure an impassive face gave no sign of the tumult in my heart.[45]

This memory is striking in its intensity, in Nusrat's absolute childhood identity as a Muslim and particularly in his conviction that Queen Victoria would be on his side. That seven-year-old child's certainty could only have been nurtured by his relatives and tutors in Murshidabad, where he had lived for the past four years. Thus, it tells us something about what the Murshidabad family wished to believe, despite the disastrous treatment Nusrat's father had suffered, namely that the Queen would have kept her promise to respect their rights if the politicians had not intervened.

When she learned of the Nawab's death, announced in the London papers, Nusrat's mother, Sarah, set about gaining custody of her children. Under English law at the time, if a child was illegitimate, the mother could claim custody, but she had no rights over children born within a legitimate marriage. In an appeal to the Court of Chancery in August 1885, Sarah therefore claimed that her marriage was not legitimate. Her lawyer argued that the case was urgent because the daughters in India were in danger of being married off as child brides: 'There could be no better case for the interference of the court,' he argued, because 'everybody knew what a Mohammedan marriage was. It was little better than a sale and purchase of the wife, who for the rest of her life would be compelled to live in the seclusion of the harem'.[46]

The defence lawyer, Mr Macnaghten, responded that the children were legitimate under Muslim law and that the boys were being educated and brought up according to the wishes of 'a great potentate'. Moreover, he declared:

The requirements of Mohammedans as to the preparation and cooking of food had been most carefully carried out [by their current guardians]. The desirability of the religion was not in question, and the only fact the court had to consider was that they had been brought up in a particular religion. It would be a disastrous thing were a Mohammedan gentleman to send his children to this country, who were legitimate according to Mohammedan law, and illegitimate according to the law of this country, and to find his whole scheme of education disarranged, and his children bastardised as well.[47]

A week later, Justice Chitty declared in favour of the defence, with the provision that any payments towards Vaheedoonissa's dowry should be immediately stopped to prevent her being betrothed at this point. Although some newspapers sympathized with Sarah's plight, viewing her as 'a woman in a humble sphere … who had been told she would be Begum of Bengal' (i.e. a legitimate wife of the Nawab), others were censorious. A reporter for *The Globe* hoped that Chitty's judgement would have 'the effect of bringing home to the minds of European women the horrors of marriage with non-Christian Orientals. Such unions, although perhaps not very numerous, are becoming far too common'.[48]

Sarah appealed to the Supreme Court. Her case was heard in October 1885 and again dismissed, unanimously, on the grounds that the marriage was legitimate, that she 'had assented to the children remaining in India with their father' and that it was in the interests of the children to remain with their appointed guardians, 'having regard to the nature of their birth, the religion in which they had been brought up, and the mode of life which had been adopted for them'.[49] Despite the ruling by both courts, and a memorandum in her favour by a lawyer appointed by the India Office, the British government was unwilling to grant Sarah a pension befitting her role as Nawab Begum, nor would they allow her the £10,000 dowry promised at the time of her marriage and reiterated in the 1875 Indenture signed before the Mayor of London by the Nawab.[50]

It is not clear whether Sarah truly believed that her daughters were in danger of being sold as child brides or simply let her lawyer refer to that commonly held belief in order to strengthen her case. The facts are that neither Miriam nor Vaheedoonissa ever married or were pressured to do so. A marriage with a member of the Oudh royal family was proposed for Miriam when she was eighteen, but Miriam refused the marriage and expressed a wish to remain single, which was respected.

Conclusion

The story of the last Nawab of Bengal and his relationship with Britain, British people and the British government is a complex one affected by varying and often contradictory political expediencies and attitudes. For the Nawab, his identity as a Muslim in terms of belief and culture was fundamental, and it linked him also to the history and political status of the Mughal Empire in the Indian subcontinent. He continued to believe that the British Queen, as Empress of India, would wish to protect that status and tradition. For the British, in India as well as in the UK, the Nawab's adherence to Islam, especially the Shi'i branch, was a cause for regret, and even suspicion, but generally had to be tolerated. But, by 1880, the Nawab's alleged failure to live as a proper 'Mahommedan nobleman' became a convenient reason for forcing his abdication. And, five years later, the purported importance of acceding to his wishes for his 'English sons' became another convenient reason for depriving his English wife of the pension and dowry the Nawab had promised her.

9

Maulana Muhammad Barakatullah Bhopali in late-Victorian England

Humayun Ansari

Introduction

Late-Victorian Britain was home to a growing number of Muslims, many with direct connections to the British Empire, others drawn there by broader networks. Some of them settled and made Britain their permanent base, while others came and went, part of the cosmopolitan traffic passing through Britain during this time. One such Indian Muslim was Maulana Muhammad Barakatullah Bhopali (c.1859–1927),[1] who spent around a decade in England at the very end of the nineteenth century, initially building connections with other pan-Islamist activists but increasingly adopting a more politically radical stance vis-à-vis the British Empire and its control over India. Barakatullah's world view was affected greatly by his ten years in the imperial metropole; his political career thereafter moved along increasingly revolutionary tracks, and he spent the rest of his life outside India challenging the status quo associated with empire.

This chapter explores how Barakatullah's stay in Victorian Britain started to reshape his outlook and political activism. It focuses in particular on two aspects of his thinking: first, his response to contemporary British criticism of Muslim beliefs and practices; and, second, his shifting engagement with the question of women's status within Islam. In both cases, his growing confidence to challenge ingrained assumptions can be associated with his years living and working in Britain in the 1890s.

This key formative phase in Barakatullah's peripatetic life has remained cloaked in relative obscurity and conjecture despite it being – for him – a profoundly formative political and intellectual experience. What we see during the 1890s is Barakatullah being drawn not only into a range of pan-Islamic but also transnational, and often secular anti-imperialist, networks that were active in Britain at that time. In response to his own experiences of hostility directed against Islam and Muslims in broader British society, he developed his critique of Muslim subjection and a concomitant vision of political liberation in which pan-Islamism and nationalism could be meaningfully interwoven.[2] For him, Islam also offered the possibility of liberation for Muslim men and women alike. More specifically, however, Barakatullah's thinking evolved in the context of the major British port cities of Liverpool and London, where a significant cluster of pan-Islamist and non-Muslim anti-colonial nationalist activists, such as Rafiuddin Ahmed (1865–1954), Mushir Hosain Kidwai (1877–1937), Dadabhai Naoroji (1825–1917), Bhikaji Cama (1861–1936) and Shyamji Krishnavarma (1857–1930), were gathering. Exposure to the day-to-day realities of being a Muslim and a colonial subject in 1890s Britain profoundly shaped Barakatullah's longer-term outlook and priorities as he operated as a transnational anti-imperialist working across continents.[3]

Defending the *umma*

British imperial domination had reached its peak by the late nineteenth century. With the Ottoman defeat at the hands of Russia in 1878 and the British occupation of Egypt in 1882, Muslims in India, as elsewhere, were acutely concerned about Islam's political decline on the world stage. It was in this context that pan-Islam emerged as an ideological movement for solidarity and reform, aimed at countering Western political and cultural hegemony. Increasingly, groups of Indian Muslims came to perceive their British rulers as antagonists, and concomitantly that the true interests of Muslims could only be secured through greater unity among Muslim peoples and nations. These Muslims were deeply influenced by the ideas of the pan-Islamist thinker and activist Saiyid Jamal al-Din al-Afghani (1838–1897).[4] Of particular appeal was al-Afghani's call for Muslim unity to resist Western power and its further expansion, and likewise his insistence that the Qur'an itself enjoined the acquisition of the most modern intellectual and technological means with which to wage this fight. For many Indian Muslims drawn to al-Afghani's political arguments, the best place to access these tools was Britain itself.

Barakatullah, who had trained as an *alim* (a learned scholar qualified to offer Islamic legal opinions) at the Madarsa Sulaimanya in the Indian princely state of Bhopal,[5] encountered al-Afghani first hand when the latter passed through

Figure 9.1 Maulana Muhammad Barakatullah Bhopali, c.1890s.
Source: Photographer unknown. Private collection.

there in 1883.⁶ What appealed to Barakatullah in al-Afghani's approach was that, in contrast to more traditionalist *ulama*,⁷ his interpretation of Islam seemed to be compatible with reason, freedom of thought and other modern 'virtues'; al-Afghani's forceful argument that Muslim freedom was possible only if the secrets of European intellectual, military, technological and political superiority had been mastered, directly appealed to him. Clearly much impressed, Barakatullah duly followed in al-Afghani's footsteps to London.⁸ What also reinforced his endeavour to move to Britain was news filtering back to India that an Englishman named William Henry Quilliam (1856–1932) had converted to Islam and was actively pursuing its propagation and institutionalization there.⁹ Abdullah Quilliam's rising profile combined with his nascent pan-Islamism, therefore, undoubtedly played a key part in drawing Barakatullah to Britain.

On his arrival in England, most likely during 1890 (the precise date remains unclear),¹⁰ Barakatullah reconnected with al-Afghani's modernist impulses at Quilliam's Liverpool Muslim Institute (LMI), arguing that Muslims in the West could play a significant, if not a leading role, in pulling Muslim peoples out of their current crisis. In a later 1893 lecture, Barakatullah set out the key reason he had felt persuaded to join the LMI. For him,

> While in the past light and learning came from the East, it is time now that the sun of Islam should rise from the West – and illumine every corner of the globe. The Muslim Institute in Liverpool and the other one in New York¹¹ promise to turn out the pioneers of civilisation in the future. The reason we look at them as fountainheads of good is simply because the Muslims in the West are Muslims by reason, not by birth. They are as free as air, unfettered by local traditions and racial superstitions, which mar the progress of our brethren in Turkey, Persia, and India. If some honest workers take up the cause in their hands seriously, … Islamic democracy will revive, and again universal brotherhood will be established.¹²

As rational as this vision appeared to him, Barakatullah must have been immediately struck by the practical challenges that confronted the pursuit of his pan-Islamic ambitions. He quickly became aware of the deeply embedded sense of Western civilizational superiority and the extent of anti-Islamic religious prejudices. Dominant discourses in late-Victorian Britain understood Islam to be a backward 'civilization', inferior to British values, customs and traditions, and inimical to science and progress. Consequently, Muslims at this time often found themselves at the receiving end of popular ridicule and official insults. Furthermore, hostility towards Muslims became entangled in anti-Ottoman sentiment, fuelled by a stream of contemporary 'horror stories' in the public sphere regarding Ottoman Turkey's persecution of its Balkan and Armenian Christian populations (see Chapter 2).[13]

Muslims in Britain thus felt compelled to resist this anti-Islamic hostility. One high-profile instance was a successful effort mounted to ban the production of Hall Caine's (1853–1931) play *Mahomet* in London in 1890.[14] 'Abd al-Hamid II (1842–1918), the Ottoman sultan and the caliph (the head of the *umma*, the universal Muslim religious community), had got the play banned in France in March 1890. The LMI members had written to the sultan expressing their appreciation of his 'efforts ... to prevent the representation of a play calculated to shock and outrage the feelings of all devout Mahomedans'.[15] Taking their cue from mounting protests in Bombay (Mumbai), Quilliam's fledgling Liverpool Muslim community joined the campaign. Newly arrived Rafiuddin Ahmad, as vice-president of the LMI, wrote to *The Times* deploring 'the proposed mockery of the prophet on the stage in a country which has pledged itself to respect [Muslim] feelings'.[16] In response to a leading article in *The Times of India* rejecting Rafiuddin's protest, Quilliam in a letter to its editor further elucidated the case for why the play should be banned. These protests were successful. The Lord Chamberlain, who was appointed by an Act of Parliament (1737) as official licenser of plays and regulated restrictions on drama, recognized 'the political exigencies involved' and informed producer Henry Irving (1838–1905) that 'such a play would not be licensed'.[17]

While the public outcry against the Ottoman Empire and Islam more generally showed no sign of abating, it did not deter Barakatullah from moving to England and settling in London, then Liverpool. It is unclear when Barakatullah first visited Liverpool, but he is known to have attended a wedding at the LMI in April 1891.[18] Following an invitation from Quilliam, in c.1893 he moved to Liverpool and became the LMI's sometime imam and *muezzin* (prayer leader and caller to prayer respectively);[19] and thereafter for most of the remainder of his stay in Britain, he operated as one of its more prominent and active members, delivering lectures, writing articles for its publications *The Crescent* and *The Islamic World*, officiating at funerals, weddings, and *'Ids* (Muslim religious festivals), where he delivered the *khutbah* (sermon), conducting prayers in Arabic, chairing meetings and reporting on the LMI's operations, especially in the vernacular press back in India. Barakatullah was also appointed vice-principal and 'Professor of Oriental Languages' at the LMI Moslem College, a school for Muslim children.[20] In this role, he took pains to promote Quilliam, publicizing the latter's recognition as the leader of Liverpool's Muslims.[21]

At the same time, Barakatullah had to deal with the vitriolic abuse and violence targeted at the LMI. Many of these attacks were physically dangerous. For instance, in November 1891, a mob numbering several hundred assembled in front of the mosque and greeted the acting *muezzin* with (as contemporary press reports put it) 'discordant howls'; worshippers were pelted with missiles, stones and filth as they left the service. As one newspaper explained, this violent opposition was proof that 'England and Liverpudlians detested Mohammed's creed'.[22]

In this patently anti-Muslim climate, Quilliam and Barakatullah's joint task of propagating Islam became extremely challenging. Strategically, they sought ways of reconciling key aspects of Islam with English culture, emphasizing that Islam was a supremely rational, ecumenical religion underpinned by reason.[23] As a means of creating a sense of receptive familiarity, they made adaptations to the previous religious practices of potential converts. Many of the LMI's activities were like the 'good works' being carried out vigorously by non-conformist Christians, especially the Unitarians, such as the LMI's annual celebration of Christmas Day by feeding the poor (see Chapter 10). The LMI also built bridges with interested Christians by adopting a form of worship to which people were accustomed to and with which they felt at home: morning and evening 'services' were organized on Sundays, when hymns, many taken from Christian evangelists but adapted by Quilliam to be suitable for English-speaking Muslim congregations, were sung accompanied by a harmonium.[24]

In December 1895, a Cape Town Muslim, Mohammed Dollie (1846–1906), an early supporter who visited the LMI and proceeded to open a mosque in London, defended these practices: 'Should the Arabic language stand in the way of making converts, I personally . . . do not see why we should not have our prayer-books and hymn-books in the English language. Nor would [I] object to pews in the Mosque.'[25] On the other hand, Yusuf Samih Asmay (d.1942), an Ottoman who also visited the LMI in 1895, formed a distinctly more negative impression of activities there. In his *Liverpool Muslims* (1896), Asmay was critical of the institute's religious ways, regarding them as non-Islamic innovation, especially the public 'Sunday Services'. Asmay dismissively described the mosque as a music 'salon'; for him, the congregational prayers lacked solemnity with their key elements set aside.[26] Barakatullah himself received his share of Asmay's censure for apparently condoning these practices and not following what Asmay regarded as prescribed rituals:

> At Eid al-Adha[27] last year, Turkish sailors . . . gathered in Quilliam's mosque . . . and asked Maulana Barakatullah to lead the prayers as imam. Then when the venerable imam led the prayers with six *takbirs* [the call of *Allahu 'akbar*, or 'God is the Greatest'], it is said they got upset and left the mosque without [sharing the traditional '*Id*] greetings. It is also said that a few times he led the [evening] prayer with four *rak'ats* [the sequence of movements in a prayer], [instead of three].[28]

The LMI secretary Thomas Omar Byrne (1856–1901) strongly rebutted Asmay's 'foolish and ill-informed' allegations in his 'ridiculous book': 'These Sunday meetings are not and have never been considered by us as Muslim services, or used in substitution for the regular prescribed prayers of Islam, neither are they held in the Mosque. … There is no organ in the mosque, nor is it or has it ever been used in connection with our prayers.'[29] Barakatullah, in two letters to Asmay dated August and October 1895, likewise disagreed with Asmay's accounts of Liverpool Muslims praying 'without ablution and [with] an organ in the mosque':

> I have taught each of the Muslims the manners of ablution and told them to come to the mosque after performing ablution at home. The presence of the music in the proximity of the mosque was due to our inability to set up the mosque except with some musical instruments therein . . . [W]e will build a mosque and there will be nothing of the Psalms in it.[30]

Hence, Barakatullah requested Asmay not to 'write these things in your book' because 'the scholars of the Orient – as they always do – . . . will give a legal opinion that the Muslims in England are infidels. And this will harm the Muslims'.[31]

While in Liverpool, Barakatullah remained supportive of Quilliam's efforts, especially the LMI's promotion of worldwide Muslim unity. Deploying his linguistic skills in Arabic, Persian and Urdu, he played a significant role in promoting its pan-Islamic profile with Muslim political leaders and philanthropists alike, writing letters 'requesting grants and donations from the wealthy and the rulers in the Islamic world'.[32] For instance, he helped to strengthen connections with Naser al-Din (1831–1896), Shah of Persia, to whom Quilliam had presented an illuminated address when the former had visited Liverpool in 1889.[33]

In 1894, at a meeting of the LMI, Barakatullah reportedly called for Quilliam to be designated as 'Sheikh-ul-Islam of the British Isles', and he was duly elected by the congregation.[34] Quilliam said that the Ottoman sultan confirmed the title (some scholars question this; see Chapter 11). In similar fashion, Abdur Rahman Khan (*c.*1844–1901), the Amir of Afghanistan, who regularly received copies of both *The Crescent* and *The Islamic World*,[35] also recognized Quilliam as the leader of British Muslims, and was 'ready to do what we can for you whenever you will need our assistance'.[36] Further recognition took place when Nasrullah Khan (1874–1920), a son of the Amir, visited Liverpool in 1895, bestowing upon Quilliam a gift of £2,500 to support the work of the LMI. Barakatullah, fluent in Persian, acted as Quilliam's interpreter during Nasrullah Khan's tour, playing a key role in communicating LMI's modernist Islam, and suggesting that 'the East . . . enveloped by the shades of tradition and imagination [withered and lifeless] . . . should take steps to follow in the wake of Great Britain in matters of new sciences and arts'.[37] Significantly, Barakatullah gained Nasrullah Khan's trust to such a degree that they came to an arrangement that the former would send the latter classified information in the form of a weekly letter in return for a fee of £10.[38] More generally, the LMI vociferously proclaimed its support for the Ottoman caliphate, a key requisite for it to become the pivot of pan-Islamic networks in England. However, its pan-Islamism was invoked within the framework of the existing imperial order, whose legitimacy was proclaimed by Britain on the basis that it was the power with the greatest number of Muslims under its rule.

Nonetheless, more widely in Britain, Muslims, and especially the Ottoman sultan, acquired a pariah status in the late nineteenth century; the Ottoman administration was repeatedly denounced for its alleged tyranny, moral decrepitude and brutality against Christians in the Balkans. Inevitably, with Quilliam's LMI forging explicit pan-Islamic connections, the mosque became the target of the press and politicians, attracting further public insult, ridicule and protest.[39] The personal experience of these violent outbursts, accompanied by jeers and abuse as the faithful were called to prayer at the LMI, would have reminded Barakatullah on a regular basis of wider antipathy towards Muslims, and so proved disillusioning as far as the wider prospects of Islam and Muslims in Britain were concerned.

From 1894, as public anger and attacks on Islam and Muslims provoked by news about the Ottoman persecution of Armenians gathered momentum, so did the riposte from Muslim circles, and the LMI become increasingly strident. When William Ewart Gladstone (1809–1898), four-times British prime minister, criticized the sultan as 'the unspeakable Turk'[40] for 'atrocities' against his Armenian Christian population, Quilliam, backed by Barakatullah, defended the Ottoman regime's actions. Pre-empting Gladstone's speech in Liverpool, in September 1896 Quilliam 'characterised the present crusade against Turkey as a mischievous agitation' which hypocritically ignored 'Christian atrocities' elsewhere: he warned that if the present one persisted 'it might be necessary to proclaim a *Jehad*,[41] which would cause every Mussulman to rally round the standard of the Prophet'. Defending the sultan, Quilliam maintained that all sects had reasonable toleration in the Ottoman Empire, and that 'Armenians were objected to because of their revolutionary political schemes'.[42] Responding to Gladstone's attacks, Mohammed Dollie wrote in *The Crescent*: 'There can be no doubt that our caliph, Abdul Hamid II, Sultan of Turkey, is the right man in the right place', while, for Barakatullah, who had left Liverpool for London, 'the genius of a statesman like Sultan Abdul-Hamid [was] quite equal to the occasion'.[43] Indeed, this response echoed sentiment at an earlier December 1894 meeting of the largest London Islamic society, the Anjuman-i-Islam, which had passed the following resolution:

> That the Moslem residents in England protest, in the name of their co-religionists, against the gross misrepresentation of the Moslem law and religion which is now being made for political purposes in connexion with the alleged Armenian atrocities. They deplore all attempts to excite religious animosity and ill-feeling between Christians and Moslems, and express their regret and indignation that this matter should have been made a subject of pulpit oratory and given a religious aspect when it is purely political.[44]

The Anjuman-i-Islam also protested against 'the indiscriminate and violent abuse of the Mohamedan religion . . . and the wholesale imputations of cruelty and inhumanity . . . which had been levelled against the Sultan and the Turkish Army without any authentic evidence of their truth'.[45] Now, in 1896, most likely following Barakatullah's counsel, Quilliam issued a defiant *fatwa* (juridical opinion), commanding Egyptian soldiers under British order who were preparing to suppress the revolt of the successor to the 'Mahdi' in the Sudan, Abdullah ibn Muhammad (1846–1899), to refuse to take up arms against their Muslim brethren, which made him vulnerable to the charge of treason.[46]

When public opinion turned firmly against the Ottoman Empire during its war with Greece over Crete in 1897, Barakatullah made speeches and wrote pieces strongly critical of British imperial campaigns and policy vis-à-vis Ottoman Turkey, increasingly causing concern to the British authorities. For instance, at a meeting in London of the Moslem Patriotic League, with Rafiuddin as president, Barakatullah seconded a resolution deploring the 'outrageous massacre of innocent Moslems in Crete', while the Anjuman-i-Islam requested 'her Majesty's Government to take immediate steps to prevent the ruthless massacre of hundreds of Mohammedan men, women and children by their Christian fellow subjects'.[47]

Throughout the 1890s, Barakatullah remained steadfast when it came to broadcasting the virtues and pan-Islamic credentials of the Ottoman sultan-caliph. At the same time he played a leading role in challenging popular and official targeting of the Ottoman Empire and its ruler, protesting strongly against 'the unjust and one-sided agitation fomented throughout the United Kingdom against Turkey' and condemning 'the unrestrained abusive language used by the press and from the pulpit and platforms ... towards the Calipha and the religion of Islam'.[48] Defending the Ottomans against the charge of committing atrocities against the Armenian population, Barakatullah demurred:

> The professional agitators ... perennially misrepresent Turkey in this country. It is to be feared that the exaggerated Armenian atrocities in our time foreshadow the repetition of the Spanish Inquisition of mediaeval ages. The much-advertised Bulgarian atrocities time [sic] and investigation have proved by unimpeachable evidence to have been falsehoods industriously circulated to aid in securing the independence of the principality, and the so-called Armenian atrocities doubtless will be proved equally false.[49]

Hence, in his response to one particularly vehement critic of Ottoman policy and Gladstone supporter, Barakatullah suggested that the Reverend Malcolm MacColl (1831–1907) should instead 'counsel the British Government to lend a helping hand to Turkey, so as to improve her power of defence both on sea and on land'.[50] Moreover, he offered another reason why Britain should offer support to the Ottomans:

> It is a well-known fact that the Muslims in India have sided with the British Government since the birth of the National Congress movement nine years ago. ... By picking quarrels with Turkey, simply to satisfy ignoramus tricksters, England will greatly shake the confidence of Muslims in the British Raj.[51]

Throughout this period, however, we can also see Barakatullah wrestling uneasily to resolve his pan-Islamic allegiances with loyalty to the British Crown. For instance, in 1892 as chairman of the Committee of Indian Mohamedans in London, he may have protested vehemently against 'monstrous calumnies ... to discredit ... the most just "Caliph of Islam"', but he also affirmed the importance of loyalty to 'our most gracious Majesty the Queen'.[52] Five years later, he was still able to second a resolution deeply regretting the outburst of fanaticism and the consequent disturbances of peace on the North-Western Frontier of India and [urged] the leaders of the Muslims to deprecate such movements, as in the opinion of this meeting the best interests of the Indian Muslims consist in their loyal support of the beneficent and impartial rule of the Queen-Empress in India.[53]

But then, contrarily, another meeting, again with Barakatullah in the chair, resolved that

considering . . . the turbulent nature of the tribes inhabiting the independent belt of land between the Indian and Afghan frontiers and their passionate love of independence and freedom, the best solution of the frontier problem is to hand over the whole independent, tribal territory . . . to the Amir of Afghanistan.[54]

Barakatullah, it seems, contended that this step would strengthen Britain's friendship with the Amir while 'no way lowering British prestige and much needed saving in the Indian Budget'.[55] Likewise, at an Anjuman-i-Islam meeting in December 1897 to consider the Indian frontier policy, many 'seditious speeches' were noted by the authorities, but Barakatullah was said to have deprecated these, advocating instead that 'differences between the Government and the tribesmen should be settled amicably by treaty'.[56]

On the broader question of British rule in India, too, we see Barakatullah's influence at work. His close friend Rafiuddin Ahmad, echoing Barakatullah's stance, stressed at a meeting of the Muslim Patriotic League that, at a time when serious attacks were being made on Imperial rule in India, it was the duty of all loyal subjects of Queen Victoria 'to come forward and freely bear testimony to the beneficent character and impartial spirit, of that government'. Barakatullah himself described talk of driving the British from India, when the huge masses were perfectly loyal, as merely fulsome nonsense. Significantly, the meeting declared that it had 'no sympathy with the revolutionary Resolution recently passed at the Conference held in Bloomsbury' by Naoroji's London Indian Society. Instead, it reaffirmed 'its loyal support to the British rule in India because, situated as India is at the present time, it is under that rule alone that the peaceful progress of the country is at all possible'. As its resolution asserted,

the withdrawal of the Queen's government from India would be a great disaster, because, though the Indian Muslims would be quite competent to take care of themselves in any emergency, [this] would give rise to a struggle for supremacy among various Indian communities so furious and prolonged that it would plunge the whole country into the darkest anarchy and the most cruel bloodshed.[57]

All the same, British intelligence continued to be suspicious of Barakatullah's expressions of loyalty, as they were of those of his close collaborator, Rafiuddin:

> In his newspaper articles the tone is loyal; even in his speeches he is generally moderate [but] it is said that his private correspondence does not reflect the loyalty of his lips. ... Hatred of everything English is said to be the tone of Rafiuddin's reports.[58]

Events in the Ottoman Empire, especially the nationalist upsurge in the Balkans and the outcry against the Ottoman sultan in Britain, thus had a massive impact on Barakatullah's political orientation. He became increasingly perplexed by 'Abd al-Hamid II's pan-Islamism that seemed totally opposed to any nationalist feeling, as revealed by the sultan's comment that 'we must not touch the question of nationality; all Mohammedans are brethren and any national partition will cause serious dissension'.[59] On the other hand, the sultan expressed deep sympathy for 'millions of Muslims under European rule' and hoped that 'one day the time for revenge will come for the Indians who then will liberate themselves from the yoke of the British . . . who are sacking and oppressing them'. But there is no evidence to suggest that the sultan ever realistically contemplated the formation of a global Muslim united front for military purposes against Christian domination, and likewise no evidence that he claimed political sovereignty over Muslims outside his domain.[60]

Quilliam, to prevent the undermining of the Ottoman Empire, continued in loyal fashion to propagate an anti-nationalist pan-Islamism in his journal, *The Islamic World*. In contrast, dismayed by anti-Muslim popular sentiment in Britain, Barakatullah's pan-Islamism was taking a progressively anti-Western turn. No doubt, he would have been reminded of al-Afghani's radical ideas, especially those that favoured a more openly anti-British pan-Islamic struggle to secure the freedom of the Islamic world from Western dominance. Slowly but surely while in Britain, Barakatullah's politics shifted more towards anti-colonial nationalism. Though still committed to the ideology of pan-Islamism, he began to understand this as an anti-imperialist project combined with Indian nationalism. Pan-Islamist ideas certainly resonated with an international Muslim audience, but nationalism was more apposite in a diasporic mixed setting. Increasingly, Indian pan-Islamists recognized the benefit of Hindu-Muslim cooperation against the British, building on al-Afghani's suggestions that Muslims should organize politically with Hindus and together force the British to leave India.[61]

With Indian nationalism on the rise, Barakatullah was drawn to the arguments of revolutionary nationalists, impatient with constitutional efforts to secure Home Rule in India. For these radicals, the main emphasis of Indian nationalists on self-rule – as embodied in the programme of the Naoroji-led British Committee of the Indian National Congress (established in 1889) – was ineffective, circumscribed as it was by the principles of loyalty to the British Empire.[62] In December 1896, Barakatullah attended a 'Conference of British Indians resident in Great Britain' (as did Rafiuddin), held under the presidency of Naoroji. While the conference

> recognise[d] the earnest and energetic efforts of the Government of India ... in mitigating the calamitous consequences of the present famine in India ... it at the same time urge[d] upon the Government the consideration of the measures which tend to restrain the drain of enormous wealth from India, which is the principal cause of the frequent recurrence of such calamities.[63]

For Barakatullah, the Government of India was 'not entitled on the present occasion' to any thanks whatsoever.[64] Then, in January 1898, Barakatullah attended another conference, again with Naoroji presiding, which – going further – passed a resolution that was trenchantly critical 'of all the evils and terrible misery that India has been suffering for a century and a half'. Such nationalist critiques denouncing the despotism of British administration, its political hypocrisy, and the 'ever-increasing bleeding' of the country's resources, will have fed into Barakatullah's own political evolution during this period of his life.[65]

Barakatullah and the status of Muslim women

As the fin de siècle approached, Barakatullah's views on other matters also evolved. By the 1890s, the place that women should occupy in British society had become a hotly debated and increasingly divisive issue, generating considerable social and political tension. Suffragists used the image of female confinement within the Islamic harem (the secluded part of a Muslim household reserved for wives, concubines and female servants) as 'caged birds' to help make their case for gender equality closer to home, invoking this trope to highlight their own restrictive experiences: no rights, no liberties and dependence on men.[66]

In response, male public figures, including members of the clergy, argued that, compared with gender inequalities in Muslim societies, those in Britain paled into insignificance. In this context, representations of the polygamous relations associated with Islam served to promote Christian monogamy as the preferred option to the assumed misery of female seclusion.

English travel writers, missionaries and scholars often described the harem as a warren of jealousy and intrigue, home to bitter rivalries but also to longings for a monogamous relationship among its denizens. Muslim women were presented as passive and docile, subject to patriarchal traditions and lacking the active agency required to change their conditions. In contrast, Muslim men were characterized by a violent promiscuous masculinity.[67] For many Victorian writers, 'Islam kept woman from any participation in public life under all circumstances, and thus hindered her intellectual and moral development. In consequence of this the Mohammedan woman has ever remained essentially a means of sensual gratification and procreation.'[68] The very well-connected Church of England clergyman Malcolm MacColl publicly lamented the experience of 'girls, [who] on reaching the age of puberty, will be sold as slaves into those unspeakable hotbeds of vice – the harems of dissolute Turks'.[69]

Leading British Muslims such as Quilliam presented a counter-narrative to the tropes associated with polygamy, veiling and the harem, and this was reflected in the LMI's own gender practices. The general atmosphere at the LMI was comparatively liberal; women and men congregated freely and without separation for prayers and community gatherings. Nor were women required to veil inside or outside the LMI, and female converts 'dressed as ordinary Englishwomen'.[70] Nonetheless, Quilliam and the members of his congregation were publicly denounced as 'apostles of polygamy and harems'.[71] But, while the British state disapproved of the Islamic weddings that Quilliam and, in due course, Barakatullah performed at the LMI, it did not deem them unlawful.[72]

All the same, there was occasional criticism from within the LMI itself. In the mid-1890s, Nafeesah M. Keep (1844–1925), an American-born Muslim convert, complained in a letter to the Ottoman sultan that 'women and men [were] standing shoulder to shoulder on the prayer carpet, men fastening the shoes of a young woman, and the same young woman greeting the young men in the mosque with a kiss'.[73] Rumours regarding Quilliam's sexual activities proliferated. Yusuf Samih Asmay, for instance, argued that 'Mr Quilliam has a regard for the fairer sex . . . they say that once he sets his eyes on a dove she cannot escape his clutches'.[74] Inevitably, perhaps, Barakatullah, who was the LMI imam at the time, came under similar suspicions. Police reports accused him of 'consorting with women of ill repute . . . and taking alcoholic drinks',[75] while others alleged that he was 'irreligious and indecent . . . visiting ladies in their houses at night for wantonness and debauchery': these were all charges that Barakatullah rejected as a lie.[76]

Indeed, Barakatullah's exposure to the freer social mingling of the sexes in Britain tested his earlier 'traditional' views about gender relations. When Barakatullah first visited the LMI in 1891, his upbringing in a conventional nineteenth-century Indian Muslim household combined with his early education meant that his ideas about gender interaction were challenged by Quilliam's modernist practices. By 1893, however, while his approach was still primarily apologetic, there were signs that his thinking had started to change. In a lecture entitled 'Seclusion of Women' given at the LMI, he pointed out that information concerning the life of women in the harem, brought to Britain by 'mere superficial observers', was largely exaggerated, and that the alleged ill-treatment of women attributed to the teachings of Islam was untrue. He conceded that – owing to local customs as well as accidental circumstances – 'the established custom of centuries made the free intercourse of the sexes, as one finds it here [in Britain], almost impossible at present in the East'. But, importantly, he also predicted that gradual change would remove all these drawbacks in the future. As he reminded his audience, the Qur'an did not order the face of a woman, nor her hands, to be covered, and women in the time of the Prophet would go to battlefields to nurse the wounded. In his view, while 'ignorant Muslims could not distinguish between what is essential and what is non-essential in the teaching of Islam . . . with the advancement of education many improvements would be carried out in the course of time'.[77]

In setting out his case in defence of the status of Muslim women during the 1890s, Barakatullah, to varying degrees and selectively, drew on arguments being elaborated at the time in British journals by modernist Muslim scholars and jurists such as Syed Ameer Ali (1849–1928) and Rafiuddin Ahmed, which challenged the perception that Muslim women occupied a subordinate status (socially and in law) relative to their English counterparts.[78] Barakatullah too felt compelled to challenge Western assumptions that Muslim women's social position was inferior to that of their British counterparts: 'European writers', he wrote,

> who seldom have real insights into Muslim harems, present to the public a terrible picture of the state of woman in Islam . . . that a Muslim harem is a pandemonium of misery, where women are caged . . . to toil and be tortured is

no less imaginary than any freak of fiction; yet their lot is far from being one of anxiety and misery. On the contrary, they enjoy themselves just as much as any women in the world can do [except that their] means of acquiring happiness is different.[79]

While he conceded that 'Mohamedan women do not have the pleasure of free intercourse with men, outside the family circles, as women do in western countries', this was 'not due to such prohibition in Islam': 'Even in the Prophet's lifetime, women used to go out freely, decently dressed'; but, as he explained, once 'Arabs came into contact with other nations . . . the laws of purity and feminine dignity became hard and fast. ... The climatic influences, the conservatism and the proverbial laziness of the East all tended in the same direction'.[80] While Barakatullah rationalized the domestic role of women, their subordination to men, their seclusion and veiling, in moral and cultural terms as sanctioned by Muhammad, it seems that he was himself not now entirely persuaded by these explanations. Muslim women, he observed regretfully, 'have up to this time, preferred social happiness to organizing for political rights of women. Nor have they yet entered into competition with men, in the field of public service, industries, or labour'. But he was hopeful that 'with the evolution of time, which works such miracles in its own mysterious ways, who knows what surprises may yet be in store for the world among the generations yet unborn'.[81]

Yet, by the end of the decade, a residue of how far Barakatullah's views on Muslim women contained some of the traditional biases associated with his upbringing can be seen in his article 'Mohamedan Women' published in 1899. In it, he still rationalizes the subordinate status of Muslim women as sanctioned by Islam and Muhammad. Though he expressed optimism that there would be change, he remained uncertain about the future, asking his readers if it was 'possible to straighten the crooked rib (of which the woman is supposed to be made) without breaking it?'[82]

Conclusion

Barakatullah had arrived in Britain at the start of the 1890s optimistic about the possibilities offered by a pan-Islamist agenda. However, by the time of Queen Victoria's death and having experienced first-hand the resentment and contempt that was directed towards Muslims in the country, he had become profoundly disillusioned about pan-Islam's prospects and, more broadly, India's chances of securing freedom without a struggle. His political profile, together with his closer association with Indian nationalists, meant that he was put under police surveillance in Britain.[83] Severely squeezed in terms of his ability to pursue a radical political course of action, whether pan-Islamic or otherwise, Barakatullah decided that he was likely to achieve greater success in the United States, a country that he knew had itself won independence from Britain through revolutionary struggle. He was especially inspired by the organizational accomplishments of other anti-colonial groups there, particularly radical Irish nationalists, whose counterparts, the Irish Home Rulers, he had encountered in London and Liverpool, and whose strategies increasingly chimed with his own.[84] The United States, where he emigrated in 1903, never to return to Britain, attracted him because – in his view – it was a place that supported colonial people's aspirations of freedom without reservation.[85]

10

Feeding hungry Christians: The Liverpool Muslim Institute on Christmas Day

Brent D. Singleton

Introduction

The history of Christmas charity in England dates to the medieval period, when manor lords held feasts for their peasantry. This practice waned dramatically by the Tudor period and all but disappeared in 1647, when Christmas festivities were outlawed by the Puritan controlled Parliament. Although the monarchy and Christmas were restored in 1660, charity during the season was diminished, a downward trend that continued into the eighteenth century as the tradition of opening aristocratic households to feed the poor was generally halted.[1] By the early nineteenth century, Christmas was neither widely celebrated nor popular. In nearly half of the years between 1790 and 1835, *The Times* did not mention Christmas.[2] Nonetheless, philanthropy during the season never fully ceased, although institutional charities and bequests had largely taken over from aristocratic households.[3]

Christmas charity made a dramatic comeback in the mid-1840s largely due to popular works of literature such as Charles Dickens's (1812–1870) novella *A Christmas Carol* (1843). Ebenezer Scrooge's 'social redemption' both encouraged and warned the middle and upper classes of their duty towards the less fortunate. As John Storey argues, 'If what was invented was commercial out of instinct, it was charitable out of a sense of fear and guilt.'[4] In the wake of Dickens's and others' intertwining Christmas, charitable giving and Englishness, a relentless onslaught of depictions of starvation in Christmas fiction arose, reinforcing this narrative.[5] Likewise, Dickens's tale brought forth a nostalgia for the imagined English Christmas traditions of widespread charitable giving, the eating of certain foods and other customs that were never truly part of English culture, such as providing meals, sweets and presents to poor children.[6]

In Liverpool, at this same point in history, increasing poverty led to the city being referred to as 'the black spot on the Mersey' and later, 'squalid Liverpool'. In response to the social crisis among impoverished Irish immigrants, the Catholic Church in the city built up a parish-based social welfare system. Many Protestant denominations responded in kind but usually met with less success. By the latter part of the nineteenth century, a large proportion of charity in Liverpool was restricted to members of denominations.[7] As a result, John Belchem states, 'There were those who fell outside any safety net, victims of the uncoordinated expansion of social intervention in Victorian Liverpool.'[8] Adding fuel to the fire, between 1891 and 1911, the population of Liverpool increased by nearly 250,000 people, or by 45 per cent.[9] There are no clear statistics of poverty or unemployment rates during this period in Liverpool; however, Lucy Kilfoyle describes the city at this time as being in its 'richest-poorest heyday'.[10]

Coinciding with this era, a new type of Christmas charity emerged in England, one 'designed to provide a festive experience for the poor'.[11] In Liverpool, the major non-denominational Christmas charity organization was the Hot Pot Charity headed by the sitting Lord Mayor and prominent citizens of the city. Starting in about 1885, the charity annually provided up to 6,000 tins with precooked meat, potatoes, onions and seasonings, purportedly enough food for a family of ten. They also distributed thousands of pounds of bread, tea, jam and coal to other people in need.[12] Nonetheless, this was not enough to help all of the hungry in the city. It was in this milieu, in the late 1880s, that the precursor to the Liverpool Muslim Institute (LMI) formed when a group of Christians converted to Islam under the leadership of Abdullah Quilliam (1856–1932). Soon after, providing Christmas meals for the needy became a hallmark of the group, but one that has not previously been examined in any detail. Beginning in 1887 or 1888, and for the next two decades, the members of the LMI would feed thousands of hungry people from the local community on Christmas Day as well as on some Islamic holidays and other special occasions.[13]

In December 1889, the Liverpool Muslims moved to their permanent quarters in Brougham Terrace, having previously held meetings in Mount Vernon Street. Their first event at Brougham Terrace was the Christmas feedings. The *Liverpool Weekly Courier* reported the occasion and thus printed what was probably the earliest mention of the meals by the press:

The new premises were inaugurated by a substantial breakfast given on Christmas morning in the future 'mosque' to 230 poor children of the neighbourhood, but chosen indiscriminately from the most destitute of that class. After the feast the youngsters were amused with songs, recitations and instrumental music and thoroughly enjoyed the treat, which is quite a departure in the history of the Moslems.[14]

Nearly a decade later, in 1898, the LMI had hit its stride in providing Christmas meals. That year, the institute's newspaper, *The Crescent* (edited by Quilliam), published unprecedented coverage detailing the events surrounding the feedings. Based on examination of descriptions from other years, albeit less detailed in each case, 1898 appears to be a typical account of Christmas Day at the LMI. Thus, the proceedings of 1898 are thoroughly examined in this chapter and supplemented with pertinent details from other years to fill in gaps. By doing so, an image emerges of what it might have been like to witness the events leading up to and on Christmas Day at the LMI in the mid-to-late 1890s.[15] This chapter also explores the LMI's motivations for the feedings, fundraising and preparations for the meals and Christmas celebrations, juxtaposed with major Islamic holidays, and analyses reaction to the feedings by other Muslims and the local press.

Motivations for the feedings

The motivations for the Christmas feedings most often expressed in *The Crescent* were helping the needy, as prescribed in Islam, and educating the public about Muslims' respect and reverence for Jesus as a non-divine prophet. These are nicely encapsulated in the opening paragraph of *The Crescent*'s coverage of Christmas Day 1899:

> Apart from the good work of assisting to feed the hungry and assist the poor and the needy, two essentially Muslim virtues, the custom is a happy one, as impressing upon the general body of the public the fact that Muslims have a sincere respect for the memory of Jesus in his true position as *Sidna-Issa* [our master Jesus], the prophet of Allah.[16]

This sort of preamble to the coverage of the feedings was typical across the years. The Christmas celebrations also attempted to allay Christian fears of Islam as foreign, and to start a conversation in the press about that faith more generally, as was related in *The Crescent* in 1898:

For centuries Islam and its Prophet have been maligned and misrepresented, until the average English man or woman has come to regard the Turk as a bloodthirsty monster, steeped to his lips in human gore, and the Mussulman as a fierce fanatic, ever hungry for the blood of the Christian. The first step, therefore, required to be taken was to remove so far as possible these deep-rooted prejudices and erroneous ideas, and replace them with a truer conception of the noble and glorious teachings of Islam.[17]

However, these efforts may have been blunted by the converts' penchant for mercilessly mocking Christians. There are countless examples, including from 1895:

The day on which Christians believe that the prophet *Isaa* [Jesus], whom they in their blind credulity worship as God incarnate in human flesh, was born, is always a day of activity among the English Muslims at Liverpool, as on that occasion they embrace the opportunity of exhibiting to the *Nasaranee* [Christians] that although they reject and condemn the false and blasphemous notions the latter hold as to the divinity of Jesus, yet that the True Believers honour and respect the memory of Christ the prophet and apostle of the One only true and undividable Deity, and further exemplify to the world, in a most practicable manner, that the religion of Islam inculcates almsgiving to the deserving poor and the needy as one of the pillars of faith.[18]

The British Muslims also used the feedings as an opportunity for *da'wah*, the propagation of Islam. Ali Köse bluntly states that 'Quilliam undertook social work in the interest of spreading Islam', including the Christmas feedings.[19] In 1896, at the culmination of Christmas Day activities, Quilliam was quoted as saying: 'Ten years ago, they called me a madman, five years ago they pelted me and my brother Muslims with mud and stones, tonight they cheer us. Perhaps in another ten years they will believe with us, *Inshallah* [God willing].'[20] Still, Quilliam was explicit about not proselytizing at the Christmas feedings, as he stated, 'Islam scorns to reach a man's heart by means of his belly!'[21] Therefore, at best, the Christmas feedings were a passive form of *da'wah*.

The British converts always straddled the culture of their birth and the culture of their adopted faith. Humayun Ansari argues that Islamicizing Christian practices was central to the converts' identity: 'By adopting rituals, such as the singing of suitable hymns at Sunday services in the mosque and celebrating Christmas as a way of conveying respect for Jesus as a prophet, we learn about how Quilliam sought to construct an indigenous British Islamic tradition, stripping it of its perception as an alien and unsuitable faith in the popular imagination.'[22] Jamie Gilham furthers this point: 'All local Muslims were able to practice a syncretic form of the school of Sunni Islamic jurisprudence (the dominant creed in the Ottoman Empire) with familiar "Christian" elements and partake in its socio-religious activities. Indeed, Quilliam himself actively encouraged fellow Muslims to develop their faith through a combination of prayer, fasting and festivals.'[23] When Cairo-based Ottoman visitor Yusuf Samih Asmay (d.1942) asked Quilliam why they held the Christmas festivities, Quilliam reportedly said, 'We have to follow the national customs of the country.'[24]

As with the other syncretic practices of the British Muslim converts, it seems reasonable to conclude that the Christmas celebrations also served as a comfort to the former Christians during the season. Their families who had not converted to Islam would have celebrated Christmas as would many of their non-Muslim friends and associates. The descriptions of the events and general cheerfulness with which they were undertaken seem to dispel the notion of a cold calculus of putting on a good face to allay fears of Islam or convert more Christians. It can be argued that they were simply enjoying the season, fellowship and ultimately the English, or British, culture of their birth.

Fundraising and logistics

Over the years, the Liverpool Muslims developed several ways to fund and otherwise supply food, sundries and services for the Christmas meals. From at least 1896 to 1899, the first event held was a concert in support of what was dubbed variously the Christmas Free Breakfast Fund, Christmas Breakfast Fund, Christmas Free Meals Fund, Christmas *Zakat* (almsgiving) Fund, *Zakat* Fund for Free Meals to Poor People, *Zakat* Feast, *Zakat* Festival or Winter Feast. The concerts were held in late November or early December in the institute's large lecture hall and occurred in place of one of the weekly group meetings such as the Liverpool Muslim Literary and Debating Society. The well-attended concerts consisted of multiple entertainments by female and male LMI members and supporters. Examples of the entertainments were electricity demonstrations, magic shows, songs, various recitations and other amusements.[25] In 1898, the concert took in 11s. 1d. and the following year, 7s. 7d.[26] The funds required to stage a feeding were between £6 and £7 in addition to other food and material donations. Thus, the concerts were not a significant source of revenue for funding the Christmas meals, however, they were a means of deferring some costs as well as providing an opportunity for light-hearted communing within the group before embarking on the Christmas preparations.

Staging an event such as the concert would have necessitated an ad hoc committee, which generally formed in one of the weekly gatherings held at the LMI. It is unclear if concert preparations were dealt with by the *Zakat* Fund Committee, which handled all aspects of *zakat* distribution, not just at Christmas, or if the concert necessitated a committee of its own. However, it appears that it was clearly differentiated from the Christmas Free Breakfast Committee, tasked with preparing for the actual meals. Although the latter committee's title varied year to year, it was often not formed until mid-December, too late to have arranged the concerts.

The committee for preparing the Christmas meals had several designations in *The Crescent* to describe its function, ranging from the Christmas Free Breakfast Committee or *Zakat* Committee to 'special' or 'executive' committees. Once again, they were formed at other group meetings. For instance, in 1895, at the LMI Amateur Dramatic Company meeting on 18 December, or in mid-December 1899 after a Sunday lecture by Quilliam.[27] The committee structure consisted of Quilliam as chairman with a secretary and treasurer, and a dozen or more other members filling out the main body. Membership of the secretary and treasurer roles changed virtually every year, and additional officers in some years included a vice-chairman and a secretary to the Ladies Committee. The officers were exclusively men except for the secretary to the Ladies Committee, despite women making up a large portion of the overall committee membership and volunteer force for the festivities.

The committee work consisted of meeting several times in the weeks leading up to Christmas to make sure that donations and preparations were on track. The week before Christmas was particularly busy for the committee in general and for individual members tasked with carrying out tasks to ensure the event's success. Issues that needed to be considered were ticket printing and distribution; adequate seating, tables, crockery and utensils; decorations; volunteer assignments for Christmas Eve preparations and both Christmas Day feedings; entertainment; food and drink purchases and delivery; and donation collection books and funds collection.

The Muslims donated to support the Christmas meals as part of their obligatory *zakat* contributions, which is set out in the Qur'an (76:8): 'And they feed, for the love of Allah, the indigent, the orphan and the captive', but they also raised funds through other means. Some members were given collection books and tasked with obtaining subscriptions specifically for the Christmas

Zakat Fund. The number of credited cash supporters in any year was relatively small compared to the membership of the LMI, especially considering that many of the contributors were not even Muslim. For instance, twenty-three people were listed as either collectors and/or contributors in 1898, thirty-seven in 1899, twelve in 1900, forty-six in 1901, thirty-five in 1902 and fourteen in 1903.[28] However, these lists were not exhaustive, as not all contributors wanted to be named. Moreover, there was often a note stating that some subscription books were outstanding, and a few contributors would have given donations in smaller amounts in the collection box or by other means. In all years mentioned above, Quilliam donated exactly £1 1s. of his own money, an amount that seems to have become his customary donation. He was also one of the chief subscription collectors, taking in an additional £1 to £2 each year. Therefore, he was responsible for nearly a third to one-half of the requisite cash donations for the feedings annually, which was in line with his overall financial support of the LMI.

Other means of cash donations included: children of members and children of the Medina Home orphanage (explained below) collecting pennies, the LMI collection box and even members no longer living in England, such as L. Hanifa Jones donating 7s. while she was in America in 1898.[29] In three of the four years enumerated, 1899, 1900 and 1903, a balance due to the treasurer to pay for the Christmas feedings was still outstanding in January, by more than £2 and £3 in the latter years. Any shortfalls were likely paid out of the general *Zakat* Fund. From 1901 to 1903, when Ramadan (the Muslim month of fasting) fell in December, Muslims were inspired to give more, with £6 to £7 collected before Christmas in those years. An account from 1903 provides us with a sample of the types of purchases the funds might cover. More than a third of the funds paid for bread, bun loaf and seed loaf (Williams and Norrie – £2 12s. 6d.); nearly a third was spent on beef and other groceries (George Fletcher – £1 9s. 1d.), tea (Pegram's – 14s.), collection books, tickets and other printing (12s. 6d.); and the remainder was spent on extra mugs, jugs, a new bench, table covers, tacks, a tin opener, postage, coal and wood and extra cleaning.[30]

There were many non-cash donations of provisions as well as discounts offered at either wholesale or at cost prices. In 1898, the following was acquired at such discounts: meat, tea, coffee, sugar, butter and mustard from John Fletcher (wholesale); milk from Billal Ambrose (at cost); and crockery from Alderman Ephraim Walker (wholesale). Also that year, Mrs. Evans lent tablecloths for the occasion and Quilliam donated a dozen spoons, five-dozen tin plates and several small banners.[31] The previous year, Poole's Golden Bonus Tea Company donated five pounds of tea.[32] In 1899, the following donations were made: Hutchinson's Karo Tea Company, ten pounds of tea; A. E. Toulzac, twenty-eight pounds of sultana cake; J. M. Hay, twenty-two pounds of sugar; and Ethel Mariam Quilliam, a length of muslin and time spent sewing tea bags from the cloth.[33]

After funding and provisions acquisition, attention was focused on the people to be fed. Although they never wanted to turn a hungry person away, to bring order to the feasts, the Muslims eventually implemented a ticket distribution system to limit the feedings to a manageable size. It is unclear when tickets were first used; however, in 1895 and 1896 respectively, a pre-set number of 500 and 600 people was mentioned prior to Christmas and at least indicates a move towards limiting the number of people to be served.[34] In 1897, it was mentioned in *The Crescent* that the LMI, 'every Christmas distributes tickets to hundreds of poor starving Christians'.[35] By then, tickets had been firmly established. Up to three weeks prior to Christmas, the poor would present themselves at the LMI or the Medina Home to apply for tickets. In 1898, there was an anecdote about Quilliam and Walid Feridoun Preston, LMI treasurer, being followed for a quarter mile by people begging for tickets, which they were apparently given.[36] In 1900, the tickets were distributed at the LMI on the evenings of 22, 23 and 24 December. There are some indications from that same year that the LMI used the demand for tickets to decide whether to have multiple sittings at each meal and thereby expand the total number of people to be fed.[37]

The final preparations for the meals began late on Christmas Eve, when two to three dozen Muslims assembled at the institute. The group mainly consisted of men, but also included women and youth from the Osmanli Regiment, a militaristic wing of the LMI's Liverpool Muslim College.[38] The disparity in gender is likely due to the nature of the manual labour required for the initial organization of the premises. The Muslims arranged tables and seating, decorated the hall with banners and other items, set up the food preparation area and arranged the fireplaces for the next day, breaking only for *salat al-'isa* (night prayer). This initial spurt of work usually lasted until nearly midnight. At around 6.00 am on Christmas Day, the next wave of work would commence, when one or two members would arrive to warm up the rooms by lighting the fires. A little while after, a handful of other helpers would arrive, including Quilliam and members of his family. By 7.00 am there would be a strong contingent of workers ready to get started with the tasks assigned to them. Duties ranged from staffing the cloakroom or the front door to prevent early arrivals from venturing into the hall, to preparing tea and coffee, setting tables, carrying trays of food and jugs of drinks and slicing loaves of bread and meat. The early arrivals included more women than the previous evening's proceedings; the adult LMI members who volunteered on Christmas Day 1898 comprised twenty-five women and forty-four men, many participating in both morning and evening feedings.[39] At around 8.00 am, the Muslims broke for *salat al-fajr* (dawn prayer) led by Quilliam, by which time more than three dozen Muslims were assembled. The group then quickly ate breakfast before opening the doors to the large crowd waiting outside the institute.[40]

Christmas feedings

The crowd would have been gathering since at least eight o'clock on Christmas Day morning, likely pondering the unfamiliar gold star and crescent above the LMI entrance as well as the green Islamic standard fluttering in the cold morning air. The sharply dressed boys of the Osmanli Regiment, parading replete with red fezzes, would have presented another striking juxtaposition with the hoard of people described as follows:

> Ill-clad Christians … old and young, boys and girls, men and women, halt and lame; the old man tottering with the aid of a stick, and the young mother with her little infant at her breast; the stalwart man and the puny child – all poor, all wretched, all ill-clad, and most of them strangers to the use of soap and water and the advantages of personal cleanliness, but all Christians.[41]

Not all of the attendees were British or Christian; some were immigrant Jews from countries such as Russia and Poland. About thirty minutes before the doors opened, those with tickets were queued according to gender and age, forming lines of boys to the left, girls to the right and the elderly up front. Each line was overseen by an officer of the Osmanli Regiment, while other LMI members officiated as required.

At nine o'clock, the LMI doors were propped open, and the groups were led in, the older adults first, followed by the youngest children, then the girls, lastly the boys and young adults. Two members of the Osmanli Regiment collected tickets and led the guests into the lecture hall, where they were presented with a cavernous space refurbished and enlarged only three years earlier, dedicated just in time for the Christmas meals of 1895. The entrance hall and openings around the stage were in the Moorish style and the lighting, cornices and frieze were Arabesque. The mouldings were salmon in colour, and the arches were fitted with wrought iron inset with azure and rose-coloured glass.[42] The walls were decorated with various banners and plaques with Arabic inscriptions as well as flags of many Islamic lands, such as the crimson with white star and crescent standard of the Ottoman Empire; the simple red and black field flags of Morocco and the Emirate of Afghanistan respectively; the sword-wielding lion and sun banner of Persia; and the striped flag of the 'Sudanese dervish'.[43] This must have presented an impressive, if not bewildering, exotic aspect for the guests. They were led to tables by members of the LMI, still separated into the groupings established before entering the hall.

The seating of over 200 guests took between ten and fifteen minutes, during which time a cacophonous 'hubbub of conversation' commenced.[44] At precisely 9.15 am, the conversation ceased when Quilliam blew a whistle and took to the stage to give a short speech. He wished the group glad tidings of the season and then described how the food would be served, and his expectations for their behaviour. Specifically, he assured them that there would be enough food for all and requested that they remain polite and patient with each other and the servers. The crowd agreed and applauded. Quilliam then assured those assembled that no religion would be preached on this occasion, but the requisite prayer of thanks in the name of 'God, the Merciful and Compassionate' was in order. Again, the crowd applauded. Quilliam asked them to repeat the following lines in unison: 'Be present at our table, Lord. Be here and everywhere adored. Thy creature bless and grant that we may feast in paradise with thee.'[45] He then proceeded to say *bismillah* (invocation: 'In the name of Allah') in Arabic and, without further delay, the food was served.

The meals for the breakfast and the evening tea were the same and went unchanged throughout the years. First, large plates of beef sandwiches and bread and butter were carried into the hall, followed by tea, coffee, milk and condiments such as mustard and sugar. Last, heaps of seed loaf and bun loaf were brought in on platters.[46] There are hints at the amount of food and drink needed for the two meals. In describing the work required to prepare the food in 1898, it was estimated that, laid end-to-end, the loaves of bread sliced by the volunteers would have reached eighty feet in length. The bun loaf, seed loaf, meat and butter were of 'similar relative quantities'.[47] Furthermore, roughly ten pounds of tea and twenty-two pounds of sugar were supplied for the feedings, along with many gallons of coffee.[48] The tea and coffee required constant attention from workers boiling water in large cauldrons and brewing the drinks before filling large jugs and urns, which were turned over to a separate detail of workers. Quilliam oversaw the entire venture.

Each table grouping was supervised by a small cadre of LMI volunteers to service the needs of the guests, serve platters of food and refill drinks. It was reported that many ate the food as if they were famished, whereas others savoured the meal as if it may have been the heartiest of the year. A cheer rose from the crowd at the appearance of both the seed loaf and the bun loaf. The crowd was allowed to linger and fill their stomachs with as much food as they wished, some apparently exclaiming 'enough' when they could hold no more.[49] When entertainment was provided in the morning, it was usually in the form of recitations or musical performances such as a pianoforte or organ solo towards the end of the sitting. In years of greater need, a second sitting would occur around 10.00 am, otherwise the event ended no later than 10.30 am.[50] The assembled cheered when Quilliam asked if they had had enough to eat, and the Osmanli Regiment escorted the crowd from the hall. On more than one occasion, a spontaneous cheer was given for Quilliam and the Muslims as the full-bellied poor filed out of the hall. Upon reaching the street, each guest was presented with the gift of an orange, and clothing was distributed to the neediest.[51] Without delay, in the hall, the men gathered up the plates, saucers and cups, while the women washed them. The tables and chairs were rearranged, and the space cleaned and prepped for the evening tea.

Perhaps, at this point, some of the Muslims made their way to the Medina Home for Children, escorting the older children of the home who had helped with the breakfast. By 1898, the home was about two years old, having been created in the last days of 1896, when Quilliam issued a notice to discuss its viability. The idea of the home was reputedly spurred when a Jewish woman approached Quilliam on the street asking to have her child taken in and brought up as a Muslim. Parents were willing to pay a small amount of money for their children to receive a good home with proper care and feeding and allow the parents to work, find lodging for themselves and carry on with their lives. Although all of the first children offered to the home had been male, Quilliam made it clear that he was in favour of taking in both boys and girls. Their parents had to sign papers waiving rights to the children and agree to them being raised as Muslims. A local Muslim convert, L. Hanifa Jones, made a motion to call the institution the Medina Home for Children, in homage to the Prophet Muhammad's fleeing Mecca for the safe confines of Medina.[52] A few years later, Yusuff Nunan described the rationale for the home's creation as, 'in order to rescue from the workhouse, from pernicious surroundings, and even from starvation, those poor, innocent little children who come into this world uncared and unasked for'.[53]

Oddly, the children of the Medina Home were treated to a more traditional celebration of Christmas than the LMI's rhetoric purported. In 1897, the children had a plum pudding, oranges, biscuits and a large cake. Furthermore, presents such as dolls, trains, other toys, furniture and clothing were given to the children by Muslims and non-Muslims alike.[54] This was acknowledged and celebrated in *The Crescent*, obviously with the support of Quilliam and the matron of the Medina Home. At Christmas 1898, the children were served special food, including a 'plump' turkey given by Quilliam, and several Muslim women gave gifts such as clothes, dolls, games, colour picture books, tea sets, rattles and more. Quilliam also donated a swing and an iron shovel. *The Crescent* was glowing in its appreciation for the donations and the happiness it brought to the children. It stated, 'One little boy got possession of a toy drum, and never ceased to play it all the day except at meal and prayer times.'[55]

At about 5.00 pm, volunteers reassembled at the LMI and the Muslims performed *salat al-magrib* (sunset prayer) before preparing food for the night's festivities. The evening tea generally had a significantly higher attendance and almost always required two sittings. Throughout the years, attendance averaged 200–300 in the morning and 300–400 in the evening. In 1908, it was claimed in *The Crescent* that, across two decades, the combined number of people fed during Christmas, *Mawlid* (Prophet Muhammad's birthday), after funerals and other occasions totalled about 22,000.[56] That figure is impossible to corroborate. Feeding 500–700 people per year at Christmas for twenty years would account for roughly 10,000–14,000 of the stated number. In 1903, the total number fed up to that point was listed at 13,000.[57] It seems unlikely that 9,000 additional people were fed in the subsequent five years, considering that the total number had been increasing by only about 1,000 per year. However, if *Mawlid* and other feedings not reported in *The Crescent* were included in the 1908 total, perhaps the number was accurate. Due to the larger number of guests, the volunteer ranks swelled up to a hundred during the tea, compared with half these numbers in the morning. In one case, fifty Indian sailors passing through Liverpool stayed to help after attending *salat al-'isa* at the institute.[58] Some of the workers would have been the same as in the morning, but many only volunteered for one service. Not all of the helpers were Muslim, but rather friends and family of members of the LMI, interested supporters and those connected to Quilliam through the Temperance Movement.[59]

After the last sitting, at about 8.00 pm, the guests were escorted out of the hall. Those who were not staying for the entertainment were given leftovers to take home.[60] With the tables cleared and the seating rearranged to face the LMI stage, the guests were readmitted for the evening's entertainment, usually to overflowing capacity. Often the entertainment included some sort of musical performance. For instance, one year, Quilliam's sons performed on the zither and fairy bells accompanied by a mandolin; another year, Mr. Fry's amateur Pierrot troupe performed.[61] Other musical entertainments were pianoforte solos performed by LMI members. Sample selections may have included the '*Hamidieh* March' (Ottoman imperial anthem) and the 'Turkish Patrol March'.[62]

Since as early as 1892, a hallmark of the evening entertainment was magic lantern shows featuring hundreds of slides. During this period, common Christmas leisure activities for adults and children were concerts, pantomimes and magic lantern slide shows.[63] Quilliam's slides often showed scenes from his travels around England, the Isle of Man, France, West Africa, Ottoman cities such as Constantinople and other 'Eastern' lands. Furthermore, in any given year, there may have been selections of comic, coloured or moving slides accompanied by appropriate piano music. Quilliam invariably provided the narration while LMI members H. Nasrullah Warren, Thomas A. Ridpath and other volunteers operated the oxy-hydrogen light source and slides.

The programme of entertainment ended between 10.00 and 10.30 pm, and the visitors were ushered to the exits. As in the morning, the events often finished with a round of cheers initiated by the appreciative audience. After the crowd had dispersed, Quilliam addressed the volunteers assembled in the lecture hall:

> Both Christ and Mahomed taught that the one who fed the hungry and assisted the poor was sure of a reward in paradise. A good conscience is a prize. The knowledge of good works done in the cause of humanity is a comforting solace to the mind, and that, I am sure, each of you must enjoy tonight.[64]

Islamic festivals and events at the LMI

The Islamic festivals and other events celebrated at the LMI were distinct from the Christmas festivities but had some features in common with them. In February 1899, less than two months after the well-covered 1898 Christmas feedings, *The Crescent* again provided unprecedented coverage of another celebration, '*Id al-Fitr* (festival of breaking the fast), marking the end of Ramadan. In July 1900, the paper also covered the celebration of *Mawlid*.[65] The Islamic events were more insular festivities. Although non-Muslims were present at '*Ids* (Muslim religious festivals), unlike at Christmas, they were not the focus of attention.

As with Christmas, LMI committees were formed to ensure the success of Islamic festivals and events, and would likely have had similar numbers of participants, each assigned a variety of duties. The difference between Christmas and 'Ids was apparent from the very beginning in 1899: at sundown, to mark the end of Ramadan, percussive fireworks were fired into the air; later that evening, the final portion of the Qur'an was read, *salat al-'isa* performed and several Muslims remained to put the finishing touches on decorations and preparations for *'Id al-Fitr*.[66] The following day, special prayers were performed and, in the evening, celebrations commenced. The LMI and Medina Home for Children were decorated as for the Christmas meals but with Ottoman and Islamic banners and bunting on the exterior and 'Bengal lights' illuminating the front of the building.[67] There were also Islamic emblems and scripture from the Qur'an adorning the interior walls, and coloured lanterns lit the hallways. Unlike Christmas, when Quilliam's sole item of Muslim clothing was generally a red fez, for the Muslim celebrations he wore flowing white and gold robes decorated with medals from the Ottoman sultan. Children and youth from the Muslim College and Medina Home wore 'Zouave' dress, likely some combination of pantaloons, vests and turbans or fezzes.[68] Attendance was also broadened for the Muslim celebrations: whereas only older members of the Medina Home for Children attended the Christmas Day meals to assist, all pupils from the Medina Home and the Muslim College were expected to attend Islamic festivals and other events.

In the lecture hall, the Muslims gathered to hear speeches and conversion testimonies. This was followed by reading letters and telegrams expressing congratulations and felicitations from afar. Then, a concert performed by several female members of the institute as well as more fireworks, musical selections and recitations filled the night. In 1903, other entertainments included a cinematograph display, a short comedy entitled '*Rubaiyeh's* Romance' written by Quilliam's elder son, Robert Ahmed (1880–1954), a mechanical contraption called 'The Flying Horse' and parlour games. The festivities ended just after midnight with the playing of the '*Hamidieh* March' in honour of the Ottoman sultan-caliph.[69]

The LMI and Medina Home were decorated for the *Mawlid* celebrations in a similar manner as at *'Id al-Fitr*. At sundown and the turning of a new day, Muslims gathered at the LMI and Quilliam would deliver a lecture in the large hall. The Muslims then moved to the mosque for a *du'a* (prayer of supplication) and a special service in honour of the Prophet Muhammad. The following day was a holiday for the Muslim school children and that evening there would be a feeding of the poor from the neighbourhood. Although not mentioned, it can be assumed that the organization, fare and preparations would have been similar to the Christmas meals since that process was virtually unchanged across this period. In 1900, it was estimated that 500 hungry people were fed on *Mawlid*. One divergence from Christmas was the participation of staff from the Ottoman consulate in Liverpool. Small amounts of money, toffee and sweetmeats were also given to children as they left. After the dinner guests dispersed, the Muslims engaged in entertainment and games until about 10.00 pm.[70]

Reactions to the feedings

Muslims from around the world participated in the Christmas festivities as they passed through Liverpool or as a result of their membership of the LMI. However, few records have emerged detailing their opinions of the Christmas celebrations, or the views of Muslims abroad. One that has recently come to light is by the Ottoman Yusuf Samih Asmay, who levelled a charge of *bid'ah* (innovation in religious matters) against Quilliam when referring to *'Id al-Fitr* and *'Id al-Adha* (feast of the sacrifice marking the end of the annual Hajj, or Pilgrimage to Mecca): 'Mr. Quilliam has increased them to three by adding to these two religious Eids the Eid of [Christ's] birth, which is called "Christmas".[71] Asmay called such perceived unorthodoxy at the LMI 'Qulliamist innovation', and regarded the community as more like a Sufi order,[72] dubbing its members 'the Quilliamiyya'.[73] Ottoman uncomfortableness with the LMI's Christmas festivities seems to be further corroborated by the lack of participation by Ottoman consulate personnel in the feedings, in contrast to their involvement on Islamic holidays.

On the other hand, the Liverpool press was supportive of the LMI's Christmas efforts. In the early years, local newspapers such as the *Liverpool Daily Post* and *Liverpool Mercury* covered the events as the reporters witnessed them, with little editorializing and a tendency to use positive terms such as 'generosity' and 'kind-hearted' while noting that the occasions were non-sectarian and not used for proselytizing.[74] In 1897, the coverage changed with the *Mercury* providing broader coverage of the event and broaching Muslim beliefs about Jesus and Islamic theology more broadly, and the *Liverpool Daily Courier* followed suit in 1898.[75] By 1899, the *Daily Post* stated: 'Islam is not anti-Christian, but rather a semi-Christian faith.'[76] In 1901 and 1902, Christmas fell in Ramadan and both the feedings and the Muslim fasting garnered special attention and admiration.[77]

These same years marked a change; it is likely that the LMI started handing out copy to reporters with details about the numbers fed, who participated and information about Muslim beliefs. This assertion is based on the local newspapers printing nearly identical articles with only minor edits differentiating them. Again, in 1907, nearly the same article covering the feedings was published in several local newspapers.[78]

Based on the Muslims' motivations for the feedings and the reaction by the local press, the Christmas Day events were a success. The Muslims were acknowledged for feeding their hungry neighbours, an act of charity that the newspapers tied directly to their Islamic faith. Further, the message that Islam respected and venerated Jesus became standard in the press coverage. Although it took nearly a decade before the press hit all the points on Islam that Quilliam and his Muslim community had hoped for since they began the feedings, the motivations for these eventually lined up rather well with their coverage in the local media.

Conclusion

From nearly its inception, the LMI made Christmas a cornerstone of its calendar of activities, philanthropy and social outreach to non-Muslims. It was a multifaceted, complex undertaking, which had become well-organized by the mid-1890s, requiring assistance from LMI members, young and old, as well as from non-Muslim supporters. Their motivations ranged from religious obligation and explaining the role of Jesus in Islam to promoting Islam more generally and keeping in touch with a central feature of British Christian culture. Nonetheless, the distinct activities during 'Ids and *Mawlid*, although still Westernized, showed an evolution towards a more Muslim cultural life, a time to celebrate as Muslims without the glare from as many outsiders or feeling obligated to tone down their 'otherness'. Although some Muslims certainly looked askance at the LMI's Christmas celebrations, the Liverpool press reaction was supportive of the Muslims' work, indicating that the Muslims were largely successful in fulfilling their aims.

11

Authority and legitimacy in Victorian Liverpool: Re-evaluating Abdullah Quilliam's title of 'Sheikh-ul-Islam of the British Isles'

Matthew A. Sharp

Introduction

In July 1901, a journalist from the British periodical *Truth* reported that Indian Muslims in Constantinople (Istanbul) vehemently rejected the numerous accounts of Ottoman Sultan 'Abd al-Hamid II (1842–1918; r. 1876-1909) having conferred the title 'Sheikh-ul-Islam of the British Isles' to Abdullah Quilliam (1856-1932), a Liverpool lawyer and the most prominent convert to Islam in Britain.[1] For the Ottomans, the office and title of 'Sheikh-ul-Islam' (Shaykh al-Islam) was the highest ranking official within the Islamic scholarly community and their religious bureaucracy.[2] The charge of the Indian Muslims in Constantinople, coupled with accusations that Quilliam had mishandled the Liverpool Muslim Institute's (LMI) finances and misused donations from the Islamic world, instigated a tussle between columnists for *Truth* and *The Crescent*, the LMI's weekly periodical, over several weeks. Writing in the latter, C. Halim Wahby George (1871–1934), an LMI member and Quilliam's close associate, defended his leader and the Liverpool Muslims on all accounts. As for Quilliam being the 'Sheikh-ul-Islam of the British Isles', George countered that 'Mr. Quilliam has never claimed any title other than [what] he is legally entitled to. It is not likely that H. I. M. the Sultan would receive Mr. Quilliam so frequently as an honoured guest, as he has done and recently confer a decoration upon him, if that gentleman was masquerading under any borrowed plumes.'[3] George further argued that attempts to delegitimize Quilliam's title not only offended Quilliam but also dishonoured the Ottoman sultan-caliph.

A respondent from the *Ceylon Muhammadan* echoed George's sentiment, suggesting that, had the title of 'Sheikh-ul-Islam of the British Isles'

> been self-assumed, the head of the Islamic religion would long ago have taken steps to proclaim the fact to the world and have checked any such presumption on the Sheikh's part, for none are more jealous of the privileges appertaining to their religion than Muhammedans, and none keener in resenting any light treatment of officers connected therewith.[4]

According to Wahby George and other Muslims, the authenticity of Quilliam's title mattered for the legitimacy of both Quilliam and the Ottoman sultan-caliph. In its subsequent issues, *Truth* provided no real rebuttal, perhaps out of disinterest. *The Crescent* never again addressed the question of Quilliam's title, although there were plenty of instances before and after, when non-Muslims and Muslims (from within the LMI and without) questioned Quilliam's authority and legitimacy. By the early twentieth century, it seemed that Quilliam had secured his position as *the* Muslim figurehead and leader in Liverpool, across the UK, and among English-speaking Muslims throughout the world – at least until he fled Liverpool in 1908, never to return to the LMI or lead a Muslim community again.[5]

A century later, Abdullah Quilliam's claim to be the 'first and last Sheikh-ul-Islam of the British Isles' found new life and validation through the first substantive scholarship on Quilliam by Ron Geaves and Jamie Gilham.[6] Based on Quilliam's and the LMI's own (self-promoting) publications and other English-language articles, these scholars reproduced the narrative formulated by Quilliam and his followers that 'Abd al-Hamid II conferred the title to him sometime between 1894 and 1895. The only significant qualification they offered was that this was an 'honorific' title, but they did not elaborate on what qualified it as an honorific title, nor did they provide independent corroborating evidence for the claim. Gilham argued that, because the British Muslim community believed that 'Abd al-Hamid II had bestowed the title on Quilliam, it made the latter 'the supreme authority on Islam in Britain and leader of British Muslims', which suggests that even though it was an honorific office, it solidified his legitimacy and authority.[7] Quilliam's version of the story is now so ubiquitous that historians, journalists and Muslim community activists – in the UK and beyond – replicate, accept and even celebrate the claim that the sultan-caliph bestowed the title upon Quilliam.[8] There is a significant attachment to this narrative in contemporary Turkey and elsewhere among individuals whose nostalgia for Ottoman history is strong and who are also fixated on the figure of 'Abd al-Hamid II, whom they deem to be the last great heroic sultan-caliph.[9]

However, the validity of the claim, its actual connection to 'Abd al-Hamid II and the Ottoman state, and Quilliam's use of it as a source of recognition, legitimacy and authority have received little scrutiny thus far. Moreover, newly discovered English and Ottoman Turkish publications and other sources, specifically documents from the Ottoman Archives of the Prime Ministry (Başbakanlık Osmanlı Arşivi), indicate that Quilliam, abetted by LMI members, invented the story. This chapter shows how this happened, and also offers some theories as to what broader insights the acceptance and contestation of the invented title tell us about Islamic authority and legitimacy in Victorian Britain.

This chapter therefore reframes the received origin story of the 'Sheikh-ul-Islam' title as a matter of legitimacy and authority. Furthermore, it contends that the title provided double legitimation because both Quilliam and his community, as well as the Ottoman sultan, benefited from the narrative. The first section explains Quilliam's connection to the Ottoman state and 'Abd al-Hamid II, which laid the foundation for the narrative's plausibility: it provides the origins of the narrative, showing that the earliest reports make no mention of the sultan as the benefactor of the title. The chapter then evaluates the varying and divergent responses to the narrative through LMI accounts, Ottoman officials in Liverpool and Constantinople, Muslim intellectuals writing in Arabic and Turkish, as well as LMI members who rejected Quilliam's story. The final part of this chapter presents the historical context of the Hamidian era, which witnessed the excessive awarding of honours and medals as a means of legitimacy. This further reveals why 'Abd al-Hamid II and the Sublime Porte willingly and deliberately permitted Quilliam to promulgate the narrative that the sultan-caliph conferred on him the title and role of 'Sheikh-ul-Islam of the British Isles'. The sultan knew that the title granted Quilliam a greater level of legitimacy and authority, which he hoped would benefit his intentions to use Quilliam for his pan-Islamic agenda, and by extension further his own legitimacy and authority among Muslims under British control.

Birth of the 'Sheikh-ul-Islam' story

For Quilliam's narrative to be plausible, then and now, there had to be a real connection between him, the Ottoman state and Sultan 'Abd al-Hamid II. The Ottoman archives indicate that the first contact between the Ottoman state and Quilliam was in early 1889; however, the Ottoman consul-general assigned to Liverpool initially showed little interest. Things changed in late 1890 when

Figure 11.1 *Carte de visite* of Abdullah Quilliam presenting as 'Sheikh-ul-Islam of the British Isles', c.1905. This image is likely to date from c.1905, when Quilliam started using the prefix 'H. E.' (His Excellency) to denote that he was Ottoman honorary consul at Douglas, Isle of Man. That same year, Quilliam was awarded the *Imtiyâz* Star (Loyalty and Bravery medal) from Ottoman Sultan 'Abd al-Hamid II. The large medallion on Quilliam's chest (bottom left of the photo) appears to be the *Imtiyâz* Star. The similar medal on the opposite side (lower right of the photo) might be a replica. The group of three medals pinned to Quilliam's chest (right of the photo) are unidentifiable. It is possible that Quilliam is wearing masonic decorations or medals presented to his children (or other members of the LMI) by the Ottoman sultan or other Muslim leaders, to exaggerate his importance.
Source: Photographer unknown. Courtesy of Jahangir Mohammed

Quilliam and the LMI's vice-president Rafiuddin Ahmed (1865–1954) publicly denounced Hall Caine's (1853–1931) play *Mahomet* (1890) because its depiction of the Prophet Muhammad was insulting to Muslims. This drew the attention of the Ottoman ambassador in London and officials in Constantinople, prompting them to instruct their consul-general in Liverpool, Dimitri Mavrokordato, to undertake a fact-finding mission regarding Quilliam and the LMI. From these early engagements, Quilliam received an official invitation to Constantinople in 1891, which established a relationship between 'Abd al-Hamid II and the Ottoman state with Quilliam, his family and the LMI that lasted nearly twenty years.

Mavrokordato's successor, Ismail Lütfi Bey (Simavı, 1862–1933), cultivated this relationship, culminating in a clear overture from Quilliam that he would place his publications at the service of the sultan-caliph and to promote Ottoman interests. Scholarship has demonstrated that 'Abd al-Hamid II and the Ottoman Foreign Ministry often bribed and enlisted European and American journalists, editors, politicians and others to participate in the Ottoman state's 'damage control and image management' policy.[10] Quilliam's contribution to this agenda was not particularly unique, but what set him apart was his willingness to perform these duties *gratis*. In addition, Quilliam declared his loyalty to 'Abd al-Hamid II due to his belief in the sultan's spiritual role as the caliph of all Sunni Muslims, and adhered to his own version of the pan-Islamic ethos that the sultan-caliph espoused. However, Quilliam's loyalty to 'Abd al-Hamid II was not absolute due to his competing loyalty to the British Crown. He maintained, especially in later years, what one might consider a doctrine of dual loyalty.[11]

In early 1894, Mahommed Shitta (1824–1895) of Lagos wrote to Quilliam, asking him to forward a petition to the Ottoman sultan on his behalf. Shitta and his community sought 'Abd al-Hamid II's caliphal favour and imperial recognition at the opening of a new mosque in Lagos, to which Shitta significantly contributed financially. Quilliam mentioned in his letter to Constantinople that he was willing to travel to Lagos as an official Ottoman representative. Although the exact details of the Sublime Porte's instructions to Quilliam have not been found, 'Abd al-Hamid II commissioned Quilliam to represent him at the mosque's opening.[12] In large part due to Quilliam's intervention, the sultan honoured Shitta with a Fourth Class *Mecîdî* Order medallion.[13]

When Quilliam returned from West Africa in the summer of 1894, LMI members hosted a celebratory event to congratulate him for his service to the sultan-caliph and to Islam in West Africa under British imperial control. It was at this event that Maulana Muhammad Barakatullah Bhopali (*c.*1859–1927; see Chapter 9), the LMI's imam (Muslim religious leader) and key instructor at the time, proposed a resolution that LMI members recognize Quilliam as the 'Sheikh-ul-Islam of the British Isles'. Barakatullah claimed that 'No man had ever more truly merited the title of Sheik[h]-ul-Islam', as evidenced by Quilliam's distinguished role in introducing Islam to Britain and his many other contributions in service to Islam.[14] Perhaps even more significant was Barakatullah's report that the Amir of Afghanistan 'had recognized Bro[ther] Quilliam's work, and addressed him with that honourable title'.[15] The 'Sheikh-ul-Islam' title for Quilliam had appeared in publications from Lahore prior to 1894.[16] Additionally, Mahommed Shitta and his brother addressed Quilliam as the 'Sheikh-ul-Islam' in their letter requesting his assistance in correspondence with 'Abd al-Hamid II, but there is no explanation for why they did this.[17] However, there is no extant evidence that Quilliam or other LMI members habitually used the title before or shortly after October 1894. Instead, they simply referred to him as 'Brother Quilliam' or 'our president'. Unfortunately, the entire 1894 run of *The Crescent* is lost, so it is unclear how the LMI community responded to Barakatullah's resolution or exactly when the title became a part of their common parlance. The majority of LMI members were recent converts and probably knew next to nothing about the religious significance of such a title. Once it became part of Quilliam's identity after 1895, there is no indication that LMI members saw it as merely an 'honorific' title.

In both *The Crescent* and the LMI's monthly journal, *The Islamic World*, between 1895 and 1896, there were a variety of self-assumed roles and titles attributed to Quilliam, such as 'Sheikh-ul-Islam of the United English and American Moslem Societies', which was a title meant to solidify allegiances with English-speaking Muslims due to a dispute between Quilliam and his American rival, Mohammed Alexander Russell Webb (1846–1916).[18] Within *The Crescent* and *The Islamic World*, there was little mention of 'Abd al-Hamid II honouring Quilliam with this title. The exact origin story for the sultan bestowing the title is far more obscure. The earliest and clearest association of the title with 'Abd al-Hamid II appeared in the editorial notes of *The Crescent* in August 1895, when it was announced that 'Sheikh Abdullah Quilliam received on Friday last from Constantinople his official seal as Sheikh-ul-Islam of the British Isles.'[19] However, if, as reported in *The Crescent*, Quilliam received an 'official seal' from 'Abd al-Hamid II, then Ottoman documents ought to either mention the event or at least in future correspondence show appropriate deference and honour to him. Such documents or correspondence have not been located in the Ottoman Archives or elsewhere.

The response of Ottoman officials in England and Constantinople

In 1896, Quilliam issued his first *fatwa* (juridical opinion) condemning Muslims who cooperated with British attempts to subdue Muslims in Sudan. As a mark of his authority and legitimacy, Quilliam signed the *fatwa* in *The Crescent* as 'Sheikh-ul-Islam of the British Isles'.[20] In documents held in the Ottoman Archives, a high-ranking Ottoman official overtly omitted 'Sheikh-ul-Islam of the British Isles' in connection with this *fatwa*. Shortly after the publication of the *fatwa* in *The Crescent*, Quilliam wrote directly to Mehmet Cemaleddin (1848–1917), the Ottoman Shaykh al-Islam, petitioning for Cemaleddin's approval and clarification on the details of the *fatwa*. In the letter translated in Ottoman Turkish, Quilliam signed it *re'is-i cemiyet-i İslamiyet* (president of the Islamic Society), but in the attached translations of the *fatwa* (in Arabic and Ottoman Turkish) he included 'Sheikh-ul-Islam of the British Isles'. The internal response from the Office of the Ottoman Shaykh al-Islam only referred to Quilliam as the *re'is-i cemiyet-i İslamiyet*, with no mention of the other title.[21] If 'Abd al-Hamid II had truly conferred the 'Sheikh-ul-Islam' title on Quilliam in 1894 or 1895, it would be assumed that the Office of the Ottoman Shaykh al-Islam would acknowledge him with his title, honorific or not, out of deference to the sultan-caliph.

Another important Ottoman figure was Esad Kenan Bey, the Ottoman consul-general in Liverpool at the time when the sultan supposedly bestowed the title upon Quilliam. Had 'Abd al-Hamid II done so, then Kenan Bey would have mentioned the matter in his communiques to London and Constantinople, but there is no such record. Rather, Kenan Bey levelled harsh criticisms at Quilliam and the Liverpool Muslims in his reports to Rüstem Paşa (d. 1895), the Ottoman ambassador in London.[22] Kenan Bey was very aware of stories about elevated titles. For example, he mentioned that, ever since the Amir of Afghanistan sent a letter to Quilliam conferring upon him the title of 'Sheikh of the Muslims of the British Isles', Quilliam often signed his name 'Sheikh Abdullah Quilliam'.[23] However, based on the content and tone of Kenan Bey's report, it is clear that he dismissed Quilliam as a legitimate leader of the Muslims in Liverpool and mocked the very idea of him being called a 'Sheikh', let alone the 'Sheikh-ul-Islam of the British Isles'.

Furthermore, among the extensive number of pages and documents pertaining to Quilliam and the LMI in the Ottoman Archives between 1889 and 1909, there is no evidence that 'Abd al-Hamid II issued an imperial *irâde* (Sultanic decree) to confer the title to Quilliam in any way, nor is there evidence of Ottoman officials referring to Quilliam, either honorifically or otherwise, as the 'Sheikh-ul-Islam of the British Isles', or even simply as a 'Sheikh-ul-Islam'. The only instances when it appears in Ottoman documents are when officials translated Quilliam's stationery, which carried the title: 'The Office of Sheikh-ul-Islam of the British Isles'. In fact, it is very difficult to find an example of Ottoman officials who willingly acknowledged Quilliam as a 'Sheikh'. Instead, most Ottoman officials, whether in Liverpool, London or Constantinople, simply referred to him as 'Mr. Quilliam' or, most commonly, '*re'is-i cemiyet-i İslamiyet*'. There are instances of officials attaching '*fahri*' (honorary), '*bey*' or '*effendi*' (both meaning lord, sir or master) to his name or the name of his eldest son, Robert Ahmed Quilliam (1880–1954); this was all part of Ottoman custom to show deference and honour to individuals by referring to them by their appointed titles, be they honorific or not.

The response of Muslim intellectuals and scholars

According to Yusuf Samih Asmay (d. 1942), an Ottoman journalist who visited the Liverpool Muslims in the summer of 1895 and interviewed Quilliam, the latter gave him a business card that read 'Sheikh al-Islam of the City of Liverpool'.[24] It would appear that, in 1895, Quilliam was not widely peddling the story of his 'Sheikh-ul-Islam of the British Isles' title, or at least it had yet to become pervasive, even at the LMI. Along with Asmay, there were other Muslim intellectuals who either responded to or seemingly overlooked Quilliam's claim to be the 'Sheikh-ul-Islam of the British Isles'. This is not to say that Muslim intellectuals and scholars outright ignored Quilliam. Indeed, there are numerous examples of Muslim scholars who commented on Quilliam's efforts to spread Islam in Britain.

In fact, several prominent Muslim intellectuals and translators in the Arabic and Ottoman Turkish-speaking world either translated some of Quilliam's works or discussed Quilliam and the LMI in their journals and religious pamphlets. They willingly overlooked many of the oddities of the practices and teaching in Liverpool in favour of promoting the fact that numerous Western Christians had embraced Islam. For many of them, converts like Quilliam and his followers proved that Islam was a universal religion that not only conformed to modern ideas of science, rationalism and progress, but more importantly actively advanced these values.²⁵ Despite their sometimes-understated approval of Quilliam, there is very little evidence that any of them considered him a viable candidate for the office of 'Sheikh-ul-Islam of the British Isles'. When the title did appear in their writings, as explained below, it appears to have been a simple case of replicating what *The Crescent* published.

Muhammad Diya of Egypt was responsible for one of the most well-received Arabic translations of Quilliam's *The Faith of Islam* in 1897.²⁶ Diya's translation was unique in several respects, not least the addition of a photo of Quilliam captioned with '*Shaykh al-Islām fī al-Jazā'ir al-Biriṭāniyah*' (Sheikh-ul-Islam of the British Isles). Diya included the image on the title page, seemingly acknowledging Quilliam's role as the 'Sheikh-ul-Islam of the British Isles' or simply affirming what Quilliam and the LMI said. There is clear evidence from *The Crescent* that Diya corresponded with Quilliam, which might explain his inclination to accept the narrative.²⁷ Muhammad Rashid Rida (1865–1935), one of the most prominent Muslim scholars and journalists of the late nineteenth and early twentieth centuries, published the only serious commentary on Diya's translation in his journal *al-Manār* (The Lighthouse) of Cairo, which had a massive readership throughout the Islamic world. In Rida's review, he described Quilliam as '*shaykh al-Muslimīn*' (Sheikh of the Muslims) and '*ra'īsihim fī Liverpool*' (their president in Liverpool). It is unthinkable that Rida missed that Diya included '*shaykh al-Islām fī al-Jazā'ir al-Biriṭāniyah*' in his translation. Rida's omission and lack of commentary suggest that he tacitly objected to the title and resisted acknowledging Quilliam to such an elevated office and role.²⁸ Rida was, after all, only mildly impressed by Quilliam's ideas in *The Faith of Islam*.

Similarly, among Ottoman Turkish-speaking Muslim translators and intellectuals, it is difficult to find anyone who acknowledged Quilliam as the 'Sheikh-ul-Islam of the British Isles'. It is particularly surprising to see the omission of the title in the writings of Ottoman scholar Mahmud Esad (Scydişehri, 1856–1918), who translated two editions of *The Faith of Islam* between 1893 and 1897, and frequently appeared in the pages of *The Crescent* as someone who contributed materials to the LMI's library and was named an honorary vice-president in 1895.²⁹ Esad, out of all the Ottoman Turkish scholars, would have been familiar with Quilliam's story of receiving the title from the sultan-caliph because he frequently read LMI publications.³⁰ He had every reason to introduce Quilliam to his readers as someone elevated by 'Abd al-Hamid II to such a distinguished title and role. In fact, at no point in his two translated editions of *The Faith of Islam* did Esad designate Quilliam as anything other than '*effendi*' or '*re'is*' (president) of the Muslim community in Liverpool. He never even mentioned him as a *şeyh* (Ottoman Turkish for shaykh).

Quilliam concocted the narrative behind the title in 1895 and then ubiquitously used it in his own publications for more than a decade. However, in the nineteenth and early twentieth centuries, Ottoman Turkish Muslim intellectuals and translators remained consistent in only recognizing him as *effendi* or *re'is* and rarely, if ever, *şeyh*.[31] It is highly unlikely that Muslim scholars and translators who wrote in Arabic and Turkish were unaware that Quilliam used the title of 'Sheikh-ul-Islam of the British Isles'. Nor were they ignorant of Quilliam promulgating the narrative that the sultan-caliph appointed him to the office and role. Nevertheless, these scholars and translators ignored Quilliam's narrative and instead merely identified him as an important figure in terms of the spread of Islam in Britain. They preferred to see him as a symbol of hope that Islam would eventually ascend in the West. Whatever legitimacy and authority these Muslim intellectuals and scholars were willing to concede to Quilliam, it certainly had nothing to do with his claim to be the 'Sheikh-ul-Islam of the British Isles'.

LMI members who rejected the narrative and title

Although, externally, few publicly questioned the authenticity of Quilliam's title and the story that it came from the sultan, internally there were individuals associated with the LMI who expressed doubts. Nafeesah M. T. Keep (1844–1925), an American convert to Islam who briefly joined the LMI in 1895, was one of the first major internal critics of Quilliam.[32] In a scathing letter to the Ottoman sultan, she disputed Quilliam's credentials to lead the Muslims, accusing him and the Liverpool Muslims of unorthodox practices and placed scare quotes around 'Sheik-ul-Islam [*sic*]', drawing attention to her scepticism.[33] When the Translation Office of the Ottoman Foreign Ministry received Keep's letter, the translator obviously doubted the title of 'Sheikh-ul-Islam' as well and decided to convey a more humble title of '*cemaat-i İslamiye şeyhi*' (the sheikh of the Islamic society) and '*cemaat-i re'isi*' (president of the society). A year later, in December 1896, the Arabic newspaper *Thamarāt al-Funūn* published a disparaging letter from Mustapha Khalil, another disgruntled LMI member, this time from Syria, who accused Quilliam of deceit and fraud.[34] That same month, in a public speech in front of the pan-Islamic London association, the Anjuman-i-Islam, Khalil refuted Quilliam's 'Sheikh-ul-Islam' title, stating that it was 'self-titled' and that it 'has not been conferred on him by any recognized personage or institution, but is self-assumed'.[35] Not surprisingly, Quilliam and the LMI committee expelled both Keep and Khalil from the institute for their sedition, and their names were virtually expunged from LMI records and future publications. There was no room in the LMI for individuals who questioned Quilliam's legitimacy and authority. Perhaps individuals like Rafiuddin Ahmed and Muhammad Barakatullah also disappeared from the LMI's institutional memory because of their later questioning of Quilliam's legitimacy and authority.

Double-legitimacy: Hamidian-era medal and honours

Despite assurances by Wahby George in 1901 and the later-received narrative in the twenty-first century, numerous Ottoman officials and LMI insiders discredited, questioned and rejected the notion that 'Abd al-Hamid II appointed Quilliam the 'Sheikh-ul-Islam of the British Isles'. Contrary to what Wahby George stated, Quilliam, in fact, did masquerade under 'borrowed plumes'. Nevertheless, 'Abd al-Hamid II and some Ottoman officials willingly allowed this charade because they believed the narrative substantiated the sultan's legitimacy as the caliph of all Sunni Muslims and elevated his authority to influence non-Ottoman Muslims, particularly British subjects. As Faiz Ahmed has noted, 'Abd al-Hamid II 'claimed a form of politico-religious jurisdiction over all Muslims – even those without Ottoman papers – based on claims to the Pan-Islamic caliphate', which resulted in the sultan-caliph becoming entangled 'in a number of diplomatic tussles with the British from the 1880s on'.[36] Additionally, by advocating for the Ottoman state in LMI publications, through the British press and on numerous official Ottoman 'damage control and image management' missions, Quilliam provided a valuable service on behalf of the sultan-caliph. He did this without bribes and payments because he viewed it as his duty to his caliph. In exchange, he received cover to circulate the story of being the 'Sheikh-ul-Islam of the British Isles', thereby validating him. Thus, Quilliam elaborately crafted and perpetuated the narrative to sustain his own legitimacy and authority, particularly in moments when doubts circulated about him, whether inside the LMI or externally. This story was and continues to be an invented tradition that performs double legitimation for both 'Abd al-Hamid II and Quilliam.

According to many then and now, it is inconceivable that 'Abd al-Hamid II knowingly allowed Quilliam to perform the role of the 'Sheikh-ul-Islam' under false pretence. However, a prominent feature of the Hamidian era helps to explain and contextualize why a story like this was not only believable but also a reasonable approach for the sultan to take with regards to Quilliam. It also demonstrates the pragmatic partnership between the two men that had developed over the years. During 'Abd al-Hamid II's reign there was a noticeable proliferation of decorations, honours and titles granted to both Ottoman and non-Ottoman subjects that greatly surpassed his predecessors. Domestically, imperial gifts were part of 'Abd al-Hamid II's political toolkit to gain sultanic legitimation.[37] Edhem Eldem argues that, in many instances, the sultan pragmatically and systematically used decorations with non-Ottoman subjects, be they Muslims or non-Muslims, as a means of diplomacy and soft power.[38] Furthermore, Eldem shows that 'Abd al-Hamid II bestowed decorations 'on journalists and editors, especially foreign, whose support was sought for the defense of the Empire's interests'.[39] Sometimes individuals appealed to 'Abd al-Hamid II or Ottoman officials to receive decorations, honours and medals, and other times the sultan granted the decorations many years after the fact. In the case of the former, there is the example of Rafiuddin Ahmed, who petitioned 'Abd al-Hamid II to honour him for his efforts to stop the 1890 *Mahomet* play, as well as his importance as a mediator between Britain and the Ottoman state.[40] In the case of the latter, many years after Mohammed Webb halted his Islamic mission in the United States, the sultan rewarded him with the Third Class *Mecîdî* Order and appointed him to the Ottoman consulate in New York as an honorary Ottoman consul.

Quilliam, his family and other LMI members were the recipients of 'Abd al-Hamid II's soft power efforts through real titles, honours, performative functions and favours. Robert Ahmed, Quilliam's son, benefited the most from 'Abd al-Hamid II's benevolence. After his first interaction with the sultan-caliph in 1891, the young Robert Ahmed received the title of *binbaşi* (Major in the Ottoman imperial cavalry) and *bey*, which the Ottoman consul-general in Liverpool originally thought was a hoax.[41] In 1898, the Quilliams returned to Constantinople, and months later Abdullah received word that six members of the LMI, including several of his children, were to receive the *Medaille des Beaux Artes* (Medal of Fine Arts).[42] Additionally, the sultan paid Robert Ahmed's tuition fees, as well as room and board, to study at the Mekteb-i Sultani, which was the Ottoman's premier school for training civil officials. At the Mekteb-i Sultani, Robert Ahmed obtained the necessary training to become a paid consul member at the Ottoman consulate in Liverpool. Based on his superb service in the Liverpool consulate, the Ottoman Foreign Ministry eventually elevated him to vice-consul.[43]

In 1905, Abdullah and Robert Ahmed both received distinguished honours and titles from 'Abd al-Hamid II. Robert Ahmed obtained a Second Class *Mütemâyiz*, awarded to Ottoman civil servants, and the Ottoman Foreign Ministry officially made him the Ottoman honorary consul-general of Liverpool, while his father became Ottoman honorary consul at Douglas on the Isle of Man and was given the *Imtiyâz* Star (the Loyalty and Bravery Medal), typically awarded for service to the Ottoman state.[44] That same year, the sultan conferred on Quilliam's daughter Bessima Khadijah (d.1965) a Third Class Imperial Order of Charity (*Şefkat*).[45] When the British Foreign Office learned of the honorary titles given to Abdullah Quilliam and his son, it created controversy and an investigation because both men lacked the required *exequatur* (royal certificate of recognition) authorizing them to exercise office. The British Foreign Office believed that Quilliam's questionable character made him unworthy of such an honour. Musurus Paşa (1841–1906), the Ottoman ambassador, protested against the British government's attempt to discredit and delegitimize 'Abd al-Hamid II's authority to bestow the titles. This kind of intervention had become a sensitive issue because the British government consistently subverted the sultan's attempt to use medals and decorations as instruments of soft power with non-Ottoman Muslims under British sovereignty.[46] It is important to note that at no time did the British Foreign Office or any important Ottoman officials mention Quilliam's 'Sheikh-ul-Islam' title, which certainly would have required an *exequatur*. The lack of discussion of an *exequatur* indicates that, from their perspective, there was no evidence or record that the sultan had conferred the title upon Quilliam. Once Quilliam fell from Ottoman grace in 1908, due to his disbarment from the law and legal problems in England after he forged evidence to help his female client in a divorce case, the Ottoman ambassador stripped him of the honorary consul title. However, there was no mention of the 'Sheikh-ul-Islam' title because it had no real connection to the sultan or the Sublime Porte.

In every instance, the imperial gifts and decorations bestowed to the Quilliam family and LMI members by the sultan-caliph carried with them an immense symbolism and were key tools for 'Abd al-Hamid II to garner allegiance. Although the symbolic power was real, the frequency and the trivialized way the sultan bestowed decorations and titles upon so many people (Ottomans and non-Ottomans, Muslims and non-Muslims) created a system in which such honours lost their prestige.[47] The banality of Ottoman decorations under 'Abd al-Hamid II helps to explain and contextualize his willingness to overlook the truth of Quilliam's story about the 'Sheikh-ul-Islam of the British Isles' title. The sultan knew it was a façade. Nevertheless, as an opportunistic and pragmatic ruler, he willingly overlooked the false narrative to gain the allegiance and the soft power influence he desired. The story of the sultan-caliph exercising his politico-religious jurisdiction as the one true caliph only strengthened 'Abd al-Hamid II's legitimacy and authority among non-Ottoman Muslims. As long as no one in the sultan's Yildiz Palace or the Sublime Porte protested, Quilliam, as a proficient 'religious entrepreneur', peddled the story to authenticate his own legitimacy and authority to lead not only the Liverpool Muslims but also potentially all Muslims under British imperial control.[48]

Conclusion

In a 1904 interview with the Indian Muslim publication *The Moslem Chronicle and Muhammadan Observer*, Quilliam revived the origin story of his 'Sheikh-ul-Islam of the British Isles' title and office. He began the story back in 1894 when he travelled to West Africa on behalf of Sultan 'Abd al-Hamid II on a mission to bestow honours upon Mohammed Shitta for the opening of the mosque in Lagos. Quilliam added a twist to the story, stating that within the sultan's instructions for his trip to Lagos was a message that 'Mr. Quilliam was named for the first time as Sheikh Abdullah Quilliam Effendi, Sheikh-ul-Islam of the British Isles.'[49] Thus, in 1904, he revitalized the story that 'Abd al-Hamid II was the benefactor and bestower of the 'Sheikh-ul-Islam of the British Isles' title. When pressed to explain what the office and title entailed, he said: 'It is difficult to define, there being nothing equivalent to it in England – I am rather like the Lord Chancellor used to be – Keeper of the King's Conscience. Also as law and religion are the same in Islam, I am in a measure the protector of the law.'[50] At no point was there talk of it being an 'honorific' title. A decade after the fact, this was the first time Quilliam articulated how he practically saw himself fulfilling this office. The article further claimed that not only 'Abd al-Hamid II recognized Quilliam as 'Sheikh of the British Isles', but two other Muslim sovereigns – the Shah of Persia and the Amir of Afghanistan – also addressed him as such. He now only waited for the Sultan of Morocco 'to complete the recognition'.[51] In point of fact, the actual record of either the Shah of Persia or the Amir of Afghanistan recognizing Quilliam in this way is questionable. According to an alleged translated letter from the Amir of Afghanistan published in the LMI's *The Islamic World* in 1894, the Amir addressed him as 'the faithful leader of the faithful (in England) Sheikh Abdullah W. Quilliam', which is not exactly the same as 'Sheikh of the British Isles' or 'Sheikh-ul-Islam of the British Isles'.[52] Over nearly two decades through the LMI's publications, Quilliam constructed various titles to express and legitimize his leadership of Muslims not only in Liverpool, but also throughout the British imperial realm and among English-speaking Muslims.

This chapter has re-evaluated this narrative. It was Maulana Muhammad Barakatullah who first conceived of calling Quilliam the 'Sheikh-ul-Islam' among the Liverpool Muslims after Quilliam returned from his trip to Lagos. And even then, there was no mention of an election among the LMI members, nor a granting of the title and office by the Ottoman sultan-caliph. Instead, Barakatullah simply deemed him worthy of the 'Sheikh-ul-Islam' title based on his efforts to spread Islam in Britain, as well as him favourably representing the British Muslim community on behalf of the sultan-caliph. Despite the statement in *The Moslem Chronicle and Muhammadan Observer* article, it is difficult to find any significant Muslim leader outside of the Liverpool Muslim community who acknowledged that Quilliam deserved the legitimacy and authority he claimed through this title. In fact, as this chapter demonstrates, Ottoman officials from Liverpool to Constantinople, Muslim scholars and intellectuals writing in Arabic and Ottoman Turkish, as well as some former members of the LMI either refuted, omitted or ignored the idea that Quilliam was the 'Sheikh-ul-Islam of the British Isles'. They saw it for what it was, a self-appointed title based on an invented story intended to grant him greater authority, authenticity and legitimacy. In some instances, however, the title certainly elevated his status in the Islamic world, particularly among Muslims under British imperial control.[53]

'Abd al-Hamid II and the Sublime Porte clearly knew that Quilliam used the title and attributed it to the sultan-caliph's benevolence and leadership. For many, then and now, this proves that Quilliam could not have lied about the title and office coming from 'Abd al-Hamid II. To do so would besmirch the honour of the sultan-caliph and question Quilliam's integrity. Scholars of the Hamidian era have demonstrated that the banal use of honours, medals and titles was so commonplace that they began to lose meaning and significance. Nevertheless, the sultan and the Sublime Porte permitted the fabricated story because it furthered the pan-Islamic-inspired soft power politics of the Hamidian era. For both sides, it was a means of constructing, achieving and maintaining authority and legitimacy.

Was there ever truly a 'Sheikh-ul-Islam of the British Isles'? Well, yes and no. On the one hand, yes, if one concedes that a small Muslim community in Victorian Liverpool had the authority to elevate Quilliam to this office and therefore allowed him to use the title. On the other hand, and as this chapter argued, no, because the actual narrative Quilliam relied on to gain legitimacy and authority was dubious and mostly fabricated. It was a self-assumed title with no real authority and legitimacy, which explains why so few of his contemporaries outside of Liverpool ever acknowledged him with the title. Perhaps now is the time that scholars and those concerned with British Muslim history critically re-evaluate much of the narratives about Quilliam and the LMI community that have thus far relied heavily upon the LMI's self-supporting, public-facing publications. We can better understand and appreciate Quilliam and his fellow British Muslims by incorporating outside sources, such as Muslim authors and scholars in the Ottoman and Arab worlds of the late nineteenth and early twentieth centuries, who provide a more expansive and critical portrayal of the people and institutions of Victorian Britain.

Notes

Introduction

1 Gerald MacLean, *The Rise of Oriental Travel: English Visitors to the Ottoman Empire, 1580–1720* (Basingstoke: Palgrave Macmillan, 2004); Gerald MacLean, *Looking East: English Writing and the Ottoman Empire before 1800* (Basingstoke: Palgrave Macmillan, 2007); Gerald MacLean and Nabil Matar, *Britain and the Islamic World, 1558–1713* (Oxford: Oxford University Press, 2011); Jerry Brotton, *This Orient Isle: Elizabethan England and the Islamic World* (London: Allen Lane, 2016).

2 Stephen Clissold, *The Barbary Slaves* (London: Paul Elek, 1977); Daniel J. Vitkus (ed.), *Piracy, Slavery, and Redemption: Barbary Captive Narratives from Early Modern England* (New York: Columbia University Press, 2001); Linda Colley, *Captives: Britain, Empire and the World, 1600–1850* (London: Jonathan Cape, 2002); Paul Auchterlonie (ed.), *Encountering Islam. Joseph Pitts: An English Slave in 17th-Century Algiers and Mecca* (London: Arabian Publishing, 2012); T. G. P. Spear, *The Nabobs: A Study of the Social Life of the English in Eighteenth Century India* (London: Milford/Oxford University Press, 1932); William Dalrymple, *White Mughals: Love and Betrayal in Eighteenth-Century India* (London: HarperCollins, 2002).

3 Nabil Matar, *Islam in Britain, 1558–1685* (Cambridge: Cambridge University Press, 1998); Nabil Matar, *Turks, Moors, and Englishmen in the Age of Discovery* (New York: Columbia University Press, 1999); Brotton, *This Orient Isle*; Nile Green, *The Love of Strangers: What Six Muslim Students Learned in Jane Austen's London* (Princeton, NJ: Princeton University Press, 2016); Martin Pugh, *Britain and Islam: A History from 622 to the Present Day* (New Haven, CT: Yale University Press, 2019).

4 Jamie Gilham, 'G. W. Leitner in England: The Oriental Institute, Islam and Muslims, 1884–1889', *Islam and Christian-Muslim Relations* 32, no. 1 (2021): 1–24; Ron Geaves, *Islam in Victorian Britain: The Life and Times of Abdullah Quilliam* (Markfield: Kube, 2010).

5 James L. Gelvin and Nile Green (ed.), *Global Muslims in the Age of Steam and Print* (Berkeley: University of California Press, 2014), 1–2.

6 Ibid., 2.

7 Pugh, *Britain and Islam*, 112–13.

8   Cited in Sushila Anand, *Indian Sahib: Queen Victoria's Dear Abdul* (London: Duckworth, 1996), 61.
9   Francis Robinson, 'The British Empire and the Muslim World', in *Oxford History of the British Empire, Volume IV: The Twentieth Century*, ed. Judith M. Brown and Wm. Roger Louis (Oxford: Oxford University Press, 1999), 402.
10 Cited in Nathalie Clayer and Eric Germain, 'Introduction', in *Islam in Inter-War Europe*, ed. Nathalie Clayer and Eric Germain (London: Hurst, 2008), 8.
11 Diane Robinson-Dunn estimates that, by the late nineteenth century, between 10,000 and 12,000 lascars (a general term for seamen from Asia, Africa and the Middle East), most of them Muslim, came to Britain annually: Diane Robinson-Dunn, *The Harem, Slavery and British Imperial Culture: Anglo-Muslim Relations in the Late Nineteenth Century* (Manchester: Manchester University Press, 2006), 155.
12 Insights about Victorian Christian attitudes towards Islam and Muslims were to be found in, among others, Norman Daniel, *Islam and the West: The Making of an Image* (Edinburgh: Edinburgh University Press, 1960); Norman Daniel, *Islam, Europe and Empire* (Edinburgh: Edinburgh University Press, 1966); Denis Wright, *The English amongst the Persians, During the Qajar Period 1787–1921* (London: William Heinemann, 1977); Edward W. Said, *Orientalism* (London: Routledge and Kegan Paul, 1978); Kathryn Tidrick, *Heart-Beguiling Araby* (Cambridge: Cambridge University Press, 1981); Maxime Rodinson, *Europe and the Mystique of Islam*, trans. Roger Veinus (London: I. B. Tauris, 1988).
13 With no dedicated scholarly or popular studies, insights were to be found in, among others, Denis Wright, *The Persians amongst the English: Episodes in Anglo-Persian History* (London: I. B. Tauris, 1985); Rosina Visram, *Ayahs, Lascars and Princes* (London: Pluto Press, 1986). In the late 1970s and 1980s, some British Muslim community historians and activists discovered and sought to revive interest in Quilliam and his Liverpool Muslim community. They included M. A. Khan-Cheema, 'Islam and the Muslims in Liverpool' (MA diss., University of Liverpool, 1979) and Muhammad Mashuq Ally, 'History of Muslims in Britain, 1850–1980' (MA diss., University of Birmingham, 1981). For a review of the 'rediscovery' of Quilliam in this period, see Yahya Birt, 'Preachers, Patriots and Islamists: Contemporary British Muslims and the Afterlives of Abdullah Quilliam', in *Victorian Muslim: Abdullah Quilliam and Islam in the West*, ed. Jamie Gilham and Ron Geaves (London: Hurst, 2017), 133–50.
14 Phillip C. Almond, *Heretic and Hero: Muhammad and the Victorians* (Wiesbaden: Otto Harrassowitz, 1989).
15 Daniel, *Islam and the West*; Daniel, *Islam, Europe and Empire*.
16 Said, *Orientalism*.
17 Almond, *Heretic and Hero*, 95.
18 Clinton Bennett, *Victorian Images of Islam* (London: Grey Seal, 1992).

19 A contested term that describes an imagined global Muslim unity that is usually contrasted with a putative – and, certainly in the nineteenth century, a broadly Christian – West. For Cemil Aydin, the idea of a 'Muslim world' does not derive from *umma* (the universal Muslim religious community): 'Muslims did not imagine belonging to a global political unity *until* the peak of European hegemony in the late nineteenth century, when poor colonial conditions, European discourses of Muslim racial inferiority, and Muslims' theories of their own apparent decline nurtured the first arguments for pan-Islamic solidarity': Cemil Aydin, *The Idea of the Muslim World: A Global Intellectual History* (Cambridge, MA: Harvard University Press, 2017), 3.

20 For example, Albert Hourani, *Islam in European Thought* (Cambridge: Cambridge University Press, 1991); Fred Halliday, *Arabs in Exile: Yemeni Migrants in Urban Britain* (London: I. B. Tauris, 1992); Billie Melman, *Women's Orients: English Women in the Middle East, 1718-1918. Sexuality, Religion and Work* (Ann Arbor: University of Michigan Press, 1992); M. A. Sherif, *Searching for Solace: A Biography of Abdullah Yusuf Ali, Interpreter of the Qur'an* (Kuala Lumpur: Islamic Book Trust, 1994); Richard I. Lawless, *From Ta'izz to Tyneside: An Arab Community in the North-East of England during the Early Twentieth Century* (Exeter: University of Exeter Press, 1995); Michael H. Fisher, *The First Indian Author in English: Dean Mahomed (1759-1851) in India, Ireland, and England* (New Delhi: Oxford University Press, 1996).

21 Gerald Parsons (ed.), *Religion in Victorian Britain, Volume 1: Traditions* (Manchester: Manchester University Press, 1988); Gerald Parsons (ed.), *Religion in Victorian Britain, Volume 2: Controversies* (Manchester: Manchester University Press, 1988); James R. Moore (ed.), *Religion in Victorian Britain, Volume 3: Sources* (Manchester: Manchester University Press/The Open University, 1988); Gerald Parsons (ed.), *Religion in Victorian Britain, Volume 4: Interpretations* (Manchester: Manchester University Press, 1988).

22 G. Beckerlegge, 'Followers of "Mohammed, Kalee and Dada Nanuk": The Presence of Islam and South Asian Religions in Victorian Britain', in *Religion in Victorian Britain, Volume V: Culture and Empire*, ed. John Wolffe (Manchester: Manchester University Press, 1997), 221–67, 336–49.

23 For example, Shahin Kuli Khan Khattak, *Islam and the Victorians: Nineteenth Century Perceptions of Muslim Practices and Beliefs* (London: I. B. Tauris, 2008); Vicky Randall, *History, Empire, and Islam: E. A. Freeman and Victorian Public Morality* (Manchester: Manchester University Press, 2020); Clinton Bennett, *Islam as Imagined in Eighteenth- and Nineteenth-Century English Literature* (London: Routledge, 2022). See also Robert Irwin, *For Lust of Knowing: The Orientalists and Their Enemies* (London: Allen Lane, 2006).

24 For example, Alan M. Guenther, 'The Image of the Prophet as Found in Missionary Writings of the Late Nineteenth Century', *The Muslim World* 90, nos. 1–2 (2000): 43–70; Avril A. Powell, *Scottish Orientalists and India: The Muir Brothers, Religion, Education and Empire* (Woodbridge: The Boydell Press, 2010); articles in David Thomas and John A. Chesworth (ed.), *Christian-Muslim Relations. A Bibliographical History. Volume 17: Britain, the Netherlands and Scandinavia (1800-1914)* (Leiden and Boston, MA: Brill, 2020). See also Andrew Porter, *Religion Versus Empire? British Protestant Missionaries and Overseas Expansion, 1700-1914* (Manchester: Manchester University Press, 2004).

25 For example, Geoffrey P. Nash, *From Empire to Orient: Travellers to the Middle East, 1830-1926* (London: I. B. Tauris, 2005); Robinson-Dunn, *Harem, Slavery and British Imperial Culture*; Pallavi Pandit Laisram, *Viewing the Islamic Orient: British Travel Writers of the Nineteenth Century* (New Delhi: Routledge, 2006); Lisa McCracken Lacy, *Lady Anne Blunt in the Middle East: Politics, Travel and the Idea of Empire* (London: I. B. Tauris, 2018).

26 This has been led by scholars at the University of Birmingham (UK), where Clinton Bennett undertook the PhD that was later published as *Victorian Images of Islam*. See, for example, Thomas and Chesworth, *Christian-Muslim Relations*; Clinton Bennett (ed.), *Christian-Muslim Relations. Volume 3: Primary Sources, 1700-1914* (London: Bloomsbury, 2023).

27 For example, see essays in the following collections: Gerald MacLean (ed.), *Britain and the Muslim World: Historical Perspectives* (Newcastle upon Tyne: Cambridge Scholars Press, 2011); David Motadel (ed.), *Islam and the European Empires* (Oxford: Oxford University Press, 2014); Justin Quinn Olmstead (ed.), *Britain in the Islamic World: Imperial and Post-Imperial Connections* (London: Palgrave Macmillan, 2019). Also see John Slight, *The British Empire and the Hajj, 1865–1956* (Cambridge, MA: Harvard University Press, 2015).

28 Studies focused on Muslims include Humayun Ansari, *'The Infidel Within': Muslims in Britain since 1800* (London: Hurst, 2004 and 2018); Geaves, *Islam in Victorian Britain*; Mohammad Siddique Seddon, *The Last of the Lascars: Yemeni Muslims in Britain, 1836–2012* (Markfield: Kube, 2014); Jamie Gilham, *Loyal Enemies: British Converts to Islam, 1850–1950* (London: Hurst, 2014); Claire Chambers, *Britain through Muslim Eyes: Literary Representations, 1780–1988* (London: Palgrave Macmillan, 2015). General studies about South Asian immigration to and immigrants in Britain, including the nineteenth century, offer fascinating insights about Muslim experiences. See, for example, Rosina Visram, *Asians in Britain: 400 Years of History* (London: Pluto Press, 2002); Michael H. Fisher, *Counterflows to Colonialism: Indian Travellers and Settlers in Britain, 1600–1857* (Delhi: Permanent Black, 2004); Rehana Ahmed and Sumita Mukherjee (ed.), *South Asian Resistances in Britain, 1858–1947* (London: Continuum, 2012); Arup K. Chatterjee, *Indians*

    in London: From the Birth of the East India Company to Independent India (London: Bloomsbury, 2020).

29 On Abdul Karim, see Shrabani Basu, *Victoria and Abdul: The True Story of the Queen's Closest Confidant* (Stroud: The History Press, 2010), which builds on Anand, *Indian Sahib*. On Quilliam and the LMI community, see Geaves, *Islam in Victorian Britain*; Gilham, *Loyal Enemies*; Gilham and Geaves, *Victorian Muslim*; Yusuf Samih Asmay, *Islam in Victorian Liverpool: An Ottoman Account of Britain's First Mosque Community*, trans. and ed. Yahya Birt, Riordan Macnamara and Münire Zeyneb Maksudoğlu (Swansea: Claritas Books, 2021). On other Victorian Muslims in Britain, see, for example, Jamie Gilham, 'Britain's First Muslim Peer of the Realm: Henry, Lord Stanley of Alderley and Islam in Victorian Britain', *Journal of Muslim Minority Affairs* 33, no. 1 (2013): 93–110; Mustafa Abdelwahid (ed.), *Duse Mohamed Ali (1866–1945): The Autobiography of a Pioneer Pan African and Afro-Asian Activist* (Trenton, NJ: The Red Sea Press, 2011); Christina Longden, *His Own Man. A Victorian 'Hidden' Muslim. The Life and Times of Robert 'Reshid' Stanley* (n.p.: Privately published, 2019); Gareth Winrow, *Whispers Across Continents: In Search of the Robinsons* (Stroud: Amberley, 2019); Lyn Innes, *The Last Prince of Bengal: A Family's Journey from an Indian Palace to the Australian Outback* (London: The Westbourne Press, 2021).

30 Halliday, *Arabs in Exile*; Fred Halliday, 'The *Millet* of Manchester: Arab Merchants and Cotton Trade', *British Journal of Middle Eastern Studies* 19, no. 2 (1992): 159–76.

1 The royal family's attitudes towards Islam and Muslims during the reign of Queen Victoria

1 British Library (hereafter BL), BL/Mss Eur D620, 'Proclamation by the Queen in Council, to the Princes, Chiefs, and People of India', 1 November 1858. https://webarchive.nationalarchives.gov.uk/ukgwa/20131107151036mp_/http://www.movinghere.org.uk//deliveryfiles/BL/Mss_Eur_D620/0/1.pdf (accessed 1 June 2022). Compare E. A. Gait, *Census of India, 1911. Vol. 1: India – Part 1: Report* (Calcutta: Superintendent of Government Printing, 1913), 141, with Todd M. Johnson and Brian J. Grim, *The World's Religions in Figures: An Introduction to International Religious Demography* (Chichester: John Wiley, 2013), 19. See also Anon, *Census of the British Empire 1901: Report with Summary* (London: HMSO, 1906), xlix.

2 Official statistics for Muslims in Britain during the nineteenth century do not exist. Those we have are based on the number of Muslim sailors arriving in British ports. See Diane Robinson-Dunn, *The Harem, Slavery and British*

Imperial Culture: Anglo-Muslim Relations in the Late Nineteenth Century (Manchester: Manchester University Press, 2006), 155, 188.

3 For instance, David Cannadine, *Ornamentalism: How the British Saw Their Empire* (London: Allen Lane, 2001); Sarah Carter and Maria Nugent (eds), *Mistress of Everything: Queen Victoria in Indigenous Worlds* (Manchester: Manchester University Press, 2016); Bernard S. Cohn, 'Representing Authority in Victorian India', in *The Invention of Tradition*, ed. Eric Hobsbawm and Terence Ranger (Cambridge: Cambridge University Press, 1983), 165–210; Shompa Lahiri, 'British Policy Towards Indian Princes in Late Nineteenth and Early Twentieth-Century Britain', *Immigrants and Minorities* 15, no. 3 (1996): 215–32.

4 Miles Taylor, *Empress: Queen Victoria and India* (New Haven, CT: Yale University Press, 2018); Shrabani Basu, *Victoria and Abdul: The True Story of the Queen's Closest Confidant* (Stroud: The History Press, 2011); *Victoria and Abdul* [Film], dir. Stephen Frears, UK, Universal Pictures, 2017.

5 Royal Collection Trust (hereafter RCT), RA/VIC/MAIN/QVJ (W), 'Queen Victoria's Journal' (hereafter QVJ), 11 February 1834 (Lord Esher's typescript). See also Molly Engelhardt, '*The Revolt of the Harem* on the English Stage: A Spectacle of Domestic Reform', *Dance Research* 33, no. 1 (2015): 32.

6 QVJ, 3 September 1835 (Esher's typescript); 3 November 1836 (Queen Victoria's handwriting).

7 QVJ, 3 November 1836 (Queen Victoria's handwriting).

8 Washington Irving, *The Alhambra: A Series of Tales and Sketches of the Moors and Spaniards*, vol. 1 (Philadelphia, PA: Carey and Lea, 1832), 55.

9 Mary Roberts, *Intimate Outsiders: The Harem in Ottoman and Orientalist Art and Travel Literature* (Durham, NC: Duke University Press, 2007), 65–6.

10 QVJ, 3 November 1836 (Queen Victoria's handwriting). Subsequent citations from QVJ are from Princess Beatrice's copies unless otherwise stated.

11 George Earle Buckle (ed.), *The Letters of Queen Victoria. Third Series. A Selection from Her Majesty's Correspondence and Journal between the Years 1886 and 1901*, vol. 1 (London: John Murray, 1930), 354.

12 Taylor, *Empress*, 49–51; Stanley Weintraub, *Uncrowned King: The Life of Prince Albert* (New York: The Free Press, 1997), 56–60; Thomas Becker, 'Prinz Albert als Student in Bonn', in *Prince Albert and the Development of Education in England and Germany in the 19th Century*, ed. Franz Bosbach, William Filmer-Sankey and Hermann Hiery (Berlin: Walter de Gruyter, 2000), 149–50.

13 Charles Hügel, *Travels in Kashmir and Panjab, Containing a Particular Account of the Government and Character of the Sikhs*, trans. T. B. Jervis (London: John Petheram, 1845), 107.

14 Ibid., 110–12.

15 RCT, RCIN 1028951, 'Alphabetical Catalogue of the Prince Consort's Library, Drawn Up in the Early 1860s', entry 1553. https://albert.rct.uk/collections/royal-archives/prince-alberts-personal-papers/alphabetical-catalogue (accessed 30 July 2022).

16 Oliver Everett, 'The Royal Library at Windsor Castle as Developed by Prince Albert and B. B. Woodward', *The Library* 3, no. 1 (2002): 58–61.

17 RCT, RCIN 1028938, 'M. S. Catalogue of Books Contained in the Library of His Royal Highness, Prince Albert, at Buckingham Palace (North Wing)', vol. 1 (1843). https://www.rct.uk/collection/1028938/m-s-catalogue-of-books-contained-in-the-library-of-his-royal-highness-prince?_ga=2.255490507.2115814016.1658960154-241048850.1658960154 (accessed 30 July 2022).

18 RCT, 'Alphabetical Catalogue'.

19 Michael Alexander and Sushila Anand, *Queen Victoria's Maharajah: Duleep Singh, 1838–93* (New York: Taplinger, 1980), 45, 53.

20 RCT, RCIN 2906685, Salted Paper Print of Farrokh Khan, 1857. https://www.rct.uk/collection/2906685/farrokh-khan-1812-71 (accessed 18 October 2022).

21 J. L., 'The Queen and Indian Ladies', *Journal of the National Indian Association* 116 (1880): 463; Lahiri, 'British Policy', 336.

22 In addition to Basu, *Victoria and Abdul*, see Sushila Anand, *Indian Sahib: Queen Victoria's Dear Abdul* (London: Duckworth, 1996).

23 QVJ, 20 January 1890.

24 QVJ, 29 December 1894.

25 Sophie Gordon, 'Travels with a Camera: The Prince of Wales, Photography and the Mobile Court', in *Sons and Heirs: Succession and Political Culture in Nineteenth-Century Europe*, ed. Frank Lorenz Müller and Heidi Mehrkens (Basingstoke: Palgrave Macmillan, 2015), 98, 101–2.

26 Cohn, 'Representing Authority', 193.

27 QVJ, 29 December 1894.

28 Anand, *Indian Sahib*, 25.

29 RCT, RCIN 2980016, 'Balmoral Tableaux Vivants: "India"', 6 October 1888. https://www.rct.uk/collection/search#/18/collection/2980016/balmoral-tableau-vivants-india (accessed 2 August 2022). See also QVJ, 6 October 1888.

30 Theresa (Mrs. William) Grey, *Journal of a Visit to Egypt, Constantinople, the Crimea, Greece, &c. in the Suite of the Prince and Princess of Wales* (London: Smith, Elder, 1869), 32.

31 Jane Ridley, *The Heir Apparent: A Life of Edward VII, The Playboy Prince* (New York: Random House, 2013), 151.

32 Ibid., 158–9.

33 Quoted in Michaela Reid, *Ask Sir James: The Life of Sir James Reid, Personal Physician to Queen Victoria* (London: Eland, 1990), 142.

34 Agatha Ramm (ed.), *Beloved and Darling Child: Last Letters between Queen Victoria and Her Eldest Daughter, 1886–1901* (Stroud: Alan Sutton, 1990), 163.
35 Ibid.
36 Quoted in Basu, *Victoria and Abdul*, 140–1.
37 Anand, *Indian Sahib*, 48.
38 Ibid., 45; Basu, *Victoria and Abdul*, 142.
39 Basu, *Victoria and Abdul*, 139, 144.
40 F. A. Neale, *Islamism: Its Rise and Its Progress, or the Present and Past Condition of the Turks*, vol. 1 (London: James Madden, 1854), 12; RCT, 'Alphabetical Catalogue'.
41 George Sale, 'Dedication', in *The Koran, Commonly Called the Alcoran of Mohammed* (London: C. Ackers, 1734), n.p. For the Royal Library's version, see *Civilisation Musulmane, Observation Historiques et Critique sur le Mahométisme* and *Le Koran, Traduction Nouvelle Faite sur le Texte Arabe*, trans. Albin de Biberstein Kazimirski, in *Les Livres Sacreés de L'Orient*, ed. Guillaume Pauthier (Paris: Société du Panthéon Littéraire, 1843), 461–746.
42 Ridley, *The Heir Apparent*, 151; Graham Fisher and Heather Fisher, *Bertie and Alex: Anatomy of a Royal Marriage* (London: Robert Hale, 1974), 91.
43 George Earle Buckle (ed.), *The Letters of Queen Victoria. First Series. A Selection from Her Majesty's Correspondence and Journal between the Years 1837 and 1861*, vol. 3 (London: John Murray, 1907), 68–9. See also Michael Ledger-Lomas, *Queen Victoria: This Thorny Crown* (Oxford: Oxford University Press, 2021), 84–5.
44 Weintraub, *Uncrowned King*, 232.
45 Ledger-Lomas, *Thorny Crown*, 10–11.
46 Quoted in Matthew Denison, *The Last Princess: The Devoted Life of Queen Victoria's Youngest Daughter* (New York: St. Martin's Press, 2007), 85.
47 Ledger-Lomas, *Thorny Crown*, 60–1.
48 Ibid., 61; Ridley, *The Heir Apparent*, 51–2.
49 RCT, 'The Prince of Wales's Journal, 6 February – 14 June 1862', 4 March 1862, fol. 21 (emphasis added). https://www.rct.uk/collection/themes/exhibitions/cairo-to-constantinople/the-queens-gallery-buckingham-palace/the-prince-of-waless-journal-6-february-14-june-1862 (accessed 9 August 2022).
50 Ibid., 1 April 1862, fol. 37.
51 BL, 'Proclamation', 2. See Taylor, *Empress*, 79–83.
52 Buckle, *The Letters*, third ser., vol. 2, 68.
53 Ibid., 69.
54 Mary Lutyens (ed.), *Lady Lytton's Court Diary, 1895–1899* (London: Hart-Davis, 1961), 38.
55 Gathorne Hardy, *The Diary of Gathorne Hardy, Later Lord Cranbrook, 1866–1892: Political Selections*, ed. Nancy E. Johnson (Oxford: Clarendon Press, 1981), 715. See also Ledger-Lomas, *Thorny Crown*, 251.

56 QVJ, 31 August 1854.
57 QVJ, 4 November 1854.
58 QVJ, 5 March 1855.
59 Mrinalini Sinha, *Colonial Masculinity: The 'Manly Englishman' and the 'Effeminate Bengali' in the Late Nineteenth Century* (Manchester: Manchester University Press, 1995), 16.
60 Freda Harcourt, 'The Queen, the Sultan and the Viceroy: A Victorian State Occasion', *London Journal* 5, no. 1 (1979): 37.
61 Quoted in Christopher Hibbert, *Queen Victoria: A Personal History* (New York: Basic Books, 2000), 347.
62 Harcourt, 'Queen', 44.
63 QVJ, 13 July 1867.
64 Wahhabism is a conservative Islamic reform movement founded in Arabia by Muhammad ibn Abd al-Wahhab (1703–1797). On the perceived Wahhabi threat in British India, see Julia Stevens, 'The Phantom Wahhabi: Liberalism and the Muslim Fanatic in Mid-Victorian India', *Modern Asian Studies* 47, no. 1 (2013): 22–52.
65 Owen Tudor Burne, *Memories* (London: Edward Arnold, 1907), 133–4, 144.
66 BL, India Office Records, L/PJ/6/363 No.1875a, 'Indians in England', Unsigned intelligence report attached to Secret Department minute paper by Lee-Warner, 'The Position of Young Indians Sent to England for Education', 29 March 1898, fol. 915.
67 Buckle, *The Letters*, third ser., vol. 2, 301–3.
68 Rafiuddin Ahmad, 'The Queen's Hindustani Diary', *The Strand Magazine: An Illustrated Monthly* 4, no. 6 (1892): 551–7.
69 Quoted in Basu, *Victoria and Abdul*, 162.
70 Ibid., 189–90.

2 Rival views on the Eastern Question, Muslims and Islam: William Ewart Gladstone, Benjamin Disraeli and Anglo-Ottoman relations

1 This chapter develops Clinton Bennett, 'William Ewart Gladstone and Benjamin Disraeli', in *Christian-Muslim Relations. A Bibliographical History. Volume 17: Britain, the Netherlands and Scandinavia (1800–1914)*, ed. David Thomas and John Chesworth (Leiden: Brill, 2020), 265–77; and Clinton Bennett, *Islam as Imagined in Eighteenth- and Nineteenth-Century English Literature* (New York: Routledge, 2023).

2   Stanford J. Shaw and Ezel Kural Shaw, *History of the Ottoman Empire and Modern Turkey*, vol. 2 (Cambridge: Cambridge University Press, 1977), 45.
3   *Hansard* HC Deb., ser. 3, vol. 142, cols. 93–4, 97, 6 May 1856. A searchable *Hansard* database is available online: https://hansard.parliament.uk/ (accessed 20 October 2022).
4   W. E. Gladstone, *Bulgarian Horrors, and the Question of the East* (London: John Murray, 1876).
5   Marmaduke Pickthall, 'The Perils of Propaganda', *The New Age* 24, no. 20 (1919): 321.
6   Bernard Lewis, for example, comments that 'Disraeli's pride in his Jewish ancestry is well known. His novels and letters amply attest his profound sympathy for the Turks, the Arabs, and Islam, and his belief in the basic kinship between Jews and Muslims': Bernard Lewis, *Islam in History* (Chicago, IL: Open Court, 1993), 140–1.
7   Robert P. O' Kell, *Disraeli: The Romance of Politics* (Toronto: University of Toronto Press, 2014), 483.
8   William Flavelle Moneypenny and George Earle Buckle, *The Life of Benjamin Disraeli, Earl of Beaconsfield*, vol. 6 (London: Macmillan, 1920), 58.
9   Anthony S. Wohl, '"Ben-JuJu": Representations of Disraeli's Jewishness in the Victorian Political Cartoon', *Jewish History* 10, no. 2 (1996): 89–133, quotes at 89.
10 Richard Aldous, *The Lion and the Unicorn: Gladstone v Disraeli* (New York: W.W. Norton, 2007), 249.
11 For example, in Kersam Aharonian, *An Historical Survey of the Armenian Case* (Watertown, MA: Baikar Publications, 1989), Aharonian describes Victoria as a 'Turcophilic' who 'hated the Russians' (34).
12 John Rusk, *The Beautiful Life and Illustrious Reign of Queen Victoria* (Boston, MA: James A. Earle, 1901), 300, 421–3.
13 *Hansard* HC Deb., ser. 3, vol. 230, cols. 425–6, 26 June 1876.
14 *Hansard* HC Deb., ser. 3, vol. 231, col. 202, 31 July 1876.
15 Ibid., cols. 172–202.
16 Gladstone, *Bulgarian Horrors*, 12.
17 Ibid., 9.
18 Ibid., 13.
19 Ibid., 14.
20 Ibid., 15.
21 Ibid., 28.
22 Ibid., 34.
23 Ibid., 43, 49–50.
24 Ibid., 55.
25 Ibid., 57–8.
26 Ibid., 61.

27 Ibid., 62.
28 W. E. Gladstone, *The Berlin Treaty and the Anglo-Turkish Convention* (Manchester: James F. Wilkinson, 1878), 28.
29 W. E. Gladstone, *Political Speeches in Scotland: March and April 1880* (Edinburgh: Andrew Elliot, 1880), 285.
30 *Hansard* HC Deb., ser. 3, vol. 272, col. 1586, 24 July 1882.
31 Simone Beate Borgstede, *'All Is Race': Benjamin Disraeli on Race, Nation and Empire* (Zurich: LIT Verlag, 2011), 15–16.
32 Benjamin Disraeli, *Coningsby; Or, The New Generation* (Leipzig: Bernh Tauchnitz Jun, 1844), 195.
33 Benjamin Disraeli, *Contarini Fleming: A Psychological Romance*, new edn (1832; London: Longmans, Green, 1881), 330.
34 Benjamin Disraeli, *Tancred: Or, The New Crusade*, new edn (1846; London: Longmans, Green, 1880), 291, 367, 433.
35 Ibid., 253, 427.
36 Disraeli, *Coningsby*, 204.
37 Disraeli, *Tancred*, 261.
38 Gladstone, *Bulgarian Horrors*, 42.
39 *Hansard* HC Deb., ser. 3, vol. 142, col. 94, 6 May 1856.
40 Martyn Frampton, *The Muslim Brotherhood and the West: A History of Enmity and Engagement* (Cambridge, MA: The Belknap Press, 2018), 161, 463.
41 Rafiq Zakaria, *Muhammad and the Koran* (Harmondsworth: Penguin, 1991), 59.
42 Akbar Ahmed, *Postmodernism and Islam: Predicament and Promise* (London: Routledge, 1992), 182.
43 E. F. Biagini, 'Exporting "Western and Beneficent Institutions": Gladstone and Empire, 1880–1885', in *Gladstone Centenary Essays*, ed. David Babbington and Roger Swift (Liverpool: Liverpool University Press, 2000), 202–24, quote at 214.
44 Richard T. Shannon, *Gladstone and the Bulgarian Agitation 1876*, new edn (1963; New York: The Harvester Press, 1975), 148.
45 Ibid., 61.
46 Ibid., 46–7.
47 Ibid., 47.
48 Ibid., 177.
49 Eastern Question Association, *Report of the Proceedings of the National Conference* (London: Eastern Question Association, 1877), 122.
50 Shannon, *Gladstone*, 26.
51 Eastern Question Association, *Report*, 90.
52 On Smith, see Clinton Bennett, 'Reginald Bosworth Smith', in *Christian-Muslim Relations*, vol. 17, ed. Thomas and Chesworth, 294–306.

53 R. Bosworth Smith, 'The Eastern Question: Turkey and Russia', *The Contemporary Review* 29 (December 1876): 147–68, quote at 148.
54 Ibid., 149.
55 Ibid., 152.
56 Ibid., 153, 155.
57 Ibid., 157.
58 Ibid., 167.
59 Lady Grogan, *Reginald Bosworth Smith: A Memoir* (London: James Nisbet, 1909), 240–1.
60 Shannon, *Gladstone*, 154.
61 Arnold received the Imperial Order of Osmanli from the Ottoman sultan in 1886 and the Order of the Lion and Sun from the Shah in 1888. On Arnold, see Clinton Bennett, 'Edwin Arnold', in *Christian-Muslim Relations*, vol. 17, ed. Thomas and Chesworth, 278-85.
62 Shannon, *Gladstone*, 154.
63 Peter Harvey, *An Introduction to Buddhism* (Cambridge: Cambridge University Press, 2013), 420.
64 *Hansard* HL Deb., ser. 3, vol. 237, cols. 3–4, 17 January 1878.
65 Arman J. Kirakossian, 'Introduction', in *The Armenian Massacres, 1894–1896*, ed. Arman J. Kirakossian (Detroit: Wayne State University, 2004), 15–46, quote at 28.
66 Roy Douglas, 'Britain and the Armenian Question, 1894–1897', *The Historical Journal* 19, no. 1 (1976): 113–33, quote at 117.
67 Wilfred Scawen Blunt, *My Diaries, Being a Personal Narrative of Events, 1888–1914. Part Two, 1900–1914* (New York: Alfred A. Knopf, 1921), 466.
68 Kirakossian, 'Introduction', 27.
69 N. Naeem Qureshi, *Pan-Islam in British Indian Politics* (Leiden: Brill, 1999), 43.
70 Douglas, 'Britain', 126.
71 Michelle Tusan, *The British Empire and the Armenian Genocide* (London: I. B. Tauris, 2020), 63.
72 Douglas, 'Britain', 123.
73 Coined by the British intelligence officer Arthur Conolly (1807–1842) in 1840, this referred to the rivalry between Russia and Britain, including spying on each other.
74 Martin Pugh, *Britain and Islam: A History from 622 to the Present Day* (New Haven, CT: Yale University Press, 2019), xi.

3 Thomas Carlyle, Islam, empire and after

1 Thomas Carlyle, *On Heroes, Hero-Worship, and the Heroic in History* (1841; London: Chapman and Hall, 1897). All subsequent references to Carlyle's *On*

Heroes are from this edition unless otherwise stated. W. Montgomery Watt, 'Carlyle on Muhammad', *Hibbert Journal* 53 (1955): 247–54, quote at 247. See also W. Montgomery Watt, *Muhammad at Mecca* (Oxford: Clarendon Press, 1953), 52.

2   Watt, *Muhammad*, 52. See also John Tolan, *Faces of Muhammad: Western Perceptions of the Prophet of Islam from the Middle Ages to Today* (Princeton, NJ: Princeton University Press, 2019), 249–58.

3   Thomas Carlyle, *Sartor Resartus: The Life and Opinions of Herr Teufelsdröckh in Three Books* (London: Chapman and Hall, 1897).

4   Frank M. Turner, *Contesting Cultural Authority: Essays in Victorian Intellectual Life* (New York: Cambridge University Press, 1991), 22.

5   Ibid., 84, 132.

6   David R. Sorensen, 'Introduction', in Thomas Carlyle, *On Heroes, Hero-Worship, and the Heroic in History*, ed. David R. Sorensen and Brent E. Kinser (New Haven, CT: Yale University Press, 2013), 7.

7   Ibid., 9. See Carlyle, *On Heroes*, 10.

8   D. S. Margoliouth, 'Introduction', in *The Koran*, trans. J. M. Rodwell (London: J. M. Dent, 1909), vii. See William Muir, *Life of Mahomet* (London: Smith and Elder, 1861); William Muir, *The Caliphate: Its Rise and Fall* (London: Smith and Elder, 1891).

9   Thomas Carlyle, *Critical and Miscellaneous Essays* (London: Chapman and Hall, 1899), vols 1–2. Edward Gibbon's account of the rise of Islam appeared in *The Decline and Fall of the Roman Empire*, ed. J. B. Bury (1900–2), 7 vols. He, in turn, relied heavily on Ockley's *History of the Saracens* (1708–18) and Sale's *The Koran, Commonly called the Alcoran of Mohammed* (1734). See Robert Irwin, *For Lust of Knowing: The Orientalists and Their Enemies* (London: Allen Lane, 2006), 120. David R. Sorensen, '"Une religion plus digne de la Divinite": A New Source for Carlyle's Essay on Mahomet', *Carlyle Studies Annual* 23 (2007): 13–42 draws attention to the French Orientalist Silvestre de Sacy's article on the life of Muhammad as a source for 'The Hero as Prophet'. See Henri d'Audiffret and Silvestre de Sacy, 'Mahomet', *Biographie Universelle Anciennne et Moderne*, vol. 26 (Paris: Michaud, 1820), 186–213.

10 Lessing's *Nathan der Weise* (1797) staged a case for religious toleration; the humanism of Goethe's *Wilhelm Meisters Lehrjahre* (1795/6), which Carlyle translated in his early career as *Wilhelm Meister's Apprenticeship and Travels* (1824), remained a lifelong point of reference for him. The phrase that Carlyle quotes in *On Heroes*: 'If this be *Islam* … do we not all live in *Islam*' (56) is derived from Goethe's statement 'If Islam means submission to God/We all live and die in Islam': see J. W. Goethe, *West-östlicher Divan*, ed. H. Birus (1814–19; Frankfurt/Main: Deutscher Klassiker Verlag, 1994). Johann Gottfried Herder, *Outlines of a Philosophy of the History of Man; Translated from the German of John Godfrey Herder, by T. Churchill*

(London: J. Johnson, 1800) provided Carlyle with a sense of the place of Islam in a European schema of history. Herder also affords to the Arabs full recognition for the transmission of Greek science and reason to Europe.

11 Carlyle, *On Heroes*, 76; Edward W. Lane, *An Account of the Manners and Customs of the Modern Egyptians, Written in Egypt during the Years 1833–1835*, new edn (1836; The Hague: East-West Publications, 1978), 124–5.
12 Carlyle, *On Heroes*, 75.
13 Cited in James Anthony Froude, *Thomas Carlyle: A History of His Life in London, 1834–1881*, vol. 1 (London: Longmans, Green, 1885), 193.
14 Clinton Bennett, *Victorian Images of Islam* (London: Grey Seal, 1992), 99.
15 William Thomson, Unsigned review of *On Heroes and Hero-Worship* in *Christian Remembrancer* (1841), repr. in *Thomas Carlyle: The Critical Heritage*, ed Jules Paul Seigel (London: Routledge and Kegan Paul, 1971), 171–92, quotes at 177, 180, 186.
16 Ruth apRoberts, '"The Lore of Heaven, The Speech of Earth": Carlyle, Mahomet, and Islam', *Carlyle Studies Annual* 23 (2007): 7–12, quote at 11.
17 Tolan, *Faces of Muhammad*, 3.
18 Ibid., 203.
19 The cube-shaped structure at Mecca.
20 Thomas Carlyle, *Oliver Cromwell's Letters and Speeches: With Elucidations*, vol. 3 (1845; London: Chapman and Hall, 1897), 72.
21 Watt, 'Carlyle on Muhammad'; C. F. Harrold, 'On the Nature of Carlyle's Calvinism', *Studies in Philology* 33 (1936): 475–86.
22 While proficient in ancient languages, even 'the most celebrated [nineteenth century] biblical scholars never set place in the Orient': Ivan Kalmar, 'Orientalism and the Bible', in *Orientalism and Literature*, ed. Geoffrey P. Nash (New York: Cambridge University Press, 2019), 133–48, quote at 147, n. 42. Sorensen believes Carlyle followed Sacy more than Sale and Gibbon, echoing his view that, far from being a charlatan, Muhammad was 'a man of truth and fidelity': see Carlyle, *On Heroes*, 46; Sorensen, '"Une religion"', 26.
23 See Geoffrey Nash, *From Empire to Orient: Travellers to the Middle East, 1830–1926* (London: I. B. Tauris, 2005); Michael D. Berdine, *The Accidental Tourist: Wilfrid Scawen Blunt, and the British Invasion of Egypt in 1882* (New York: Routledge, 2005); Lisa McCracken Lacy, *Lady Anne Blunt in the Middle East: Politics, Travel and the Idea of Empire* (London: I. B. Tauris, 2018).
24 Carlyle, *On Heroes*, 76–7, 44.
25 See Ian Barnes, *World Religions* (Royston: Cartographical Press/Eagle Editions, 2008).
26 C. S. I. Graham, *The Life and Work of Syed Ahmed Khan* (Edinburgh: Blackwood, 1885), 98–9.
27 Bennett, *Victorian Images of Islam*, 45.

28 Shaden M. Tageldin, 'Secularizing Islam: Carlyle, al-Siba'i, and the Translations of "Religion" in British Egypt', *PMLA* [Publications of the Modern Language Association of America] 126, no. 1 (2011): 123–39, quote at 133.
29 Jamie Gilham, *Loyal Enemies: British Converts to Islam, 1850–1950* (London: Hurst, 2014), 21.
30 Ian Campbell, Kenneth J. Fielding, Sheila McIntosh and David R. Sorensen (eds), *The Collected Letters of Thomas and Jane Welsh Carlyle: January 1854-June 1855*, vol. 29 (Durham, NC: Duke University Press, 2001), xiv–xv. Carlyle's view of 'the Turks' during the Eastern Crisis of 1876–7 was that they were 'barbarians, decrepit, and incurable': see Froude, *Thomas Carlyle*, vol. 2, 440. Moncur Conway wrote of him as 'the man whose voice helped to arrest the schemes to obtain English aid for the European slave-trader, "the unspeakable Turk"': see Moncur Daniel Conway, *Thomas Carlyle* (London: Chatto and Windus, 1881), 94.
31 However, when Carlyle wrote to Edward FitzGerald of Norton's disclosure about 'your notable Omar Khayyam', he said 'the Book itself [is] a kind of jewel in its way': Alfred McKinley Terhune, *Life of Edward FitzGerald* (New Haven, CT: Yale University Press, 1947), 211–12.
32 Alfred Lord Tennyson, *Tiresias, And Other Poems* (London: Macmillan, 1895), 3.
33 Tareq Y. Ismael and Andrew Rippin, *Islam in the Eyes of the West: Images and Realities in an Age of Terror* (London: Routledge, 2010), 8.
34 John Morrow, *Thomas Carlyle* (London: Hambleton Continuum, 2006), 112.
35 On Carlyle's response to the Crimean War, see 'Introduction', in *The Collected Letters of Thomas and Jane Welsh Carlyle*, vol. 29. The editors of Carlyle's collected letters note: 'There is no satisfaction for [Carlyle] when the [Indian] rebellion is put down and he is appalled at the brutality with which it is done. He writes to John Strachey, 13 September 1857: "I cannot bear to read those inhuman details in the Newspapers. … To punish the Sepoys, and mince them all to pieces &c &c"': Ian Campbell, Kenneth J. Fielding, Sheila McIntosh and David R. Sorensen (eds), *The Collected Letters of Thomas and Jane Welsh Carlyle: August 1857-June 1858*, vol. 33 (Durham, NC: Duke University Press, 2001), xxi–xxii.
36 Albert Hourani, *Europe and the Middle East* (Berkeley: University of California Press, 1980), 64.
37 Edward W. Said, *Orientalism: Western Conceptions of the Orient*, new edn (1978; London: Penguin, 2003), 152.
38 K. Humayun Ansari, 'The Muslim World in British Historical Imaginations: Re-thinking "Orientalism"?', *British Journal of Middle Eastern Studies* 3, no. 1 (2011): 73–93, quotes at 81, 83; Watt, 'Carlyle on Muhammad', 247.
39 Carlyle, *On Heroes*, 43 (emphasis added).
40 Ibid., 112.
41 Tageldin, 'Secularizing Islam', 134.

42 Ibid., 124.
43 Ibid., 128.
44 Ibid.
45 Ibid., 130–1.
46 Ameen Rihani, *Around the Coasts of Arabia*, new edn (1930; Delmar, NY: Caravan Books, 1983), 50.
47 Gilham, *Loyal Enemies*, 60–1; Geoffrey Nash, 'Abdullah Quilliam, Marmaduke Pickthall and the Politics of Christendom and the Ottoman Empire', in *Victorian Muslim: Abdullah Quilliam and Islam in the West*, ed. Jamie Gilham and Ron Geaves (London: Hurst, 2017), 83.
48 Fred Kaplan, *Thomas Carlyle: A Biography* (Berkeley: University of California Press, 1983), 529.
49 Ian Campbell, *Thomas Carlyle* (Harlow: Longman/British Council, 1978), 27.
50 Morrow, *Thomas Carlyle*, 136.
51 A. Dwight Culler, 'Mill, Carlyle, and the Spirit of the Age', in *Modern Critical Views: Thomas Carlyle*, ed. Harold Bloom (New York: Chelsea House, 1986), 127–60, quote at 58.
52 Sayyid Qutb, *Milestones*, new edn (1964; New Delhi: Islamic Book Service, 2001).
53 Sharough Akhavi, 'Islam and the West in World History', *Third World Quarterly* 24, no. 3 (2003): 545–62, quote at 554–5.
54 Ibid., 555.
55 David R. Sorensen, 'Carlyle, Mahomet, and the Force of History', in Thomas Carlyle, *On Heroes*, ed. Sorensen and Kinser, 209; Carlyle, *On Heroes*, 118; Francis Fukuyama, *The End of History and the Last Man* (New York: Free Press, 1992), 48.
56 Sorensen, 'Carlyle, Mahomet', 209; Carlyle, *On Heroes*, 108.
57 Sorensen, 'Carlyle, Mahomet', 220; Carlyle, *On Heroes*, 121.
58 See Bassam Tibi, *Islam and Islamism* (New Haven, CT: Yale University Press, 2012).

4 'Permission to go and see the ancient city': Women travellers' encounters with Islam in the nineteenth century

1 Clinton Bennett, 'Islam and the Victorians: Nineteenth Century Perceptions of Muslim Practices and Beliefs' [Review], *Victorian Studies* 51, no. 2 (2009): 356–7, quote at 357.
2 The period between the publication of Lady Sale's journal in the early 1840s and Edwards' book in the 1870s witnessed a hardening of imperialist attitudes in Britain and aggressive foreign policy. See Patrick Brantlinger, *Rule of Darkness: British Literature and Imperialism, 1830–1914* (Ithaca, NY: Cornell University Press, 1988). For a useful overview of imperial practices in the

period, see P. J. Cain and A. G. Hopkins, *British Imperialism, 1688–2000* (London: Routledge, 2002). At the same time, and particularly from mid-century, there was an increasing preoccupation with the 'Woman Question', as women began to campaign for legal and economic rights, and access to higher education. This arguably contributed to the burgeoning of female-authored travel writing in the Victorian period, with women taking advantage of increased freedoms and shifting attitudes about women's roles. See Mary Lyndon Shanley, *Feminism, Marriage, and the Law in Victorian England, 1850–1900* (Princeton, NJ: Princeton University Press, 1989).

3 The Simla Manifesto effectively made explicit British ambition to dethrone the Afghan ruler Dost Mohammad Khan in response to his political overtures to Russia. Ostensibly, the aim was to have the 'integrity and independence of Afghanistan established'. Tamim Ansary notes that this claim 'would become grindingly familiar over the next 150 years': Tamim Ansary, *Games without Rules* (New York: Public Affairs, 2012), 45.

4 Some of Sale's letters to her husband were published in newspapers while she was still in captivity. After General Sale's defence of Jalalabad in late 1842, he defeated the Afghans, who were laying siege to the fortress, and was part of an attacking force that re-invaded Afghanistan, finally bringing his wife to safety – ironically, in Kabul – on 19 September 1843.

5 Dea Birkett, *Spinsters Abroad: Victorian Lady Explorers* (Oxford: Blackwell, 1989), 164.

6 Carl Thompson, 'Journeys to Authority: Reassessing Women's Early Travel Writing, 1763–1862', *Women's Writing* 24, no. 2 (2017): 131.

7 Sara Mills, *Discourses of Difference: An Analysis of Women's Travel Writing and Colonialism* (London: Routledge, 1991), 99.

8 Susan Bassnett, 'Travel Writing and Gender', in *The Cambridge Companion to Travel Writing*, ed. Peter Hulme and Tim Youngs (Cambridge: Cambridge University Press, 2002), 239.

9 Lady Florentia Wynch Sale, *A Journal of the Disasters in Afghanistan, 1841–2* (London: John Murray, 1843), 191.

10 The non-Muslim tribes of the Hindu Kush, such as the Kafiristani, were not involved in the conflict and not forcibly converted to Islam until the end of the nineteenth century.

11 Sale, *A Journal*, 29.

12 Bijan Omrani, '"Will We Make It to Jalalabad?": 19th Century Travels in Afghanistan', *Asian Affairs* 37, no. 2 (2006): 170.

13 Sale, *A Journal*, 75. Jane Austen was Emily Eden's favourite author and, like Sale, her use of irony and light sarcasm is also comparable to Austen. In her lifetime, Eden was known more as a novelist and poet than for her letters. The two volumes that

followed *Up the Country*, and included her reaction to the retreat from Kabul, were published after her death.
14 Sale, *A Journal*, 74.
15 Ibid., 29.
16 Ibid., 19 (emphasis added). This is perhaps an example of what Edmund Yorke refers to as her 'occasional unjustified personal prejudices': Edmund Yorke, *Playing the Great Game: Britain, War and Politics in Afghanistan from 1839* (London: Robert Hale, 2012), 168.
17 Sale, *A Journal*, 61.
18 Emily Eden, *Up the Country: Letters Written to Her Sister from the Upper Provinces of India* (London: R. Bentley, 1867), 96.
19 Sale, *A Journal*, 77.
20 Eden, *Up the Country*, 202.
21 Ibid., 62.
22 The first *sura* (chapter) of the Qur'an, which is recited during daily prayers.
23 Sale, *A Journal*, 66.
24 Ibid., 46–7.
25 Ibid., 134.
26 Ibid., 149.
27 Ibid., 117.
28 Ibid., 91.
29 Ibid., 200.
30 Ibid., 199.
31 Ibid., 363. The term *ghazeeas* is derived from *ghazis*, or Muslim warriors who fight in a war against non-Muslims; also used by Western Victorian writers to denote a religious fanatic. In the Qur'an and Islamic belief, *houris* are women with beautiful eyes described as a reward for faithful Muslim believers in Paradise.
32 Corinne Fowler, *Chasing Tales: Travel Writing, Journalism and the History of British Ideas about Afghanistan* (New York: Rodopi, 2007), 29–30, 186.
33 Eden, *Up the Country*, 281.
34 Ibid., 286.
35 Ibid., 297.
36 Bassnett, 'Travel Writing and Gender', 239.
37 Carl Thompson, *Travel Writing* (Abingdon: Routledge, 2011), 194. Thompson quotes Indira Ghose, *Memsahibs Abroad: Writings by Women Travellers in Nineteenth Century India* (New Delhi: Oxford University Press, 1998), 5.
38 Many of the more uncomfortable moments of Duff Gordon's letters relate to her objectification of the bodies of black and Arab people, which range from attraction to repulsion but are always problematic in their assumption of the colonizer's gaze. While still in the Cape, Duff Gordon writes: 'Yesterday, I should have bought a black

woman for her beauty, had it still been possible': Janet Ross (ed.), *Three Generations of Englishwomen*, revised edn (London: T. Fisher Unwin, 1893), 482. She goes on to admit that 'such stupendous physical perfection I never even imagined', and compares the woman to the Sphinx. Almost in the same breath, Duff Gordon comments that 'the ordinary blacks, or Mozambiques, as they call them, are hideous'.

39 Lady Duff Gordon, *Letters from Egypt, 1863–1865* (London: Macmillan and Company, 1865), 56.
40 Ibid., 59.
41 Ibid., 51.
42 Ibid., 36.
43 Sarah Austin, 'Preface', in Duff Gordon, *Letters from Egypt*, vii.
44 Duff Gordon, *Letters from Egypt*, 528.
45 Ibid., 36.
46 Ibid., 353.
47 Ibid., 20.
48 Ross, *Three Generations of English Women*, 520.
49 Bassnett, 'Travel Writing and Gender', 229.
50 Lucie Duff Gordon, *Last Letters from Egypt*, new edn (1875; New York: Cambridge University Press, 2010), 181. In her 1865 'Preface', Sarah Austin, with a strange mixture of defensiveness and defiance, admits that her daughter's letters contain 'passages illustrative of the manners and morals of Arabs which I at first determined to omit; but farther reflection convinced me that to do so would be to rob this little volume of much of its value' (Austin, 'Preface', ix). Austin does not specify which passages she was initially tempted to remove, but it is likely that she was cautious about both her daughter's outspokenness and her unconventional (and potentially controversial) racial attitudes.
51 Mervat Hatem, 'Through Each Other's Eyes: The Impact on the Colonial Encounter of the Images of Egyptian, Levantine-Egyptian, and European Women, 1862–1920', in *Western Woman and Imperialism: Complicity and Resistance*, ed. Nupur Chaudhuri and Margaret Strobel (Bloomington: University of Indiana Press, 1992), 49.
52 Amelia B. Edwards, *A Thousand Miles Up the Nile* (New York: A. L. Burt, 1890), 409.
53 Patricia O'Neill, 'Destination as Destiny: Amelia B. Edwards's Travel Writing', *Frontiers: A Journal of Women Studies* 30, no. 2 (2009): 43.
54 Edwards, *A Thousand Miles Up the Nile*, 27.
55 O'Neill, 'Destination as Destiny', 61.
56 Edwards, *A Thousand Miles Up the Nile*, v–vi (emphasis added).

57 Billie Melman, *Women's Orients, English Women and the Middle East, 1718–1918: Sexuality, Religion, and Work* (Ann Arbor: University of Michigan Press, 1992), 48.
58 O'Neill, 'Destination as Destiny', 61.
59 Bassnett, 'Travel Writing and Gender', 234.
60 Edwards, *A Thousand Miles Up the Nile*, 17.
61 The five 'pillars' are: the Islamic testimony of faith (*shahada*), worship/ritual prayer (*salat*), almsgiving (*zakat*); fasting/abstinence during Ramadan, the Muslim month of fasting (*sawm*), and pilgrimage to Mecca (Hajj).
62 See Jamie Gilham, 'Professor G. W. Leitner in England: The Oriental Institute, Woking Mosque and Relations with Muslims, 1884–1899', *Islam and Christian-Muslim Relations* 32, no. 1 (2021): 1–24. Gilham has also shown that conversion among the British, especially abroad, declined as imperialism increased in the mid-nineteenth century, although there were still significant instances: 'As imperialism advanced, Britons increasingly defined themselves against the colonial peoples (many of them Muslim) they conquered – peoples who appeared manifestly alien in terms of colour, culture, and religion. Concurrently, relations with both colonized and free Muslim countries and populations ... deteriorated and adversely affected British attitudes towards Muslims and Islam': Jamie Gilham, 'Britain's First Muslim Peer of the Realm: Henry, Lord Stanley of Alderley and Islam in Victorian Britain', *Journal of Muslim Minority Affairs* 33, no. 1 (2013): 93.
63 Christine Bolt, *Victorian Attitudes to Race* (London: Routledge and Kegan Paul, 1971), 110.
64 Sale, *A Journal*, 423.

5 Translators, publishers and popular readerships: The Qur'an on the Victorian bookshelf

1 The University of Edinburgh Archives, Correspondence and Photographs of Sir William Muir, Dk.2.14, f.121, George Douglas Campbell, Duke of Argyll, to Sir William Muir, 7 Dec 1877.
2 Ibid.
3 For an overview of the various Asian texts available at this time to the English reading public in popular, cheap editions, see Alexander Bubb, *Asian Classics on the Victorian Bookshelf: Flights of Translation* (Oxford: Oxford University Press, 2023).
4 Ziad Elmarsafy, *The Enlightenment Qur'an: The Politics of Translation and the Construction of Islam* (Oxford: Oneworld, 2009), 1, 64–5.
5 An earlier English version had appeared in London during the reign of Charles I (r. 1625–49), 'for the fatisfaction of all that defire to look into the Turkiſh

vanities', though it was wholly based on the 1647 French text of André du Ryer (c.1580–c.1660). See Sieur Du Ryer, *The Alcoran of Mahomet* (London: [n. publ.], 1649). Sale's was the first translation founded at least in part on the original Arabic, though Ludovico Maracci's (1612–1700) Latin edition of 1698 was no doubt constantly at his elbow.

6 Arthur King and Albert Frederick Stuart, *The House of Warne: One Hundred Years of Publishing* (London: Frederick Warne, 1965), 5.
7 University of Reading, Special Collections, Frederick Warne Archive, MS 5337/27, Publication Book A-H, c.1904–1949.
8 The third text was Laura Valentine's *The Old, Old Fairy Tales*.
9 University College London Archives, Routledge and Kegan Paul Archive, ROUTLEDGE/A/11, George Routledge and Co. Publication Book, vol. 6.
10 Terry Seymour, *A Printing History of Everyman's Library, 1906–1982* (Bloomington, IN: AuthorHouse, 2011), 164.
11 *The Crescent* (hereafter *TC*), 3 November 1897, 700.
12 Jamie Gilham, *Loyal Enemies: British Converts to Islam, 1850–1950* (London: Hurst, 2014), 53. An observer, James Monro, noticed several copies of Sale's edition within the Liverpool Muslim Institute, 'the bindings of which showed marks of usage': see James Monro, *Moslems in Liverpool* (Calcutta: Joseph Culshaw, 1901), 6.
13 *TC*, 21 November 1900, 323.
14 E. H. Palmer (trans.), *The Qur'ân*, vol. 1 (Oxford: Clarendon Press, 1880), 65, 135.
15 Anon, 'Palmer's Koran', *Saturday Review* 51, no. 1320 (12 February 1881): 213.
16 George Sale (trans.), *The Koran, Commonly called the Alcoran of Mohammed*, new edn (1734; London: Frederick Warne, 1887), 450.
17 J. M. Rodwell (trans.), *The Koran*, new edn (1861; London: J. M. Dent, 1909), 19–20.
18 Palmer, *The Qur'ân*, vol. 2, 336.
19 Relatively little is known of Rodwell's life but for an autobiographical fragment that reveals something of the origins of his interest in the Qur'an. See London Metropolitan Archives, P69/ETH/A/002/MS04238, Parish Register of St Ethelburga. That he intended his translation to be read by missionaries is shown in a letter in University of Cambridge Library, Manuscripts, MS Add.7603/64, J. M. Rodwell to Mrs Cecil Bendall, 8 August 1890.
20 The Huntington Library, San Marino CA, 634991, J. M. Rodwell (trans.), *El-Korân; Or, The Korân: Translated from the Arabic*, new edn (1861; London: Quaritch, 1876), xxii–xxiii, 251.
21 Wilson Library, University of North Carolina, J. M. Dent Records, Folder 5201, History Files: Everyman's Library, Hugh R. Dent, 'The Story of "Everyman's Library"' [typescript], 28. In an ironic twist, this came back to haunt Shaw two

decades later, when he engaged the Islamic scholar Muhammad Abdul Aleem Siddiqui (1892–1954) in a remarkable debate (later published) at Mombasa. After Shaw expressed his preference for Rodwell, Siddiqui rebuked the translation for its 'flagrant mistakes' and the injurious effect it was having on Western perceptions of Islam. See Anon, 'A Shavian Meets a Theologian', *Genuine Islam: Organ of the All-Malaya Muslim Missionary Society* 1, no. 1 (1936): 23.

22 Anon, 'The Korān', *The Edinburgh Review* 154, no. 316 (1881): 357–8.
23 New York Public Library, Berg Collection, Correspondence, Lafcadio Hearn to W. D. O'Connor, 29 June 1884. Hearn was mistaken about the 'Sacred Books of the East' – the series was published by Oxford University Press, not Macmillan.
24 Anon, 'The Korān', 357.
25 Elmarsafy, *The Enlightenment Qur'an*, 8.
26 Maria Westman Chapman (ed.), *Harriet Martineau's Autobiography*, vol. 1 (Boston, MA: Houghton, Osgood, 1877), 115.
27 Emanuel Deutsch, 'The Talmud', *The Quarterly Review* 123, no. 246 (1867): 418.
28 Brian Crowley, '"His Father's Son": James and Patrick Pearse', *Folk Life: Journal of Ethnological Studies* 43, no. 1 (2004): 73–4.
29 Thanks to Brian Crowley for facilitating my viewing of this book in 2018. It contains J. Darcy's stamp but no other markings.
30 Bateman's, East Sussex (National Trust), George Sale (trans.), *The Koran, Commonly called the Alcoran of Mohammed*, vol. 2 (1734; London: L. Hawes, W. Clarke and T. Wilcox, 1764), 117, 130, 190.
31 Rudyard Kipling, 'The Two-Sided Man', in Rudyard Kipling, *Selected Poems* (London: Penguin, 2006), 4.
32 Thomas Pinney (ed.), *The Letters of Rudyard Kipling. Volume 4, 1911–19* (Basingstoke: Palgrave Macmillan, 1998), 294. Hatim Tai is a familiar character in Persian and Arabic fiction, proverbial for his generosity.
33 Gilham, *Loyal Enemies*, 34–5.
34 AVaTAR Books website, Ar.S.4a, Sir William Muir, *Mahomet and Islam: A Sketch of the Prophet's Life from Original Sources, and a Brief Outline of His Religion* (London: Religious Tract Society, 1887). This book, and others cited below, are items in my personal collection, catalogued online with photographs of the books and the marginalia they contain in AVaTAR: Archive of Victorian Translations from Asia and their Readerships. www.avatar-books.com (accessed 25 October 2022).
35 Identification based on the Census of England and Wales, 1901, 1911 and 1921; Newham Archives and Local Studies Library, London, West Ham Municipal Central Secondary School Papers, Box 5, Item 2, Length of School Life and After-careers of Pupils, Girls.

36 AVaTAR Books website, Ar.S.3b, J. M. Rodwell (trans.), *The Koran*, new edn (1861; London: J. M. Dent, 1909), 508, 341, 390, viii.
37 Anon, 'Margoliouth, George', in Anon, *Crockford's Clerical Directory, 1916–17* (London: Horace Cox, 1916), 1009.
38 Leah Price, *How to Do Things with Books in Victorian Britain* (Princeton, NJ: Princeton University Press, 2012), 163.
39 For an indication, see the front page headline of the *Daily Express* (London) for 25 March 2008: 'Fury Over Plan to Teach the Koran in Schools'.
40 Repr. in Anon, *The 100 Best Books: Sir John Lubbock's List* (London: Amalgamated Press, 1899), 10.
41 British Library, Western Archives and Manuscripts, Avebury Papers, Add MS 49678, J. R. Shannon to Sir John Lubbock, 18 October [no year].
42 Stuart Wood, *Shades of the Prison House: A Personal Memoir* (London: Williams and Norgate, 1932), 44. The verse quoted is *sura* (chapter) Al-Isra, 17:13, in Sale's translation. The author's name is a pseudonym.
43 AVaTAR Books website, Ar.S.2a, George Sale (trans.), *The Koran, Commonly called the Alcoran of Mohammed* (1734; London: Frederick Warne, 1887).
44 *Hansard* HC Deb., ser. 3, vol. 234, col. 654, 8 May 1877.
45 Anon, 'Literary Intelligence', *The Publishers' Circular, and General Record of British and Foreign Literature* 40, no. 949 (1877): 230.
46 Dowager Duchess of Argyll (ed.), *George Douglas, Eighth Duke of Argyll: Autobiography and Memoirs*, vol. 1 (London: John Murray, 1906), 323.
47 George Douglas Campbell, *The Eastern Question*, vol. 2 (London: Strahan, 1879), 26.

6 Saiyid Mustafa Ben-Yusuf, an Arab Muslim convert to Christianity in Victorian Britain

1 Based on a search of the British Newspaper Archive (British Library), November 2020 to March 2021.
2 Ben-Yusuf often gave two lectures on the same day (afternoon and evening) in the same venue. To avoid erroneous 'double-counting', second lectures are only recorded separately when they are explicitly mentioned in press reports or advertisements.
3 *The Isle of Wight Observer*, 5 September 1868, 3.
4 General Register Office, England (hereafter GRO), Southport, 1871 Census of England and Wales; GRO, Death Certificate of Henry Crane, 1931. An enumerator for the 1871 Census added, incorrectly, that Ben-Yusuf was a British subject.
5 *The Shepton Mallet Journal*, 23 January 1874, 3.

6 *The Isle of Wight Observer*, 5 September 1868, 3.
7 Ibid.
8 *Portsmouth Times and Naval Gazette*, 5 September 1868, 8.
9 *The Hampshire Advertiser County Newspaper*, 10 September 1870, 8.
10 *The Isle of Wight Observer*, 5 September 1868, 3.
11 *Portsmouth Times and Naval Gazette*, 5 September 1868, 8.
12 The exhibition included 28,000 exhibitors from almost forty countries and attracted more than 6 million visitors: see Bureau International des Expositions website. https://www.bie-paris.org/site/en/1862-london (accessed 6 December 2021).
13 *The Isle of Wight Observer*, 5 September 1868, 3.
14 Ibid.
15 *The Hampshire Advertiser County Newspaper*, 10 September 1870, 8. An alternative version of this story states that he was given two copies, one in French and another in Hebrew: *The Isle of Wight Observer*, 5 September 1868, 3.
16 Ibid.
17 *The Essex Standard*, 29 October 1875, 3.
18 *The Isle of Wight Observer*, 5 September 1868, 3.
19 Martin Pugh, *Britain and Islam: A History from 622 to the Present Day* (New Haven, CT: Yale University Press, 2019), 113; G. A. Oddie, *Social Protest in India: British Protestant Missionaries and Social Reforms 1850–1900* (New Delhi: Manohar, 1979), 10.
20 *The Hampshire Advertiser*, 26 September 1868, 6.
21 Repr. in *The Bedford Times and Bedfordshire Independent*, 4 February 1871, 5.
22 Ibid.
23 On El-Karey's early life, see *The Hereford Journal*, 23 June 1866, 7.
24 *Islington Gazette*, 13 November 1866, 1.
25 *Portsmouth Times and Naval Gazette*, 5 September 1868, 8.
26 Ibid.
27 *Birmingham Daily Post*, 15 June 1868, 1.
28 *Portsmouth Times and Naval Gazette*, 5 September 1868, 8.
29 *The Isle of Wight Observer*, 5 September 1868, 3.
30 Ibid.
31 *The South Eastern Advertiser*, 5 October 1872, 3.
32 *The Wrexham Advertiser*, 23 September 1871, 4.
33 *The Stratford Times*, 10 May 1876, 8.
34 A search of the British Newspaper Archive revealed just one reference in this period to Ben-Yusuf's Jewish heritage: an advertisement for an 1869 lecture which described him as 'an Algerian Jew'. See *The Aberdeen Free Press*, 24 September 1869, 4.
35 *The Bedfordshire Mercury*, 8 February 1873, 5.

36 See Sadiah Qureshi, *Peoples on Parade: Exhibitions, Empire, and Anthropology in Nineteenth-Century Britain* (London: University of Chicago Press, 2011).
37 Ibid., 106, 3, 54.
38 Ibid., 105.
39 Ibid., 8.
40 *The Banbury Advertiser*, 24 December 1873, 4.
41 See Kathryn Tidrick, *Heart-Beguiling Araby* (Cambridge: Cambridge University Press, 1981).
42 *The Wrexham Advertiser*, 23 September 1871, 4.
43 *Sheffield and Rotherham Independent*, 30 April 1869, 2.
44 *The Morning Post*, 7 June 1869, 1.
45 GRO, Marriage Certificate for Mustapha Moussa Ben-Youseph Nathan and Anna Hermine Charlotte Kind, 17 August 1869.
46 *The Aberdeen Free Press*, 24 September 1869, 5.
47 GRO, 1871 Census for England and Wales; *Chester Courant*, 14 June 1871, 6.
48 J. Muhleisen-Arnold, *The Society for Propagating the Gospel among the Moslems, in Connection with the Church of England; Its First Appeal* (London: Rivingtons, 1860), 4.
49 Ibid., 8.
50 *The Atlas*, 13 April 1861, 14.
51 Anon, *Statement of The Moslem Mission Society*, 3rd edn (London: Rivingtons, 1862), 2.
52 University of Cambridge, A Cambridge Alumni Database. http://venn.lib.cam.ac.uk/cgi-bin/search-2018.pl?sur=&suro=c&fir=mustafa&firo=c&cit=&cito=c&c=all&z=all&tex=&sye=&eye=&col=all&maxcount=50 (accessed 8 January 2022).
53 *The Wrexham Advertiser*, 23 September 1871, 4.
54 *The Wrexham Guardian*, 9 September 1871, 7.
55 *The Hampshire Chronicle*, 10 September 1870, 4.
56 *The Shepton Mallet Journal*, 23 January 1874, 3.
57 *The Wrexham Advertiser*, 19 November 1870, 4.
58 *The Hampshire Advertiser County Newspaper*, 10 September 1870, 8.
59 *The Wrexham Advertiser*, 19 November 1870, 4.
60 Ibid.
61 *The Chester Chronicle*, 17 June 1871, 8.
62 *The Wrexham Advertiser*, 23 September 1871, 4.
63 *The Chelmsford Chronicle*, 7 May 1875, 6.
64 *The Wrexham Advertiser*, 19 November 1870, 4.
65 *Bolton Evening News*, 19 April 1871, 4.
66 Ibid.
67 *The Shepton Mallet Journal*, 23 January 1874, 3.

68 *The Bath Chronicle*, 29 January 1874, 7.
69 *The Framlingham Weekly News*, 2 October 1875, 4.
70 Ibid.
71 Anon, *A Plea for 75 Members of a Church of England Missionary Brotherhood, to Be Sent to India, Central Africa and Syria, in Connection with The Moslem Missionary Society* (London: Wells Gardner, 1873), 17.
72 *The Bath Chronicle*, 22 January 1874, 3.
73 *Southern Times*, 26 September 1874, 6.
74 *The Lincoln, Rutland, and Stamford Mercury*, 5 December 1873, 4.
75 *The Shepton Mallet Journal*, 23 January 1874, 3.
76 *The Bath Chronicle*, 29 January 1874, 7.
77 *The Shepton Mallet Journal*, 23 January 1874, 3.
78 *Leicester Journal*, 11 July 1873, 7.
79 *The Chelmsford Chronicle*, 5 March 1875, 8.
80 *Derby Mercury*, 16 July 1873, 5.
81 *The Star* [Guernsey], 19 August 1880, 2.
82 See *Leicester Journal*, 19 December 1879, 3.
83 *Southern Times*, 31 March 1877, 6.
84 Anna became a milliner in Boston and wrote a popular reference book on the subject (1909). She moved to New York City, where Zaida found success as a portrait photographer.
85 *The Chelmsford Chronicle*, 2 November 1876, 5.
86 *The Ipswich Journal*, 18 November 1876, 5.
87 *The Coleraine Chronicle*, 13 November 1880, 4.
88 *The Islington Gazette*, 7 May 1888, 1.
89 The charge against him was dismissed in court: see *The Islington Gazette*, 30 May 1892, 3.
90 *The South London Press*, 29 June 1895, 6.
91 Ibid.
92 *St. James's Gazette*, 15 January 1896, 6; *Lloyd's Weekly Newspaper*, 19 January 1896, 15.
93 *Eastern Evening News*, 3 February 1896, 3.
94 *The Hackney Express*, 5 September 1896, 4.
95 *Lloyd's Weekly Newspaper*, 26 July 1896, 3.
96 *The Hackney Express*, 5 September 1896, 4.
97 Ibid.
98 GRO, 1901 Census of England and Wales.
99 GRO, 1911 Census of England and Wales.
100 *The Weekly Herald* [Tottenham and Edmonton], 12 February 1904, 4.
101 Ibid.

102 Ibid., 23 March 1906, 10.
103 Ibid.
104 GRO, England and Wales Death Index, 1916–2007.

7 From Arab *millet* to British Islam: Syrian Muslims in Victorian Manchester

1 Fred Halliday, 'The *Millet* of Manchester: Arab Merchants and Cotton Trade', *British Journal of Middle Eastern Studies* 19, no. 2 (1992): 159–76.
2 Ibid., 168.
3 *The Liverpool Mercury*, 14 December 1892, 6.
4 By 'Syria' I mean the Ottoman sub-provinces of Aleppo, Damascus and Beirut, in addition to the two special districts of Mount Lebanon and Jerusalem.
5 Fruma Zachs, *The Making of a Syrian Identity: Intellectuals and Merchants in Nineteenth Century Beirut* (Leiden: Brill, 2005), 40–4.
6 Geyikdağı, V. Necla, *Foreign Investment in the Ottoman Empire: International Trade and Relations, 1854–1914* (London: Tauris Academic Studies, 2011), 23.
7 See Giorgio Riello, *Cotton: The Fabric that Made the Modern World* (Cambridge: Cambridge University Press, 2014).
8 Roger Lloyd-Jones and A. A. Le Roux, 'The Size of Firms in the Cotton Industry: Manchester 1815–41', *The Economic History Review* 33, no. 1 (1980): 72–82.
9 Riello, *Cotton*, 228.
10 See Anon, *The Export Merchant Shippers of London, Liverpool, Sheffield [etc.], with Their Respective Trading Ports, Classification of Exports [etc.]* (London: Dean, 1880).
11 Zachs, *The Making of a Syrian Identity*, 51–67.
12 Halliday, 'The *Millet* of Manchester'.
13 Ibid., 127.
14 Ibid., 161.
15 See May Ydlibi and Bahru Zewde, *With Ethiopian Rulers: A Biography of Hasib Ydlibi* (Addis Ababa: Addis Ababa University Press, 2006); *The Times*, 18 August 1853, 8.
16 *The Evening Chronicle*, 28 December 1846, 9.
17 Moss Side was to grow substantially during the nineteenth century, becoming an important residential centre for immigrants and developing a strong multicultural working-class culture and identity. In the early 1850s, there were 131 inhabited houses for a population of 943 individuals; by the turn of the new century, the township had amalgamated with Manchester, with a population of 26,677. See *The Manchester Guardian*, 18 November 1901, 4.

18 *The Guardian*, 11 June 1885, 5.
19 Louis M. Hayes, *Reminiscences of Manchester and its Surrounding Areas from 1840*, new edn (1905; Manchester: Empire Publications, 2009), 212. The first reference to Ydlibi attending the Royal Manchester Exchange is 1853: see Anon, *A New Alphabetical and Classified Directory of Manchester & Salford* (Manchester: Whellan, 1853), 549.
20 See *The Guardian*, 5 April 1886, 5.
21 On the merchant-consul figure, see Philip D. Curtin, *Cross-Cultural Trade in World History* (Cambridge: Cambridge University Press, 1984), 115, 130, 245; Ferry de Goey, 'Les consuls et les relations internationales au xixe siècle', *Cahiers de la Méditerranée* 93 (2016): 61–75.
22 *Manchester Courier and Lancashire General Advertiser*, 24 January 1852, 9.
23 *The Manchester Weekly Times and Examiner*, 31 January 1852, 5.
24 *Manchester Courier*, 15 January 1855, 3.
25 *The Standard*, 25 September 1848, 2.
26 *The Morning Post*, 22 October 1852, 3.
27 See D. A. Farnie, *The English Cotton Industry and the World Market, 1815–1896* (Oxford: Clarendon Press, 1979), 145–67.
28 *The Guardian*, 29 October 1863, 2.
29 *The Guardian*, 11 June 1885, 5.
30 Hayes, *Reminiscences*, 309.
31 *Manchester Courier*, 18 November 1854, 1.
32 Ydlibi and Zewde, *With Ethiopian Rulers*, n.p. [preface]. Another version states that he returned to settle a dispute regarding money that he was owed by the Ottoman government. When Hayes met him in Constantinople, he was 'at the stage of hopeless despair', haunting the courts 'like a restless spirit longing and hoping for the verdict in his favour, which was never to be given' (Hayes, *Reminiscences*, 309).
33 With no Islamic institution, imam or *qadi* (magistrate, judge) officiating religious weddings in Lancashire prior to Quilliam's LMI, it is unclear how they were married.
34 Gladys (b. 1887), Lillie (b. 1888), Mustapha Cecil (b. 1889), Eminie (b. 1891), Rudah (b. 1893), Mohamed Yusuff (b. 1895), Leilah (b. 1898) and Fizie (b. 1899).
35 *The Guardian*, 29 August 1900, 9.
36 *The Liverpool Mercury*, 14 November 1892, 6.
37 *The Crescent* (hereafter *TC*), 21 August 1907, 122.
38 Author's correspondence with Fady Mokaiesh, August 2020.
39 *The Brooklyn Daily Eagle*, 7 June 1909, 18.
40 See Albert Hourani, 'Ottoman Reform and the Politics of Notables', in *Beginnings of Modernization of Middle East: The Nineteenth Century*, ed. William R. Polk and Richard L. Chambers (Chicago, IL: University of Chicago Press, 1968), 41–68.

41 *The Manchester Courier*, 20 February 1896, 6.
42 See Hugh McLeod, *Class and Religion in the Late Victorian City* (London: Croom Helm, 1974), 2.
43 Simon Taylor, Malcolm Cooper and P. S. Barnell, *Manchester, The Warehouse Legacy. An Introduction and Guide* (London: English Heritage, 2002), 21–4.
44 Anon, *The Export Merchant Shippers of London*, 76–111.
45 *TC*, 5 May 1902, 155.
46 Essiedene (Azzeddine, 1904–1975) and Partmie (Fatimeh, 1910–2002).
47 Assets that are an inalienable charitable endowment under Islamic law. Author's correspondence with Fady Mokaiesh, August 2020.
48 Christopher O'Brien, *Cardus Uncovered* (Nottingham: Whitethorn Range Publishing, 2014), 23‑5.
49 *The Guardian*, 22 April 1902, 5.
50 *Dundee Evening Post*, 22 April 1902, 2.
51 The Anzarut brothers were among the founding members of the Spanish and Portuguese Synagogue (now Manchester Jewish Museum) with other well-to-do philanthropic members of the Levantine Sephardic community, such as Baghdad-born Charles I. Sassoon.
52 The first mosque and Islamic cultural centre in Manchester opened to the public in September 1949: see *Manchester Evening News*, September 17, 1949, 4.
53 Ron Geaves, *Islam in Victorian Britain: The Life and Times of Abdullah Quilliam* (Markfield: Kube, 2010), 69-71.
54 The earliest known list of members was provided by Elisabeth Fatima Cates for *The Allahabad Review* 3 (1892): 22.
55 *The Isle of Man Times and General Advertiser*, 8 July 1893, 5; *TC*, 18 May 1898, 331.
56 *The Liverpool Mercury*, 21 September 1892, 6.
57 *The Liverpool Mercury*, 14 December 1892, 6.
58 *TC*, 12 September 1900, 163-4.
59 *TC*, 18 March 1896, 597-9.
60 *TC*, 13 April 1898, 227.
61 Durham University Library, SAD-263/1/329–330, 'Paper Read by Mr. Mustapha Khalil at a Meeting of the Anjuman-i-Islam of London', 27 December 1896.
62 For instance, Yusuf Samih Asmay, *Islam in Victorian Liverpool: An Ottoman Account of Britain's First Mosque Community*, trans. and ed. Yahya Birt, Riordan Macnamara and Münire Zeyneb Maksudoğlu (Swansea: Claritas Books, 2021). Asmay (d. 1942), who was an Ottoman subject, had his harsh account of Quilliam and the LMI banned by order of the sultan.
63 Quilliam, for instance, later intercepted Bibles shipped from Liverpool to Constantinople that contained hidden tracts targeting the central Ottoman power (*St. James's Gazette*, 10 January 1905, 10). On Quilliam as a soft-power actor for the

Ottoman Porte, see Matthew A. Sharp, '"On Behalf of the Sultan": The Late Ottoman State and the Cultivation of British and American Converts to Islam' (PhD thesis, University of Pennsylvania, 2020).
64 Hourani, 'Ottoman Reform', 48.
65 Geaves, *Islam in Victorian Britain*, 72.
66 Hourani, 'Ottoman Reform', 46.
67 Asmay, *Islam in Victorian Liverpool*, 74.
68 The act of inviting or calling to people to embrace Islam.
69 *The Liverpool Daily Post*, 16 August 1897, 7.
70 Jamie Gilham, *Loyal Enemies: British Converts to Islam, 1850–1950* (New York: Oxford University Press, 2014), 91–2.
71 *TC*, 28 January 1893, 14–16.
72 Shahin Kuli Khan Khattak, *Islam and the Victorians: Nineteenth-Century Perceptions of Muslim Practices and Beliefs* (London: Tauris Academic Studies, 2008), 34–43.
73 Ali Özuyar, *Knockaloe ve Meçhul Türkler: Modern Tarihin İlk Sivil Esir Kampı* (Istanbul: Emre Yalçın, 2008), 69. See also Matthew Stibbe, *Civilian Internment during the First World War* (London: Palgrave Macmillan, 2019); Panayi Panikos, *Prisoners of Britain: German Civilian and Combatant Internees during the First World War* (Manchester: Manchester University Press, 2013), 99.
74 *Daily Gazette for Middlesbrough*, 19 July 1916, 4; Rudolf Hartmann, *Bilder aus dem Gefangenenlager Knockaloe in England* (Bad Nassau: Blättervereinigung, 1918), 81. The Kirk Patrick Cemetery, next to Knockaloe Camp, contains a small Muslim plot with seven graves containing Turkish civilian internees from this period.
75 See 'Aliens Restriction (Amendment) Act, 1919'. http://www.legislation.gov.uk/ukpga/1919/92/pdfs/ukpga_19190092_en.pdf (accessed 25 October 2022).

8 The last Nawab of Bengal: India and England, 1838–84

1 This chapter expands on Lyn Innes, *The Last Prince of Bengal: A Family's Journey from an Indian Palace to the Australian Outback* (London: The Westbourne Press, 2021). Much of the original research for the book was carried out with the financial aid of a Leverhulme Emeritus Fellowship, and I am grateful to the Leverhulme Trust for this assistance.
2 Anon, *Indian Records, with a Commercial View of the Relations between the British Government and the Nawab Nazim of Bengal, Behar and Orissa* (London: G. Bubb, 1870), 110.
3 The first and most important division in the *umma* (the universal Muslim religious community) occurred after the death of Muhammad in relation to his successor. Unlike the vast majority of Muslims (Sunnis), Shi'is believe in the succession of the

direct descendants of Muhammad through the line of the Prophet's cousin and son-in-law Ali ibn Talib (601–61) rather than the caliphate.

4 Philip Mason, *A Matter of Honour: An Account of the Indian Army* (London: Macmillan, 1986), 240–1.
5 Quoted by Norman Daniel, *Islam, Europe and Empire* (Edinburgh: Edinburgh University Press, 1966), 246.
6 J. Datta Gupta and Sanat Kumar Bose (eds), *West Bengal District Records. New Series. Murshidabad Nizamut. Letters Issued. Part II. 1834–1872* (Calcutta: Government of West Bengal Publications, 1969), 230.
7 Daniel, *Islam*, 267.
8 Macaulay served on the governor-general's Supreme Council, 1834–8. Minute by T. B. Macaulay, 2 February 1835. http://www.columbia.edu/itc/mealac/pritchett/00generallinks/macaulay/txt_minute_education_1835.html (accessed 10 September 2022).
9 Gupta and Bose, *West Bengal*, 386.
10 British Library (hereafter BL), India Office Records (hereafter IOR), IOR/L/PS/6/530, Coll 30/2: India Political Collections to Dispatches 1861.
11 Ibid.
12 Ibid.
13 Ibid.
14 Ibid.
15 Barbara Daly Metcalf, *Islamic Revival in British India: Deoband, 1860–1900*, new edn (1982; Princeton, NJ: Princeton University Press, 2002), 56–7.
16 Gupta and Bose, *West Bengal*, iii.
17 Ibid., 306.
18 Ibid.
19 BL, IOR, IOR/L/PS/6/530, Coll 30/2, India Political Collections to Dispatches, 1861.
20 Ibid.
21 Gupta and Bose, *West Bengal*, 312.
22 Henry W. Torrens, *A Selection from the Writings, Prose and Poetical, of the Late Henry W. Torrens*, ed. James Hume, vol. 1 (Calcutta: C. R. Lepage, 1854), cix.
23 Ibid., ci, cii.
24 Ibid., 77.
25 Ibid.
26 Kenneth Ballhatchet, *Race, Sex and Class under the Raj: Imperial Attitudes and Policies and their Critics, 1793–1905* (London: Weidenfeld and Nicolson, 1980), 7.
27 Helen Mackenzie, *Storms and Sunshine of a Soldier's Life: Lt.-General Colin Mackenzie*, vol. 1 (Edinburgh: David Douglas, 1884), 152–3.
28 Gupta and Bose, *West Bengal*, 640.
29 Ibid., 645.

30 Ibid.
31 BL, IOR, IOR/L/PS/6/530, Coll 30/2: India Political Collections to Dispatches, 1861.
32 1871 Census of England and Wales (Knightsbridge, London).
33 *The Illustrated Times Weekly Newspaper*, 14 April, 1869, 227.
34 Ibid.
35 The *Dundee Courier* 12 April 1869, 3; *Greenock Telegraph and Clyde Shipping Gazette*, 10 April 1869, 5.
36 *The Leeds Mercury*, 27 May, 1869, 3.
37 *The Tralee Chronicle*, 17 May 1870, 1.
38 See Innes, *The Last Prince*, 92–7.
39 Anon, *British Policy in India, With Special Reference to the Nawab Nazim of Bengal. By an Englishman* (London: J. Burbridge, 1870).
40 *Vanity Fair*, 16 April 1870, n.p.
41 *The Tomahawk*, 16 April 1870, 11.
42 BL, IOR and Private Papers, Mss Eur 467, Private letters from the Earl of Mayo to the Duke of Argyll (microfilm), Letter from Argyll to Mayo, 26 April 1870.
43 Hafiz Ahmed Hassan, *Pilgrimage to the Caaba and Charing Cross* (London: W. H. Allen, n.d. [1871]), 139.
44 Quoted in Humayun Mirza, *From Plassey to Pakistan: The Family History of Iskander Mirza, the First President of Pakistan* (Lanham, MD: University Press of America, 2002), 105.
45 *Daily Mail*, 1 June 1921, 6.
46 *The Morning Post*, 5 August 1885, 6.
47 Ibid.
48 *The Globe*, 12 August 1885, 1.
49 *The Evening Standard*, 29 October 1885, 2.
50 With the support of the Nawab of Murshidabad, Mansour Ali Khan's elder son, Sarah eventually gained custody of her sons in 1887 following the death of one of their appointed guardians, Mowbray Walker. In 1889, she was able to visit her two daughters in Murshidabad.

9 Maulana Muhammad Barakatullah Bhopali in late-Victorian England

1 Barakatullah's name has been spelled in a number of ways, such as 'Barkatullah' and 'Barakat-Ullah'. This chapter uses the format that he used himself most frequently during the period under discussion, namely the 1890s. Bhopali indicates his place of origin in India, the princely state of Bhopal. His year of birth is contested, but generally given as 1859. Maulana is a title given to a Muslim religious scholar.

2 Pan-Islamism emerged in the late nineteenth and early twentieth centuries as a political movement and ideology aimed at the worldwide unity of Muslims. For a definitive study of pan-Islam, see Jacob Landau, *The Politics of Pan-Islam: Ideology and Organization* (New York: Oxford University Press, 1990).

3 For more details about Barakatullah's later political career, see Humayun Ansari, 'Maulana Barkatullah Bhopali's Transnationalism: Pan-Islamism, Colonialism and Radical Politics', in *Transnational Islam in Interwar Europe: Muslim Activists and Thinkers*, ed. Gotz Nordbruch and Umar Ryad (New York: Palgrave Macmillan, 2014), 181–210.

4 Nikki R. Keddie, *An Islamic Response to Imperialism: Political and Religious Writings of Saiyid Jamal al-din 'al-Afghani'* (Los Angeles: University of California Press, 1968), 39–41.

5 On Barakatullah's qualification, see Charles Brodie Patterson, 'Mohammad Barakatullah: A Biographical Sketch' *Mind* 12, no. 7 (1903): 495.

6 Accused of seditious activities in Egypt, al-Afghani was, under British pressure, expelled by the Khedive (the Ottoman viceroy) in August 1879. See Keddie, *An Islamic Response*, 21.

7 Plural of *alim*.

8 Al-Afghani was in London in 1883 and again in 1891–2, when he attacked Persia's autocratic oppression (see Keddie, *An Islamic Response*, 24). For details of al-Afghani's activities in London, see Nikki R. Keddie, *Sayyid Jamal ad-Din 'al-Afghani': A Political Biography* (Los Angeles: University of California Press, 1972), 355–72. On al-Afghani in India, see M. Irfan, *Aik Jahan Gasht Inqilabi: Barkatullah Bhopali* (Bhopal: A'fan Publisher, 1969), 51–2.

9 Anon, 'Sheikh-ul- Islam, Mr. Quilliam,' *Paisa Akhbar* [Lahore], 11 May 1891, 3.

10 A close friend of Barakatullah, Abdul Rahman Siddiqui, provides details of Barakatullah travelling to England in 1890 on the same ship as Maulvi Riazuddin, editor of the Indian periodical, *Al-Riaz*. See Abdul Rahman Siddique,'Maulana Barkatullah Marhum', *Urdu* (July 1941): 393.

11 Led by an American convert to Islam, Mohammed Russell Webb (1846–1916). See Umar F. Abd-Allah, *A Muslim in Victorian America: The Life of Alexander Russell Webb* (New York: Oxford University Press, 2006), 160–1.

12 *The Crescent* (hereafter *TC*), 3 June 1893, 160.

13 W. E. Gladstone, *Bulgarian Horrors, and the Question of the East* (London: John Murray, 1876); J. Salt, *Imperialism, Evangelism and the Ottoman Armenians, 1878–1896* (London: Frank Cass, 1993).

14 See Ron Geaves, *Islam in Victorian Britain: The Life and Times of Abdullah Quilliam* (Markfield: Kube, 2010), 69–71.

15 *Home News for India, China and the Colonies*, 26 December 1890, 25.

16 *The Times*, 26 September 1890, 7.

17 *Liverpool Mercury*, 10 October 1890, 6. See also Kristan Tetens, 'The Lyceum and the Lord Chamberlain: The Case of Hall Caine's Mahomet', in *Henry Irving: A Re-Evaluation of the Pre-Eminent Victorian Actor-Manager*, ed. Richard Foulkes (London: Routledge, 2008), 49–63.
18 See *The Times*, 21 April 1891, 4.
19 *TC*, 18 November 1893, 349.
20 *TC*, 20 May 1893, 139; *TC*, 2 January 1895, 1 and back matter; *TC*, 5 June 1895, 182. For an index of Barakatullah's lectures, articles and other activities at the LMI, see Brent D. Singleton, 'Index to The Crescent (Weekly of the Liverpool Moslem Institute) for January 14, 1893–December 30, 1893; and January 2, 1895; March 6, 1895', *CSUSB Library Faculty Publications*, Paper 26 (2014). Available online: https://scholarworks.lib.csusb.edu/library-publications/26/ (accessed 10 June 2022).
21 See, for example, Barakatullah's piece on Quilliam's return from Constantinople in *Paisa Akhbar* [Lahore], 20 July 1891, 5; also translated in *The Liverpool Echo*, 5 June 1891, 3, which followed up on an earlier bulletin regarding an invitation to Constantinople from 'The Lord Chamberlain of the Sultan of Turkey to the leader of the Mohameden sect in Liverpool to attend an International Conference on Islam' (see *The Huddersfield Chronicle*, 15 April 1891, 3).
22 *Liverpool Review*, 28 November 1891, 7.
23 Writing about the concepts of heaven and hell, Barakatullah referred to the verse in the Qur'an that regarded their expression as 'parabolical' rather than material (*TC*, 6 November 1895, 298–9).
24 See Jamie Gilham, *Loyal Enemies: British Converts to Islam, 1850–1950* (London: Hurst, 2014), 90–1.
25 *TC*, 18 December 1895, 387.
26 Yusuf Samih Asmay, *Islam in Victorian Liverpool: An Ottoman Account of Britain's First Mosque Community*, trans. and ed. Yahya Birt, Riordan Macnamara and Münire Zeyneb Maksudoğlu (Swansea: Claritas Books, 2021), 9–12.
27 'Id al-Adha is the feast of the sacrifice celebrating the end of the annual Hajj, or Pilgrimage to Mecca.
28 Asmay, *Islam in Victorian Liverpool*, 86.
29 See the report of the 1896 Annual Meeting of the LMI in ibid., 138.
30 Ibid., 89.
31 Ibid.
32 Ibid., 86.
33 *Liverpool Mercury*, 16 July 1889, 5.
34 See *Liverpool Mercury*, 27 September 1894, 6; *Mona's Herald*, 10 October 1894, 5.
35 As reported in *The Islamic World*, May 1894, 24.
36 Quoted in *The Islamic World*, October 1894, 187–9.

37 Quilliam's welcoming speech (translated into Persian by Barakatullah), echoing Barakatullah's thoughts, in *TC*, 3 July 1895, 5.
38 British Library (hereafter BL), India Office Records (hereafter IOR), Political and Secret Department Papers, L/PS/19/168, Thugee and Dakaiti Department, C.S.B. Memoranda etc., 1897–8.
39 As is well-known, among the most vitriolic of the late Victorian politicians was William Ewart Gladstone. Victorian clergymen too raised the temperature by drawing attention to 'those unspeakable hotbeds of vice – the harems of dissolute Turks', denouncing Islam as that 'most nauseous abomination'. Drawing on medieval vocabulary, they denounced the character and conduct of Muhammad as a demonic, heretic imposter. See Richard T. Shannon, *Gladstone and the Bulgarian Agitation 1876* (London: Thomas Nelson, 1963), 35, 33. Later, Winston Churchill (1874–1965) condemned Islam's 'fatalistic apathy', its 'degraded sensualism' and its demeaning treatment of women 'as absolute property'; indeed, he likened the dangerous 'fanatical frenzy' of Muslims to 'hydrophobia [rabies] in a dog': see Winston Churchill, *The River War: An Historical Account of the Reconquest of the Soudan, Vol. II* (London: Longmans, Green and Company, 1899), 248–9.
40 See *Punch*, 18 January 1896, 26.
41 *Jihad*, striving or struggling in the path of God. Here, Quilliam is threatening the lesser *jihad* – armed struggle or 'holy war'.
42 *The Newcastle Evening Chronicle*, 24 September 1896, 3.
43 *TC*, 15 January 1896, 459; *TC*, 9 September 1896, 1004. It is currently unclear when and why Barakatullah left Liverpool. His letters to Asmay, dated 15 August 1895 and 11 October 1895 (discussed above), were written from Liverpool. Newspapers reporting him chairing meetings in London suggest that he had moved there in 1896. In the absence of any hard evidence, it remains largely a matter of conjecture why he left Liverpool. However, his two letters to Asmay indicate that he was becoming increasingly unhappy with the tensions emerging at the LMI. Moreover, the pan-Islamic political activism of Muslims in London, as well as the opening of a mosque there by Mohammed Dollie in late 1895 (see *TC*, 18 December 1895, 387), whom he had earlier met in Liverpool, would likely have prompted his move.
44 *The Times*, 22 December 1894, 7.
45 *The Morning Post*, 16 May 1895, 2.
46 See *TC*, 25 March 1896, 617; Gilham, *Loyal Enemies*, 69–71.
47 *The Morning Post*, 22 February 1897, 3. Referring to some British newspapers 'advocating that English people should volunteer their services as soldiers to help the Greeks [in Crete]', Quilliam stated that 'it might be his duty to call upon the Muslims in England, India, and West and South Africa to volunteer to serve under the banner of the Sultan, the Caliph of Islam': *TC*, 10 March 1897, 155.
48 *The Morning Post*, 1 September 1896, 5.

49 *The Islamic World*, March 1895, 325.
50 Ibid., 324. See also Rev. Malcolm MacColl, 'Russia and England', *The Contemporary Review* 67 (January 1895): 1–16.
51 *The Islamic World*, March 1895, 324–5.
52 *The Standard*, 9 September 1892, 2.
53 BL, IOR, L/PS/19/168, C.S.B. Memoranda, 1897–8.
54 Ibid.
55 Ibid.
56 Ibid.
57 *London Evening Standard*, 10 January 1898, 4. The London Indian Society was established in 1865 with Dadabhai Naoroji as president: see *The Homeward Mail*, 5 April 1865, 289.
58 BL, IOR, L/PS/19/168, Memoranda by Lee-Warner, 5 April 1897 and 25 January 1898.
59 Quoted in Azmi Ozcan, *Pan-Islamism: Indian Muslims, the Ottomans and Britain (1877–1924)* (Leiden: Brill, 1997), 47.
60 Ibid., 51–2.
61 *The Pall Mall Gazette*, 19 December 1891, 2.
62 S. N. Sen, *History of the Freedom Movement in India (1857–1947)* (New Delhi: New Age International Publishers, 1997), 69–70.
63 *The Morning Post*, 29 December 1896, 5; *The Standard*, 14 January 1898, 3.
64 Ibid.
65 For the full resolution, see *The Standard*, 29 December 1897, 3. Rafiuddin was present at the conference, though he later claimed that he had dissociated himself from the resolution: see his reply in *The Standard*, 14 January 1898, 3, to Naoroji's earlier letter in *The Standard*, 12 January 1898, 2. In contrast, other Muslims, such as H. S. Khalil, sessional president of the Anjuman-i Islam, and Barakatullah, supported it.
66 Diane Robinson-Dunn, *The Harem, Slavery and British Imperial Culture: Anglo-Muslim Relations in the Late Nineteenth Century* (Manchester: Manchester University Press, 2006), 119.
67 Rana Kabbani, *Europe's Myths of Orient: Devise and Rule* (London: Pandora, 1986), 14–36.
68 Charles G. Chaddock (trans.), *Psychopathia Sexualis* (London: F. J. Rebman, 1894), 5.
69 Malcolm MacColl, *The Sultan and the Powers* (London: Longmans, Green and Company, 1896), ix.
70 Matthew A. Sharp, '"On Behalf of the Sultan": The Late Ottoman State and the Cultivation of British and American Converts to Islam' (PhD thesis, University of Pennsylvania, 2020), 8–9; Gilham, *Loyal Enemies*, 95.

71 *The Manx Sun*, 31 March 1900, 2.
72 Ibid.
73 Quoted in Sharp, '"On Behalf of the Sultan,"' 9.
74 Asmay, *Islam in Victorian Liverpool*, 99.
75 BL, IOR, L/PJ/12/213, New Scotland Yard Report on 'Maulvie Mahomed Barkatullah', 30 July 1924, f. 1. Another note reported that Barakatullah had married in London: see BL, IOR, L/PS/19/168, C.S.B. Memoranda, 1897–8.
76 Asmay, *Islam in Victorian Liverpool*, 88.
77 *TC*, 21 October 1893, 315.
78 Sayyid Amir Ali, 'The Real Status of Women in Islam', *The Nineteenth Century* 30, no. 175 (1891): 387–99; Rafiuddin Ahmad, 'Are English Women Legally Inferior to their Mahomedan Sisters?', *Imperial and Asiatic Quarterly Review and Oriental and Colonial Record* 1 (January–April 1891): 410–29.
79 Mohammad Barakatullah, 'Mohamedan Women', in *India, Ceylon, Straits Settlements, British North Borneo, Hong Kong. The British Empire Series*, ed. Anon, vol. 1 (London: Kegan Paul, 1899), 384.
80 Ibid.
81 Ibid.
82 Ibid., 378.
83 BL, IOR, New Scotland Yard Report, 30 July 1924, f. 5.
84 On arrival in New York, Barakatullah connected with George Freeman and John Devoy, both radical Irish republican activists. See J. Campbell Ker, *Political Trouble in India, 1907–1917* (Calcutta: Superintendent Government Printing, 1917), 221–3.
85 See Ansari, 'Maulana Barkatullah Bhopali's Transnationalism', 186–205.

10 Feeding hungry Christians: The Liverpool Muslim Institute on Christmas Day

1 Neil Armstrong, *Christmas in Nineteenth Century England* (Manchester: Manchester University Press, 2010), 100.
2 J. M. Golby and A. W. Perdue, *The Making of the Modern Christmas* (Athens, GA: University of Georgia Press, 1986), 40.
3 Armstrong, *Christmas*, 102.
4 John Storey, 'The Invention of the English Christmas', in *Christmas in Ideology and Popular Culture*, ed. Sheila Whiteley (Edinburgh: Edinburgh University Press, 2008), 17–31, quote at 17.

5 For more on this, see Tara Moore, 'Starvation in Victorian Christmas Fiction', *Victorian Literature and Culture* 36, no. 2 (2008): 489–505.
6 Armstrong, *Christmas*, 118.
7 For more on the Catholic and competing welfare structures, see the chapter 'Charity, Ethnicity and the Catholic Parish,' in John Belchem, *Merseypride: Essays in Liverpool Exceptionalism*, 2nd edn (Liverpool: Liverpool University Press, 2006), 101–28.
8 Ibid., 127.
9 Ibid., 4.
10 Lucy Kilfoyle, 'Beyond Her Benny: Reimagining the "Street Arab" in Victorian Liverpool', *Transactions of the Historic Society of Lancashire and Cheshire* 166, no. 1 (2017): 75–92, quote at 77.
11 Armstrong, *Christmas*, 105.
12 Arthur Birnage, 'Liverpool's Hot Pots: A Remarkable Christmas Charity', *The Harmsworth Magazine* 5 (August 1900–January 1901): 299–301.
13 The date of the start of feedings is given variously as 1887 or 1888 in contemporaneous accounts.
14 *Liverpool Weekly Courier*, 28 December 1889, 6.
15 Unless otherwise noted or quoted, the following description of events comes from *The Crescent* (hereafter *TC*), 28 December 1898, 387–91.
16 *TC*, 27 December 1899, 404.
17 *TC*, 28 December 1898, 387.
18 *TC*, 1 January 1896, 427.
19 Ali Köse, *Conversion to Islam: A Study of Native British Converts* (London: Kegan Paul, 1995), 12.
20 *TC*, 30 December 1896, 1262.
21 *TC*, 29 December 1897, 820.
22 Humayun Ansari, 'Preface', in *Victorian Muslim: Abdullah Quilliam and Islam in the West*, ed. Jamie Gilham and Ron Geaves (London: Hurst, 2017), xxi.
23 Jamie Gilham, '"Upholding the Banner of Islam": British Converts to Islam and the Liverpool Muslim Institute, c.1887–1908', *Immigrants and Minorities* 33, no. 1 (2015): 23–44, quote at 32.
24 Yusuf Samih Asmay, *Islam in Victorian Liverpool: An Ottoman Account of Britain's First Mosque Community*, trans. and ed. Yahya Birt, Riordan Macnamara and Münire Zeyneb Maksudoğlu (Swansea: Claritas Books, 2021), 93.
25 *TC*, 9 December 1896, 1208.
26 *TC*, 11 January 1899, 26; *TC*, 27 December 1899, 406.
27 *TC*, 25 December 1895, 409; *TC*, 20 December 1899, 393.

28 *TC*, 28 December 1898, 391; *TC*, 27 December 1899, 406; *TC*, 26 December 1900, 409; *TC*, 25 December 1901, 410; *TC*, 24 December 1902, 412; *TC*, 13 January 1904, 26.
29 *TC*, 28 December 1898, 391.
30 *TC*, 13 January 1904, 26.
31 *TC*, 28 December 1898, 391.
32 *TC*, 29 December 1897, 821.
33 *TC*, 27 December 1899, 405.
34 *TC*, 25 December 1895, 409; *TC*, 16 December 1896, 1225.
35 *TC*, 29 December 1897, 820.
36 *TC*, 28 December 1898, 387.
37 *TC*, 26 December 1900, 410.
38 Of the participants named, four were female and eighteen were male: *TC*, 28 December 1898, 388.
39 Ibid., 394–5.
40 *TC*, 30 December 1896, 1260.
41 Ibid.
42 *TC*, 4 December 1895, 364.
43 *TC*, 29 December 1897, 822.
44 *TC*, 28 December 1898, 389.
45 Ibid.
46 *TC*, 27 December 1899, 405. That year, a donation was described as sultana cake and may have represented the typical bun loaf served: *TC*, 30 December 1893, 395.
47 *TC*, 28 December 1898, 388.
48 *TC*, 20 December 1899, 393.
49 *TC*, 30 December 1896, 1261.
50 This occurred on several occasions, including 1901: see *TC*, 1 January 1902, 10.
51 *TC*, 30 December 1896, 1261.
52 Account of the initial meeting to establish the Medina Home comes from *TC*, 6 January 1897, 11–14.
53 *TC*, 15 February 1899, 102.
54 *TC*, 29 December 1897, 823.
55 *TC*, 28 December 1898, 394.
56 *TC*, 1 January 1908, 7.
57 *TC*, 30 December 1903, 427.
58 *TC*, 27 December 1899, 405.
59 *TC*, 28 December 1898, 390.
60 *TC*, 14 January 1893, 5.
61 *TC*, 2 January 1895, 3; *TC*, 27 December 1905, 413.
62 *TC*, 28 December 1898, 390.

63 Armstrong, *Christmas*, 130–1.
64 *TC*, 28 December 1898, 390.
65 'Id al-Fitr is often referred to as the Lesser *Bairam* (Ottoman Turkish) in *TC*. Unless otherwise noted, accounts of both celebrations come from *TC*, 15 February 1899, 99–103; *TC*, 11 July 1900, 26–7.
66 *TC*, 14 January 1903, 26–7.
67 Bengal lights are a type of firework used for signalling or lighting, also called sparklers.
68 *TC*, 11 July 1900, 27.
69 *TC*, 14 January 1903, 27.
70 *TC*, 11 July 1900, 26–7.
71 Asmay, *Islam in Victorian Liverpool*, 93.
72 Historically, Sufis (followers of Islamic mysticism) have belonged to an order, also known as a *tariqa*, guided by a spiritual teacher.
73 Asmay, *Islam in Victorian Liverpool*, 9.
74 All succeeding notes on coverage from Liverpool papers are from reprints in *TC*: *TC*, 14 January 1893, 4; *TC*, 2 January 1895, 4.
75 *TC*, 29 December 1897, 822; *TC*, 28 December 1898, 395–6.
76 *TC*, 3 January 1900, 13.
77 *TC*, 1 January 1902, 10–12; *TC*, 7 January 1903, 12–13.
78 See *TC*, 1 January 1908, 7–8.

11 Authority and legitimacy in Victorian Liverpool: Re-evaluating Abdullah Quilliam's title of 'Sheikh-ul-Islam of the British Isles'

1 *Truth* 50, no. 1279 (4 July 1901): 6.
2 Richard W. Bulliet, 'The Shaikh al-Islam and the Evolution of Islamic Society', *Studia Islamica* 35 (1972): 53–67; J. H. Kramers, R. Bulliet and R. C. Repp, 'Shaykh al-Islām', in *Encyclopaedia of Islam, Second Edition*, ed. P. Bearman, Th. Bianquis, C. E. Bosworth, E. van Donzel and W. P. Heinrichs (Brill Online, 2012). Available online: https://referenceworks.brillonline.com/entries/encyclopaedia-of-islam-2/shaykh-al-islam-COM_1052 (accessed 18 November 2022).
3 C. Halim Wahby George's response in *Truth* 50, no. 1280 (11 July 1901): 78.
4 Reprinted in *The Crescent* (hereafter *TC*), 28 August 1901, 139.
5 On Quilliam's departure, see Ron Geaves, *Islam in Victorian Britain: The Life and Times of Abdullah Quilliam* (Markfield: Kube, 2010), 253–64.
6 Geaves, *Islam in Victorian Britain*; Jamie Gilham, *Loyal Enemies: British Converts to Islam, 1850–1950* (New York: Oxford University Press, 2014), chapters 2 and 3;

Jamie Gilham, 'Abdullah Quilliam, First and Last "Sheikh-ul-Islam of the British Isles"', in *Victorian Muslim: Abdullah Quilliam and Islam in the West*, ed. Jamie Gilham and Ron Geaves (London: Hurst, 2017), 97–112.

7   Gilham, 'Abdullah Quilliam', 97.
8   Aydin Bayram, 'Osmanlı'nın Britanya'daki İlk ve Tek Şeyhülislamı Abdullah Quilliam ve Liverpool İslâm Estitüsü', *Ondokuz Mayıs Üniversitesi İlahiyat Fakültesi Dergisi* 42 (2017): 163–94. A simple internet search of Quilliam's name in Arabic and Turkish will produce countless journal articles, popular Muslim history websites, news stories and the like that recount the story of the 'first and last Sheikh ul-Islam of the British Isles'.
9   For the most comprehensive treatment on Ottomania, neo-Ottomanism and nostalgia over Ottoman history, see M. Hakan Yavuz, *Nostalgia for the Empire: The Politics of Neo-Ottomanism* (New York: Oxford University Press, 2020).
10 Selim Deringil, *The Well-Protected Domains: Ideology and the Legitimation of Power in the Ottoman Empire, 1876–1909* (New York: I. B. Tauris, 2011), 135–49; Houssine Alloul and Roel Markey, '"Please Deny These Manifestly False Reports": Ottoman Diplomats and the Press in Belgium (1850–1914)', *International Journal of Middle East Studies* 48, no. 2 (2016): 267–92.
11 See Gilham, *Loyal Enemies*, 65–71.
12 Başbakanlık Osmanlı Arşivi (Ottoman Archives of the Prime Ministry; hereafter BOA), HR.SFR.3 427/9.
13 Sultan 'Abd al-Mecid I (1823–61, r. 1839–61) instituted the Mecîdî Order in 1851 as both a military and civilian award for service: see Edhem Eldem, *Pride and Privilege: A History of Ottoman Orders, Medals and Decorations* (Istanbul: Ottoman Bank Archives and Research Centre, 2004), 176–91.
14 *Mona's Herald*, 10 October 1894, 5.
15 Ibid.
16 Maulvi Karim Bakhsh, *Islam in England* (Lahore: Islamia Press, 1892); Hamid Snow, *The Prayer Book for Muslims* (Lahore: Islamia Press, 1893), 5.
17 BOA, Y.PRK.AZJ 56/7, Letter to 'Abd al-Hamid II requesting assistance.
18 *TC*, 20 February 1895, 57. Sometimes it was simply 'Sheikh of the United English and American Moslem Societies'.
19 *TC*, 14 August 1895, 105.
20 *TC*, 25 March 1896, 617.
21 BOA, Y.PRK.MŞ 6/41.
22 Matthew A. Sharp, '"On Behalf of the Sultan": The Late Ottoman State and the Cultivation of British and American Converts to Islam' (PhD thesis, University of Pennsylvania, 2020), 64–9; BOA, HR.SFR.3 446/50, 14 and 18 June 1895.
23 BOA, HR.SFR.3 446/50, 14 June 1895.

24 Yusuf Samih Asmay, *Islam in Victorian Liverpool: An Ottoman Account of Britain's First Mosque Community*, trans. and ed. Yahya Birt, Riordan Macnamara and Münire Zeyneb Maksudoğlu (Swansea: Claritas Books, 2021), 98.
25 For more on Muslim intellectuals' engagement with converts like Quilliam and Webb, see Sharp, "'On Behalf of the Sultan,'" 191–286.
26 Abdullah Quilliam, *al-ʿAqīda al-Islāmiyah*, trans. Muhammad Diya (Cairo: Matbaʿah Hindiyah, 1315/1897).
27 See an example of Diya requesting a photo from Quilliam in *TC*, 3 November 1897, 697. *TC* also congratulated Diya on his translation with mention of the photos of the 'Sheikh-ul-Islam of the British Isles': see *TC*, 5 January 1898, 9.
28 Muhammad Rashid Rida, 'al-ʿAqīdah al-Islāmiyah', *al-Manār* 1, no. 25 (September 1898): 472–4.
29 Abdullah Quilliam, *Dîn-i İslâm*, trans. Mahmud Esad (Seydişehri), 1st and 2nd edn (Izmir: Kitapçı Arakel, 1311/1893–1894 and 1314/1896–1897); *TC*, 12 June 1895, 186–7; *TC*, 21 August 1895, 116.
30 For example, he discussed Quilliam and translated part of *TC* in Mahmud Esad (Seydişehri), *Şü'ûn-ı İslamiye* (Constantinople: Nişan Berberyan Matbaası, 1311/1894).
31 Examples of later omissions of 'Sheikh-ul-Islam' include Ali Rıza Seyfi's translations of *The Religion of the Sword* ('Kılıç Dini') that first appeared in the Ottoman Turkish Islamic journal *Sebîlü'r-Reşâd*, starting in April 1912 and ending in October 1912; Tevfikîzâde İsmail Tevfik, *Medeniyet-i İslâmiye ve İngiliz Müslümanları* [Islamic Civilization and English Muslims] (Constantinople: Matbaa-ı Der Nersisyan, 1326/1910–1911); Ahmet Hamdi Akseki, *Ulemâ-yı İslâmiye'ye Bir Suʾâl ve Abdullah Quilliam Efendi'nin Cevabı* [A Question to Islamic Scholars and Abdullah Quilliam Efendi's Answer] (Constantinople: Tevsi-yi Tıbâat Matbaası, 1332/1913).
32 See Matthew A. Sharp, 'Dynamism and Discontent: Nafeesah M. T. Keep and Female Muslims in Victorian Liverpool', in *Muslim Women in Britain, 1850–1950: 100 Years of Hidden History*, ed. Sariya Cheruvallil-Contractor and Jamie Gilham (London: Hurst, 2023).
33 BOA, Y.A.HUS 335/83, Nafeesah M. T. Keep to Sultan ʿAbd al-Hamid II, 3 August 1895.
34 Sharp, "'On Behalf of the Sultan,'" 214–16. Two years later, in 1898, Khalil also wrote to the Ottoman embassy in London accusing Quilliam of being a spy: see Sharp, "'On Behalf of the Sultan,'" 75–8.
35 Durham University Library, SAD-263/1/329–330, 'Paper Read by Mr. Mustapha Khalil at a Meeting of the Anjuman-i-Islam of London', 27 December 1896.
36 Faiz Ahmed, 'The British-Ottoman Cold War, c. 1880–1914: Imperial Struggles over Muslim Mobility and Citizenship from the Suez Canal to the Durand Line', in *The*

Subjects of Ottoman International Law, ed. Lâle Can, Michael C. Low, Kent F. Schull and Robert Zens (Bloomington: Indiana University Press, 2020), 159.

37 Nadir Özbek, 'Imperial Gifts and Sultanic Legitimation during the Late Ottoman Empire, 1876–1909', in *Poverty and Charity in Middle Eastern Contexts*, ed. Michael Bonner, Mine Ener and Amy Singer (Albany, NY: State University of New York Press, 2003), 203–20.
38 On honours and medals during 'Abd al-Hamid II's reign, see Eldem, *Pride and Privilege*, 252–9.
39 Ibid., 345.
40 BOA, Y.PRK.EŞA 15/27, 14 February 1892.
41 Sharp, '"On Behalf of the Sultan,"' 52.
42 BOA, HR.SFR.3 470/58, 29 September 1898. The *Medaille des Beaux Artes* was likely the equivalent to the *Sanâyi-i Nefîse Madalyası* (Medal of Fine Arts), awarded to individuals who distinguished themselves in the arts, crafts or sciences: Eldem, *Pride and Privilege*, 290.
43 Sharp, '"On Behalf of the Sultan,"' 91–2.
44 Ibid., 97–9; Eldem, *Pride and Privilege*, 289–93.
45 BOA, HR.SFR.3 557/47, 6 September 1905.
46 Sharp, '"On Behalf of the Sultan,"' 121, particularly n. 432 and n. 433. Faiz Ahmed, 'Meddling with Medals, Defending the Dead: Late Ottoman Soft Power from South Asia to North America', *The International History Review* 43, no. 5 (2021): 1041–59.
47 On the debate over 'Abd al-Hamid II's overuse of decorations to the point of debasement while still maintaining some symbolic power, see Eldem, *Pride and Privilege*, 332–57.
48 On Muslim 'religious entrepreneurs', see Nile Green, *Terrains of Exchange: Religious Economies of Global Islam* (New York: Oxford University Press, 2014).
49 *The Moslem Chronicle and the Muhammadan Observer*, 23 January 1904, 53.
50 Ibid.
51 Ibid.
52 *The Islamic World*, October 1894, 187.
53 For example, the letter to Quilliam from Ceylon (Sri Lankan) Muslims requesting that he petition the Ottoman government for a favour: see Sharp, '"On Behalf of the Sultan,"' 96–7 and BOA, HR.SFR.3 548/7.

Select bibliography

Abd-Allah, Umar F. *A Muslim in Victorian America: The Life of Alexander Russell Webb.* New York: Oxford University Press, 2006.
Akhavi, Sharough. 'Islam and the West in World History'. *Third World Quarterly* 24, no. 3(2003): 545–62.
Almond, Phillip C. *Heretic and Hero: Muhammad and the Victorians.* Wiesbaden: Otto Harrassowitz, 1989.
Anand, Sushila. *Indian Sahib: Queen Victoria's Dear Abdul.* London: Duckworth, 1996.
Anon, *Indian Records, With a Commercial View of the Relations between the British Government and the Nawab Nazim of Bengal, Behar and Orissa.* London: G. Bubb, 1870.
Ansari, Humayun. 'Maulana Barkatullah Bhopali's Transnationalism: Pan-Islamism, Colonialism and Radical Politics'. In *Transnational Islam in Interwar Europe: Muslim Activists and Thinkers*, edited by Gotz Nordbruch and Umar Ryad, 181–210. New York: Palgrave Macmillan, 2014.
apRoberts, Ruth. '"The Lore of Heaven, The Speech of Earth": Carlyle, Mahomet, and Islam'. *Carlyle Studies Annual* 23 (2007): 7–12.
Armstrong, Neil. *Christmas in Nineteenth Century England.* Manchester: Manchester University Press, 2010.
Asmay, Yusuf Samih. *Islam in Victorian Liverpool: An Ottoman Account of Britain's First Mosque Community.* Translated and edited by Yahya Birt, Riordan Macnamara and Münire Zeyneb Maksudoğlu. Swansea: Claritas Books, 2021.
Ballhatchet, Kenneth. *Race, Sex and Class under the Raj: Imperial Attitudes and Policies and Their Critics, 1793–1905.* London: Weidenfeld and Nicolson, 1980.
Bassnett, Susan. 'Travel Writing and Gender'. In *The Cambridge Companion to Travel Writing*, edited by Peter Hulme and Tim Youngs, 225–41. Cambridge: Cambridge University Press, 2002.
Basu, Shrabani. *Victoria and Abdul: The True Story of the Queen's Closest Confidant.* Stroud: The History Press, 2011.
Beckerlegge, G. 'Followers of "Mohammed, Kalee and Dada Nanuk": The Presence of Islam and South Asian Religions in Victorian Britain'. In *Religion in Victorian Britain, Volume V: Culture and Empire*, edited by John Wolffe, 221–67. Manchester: Manchester University Press, 1997.
Bennett, Clinton. 'Islam and the Victorians: Nineteenth Century Perceptions of Muslim Practices and Beliefs' [Review]. *Victorian Studies* 51, no. 2 (2009): 356–7.
Bennett, Clinton. *Victorian Images of Islam.* London: Grey Seal, 1992.

Bolt, Christine. *Victorian Attitudes to Race*. London: Routledge and Kegan Paul, 1971.

Bubb, Alexander. *Asian Classics on the Victorian Bookshelf: Flights of Translation*. Oxford: Oxford University Press, 2023.

Carlyle, Thomas. *On Heroes, Hero-Worship, and the Heroic in History*. New edn 1841. Reprint. London: Chapman and Hall, 1897.

Carlyle, Thomas. *On Heroes, Hero-Worship, and the Heroic in History*, edited by David R. Sorensen and Brent E. Kinser. New Haven, CT: Yale University Press, 2013.

Cohn, Bernard S. 'Representing Authority in Victorian India'. In *The Invention of Tradition*, edited by Eric Hobsbawm and Terence Ranger, 165–210. Cambridge: Cambridge University Press, 1983.

Daniel, Norman. *Islam and the West: The Making of an Image*. Edinburgh: Edinburgh University Press, 1960.

Daniel, Norman. *Islam, Europe and Empire*. Edinburgh: Edinburgh University Press, 1966.

Deringil, Selim. *The Well-Protected Domains: Ideology and the Legitimation of Power in the Ottoman Empire, 1876–1909*. New York: I. B. Tauris, 2011.

Douglas, Roy. 'Britain and the Armenian Question, 1894–1897'. *The Historical Journal* 19, no. 1 (1976): 113–33.

Duff Gordon, Lady Lucie. *Letters from Egypt, 1863–1865*. London: Macmillan, 1865.

Eden, Emily. *Up the Country: Letters Written to Her Sister from the Upper Provinces of India*. London: R. Bentley, 1867.

Edwards, Amelia B. *A Thousand Miles Up the Nile*. New York: A. L. Burt, 1890.

Eldem, Edhem. *Pride and Privilege: A History of Ottoman Orders, Medals and Decorations*. Istanbul: Ottoman Bank Archives and Research Centre, 2004.

Elmarsafy, Ziad. *The Enlightenment Qur'an: The Politics of Translation and the Construction of Islam*. Oxford: Oneworld, 2009.

Fowler, Corinne. *Chasing Tales: Travel Writing, Journalism and the History of British Ideas about Afghanistan*. New York: Rodopi, 2007.

Geaves, Ron. *Islam in Victorian Britain: The Life and Times of Abdullah Quilliam*. Markfield: Kube, 2010.

Gelvin, James L., and Nile Green (eds). *Global Muslims in the Age of Steam and Print*. Berkeley: University of California Press, 2014.

Gilham, Jamie. 'Britain's First Muslim Peer of the Realm: Henry, Lord Stanley of Alderley and Islam in Victorian Britain'. *Journal of Muslim Minority Affairs* 33, no.1 (2013): 93–110.

Gilham, Jamie. *Loyal Enemies: British Converts to Islam, 1850–1950*. London and New York: Hurst and Oxford University Press, 2014.

Gilham, Jamie. 'Professor G. W. Leitner in England: The Oriental Institute, Woking Mosque and Relations with Muslims, 1884–1899'. *Islam and Christian-Muslim Relations* 32, no. 1 (2021): 1–24.

Gilham, Jamie, and Ron Geaves (eds). *Victorian Muslim: Abdullah Quilliam and Islam in the West*. London and New York: Hurst and Oxford University Press, 2017.

Gladstone, W. E. *Bulgarian Horrors, and the Question of the East*. London: John Murray, 1876.

Halliday, Fred. *Arabs in Exile: Yemeni Migrants in Urban Britain*. London: I. B. Tauris, 1992.

Halliday, Fred. 'The *Millet* of Manchester: Arab Merchants and Cotton Trade'. *British Journal of Middle Eastern Studies* 19, no. 2 (1992): 159–76.

Innes, Lyn. *The Last Prince of Bengal: A Family's Journey from an Indian Palace to the Australian Outback*. London: The Westbourne Press, 2021.

Irwin, Robert. *For Lust of Knowing: The Orientalists and their Enemies*. London: Allen Lane, 2006.

Kabbani, Rana. *Europe's Myths of Orient: Devise and Rule*. London: Pandora, 1986.

Khattak, Shahin Kuli Khan. *Islam and the Victorians: Nineteenth-Century Perceptions of Muslim Practices and Beliefs*. London: Tauris Academic Studies, 2008.

Landau, Jacob. *The Politics of Pan-Islam: Ideology and Organization*. New York: Oxford University Press, 1990.

McLeod, Hugh. *Class and Religion in the Late Victorian City*. London: Croom Helm, 1974.

Melman, Billie. *Women's Orients, English Women and the Middle East, 1718–1918: Sexuality, Religion, and Work*. Ann Arbor, MI: University of Michigan Press, 1992.

Muhleisen-Arnold, J., Rev. *The Society for Propagating the Gospel among the Moslems, in Connection with the Church of England; Its First Appeal*. London: Rivingtons, 1860.

Nash, Geoffrey. *From Empire to Orient: Travellers to the Middle East, 1830–1926*. London: I. B. Tauris, 2005.

Oddie, G. A. *Social Protest in India: British Protestant Missionaries and Social Reforms 1850–1900*. New Delhi: Manohar, 1979.

Omrani, Bijan. '"Will We Make It to Jalalabad?": 19th Century Travels in Afghanistan'. *Asian Affairs* 37, no. 2 (2006): 161–74.

O'Neill, Patricia. 'Destination as Destiny: Amelia B. Edwards's Travel Writing'. *Frontiers: A Journal of Women Studies* 30, no. 2 (2009): 43–71.

Ozcan, Azmi. *Pan-Islamism: Indian Muslims, the Ottomans and Britain (1877–1924)*. Leiden: Brill, 1997.

Palmer, E. H. (trans.). *The Qur'ân*, 2 vols. Oxford: Clarendon Press, 1880.

Pugh, Martin. *Britain and Islam: A History from 622 to the Present Day*. New Haven, CT: Yale University Press, 2019.

Qureshi, Sadiah. *Peoples on Parade: Exhibitions, Empire, and Anthropology in Nineteenth-Century Britain*. London: University of Chicago Press, 2011.

Robinson-Dunn, Diane. *The Harem, Slavery and British Imperial Culture: Anglo-Muslim Relations in the Late Nineteenth Century*. Manchester: Manchester University Press, 2006.

Rodwell, J. M. (trans.). *The Koran*. New edn 1861. Reprint. London: J. M. Dent, 1909.

Said, Edward W. *Orientalism: Western Conceptions of the Orient*. New edn 1978. Harmondsworth: Penguin, 1995.

Sale, George (trans.). *The Koran, Commonly Called the Alcoran of Mohammed*. New edn 1734. Reprint. London: Frederick Warne, 1887.

Sale, Lady Florentia Wynch. *A Journal of the Disasters in Afghanistan, 1841–2*. London: John Murray, 1843.

Salt, J. *Imperialism, Evangelism and the Ottoman Armenians, 1878–1896*. London: Frank Cass, 1993.

Shannon, Richard T. *Gladstone and the Bulgarian Agitation 1876*. London: Thomas Nelson, 1963.

Sharp, Matthew A. '"On Behalf of the Sultan": The Late Ottoman State and the Cultivation of British and American Converts to Islam'. PhD thesis, University of Pennsylvania, 2020.

Tageldin, Shaden M. 'Secularizing Islam: Carlyle, al-Sibaʿi, and the Translations of "Religion" in British Egypt'. *PMLA* [Publications of the Modern Language Association of America] 126, no. 1 (2011): 123–39.

Taylor, Miles. *Empress: Queen Victoria and India*. New Haven, CT: Yale University Press, 2018.

Thomas, David and John Chesworth (eds). *Christian-Muslim Relations. A Bibliographical History, Vol. 17: Britain, the Netherlands and Scandinavia (1800–1914)*. Leiden: Brill, 2020.

Thompson, Carl. 'Journeys to Authority: Reassessing Women's Early Travel Writing, 1763–1862'. *Women's Writing* 24, no. 2 (2017): 131–50.

Tidrick, Kathryn. *Heart-Beguiling Araby*. Cambridge: Cambridge University Press, 1981.

Turner, Frank M. *Contesting Cultural Authority: Essays in Victorian Intellectual Life*. New York: Cambridge University Press, 1991.

Watt, W. Montgomery. 'Carlyle on Muhammad'. *Hibbert Journal* 53 (1955): 247–54.

Wohl, Anthony S. '"Ben-JuJu": Representations of Disraeli's Jewishness in the Victorian Political Cartoon'. *Jewish History* 10, no. 2 (1996): 89–133.

Index

Note: Figures are indicated by page number followed by 'f'. Endnotes are indicated by the page number followed by 'n' and the endnote number; e.g., 210 n.1 refers to endnote 1 on page 210.

'Abd al-Aziz, Sultan 19, 25, 26, 33, 128
'Abd al-Hamid II, Sultan 10, 26, 43, 130, 131, 163, 170, 194–5, 197–200, 203–6
Abd al-Wahhab, Muhammad ibn 217 n.64
Abdul Aleem Siddiqui, Muhammad 229–30 n.21
Achmet, Ali 21
adhan (Muslim call to prayer) 137
Afghanistan 62, 63, 70, 71, 166, 186, 198, 199, 206, 225 n.4
  Muslims in 7
Africa 19, 52, 61–4, 80, 121, 189, 197, 210 n.11
  travel literature from 16
Ahmed, Akbar 39
Ahmed, Faiz 203
Ahmed, Rafiuddin 26, 160, 163, 169, 170, 173, 197, 203, 204
Akhavi, Sharoukgh 57, 58
al-Afghani, Jamal al-Din 57, 160
Albert, the Prince Consort 15, 21–2
  passion for visual arts 16–17
Al-Chamaa, Fawzie 131
Al-Chamaa, Rushdi 131
Alexandra, the Princess of Wales 17, 19, 21, 43, 152
Al-Faransawi, Soliman Pasha 24
Algeria 7, 101, 105, 111, 114, 119, 121
Algiers 101
The Alhambra (Irving, Washington) 15
Ali, Muhammad 24
Ali, Syed Ameer 173
alim (a learned scholar qualified to offer Islamic legal opinions) 160
al-Manār (The Lighthouse) 201
Almond, Phillip C. 3
al-Siba'i, Muhammad 54–5
Anglican Christianity 16, 21, 23, 47, 49, 50

Anglo-Ottoman relations 6, 29, 44
Anglo-Persian War (1856–7) 17
Anglo-Russian Agreement of 1904 43–4
Anjuman-i-Islam 136, 167–9, 202
Ansari, Humayun 9, 54, 180
anti-Christian violence 126, 127
Arabia 6, 51, 54, 88, 107, 113–14, 121
Arabian Nights 19, 61, 82, 145
Arabic 8, 142
Ardati, Ali 132
Ardati, Muhieddine 132–3
Argyll (Duke of) 81, 84, 90, 94, 150
Armenian Christians 42, 163, 166
Armenian massacres of 1894–5 6, 30, 41–3
Arnold, Sir Edwin 41, 84
Asia 19, 36, 63, 84, 93, 125
  travel literature from 16
Asmay, Yusuf Samih 164–5, 172, 181, 191, 200, 243 n.43
Assha, Damascene Said 133
Auckland (Lord) 63, 139, 142
Austen, Jane 67, 225 n.13
Austin, Sarah 71, 74, 227 n.50
Australasia 53
Azeem, Meerza Ali 142, 143

Balkan Slavs 32, 34, 36, 41, 94, 163, 170
Barelvi, Saiyid Ahmad 143
Baring, Walter 34
Barton, William 89
Basevi, Maria 31
Bassnett, Susan 64, 72, 73, 75, 79
Battle of Balaclava (October 1854) 24
Battle of Plassey (1757) 140
Beatrice (Princess) 19, 22, 27, 134
Beirut 124, 125
Belchem, John 178
Bengal 8, 139, 141, 142, 153, 155, 158, 190

Bennett, Clinton 3, 6, 49–50, 61, 224 n.1
Bennett, Eliza 67
Bentham, Jeremy 49
   Utilitarianism 45, 48
Ben-Yusuf, Saiyid Mustafa 8, 99, 231 n.2
   conversion to Christianity 101–3
   early years 101–3
   independent missionary 114–18
   later years 118–20
   Moslem Mission Society 109–114
   Palestine Christian Union Mission to the Arabs 103–4
Berlin 36
bey (meaning lord, sir or master)
Bhopali, Maulana Muhammad Barakatullah 9, 136, 161f, 203, 207, 240 n.1
   defending *umma* 160–71
   in late-Victorian England 159
   and status of Muslim women 171–4
Biagini, Eugenio 39
Bihar 8
Birkett, Dea 63
Blunt, Lady Anne 51
Blunt, Wilfrid Scawen 51
Bolt, Christine 80
Bosnia 32, 34, 36
Bostock, Emilie 133–4
Brexit 44
Bright, Canon William 40
British monarchy 13, 22
   Islam as a political issue for 24–7
Buddhism 16, 41
Bulgaria 31–7, 41
Bulgarian agitation 39, 41
Bulgarian Horrors, And the Question of the East (Gladstone, W. E.) 31–7, 52, 94, 138
Burton, Sir Richard F. 51, 61, 86–7, 92
Byrne, Thomas Omar 134, 165
Byron (Lord) 31, 34, 145

Caine, Hall 163, 197
Cairo 49, 78, 112, 128, 181, 201
Cama, Bhikaji 160
Campbell, George 81
Canada 53
Canning, Earl (Lord) 147–8, 150
Carlyle, Thomas 6, 7, 40, 51, 90, 92
   Islam and Victorian world 45, 51–3
   On Heroes in context 45–9
   Orientalism and empire 53–5
Cates, Fatima 84
Caulfield, James 141–2
Chamberlain (Lord) 163
'Chandos Classics' 83, 84, 93, 94
Chartism (Carlyle, Thomas) 56
Chitty, Justice 157
Christianity 8, 47
   and Islam 2
   response and national debate 38
   truth of 23
Christians 37
   and Muslim relations 3–4, 74
   missionaries 4, 106
   monogamy 172
A Christmas Carol (Dickens, Charles) 177
A Chronicle of the Conquest of Granada (Irving, Washington) 15
Church Missionary Society (CMS) 107, 115, 117
Churchill, Winston 243 n.39
Cockerell, Horace 155
Cohn, Bernard S. 19
Coleridge, Samuel Taylor 50
Coningsby (Disraeli, Benjamin) 38
Conservative Party 32, 42
Constantinople 16, 26, 33, 36, 43, 193
Contarini Fleming (Disraeli, Benjamin) 38
Crane, Henrietta 118–20
Crane, Henry, *see* Ben-Yusuf, Saiyid Mustafa
Crimean War (1853–6) 24, 29, 52, 53, 127
Curtis, William J. 93
Cyprus Convention 36, 37

D'Israeli, Isaac 31
da'wah ('invitation') 137, 180
Dalhousie (Lord) 146–7
Damascus 124, 125–6, 131, 136
Daniel, Norman 3
dar al-Islam (territory of Islam) 57
Darwin, Charles 21
Deutsch, Emanuel 88–9
Dickens, Charles 61, 72, 177–8
Disraeli, Benjamin 6, 7, 29, 33–4
   Eastern policy 40
   family and childhood 31
   literary career 31
   political career 31–2

pro-Ottoman policy 103
pro-Turkish view 38
Turcophile policy 44
Dole, Nathan Haskell 84
Dollie, Mohammed 164, 167, 243 n.44
Doughty, Charles M. 51
du'a (prayer of supplication) 190
Duff, M. E. Grant 153
Duff Gordon, Lucie 7, 53, 61, 62, 63, 71–6, 226 n.38
Duff Gordon, Sir Alexander Cornewall 71
Dunlop, Douglas 39
Durrani, Shah Shuja 63, 69

East India Company (EIC) 13, 22, 109, 140, 144
'Eastern Question' 6, 29, 40, 94
  rival politicians and 33–8
  see also Ottoman Empire
Eden, Emily 7, 61, 62, 63, 64–71, 73, 79, 225 n.13
Edward VII 17, 22
Edwards, Amelia B. 7, 61–2, 63, 76–80
effendi (meaning lord, sir or master) 200, 202
Egypt 5, 7, 19, 21, 25, 37, 39, 43, 51, 62, 71, 73, 75–6, 78–80, 125, 130, 131, 133, 146, 160, 201
  culture and archaeology 76
  Muslims in 7
Egyptian hieroglyphic symbol 76
Egyptology 76, 80
Eliot, George 61, 83
El-Karey, Youhannah 104, 105
Elmarsafy, Ziad 82
Elphinstone, William 62, 67, 69
Emerson, Ralph Waldo 47
Essex 118
European Union (EU) 44
Evans, Selim 134
'Everyman's Classics' 87

The Faith of Islam (Quilliam) 201
fanaticism 59, 74
fatwa (juridical opinion) 167, 199
First Anglo-Afghan War (1838–42) 62, 71
FitzGerald, Edward 52–3, 223 n.31
Forster, William Edward 33–4
Fowler, Corinne 70
Fox, William 150, 152

France 24, 36, 42, 43, 44, 56, 125, 128, 131, 163, 189
Fraser, James 40

Galton, Francis 48
Geaves, Ron 194
Gelvin, James L. 1–2
George, C. Halim Wahby 193–4, 203
Germany 30, 36, 37, 43, 44, 109
ghazeeas 70, 226 n.31
Gibbon, Edward 16, 49, 82
Gilham, Jamie 7, 52, 90, 181, 194, 228 n.62
Gladstone, Sir John 30
Gladstone, William Ewart 6, 7, 29, 30, 32, 38–41, 166, 243 n.39
  anti-Turkish view 33–7
  family 30
global Muslim unity 211 n.19
Gouramma of Coorg (Princess) 21
Grey, Theresa 19
Gupta, J. Datta 144

hadith (the traditions of Muhammad) 90
Hakki Bey, Ibrahim 135
Hall, Michael 137
Hallaby, Mohamed 133
Halliday, Fred 8, 123
'Hamidieh March' (Ottoman imperial anthem) 189, 190
Hanowye, Selim 133, 134
Harcourt, Freda 25
Harcourt, William 42
Harris, Lady 23
Harrold, C. F. 56
Hassan, Hafiz Ahmed 153
Hassan, Sultan 78
Hatem, Mervat 75
Hearn, Lafcadio 87
Henry of Battenberg (Prince) 19
Henry, Mitchell 94
Herder, Johann Gottfried 49, 221–2 n.10
Herzegovina 32, 34
Hindu Kush 67, 225 n.10
Hinduism 3, 16, 23, 64, 171
  and Muslim cooperation 171–2
  religious practices 140
  and Sikhs 21, 64
  solar calendars 26
  theological texts 89

History of Frederick the Great (Carlyle, Thomas) 59
History of the French Revolution (1835) 47
Hourani, Albert 54
Hume, James 146
Husayn, imam 143
Huth, F. H. 90
Huxley, T. H. 48

Ibn Muhammad, Abdullah 167
Ibn Talib, Ali 239 n.3
'Id al-Adha (feast of the sacrifice marking the end of the annual Hajj) 165, 191, 242 n.27
'Id al-Fitr (festival of breaking the fast) 135, 136, 189, 190, 191, 248 n.65
Iddleby, James 128
Iliahoo, Joseph 134
imam (Muslim religious leader) 134–6, 163, 197
India 5, 8–9, 14, 19, 29, 37, 53, 62, 67, 71, 153, 158, 171
  and England 139
  'Indian Mussulman' 146
  Muslims in 7, 160, 193
  and Ottoman Turkey 6
Indian Rebellion of 1857–8 53, 139
Iraq 143
  Shi'i-Sunni tensions in 44
Ireland 53, 99, 100, 115, 118, 121, 145
Irving, Henry 163
Irving, Washington 14–15
Islam 45
  architecture 68
  over conventional Christianity 86–7
  countries and societies 4
  culture in Arabic script 20
  festivals and events at LMI 189
  five 'pillars' of faith 228 n.61
  history in Victorian Britain 2–5
  as political issue for British monarchy 24–7
  and Victorian world 2–3, 51–3
Ismail Pasha of Egypt 19, 25

J. Darcy books 89
J. M. Dent and Company 83, 91
Jafar, Mir 140, 143, 146
Jah, Feradun 139
Jah, Nawab Humayun 140–1

Jefferson, Thomas 82
Jews 8, 32, 37, 41, 88, 138, 185
jihad (striving or struggling in the path of God) 57, 167, 243 n.41
Jones, L. Hanifa 183, 187

Kabul 62, 64, 68, 69, 225–6 n.13
Kafiristani 225 n.10
kalima (Islamic statement of faith) 51
Karim, Abdul Mohammad 4, 6, 13, 14, 18f, 26, 27, 213 n.29
  as *munshi* (instructor, attendant) 17
  in *tableaux vivants* (living pictures) 17
Karsa, Cecil Mustapha 130
Karsa, Eminie 130, 132–3
Karsa, Mustapha 124, 128–31, 132, 134, 136, 137
Keats, John 47
Keep, Nafeesah M. T. 172, 202
Kenan Bey, Esad 199
Khalil, Mustapha 136, 202–3
Khan, Abdur Rahman 166
Khan, Akbar 62
Khan, Dost Mohammad 63, 225 n.3
Khan, Farrokh 16–17
Khan, Mansour Ali 8, 139, 151–2, 155
Khan, Nasrullah 166
Khan, Syed Ahmad 52
Khan, Zeman Shah 70
Kidwai, Mushir Hosain 160
khutbah (sermon) 134, 163
Kilfoyle, Lucy 178
Kind, Anna 109
King James Bible 85
Kipling, Rudyard 70, 89–90
kitabi (one who believes in a book of sacred scripture) 152
Koory, Kallil Hanna 128
The Koran, Commonly called the Alcoran of Mohammed (Sale, George) 82, 88, 89
Kose, Ali 180
Krishnavarma, Shyamji 160

Lalla Rookh (Moore, Thomas) 145
Lane, Edward William 49, 51, 84
Lansdowne (Lord) 26
Layard, Frederick 150
Lebanon 8
Lessing, Gotthold Ephraim 49
Levant 8

Levi, R. M. 133
Levy-Lawson, Edward 41
Lewis, Julia 155
Liberal Party 30–1, 41, 42
Liddon, Canon Henry 40
The Life of Mahomet (Muir, William) 81
The Life of Wellington 145
Lincoln's Inn 30, 31
Lippincott 83
Liverpool Muslim Institute (LMI) 1, 8, 123, 134, 162, 178, 193, 199, 200, 206, 207
  members 202
  Islamic festivals and events at 189–91
  fundraising and logistics 181–5
Livingstone, David 61
London 9, 16, 25, 31, 36, 40–2, 47, 67–68, 102–3, 109, 114, 117, 120, 136, 142, 152, 156, 162, 167, 197, 199, 200, 202
Louise (Princess) 33
Lubbock, Sir John 83, 92
Lutfi Bey, Ismail 197

Macaulay, Thomas Babington 141
MacColl, Canon Malcolm 40, 168, 172
MacGahan, J. A. 33
Mackenzie, Colin 147, 148
MacPherson, Crawford B. 57
Maharaja of Kutch 15
Mahomet (Caine, Hall) 163, 197, 204
Mahomet and Islam (Muir, William) 90
The Man Who Would be King (Kipling, Rudyard) 70
Maracci, Ludovico 228–9 n.5
Margoliouth, D. S. 48
Margoliouth, George 91, 92
Martineau, Harriet 88
Maurice, F. D. 48
Mavrokordato, Dimitri 197
Mawlid (Prophet Muhammad's birthday) 137, 188, 189, 190–2
Mayo (Lord) 26, 151
Mecidi Order medallion 197, 204
Melman, Billie 78–9
Menelik II 128
Milestones (Qutb, Sayyid) 56
Mill, John Stuart 48, 49, 83
millet (an Ottoman semiautonomous minority community) 8, 123
Mills, Sara 64

Minto (Lord) 140
Minute on Education (1835) 141
mohurs (gold coins) 148
Mokaiesh family 131–3
Mokaiesh, Ali 131–3, 134
Mokaiesh, Amy 131–3, 135
Mokaiesh, Selim 131, 132
Montenegro 34, 36
Montriou, William Austin 149
Moore, Thomas 145
Morley, John 48
Morocco 186, 206
Moslem Mission Society (MMS) 109–14
muezzin (prayer caller) 135, 163, 164
Muhammad (Prophet) 3, 21, 45, 55, 59, 100, 187, 190, 197
Muharram (the first month of the Islamic calendar) 143, 148
Muhayyeş family, *see* Mokaiesh family
Muhayyeş, Mohamed Darwiche 131
Muhleisen-Arnold, Reverend John 109–10
Muir, Sir William 48, 81, 82, 84, 90, 94
mullahs (religious leaders) 69, 70
Muller, Max 15–16
Murad V, Sultan 33
Murrow, John 53
Murshidabad 139, 140, 142, 145, 147–8, 151, 153, 155, 156
Muslims 37
  and Christians 74
  holy sites 22
  immigrants 8
  in India 2
  Indian culture 20–1
  intellectuals and scholars 200–2
  and Islam 29
  and non-Muslims 1, 187–8
  Victorian attitudes to 2–3
  women in purdah 19–20

namaz (ritual prayer) 135, 137
Naoroji, Dadabhai 160, 169, 171
Napoleon III 24–5, 150
Naser al-Din, Shah 25, 165
natural supernaturalism 47
Nawab of Bengal 9, 139
  British during rebellions 147–8
  British government and public 152–4
  education policies 141–3
  finance and fraud 145–7

forced abdication 155
'harmful' influences 144–5
marriage to Englishwoman 151–2
petitioning Queen Victoria 154f
rupture 148–9
Shi'i traditions 143–4
visit to Britain 149–51
wife and children 155–7
Nawab of Murshidabad 153, 240 n.50
New Testament 104, 121
  and Christianity 103
Newman, Francis William 48
Newman, John Henry 48
nikah (religious marriage ceremony) 133, 144, 152
nikah mut'ah (temporary marriage contract) 144, 155
non-Muslims 23, 192, 204
  and Muslims 188, 194
  tribes 225 n.10
North Africa 62, 63, 121
Norton, Charles Eliot 52
Nunan, Yusuff 187

O'Neill, Patricia 78, 79
Ockley, Simon 49, 221
Old Testament 85
Oliver Cromwell's Letters and Speeches (Carlyle, Thomas) 50, 56
Omar Khayyam 52, 53
Omrani, Bijan 67
On Heroes, Hero-Worship, and the Heroic in History (Carlyle, Thomas) 45, 90
One Thousand and One Nights 61
  see also *The Thousand and One Nights*
Orientalism 3, 46, 78
  and empire 53–5
Orissa 8, 139, 140, 149, 153
Ottoman and non-Ottoman subjects 204
Ottoman Empire 6, 8, 10, 24, 29, 37, 38, 42–3, 103–4, 106, 126, 130, 170, 186
  Muslims in 5
  Turkish soldiers 24–5
  see also Eastern Question
Oudh (Awadh) 147, 157

Palestine Christian Union Mission to the Arabs (PCUMA) 103–7, 109, 110–11
Palestine 5, 38, 103, 105, 120
  non-Jewish population 44

Palgrave, William Gifford 51
Palmer, Edward Henry 82, 85–6
Palmerston, Viscount 21
Pan-Islam 9, 159, 160, 162, 165, 166, 168, 170, 174, 175, 195, 197, 202, 203, 207, 211 n.19, 241 n.2, 243 n.43
Parry, Edward 140
Parsi theological texts 89
Parsi Zoroastrianism 23
Paşa, Musurus 205
Paşa, Rustem 199
Past and Present (Carlyle, Thomas) 56
Pearls of the Faith (Arnold, Edwin) 84
Pears, Edwin 33
Pearse, James 89
Pemberton, Robert 142
Persia (Iran) 43
Pickthall, Marmaduke 31, 39, 94
Poland 185
polygamy 87, 134, 172
Ponsonby, Henry 19, 25
Preston, Walid Feridoun 184
Price, Leah 92
Priestley, Joseph 82
Protestants 21, 22–3, 81, 103, 117, 119, 128, 178

Queen Victoria 1, 2, 5–6, 9, 19, 24, 30, 32, 41–3, 48, 139, 147, 149, 152–4, 169, 174
  early encounters with Islamic culture 13
  munshi (Muslim instructor-attendant) 4
  passion for visual arts 16–17
Quilliam, W. H. Abdullah 1, 8, 9, 56, 84, 123, 133, 135, 178, 193, 194, 205
  as 'Sheikh-ul-Islam of the British Isles' 193
Quilliam, Bessima Khadijah 205
Quilliam, Robert Ahmad 136, 190, 200, 204, 205
Qur'an
  ayahs 85, 86
  choice of translations 83–7
  experiencing 88–95
  popular readerships 81
  publishers 81, 82–7
  qaraa 86
  suras 85, 86
  translators 81, 82–7
  on Victorian bookshelf 81

Qureshi, Sadiah 106–7
Qutb, Sayyid 56

Ramadan (the Muslim month of fasting) 135–6, 183, 189–90, 191
Raper, Felix Vincent 142, 144, 145
Reid, James 26–7
Rekab, Mustapha 133
Religion of the Koran (Wollaston, Arthur N.) 84
religious conversion 84, 121
The Revolt of the Harem (Engelhardt, M.) 14
Rida, Muhammad Rashid 201
Ridpath, Thomas A. 189
Rihani, Ameen 55
Robertson, Anne MacKenzie 30
Rodwell, John Medows 82–7, 92
Romania 34, 36
Rosebery (Lord) 41–3
royal family 5, 13
  imagination, Islamic world in 14–20
  tolerant of non-Christian religions 14
  towards Islam as religion 21–4
Royal Library 16, 21
Rubaiyat (Omar Khayyam) 52–3, 61
Rubaiyat of Omar Khayyam (FitzGerald, Edward) 52–3
Rushdie, Salman 2
Russia 26, 29, 34, 36, 37, 41, 42, 43, 52, 185
Russo-Turkish War (1877–8) 32, 34, 36, 41, 130
Rutherford, Mark 48

de Sacy, Silvestre 49, 221 n.9
Sagar, Marion Amina 133
Said, Edward W. 3, 54
Saladin, Sultan 16
salat al-'isa (night prayer) 137, 184, 188, 190
salat al-janazah (Islamic funeral prayers) 130
salat al-jum'a (Friday prayer) 135
salat al-magrib (sunset prayer) 188
Sale, Florentia 7, 61, 62, 64–71, 224 n.2
Sale, George 21, 49, 82, 85
Sale, Robert 63
Salisbury (Lord) 2, 26, 32, 41–3
Sanskrit 15–16, 142
Sartor Resartus (Carlyle, Thomas) 47

The Satanic Verses (Rushdie, Salman) 2
Saunders, Helen 128
Schlegel, Friedrich 49
Schuyler, Eugene 35
Scotland 30, 82, 100, 104, 107, 109, 115
Scott, C. G. 103
Scott, Sir Walter 16
Seddon, Felix 142
Selections from the Koran of Mohammed (Dole, Nathan Haskell) 84
Serbia 34, 36
Shades of the Prison House (Wood, Stuart) 93
Shaftesbury (Lord) 107, 109
Shannon, Richard 40
Shaw, George Bernard 87
'Sheikh-ul-Islam of the British Isles' 193–4
Shekoor, Moollah 69
Shi'i Muslim/Islam 8, 44, 152
  traditions 143–4
Shirley, Alice 133
Shitta, Mahommed 197, 198, 206
Siddiqui, Abdul Rahman 241 n.10
Sikhs 64
Silas Marner (Eliot, George) 83
Simla Manifesto 63, 225 n.3
Singh, Duleep (Maharaja) 16, 21
  from Sikhism to Anglican Christianity 16
Sinha, Mrinalini 24
Siraj-ud-Duala 140
Smith, Reginald Bosworth 40, 41, 219 n. 52
Sorensen, David R. 48, 58, 59
South Africa 72–3, 243 n.47
Speke, John Hanning 61
Spencer, Herbert 48
Spurgeon, Charles Haddon 39, 103
Stanley, Henry Morton 61
Stephen, Leslie 48S
Storey, John 177
Sufis (followers of Islamic mysticism) 248 n.72
sunna (custom, practice of Muhammad) 137
Sunni Islam 39, 44, 203
Syria 5, 8, 51, 131
  Christians 126
  Jews in 134–5

Syrian Muslims 137
   Karsa, Mustapha 128–31
   Mokaiesh family 131–3
   Ottoman Syria-British trade 124–5
   religious life 134–7
   social and family life 133–4
   in Victorian Manchester 123
   Ydlibi, Abdullah 125–8

taʿziehs (miniature mausoleums) 143
tableaux vivants (living pictures) 17, 19, 27, 112
Tageldin, Shaden 52, 54
The Talisman (Scott, Sir Walter) 17
Tancred (Disraeli, Benjamin) 38
tariqa 248 n.72
Taweel, Hassan 133
Taylor, Miles 13–14
Tegg, William 94
Tennyson, Alfred 53, 72, 145
Terry, Seymour 83
Thackeray, William Makepeace 72
Thompson, Carl 63–4, 73
Thomson, William 50
The Thousand and One Nights 16
   see also *One Thousand and One Nights*
A Thousand Miles up the Nile 76, 78
Tipu Sultan of Mysore 140, 143–4
Tolan, John 50, 51
Torrens, Henry Whitelock 145, 146
Tractarian 48
Travels in Kashmir and Panjab (von Hugel, Carl) 16
Treaty of Balta Liman 124
Treaty of Berlin 32, 37, 42
Treaty of Paris 30–1, 39
Tsar Nicholas II 43
Turcophile 33
Turkey 5, 44
   'administrative system' 35
   see also Ottoman Empire
The Turkish Atrocities in Bulgaria (MacGahan, J. A.) 33
Turner, Francis 48
Turner, Nellie 91, 92
Tyndall, John 48

ulama (plural of *alim*) 162
umma (the universal Muslim religious community) 137, 160, 163, 211 n.19, 238 n.3
United Kingdom 99, 107, 120, 146, 168, 194
   terrorist attacks in 3
United States 3, 42, 76, 117–18, 175, 204
   terrorist attacks in 3
Urdu 20, 26, 165

Vellore Mutiny 140
Vennell, Sarah 152
Victoria, Princess Royal 20
Vivien Grey (Disraeli, Benjamin) 31
Voltaire 82
von Goethe, J. G. 47
von Hugel, Carl 16
von Schlegel, August Wilhelm 15

Wahhabism 217 n.64
Wales 100, 101, 104, 110, 115, 128
Walker, Mowbray 156, 240 n.50
waqf property 134
Warne, Frederick 82, 83
Warren, H. Nasrullah 189
Watt, W. Montgomery 45, 49
Webb, Mohammed Russell 198, 204, 241 n.11
West Indies 53
William IV 146
Winterhalter, Franz Xaver 16
Wollaston, Arthur N. 84
women travellers'
   Duff Gordon, Lucie 71–6
   Eden, Emily 64–71
   Edwards, Amelia B. 76–80
   Sale, Lady Florentia 64–71
Wood, Stuart 93

Ydlibi, Abdullah 124, 125–8
Ydlibi, Ali 128
Ydlibi, Selim 137

Zakaria, Rafiq 39
Zakat (almsgiving) 181–2

www.ingramcontent.com/pod-product-compliance
Lightning Source LLC
Chambersburg PA
CBHW071810300426
44116CB00009B/1263